the Longer-Lasting
Inspirational Bathroom Book

the *Longer-Lasting*
Inspirational
Bathroom
Book

W. B. Freeman

Faith
Words
™

New York   Boston   Nashville

Editor: Lila Empson
Associate Editor: Holly Halverson
Assistant Editor: Robin Schmitt
Cover & Interior Design: Diane Whisner
Manuscript: W. B. Freeman Concepts, Inc.

FaithWords
Hachette Book Group USA
237 Park Avenue
New York, NY 10017

Visit our Web site at www.faithwords.com.

The FaithWords name and logo are trademarks of the Hachette Book Group USA.

Printed in the United States of America

First Edition: November 2007

10 9 8 7 6 5 4 3 2 1

ISBN: 0-446-69813-X

978-0-446-69813-9

He who lives up to a
little knowledge shall
have more knowledge.

THOMAS BROOKS

CONTENTS

Introduction 15

LISTS IN A HURRY

Lost (and Found) in
Translations 18
You Are Invited!
Please RSVP! 18
Phone Home! 47
Why Do Good People
Suffer? 57
Big Blessings 57
What's God Like? 95
Questions God Asks Us! 95
Courage! It's
Commanded! 111
Author! Author! 111
God Bless You! 123
Jerusalem by Any
Other Name 145
Positive Commands 145
The Forties 155
Founding Fathers You'd
Have Seen in Church 155
Religion Rocks 198
Shakespeare or
the Bible? 198
"Colorful" Theology 208
Murmur, Murmur,
Complain, Complain 208
Terms of Endearment 252
Angels from All Angles 252
What a Guy! 282
Follow the Leader? 282
Facets of Praise 292
Unceasing Praise! 292
Putting on the Feedbag 319
Cry Me a River 319
Sounds Like a Job for
the Holy Spirit! 330
The To-Love List 330

LISTS WITH TIME TO SPARE

The Twenty Tallest
Churches in the World 43
Jesus and the Psalms 81
A Partridge in a
Pear Tree? 133
To Believe or Not
to Believe 177
Facing Suffering
the "Bible" Way 194
Dynamic Duo 278
Begging Off 314
Prevent Spiritual
Identity Theft 354

LISTS FOR THE LONG SOAK

Infinite Freedom 35
Worth a Thousand
Words 51
Let's Party! 74
What a Woman! 99
Just Add Water 126
Will the Real Messiah
Please Stand Up? 149
Things God Won't Do 170
Broadcasting the
Good News 202
What's a Wise
Person to Do? 221
Signs of the End 236
Get God in the Act! 269
How to Spell Paradise?
H-E-A-V-E-N 286
Memory Like an
Elephant 307
A Different Order 323
They Saw Angels 347

TELL-ME-MORE LISTS IN A HURRY

God's Trading Post 86

Jesus and Deuteronomy 130

Rev Up! 134

Hold Still! Don't
    Move Those Dates! 141

The Ten Largest
    Protestant Congregations
    in the U.S. 174

Is It Good or Bad
    to Be a Pillar? 225

The Chain Gang 228

They Received
    Paul's Letters 228

It Just Takes Two 229

Unpopular Bible
    Preachers 275

What About "No" Don't
    You Understand? 311

Are We There Yet? 350

TELL-ME-MORE LISTS WITH TIME TO SPARE

Just Can't Trust
    Anybody 30

A Biblical Orchestra? 70

If Trees Could Talk 121

Real Rest Stops 167

Ten Old Testament
    Cheaters and Liars 186

If You Can't Stand
    the Heat 218

Bible Bugs 264

"Up" with God! 304

It's All in the Name 344

TELL-ME-MORE LISTS FOR THE LONG SOAK

Wedding
    Announcements 31

How They Met Jesus 39

Small but Important 45

Her Majesty 83

"Signs" of the Times 179

Count Your Blessings! 230

What Did You
    Call That? 280

Apparitions or
    Inspirations? 316

The Perfect Gift 356

LITTLE-KNOWN FACTS TO SOAK UP

He Didn't Start the Fire 26

The Key to Good Writing 26

Water from the Sky 26

Pharaoh's Daughter 49

Bless This Horse 49

God in Every State 49

Oldest City in the World 66

Saint Luke's Little
    Summer 66

Blind or Dazzled? 66

Biblical Support for the
    Antichrist 97

Lord of the Flies 97

The Carpenter's
    Calling Card 97

Exceedingly Beautiful
    Women 117

Which Laws Did
    They Break? 117

Their Fees Were
    Too High 117

Toys for Little Jesus 147

The Snakes of Ireland 147

Longest Press Run 147

Pass the Curds, Please 163
Her Honor, Candace 163
Low but Not Lowly 163
Thslttllghtfmn 200
First Waves 200
What's the Tanakh? 200
Nothing on His Own 214
Two Types of Coins 214
Fasten Your Bible Belt! 214
Cave Yen? 234
Star Power 234
The Best Bible 234
America's First Bible to
    America's First People ... 260
Abraham Wasn't Jewish 260
One-Hundred-Year
    Prayer Meeting 260
Truth Is Stranger
    Than Fiction 284
Little-Known Bible
    Word Facts 284
Gezhundheit! 284
Fringe Bereft 300
Psalms 24/7 300
All Is Forgiven . . .
    350 Years Later 300
The Star That Never
    Steered Them Wrong 321
Sabbath Rest 321
Know How to Fold 'Em 321
Make a Joyful Noise 340
God and the Pledge 340
Still Vivid After All
    These Years 340

GOOD WORDS—NO SOAP NEEDED

Bleep! 21
Opening Up the
    Word *Cloister* 21
Eschatology 52
Shekinah 52
Is Enthusiasm Good or Bad? 60

Atonement =
    "At-One-Ment" 60
What Is Deism? 78
The End 78
180-Degree Change 87
Holy Paradox 87
No Apology for
    Apologetics 114
Who Qualifies for
    Sainthood? 114
Pulling in the Same
    Direction 137
Another Word for
    "Word" 137
Gnot So Smart 150
A Costly
    Mispronunciation 150
Insight into "Truth" 158
Eye of a Needle 158
Learn, Study, and
    Pass It On 188
Megachurch 188
Raise Your Ebenezer! 203
Not Rocket Science 203
Being a Witness 211
Maranatha! 211
Who Gets the Glory 211
Ya Gotta Have It 237
Live the Passion 237
A to Z 255
Your Future Home? 255
You Don't Want to
    Go There 255
Open Hearts and
    Open Homes 287
A Ten-Dollar Word for
    "Work Together" 287
The Perfection of
    Paradise 295
More Balm, Please 295
City of Refuge 295
Ah-h-h-h-h 324
Evensong 324
Something's Missing 333
Get It Rite 333

STORIES IN A HURRY

A Short Life, Well Spent 94
A Russian Grandmother's
  Bible 94
The Rest, They Say 103
Soul Surfer 103
The Cross and the
  Hurricanes 144
Who Started Christmas? 144
For God and for Country 197
A Coded Message 197
A Penny's Worth of
  Wisdom 242
Four Lines Worth
  Singing . . . Over
  and Over Again 242

STORIES WITH TIME TO SPARE

Please Don't Leave, Lord 19
Faithful to the
  Finish Line 58
It Is No Secret 89
Even the Wave Obeys 112
"You Will Go Forth" 156
The Tears of the Russian 190
An Unlikely but
  Effective Evangelist 209
Retirement Home
  Becomes Tourist
  Attraction 248
The Right Frame
  of Mind 253
Mrs. Goodnest 293
A Mountain-Sized
  Dilemma 331

STORIES FOR THE LONG SOAK

The New Good Samaritan 28
One Saint's Life 68

She Used Every Vessel
  She Could Find 119
An Offering of Fifty-
  Seven Cents 165
A Promise Is a Promise 216
Not Down and Not
  Under 262
Ruby Bridges: Bridge
  Builder 302
God's Plan and a Bet
  Gone Wrong 342

INFORMATION IN A HURRY

The Road to Heaven
  Was Paved . . . with
  Concrete? 44
Just What the Doctor
  Ordered 44
Tyndale's Translation 55
Jesus in the Sand 55
Come As a Little Child 82
The Devil Knew His
  Music 82
Come Sail Away 85
Absalom: Handsome
  but Treacherous 85
The Rosetta Stone and
  the Bible 93
First Printing 101
Save Our Sea 101
Time Is Everything 107
A Layer Cake Made
  of Dirt 107
What Makes a Monk
  a Trappist? 125
Bringing in the
  Sheaves 125
Is the Stable a Fable? 129
Church: An Inoculation
  Against Divorce? 129
How Old Is That Scroll? 153
Dowry Veils 153

Holy Hieroglyphics? 178
Let It Snow! 178
Not That Guy 185
Clerical Fashion Show 185
Family Resemblance 206
Awe-full Blessing 206
So Much Focus on a
    Place So Small 240
God Bloggers 240
The Name Above All
    Others 246
They Can Go Home
    Again 246
The Mount of Olive
    Trees 266
Teaching in Parables 266
Private Gardens 279
An Amazing Rod 279
Nero the Depraved 290
Shema Yisrael 290
At the Corner of Shiphrah
    and Puah 315
All in a Name 315
Modern Illumination 327
Lift Every Voice 327
Enjoy the Sabbath 355
Are You High or Low
    Church? 355

INFORMATION WITH
TIME TO SPARE

Built and Rebuilt to Last 17
Give Us This Day
    Our Daily 22
And Then What
    Happened? 27
The Salty Personality 34
Bitter Herbs or
    Just Salad? 38
An Offering of Herbs? 48
What Time of Year Is
    That in Hebrew? 50

Pomegranates 61
Go Ye, Everyday
    Evangelists 67
Life on the Line 73
Skilled with Bow and
    Arrow 77
Get Real! 96
Megahit Chronicled 98
Do You *Believe* It? 100
A Folded Napkin 104
Lake or Sea? 106
Who Are the Moravians? 108
The Crystal Quartz
    Cross 110
Sweeping for a Lost
    Coin 115
It's a Deal! 118
Nothing to Sniff At 143
Dead Sea Vitality 146
Speed-Reading Bibles 148
Don't Tell 159
What Did Jesus Really
    Look Like? 164
Glowing with Goodness 169
How Were Your
    Godparents Involved? 173
The Weighty Soul 189
Was Jesus a Real Person? 196
The Long and Short
    of It 199
Do Not Pass Go 201
Exchanging Gifts 212
The Mystery of the
    Staircase 215
An Overlooked Center
    of Christianity 220
Would You Have Gone
    to Keswick? 224
Christmas Dating 233
Sacred Sites 235
Is There a Pastor in the
    House (and Senate)? 243
It's a Good Day to Pray 245
Oye! 247
Baptizing the Baby 249

A Knight's Son and the
    Cathedral 251
Dinner at Solomon's
    House 256
Tune in Next Week for
    the Rest of the Story 261
The Rose As a Symbol
    of Faith 268
Iraq Is Noteworthy
    Throughout the Bible 274
Lighten Up 283
Life at the Top 285
America's First Church 296
Can't Get Enough of
    Prayer 301
What Kind of Chariot
    Would You Have
    Driven? 306
Going Round in Circles 310
Close Encounters 320
"And Where Do You
    Go to Church?" 322
Not a Thing to Wear 334
There's Nothing to Fear 337
What's That Ringing
    Sound? 341
How Secure Were They? 346

God's Astronomy Lesson:
    Ahead of Its Time 79
The Beautiful Irish
    Books 127
Prove It! 131
The Wedding Planner 139
Infallible? 151
The Dreaded Philistines 161
Is It a Hymn or a
    Gospel Song? 171
What's *That* Mean? 175
Faith and Work 192
Alone Together 204
Raise the Flag, Salute
    the Faith 222
Ancient Words,
    Ever New 226
The Big Picture 238
The Sign of the Cross 258
O Say, Can You Sing? 272
Christmas Bookends 276
What Not to Worship 288
Who Names This Child? 298
"Highest Praise" in the
    Nation's Capital 308
Figuratively Speaking 312
"With Malice Toward
    None, with Gratitude
    for All" 325
Is It in the Book? 338
The Song Heard Around
    the World 348
Prepress Production 352

INFORMATION FOR THE LONG SOAK

A Totally Dysfunctional
    Family 24
Masada: Fortified for
    Survival—and Luxury 36
Special Rules Regarding
    the Poor 41
Who Were They and
What Were They
Following? 53
A Deity by Any Other
    Name Is Called 64
Go Figure! 75

CLEANED-UP LIVES IN A HURRY

Faith Conquers Death 33
A Change of Heart That
    Changed History 33
He Had a Dream 72
Ultimate Survivors 72
No Horsing Around
    About God 92

Having a Ball and
  Helping Others 92
Brother to All 105
Each One Teach One 105
An Unlikely Participant 124
Three Generations of
  Prolific Writers 124
Now, That's a Nice
  Neighborhood 142
One-of-a-Kind Teacher 142
Printer, Phrasemaker, and
  Commentator 184
Voice of Praise and
  Rescue 184
Hardship and Heroism 195
Share the Healing 195
A Poet Against All Odds . . . 219
One for the Book 219
Fearless and Faith-full 244
A Unified Sneeze 244
Thomas A. Dorsey: From
  Blues to Gospel 267
Siberian Convert 267
From the Bottom to
  the Top 305
Lady Sings the "Go
  Away, Blues!" 305
A University for the
  New World 345
Billy Sunday: From
  Stolen Bases to
  Temperance 345

Dr. Livingston,
  I Presume 250
Rest Assured, This
  Woman Could Write 254
Hands That Bring
  Healing 294
The Eternity Man 332

CLEANED-UP LIVES FOR THE LONG SOAK

A Monumental Charitable
  Gift 135
What Did He Really
  Believe? 271

ONE-LINERS TO SOAK UP

Ageless Prayer 23
Why Worship? 56
A Most Valuable Book 62
The Presidents Speak
  of God 90
Talk About Church! 102
Commanded but Hard
  to Do 116
Boot Camp for God's
  Army 138
For the Sake of Others 154
Kindness 160
Life in a Nutshell 191
Movers and Shakers 207
Humility 213
The Essence of
  Friendship 241
Obedience 257
In Times of Trouble,
  Call on the Big Guy 291
Self-Control 297
Talk About Heaven 328
Case Closed 335

CLEANED-UP LIVES WITH TIME TO SPARE

Still Popular a Hundred
  Years Later 20
Better Than Legend 59
"God's Friend" 109
A Woman of Substance 113
Rebel with a Cause! 157
The "Fantastic" Voyage
  of George MacDonald . . . 210

WATERMARKS—PENCIL REQUIRED

The Path to Heaven 365
A Prophet's Job 366
Be an Action Hero 368
Jesus, aka the Vine 370
Bible Brain Twister 377
Jacob's Boys 381

TICKLE YOUR FUNNY BONE

Do You Go to Church? 358
Awake All Night 358
The Church Chandelier 358
The Substitute Organist 359

Pay Attention! 359
The B-I-B-L-E 360
Sees All and Knows All 362
Why Waste Time? 362
Biblical Theme Songs 363
Twenty-five Pearls of
    Wisdom 364

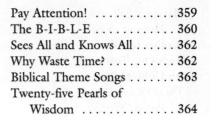

TEST THE WATER

Which Woman? 372
Matched Pairs 374
Name That Enemy 375
All Wrapped Up 376
Are You Sure? 378
Travelocity Bible-Style 380

INTRODUCTION

The apostle John, one of Jesus' closest disciples, ended his account of Jesus' life this way: "There are many other things that Jesus did. If they were all written down one by one, I suppose that the whole world could not hold the books that would be written" (*John 21:25 GNT*).

Certainly the same thing could be said for all of the things that have been written about what Jesus said and did, or about the Bible as a whole, God the Creator, the church, or believers through the millennia!

This book is a small sampling of things serious and humorous, important and trivial, fictional and factual from the Bible, about the Bible, and about people who have believed in and attempted to live by the Bible.

Most of the entries can be read in a matter of seconds, not minutes. A few will require a little more time and thought.

Sometimes it only takes a "little" to jump-start your morning, get you through an emotional hiccup, help you wait out an appointment or delay, or help you regroup and transition from one thing to the next. Those are optimal times to pick up this book and add a little bit of inspiration—and a little glimpse into things eternal—to your day.

You'll find jokes and quizzes, stories and lists, quotes and biographical sketches, vocabulary builders and puzzles, and lots and lots of bits of information—small and large. You'll find a few things that may bring tears to your eyes, some statements that may cause an "aha!" moment, and some entries that are likely to make you laugh out loud. Some entries have the potential to build your faith, some to challenge your mind, and some to pull things out of your memory. We also hope you'll find countless entries that inspire you to want to read the Bible for yourself and apply its message to your life.

Enjoy!

—W. B. Freeman

BUILT AND REBUILT TO LAST

The separation of church and state is a familiar concept in the United States in the twenty-first century, but in London in the late seventeenth century, few people questioned whether the government should help the church. London had dozens of churches at that time affiliated with the Church of England (Anglican), and many of them were in need of extensive repair. In the Great Fire of 1666, more than eighty of London's churches suffered devastating damage or were completely destroyed, including St. Paul's.

The government stepped in—first with the Rebuilding Act of 1667. The city imposed a tax on all the coal arriving at the Port of London, with the intent that the tax would be used to pay for rebuilding public buildings.

In 1670 a second Rebuilding Act increased the tax on coal. Most of this tax money was earmarked for rebuilding the city's churches. Christopher Wren, the surveyor-general, was the primary player in this project. About two-thirds of the churches were rebuilt within the next two decades, and some are still standing today.

And old St. Paul's? The rebuilding began in 1675. The coal tax was extended to help cover costs. By 1707 work was completed. Nearly destroyed during World War II, the church was again repaired. It is still standing today and is the final resting place of the city's most famous architect, Christopher Wren—a man, by the way, who never received any formal training in architecture.

LOST (AND FOUND) IN TRANSLATIONS

Which versions of the Bible are the most popular? The data change from month to month, but in February 2005, as an example, these were the top ten best sellers at U.S. and Canadian Christian retail stores (as reported in April of that year):

Christian Marketplace Top Seller List, April 2005
General Versions and Translations

1. New International Version (various publishers)
2. King James Version (various publishers)
3. New Living Translation (Tyndale)
4. New King James Version (various publishers)
5. Holman Christian Standard Bible (Broadman & Holman)
6. New Century Version Nelson Bibles (Nelson)
7. New American Standard Bible update (various publishers)
8. Reina Valera 1960 (Spanish) (various publishers)
9. The Message (Eugene Peterson, Nav Press)
10. New International Reader's Version (Zondervan)

Note: This list is based on actual sales in Christian retail stores in the United States and Canada during February, using STATS as the source for data collection. All rights reserved. Distribution and copyright © 2005 CBA and ECPA. Used by permission.

YOU ARE INVITED! PLEASE RSVP!

Jesus came to issue God's invitation to a great heavenly banquet. Jesus said that all those who came to him, he would not reject. The Gospels contain some of Jesus' own words of invitation. So who is invited?

1. Everyone who thirsts (*John 7:37*)
2. All who are weary and burdened (*Matthew 11:28*)
3. Those who are spiritually poor (*Matthew 5:3*)
4. Anyone who seeks righteousness (*Matthew 5:6*)
5. People willing to be self-sacrificing (*Matthew 16:24*)
6. Little children (*Matthew 19:14*)
7. The "empty" who want to be complete (*Matthew 19:21*)
8. Those willing to "fish for people" (*Matthew 4:19* NLT)
9. Wrongdoers (*Mark 2:17*)
10. Whoever wants to follow Jesus (*Mark 8:34* NLT)

PLEASE DON'T LEAVE, LORD

Pain and suffering can make or break a man. In the case of Henry Lyte (1793–1847), a Scottish minister, poet, and musician, it made him stronger. It also resulted in a hymn that has brought comfort to countless suffering souls since the mid-1800s:

> *Abide with me—fast falls the eventide.*
> *The darkness deepens—Lord, with me abide.*
> *When other helpers fail and comforts flee,*
> *Help of the helpless, O abide with me!*

It is said that this hymn, "Abide with Me," was written by Lyte at a time when he was preparing to leave his congregation and move to Italy. The climate of the English town where he was living only caused him greater physical suffering as he fought against the ravages of asthma and tuberculosis.

Considering the popularity of "Abide with Me" in the twenty-first century, it is somewhat surprising that the hymn was not well known in England until several years after Lyte's death in 1847. It took a book, called *Lyte's Remains*, to spread the words across England in 1850, and another book, Henry Ward Beecher's *Plymouth Collection of Hymns*, to get the words out in America beginning in 1855.

Another hymn writer, William Henry Monk, discovered the hymn and placed it in his well-regarded hymnal *Hymns Ancient and Modern* in 1861. Before doing so, it is said, he wrote a new tune for the hymn, which continues to be used today.

The words of the hymn come from Luke 24:29, where two disciples said to Jesus after walking with him along the road to Emmaus, "Abide with us" (*KJV*).

Source: Kenneth W. Osbeck, *101 Hymn Stories* (Grand Rapids, MI: Kregel, 1982), 16–17.

STILL POPULAR A HUNDRED YEARS LATER

Andrew Murray was born in South Africa in 1828 and was sent to study in England at the age of ten. When he returned to South Africa as a pastor and evangelist, he led a revival that shook the entire nation. He served as a Dutch Reformed pastor in four cities: Bloemfontein, Worcester, Cape Town, and Wellington. A theological conservative, he opposed the liberal trends he saw in the Dutch Reformed denomination, and although he was not a Pentecostal, his high regard for the Methodist holiness tradition and his writings helped to shape South African Pentecostalism.

Murray touched not only the southern tip of Africa but also the entire world through a legacy of writings that have become Christian classics, most notably *With Christ in the School of Prayer, Abide in Christ,* and *Raising Your Children for Christ.* In all, Murray wrote more than 250 books aimed at deepening the personal devotional life of the layperson.

Lesser known is Murray's influence on education. He founded the Huguenot Seminary in 1874 and the Mission Institute at Wellington in 1877. He was bold in debating his theological positions at the Keswick Convention—an annual summer meeting of evangelicals at Keswick in the English Lake district. In recent years Murray's writings have been republished with great popularity in the United States and England. Some of his works have been more popular a hundred years after their initial publication than they were during his lifetime.

BLEEP!

*B*lasphemy is often popularly used to refer to things that have nothing to do with God. The true meaning of the word has been watered down to the extent that many "respectable" people commit blasphemy publicly and regularly.

Blasphemy is the act of insulting God, showing contempt or lack of reverence for him, or claiming his attributes for one's self or another entity. Using the name of God in a way that has nothing to do with his true attributes is blasphemy, as is using his name as part of an expletive or exclamation of any kind. The Bible also references blasphemous deeds—those committed with deliberate disobedience to God's commands.

OPENING UP THE WORD *CLOISTER*

*I*t's a noun! It's a verb! The word *cloister* comes from the Latin word *claustrum*, which describes an enclosed place. In times past, a cloister might be any area set aside for prayer, such as a garden, an open court, or a walkway that linked a monastery's many buildings.

The verb *cloister* denotes pulling away from the everyday world. In the case of a monk or a nun, the decision to be cloistered indicates a choice to live in the closest possible intimacy with God. Cloistered communities may be closed to outside visitors or open to visitors only on designated days.

GIVE US THIS DAY OUR DAILY . . .

B read is something easily taken for granted. Go to the grocery store, pick up a loaf (sliced or not), and enjoy. When it gets stale or moldy, throw it out.

In ancient times bread, a food that nourished and strengthened, was too precious to waste. It took time to grind the grain (by hand), mix the ingredients (homegrown or produced), knead the dough, and bake it—on a hot rock, in a pan (crafted by hand), or in an oven made of iron or clay.

With more limited food choices, bread became known as "the staff of life." This is probably why Jesus called himself the Bread of Life (John 6:35), a term that would strike a chord with people of his day. Jesus said he came to earth to give people a full life—a life that lacks nothing (John 10:10). Talk about daily, fresh bread!

> ### THE LORD'S PRAYER
> Our Father in heaven,
> Hallowed be Your name.
> Your kingdom come.
> Your will be done
> On earth as it is in heaven.
> Give us this day our daily bread.
> And forgive us our debts,
> As we forgive our debtors.
> And do not lead us into temptation,
> But deliver us from the evil one.
> For Yours is the kingdom and the
> power and the glory forever. Amen.
> —*Matthew 6:9–13* NKJV

Ageless Prayer

Prayer is the opportunity to express the inexpressible; to give "place" to God, the One who is infinitely other and intimately present. To pray is to express hope beyond one's recognized and acknowledged limitations. It is breath, roots, and wings—all in one.

1. "Don't fret or worry. Instead of worrying, pray."—*Philippians 4:6 MSG*

2. "If God seems slow in responding, it is because He is preparing a better gift. He will not deny us. God withholds what you are not yet ready for. He wants you to have a lively desire for His greatest gifts. All of which is to say, pray always and do not lose heart."—*Saint Augustine (354–430)*

3. "When we are linked by the power of prayer, we, as it were, hold each other's hand as we walk side by side along a slippery path; and thus by the bounteous disposition of charity, it comes about that the harder each one leans on the other, the more firmly we are riveted together in brotherly love."—*Gregory the Great (540–604)*

4. "However great may be the temptation, if we know how to use the weapon of prayer well we shall come off conquerors at last, for prayer is more powerful than all the devils. He who is attacked by the spirits of darkness needs only to apply himself vigorously to prayer and he will beat them back with great success."—*Saint Bernard of Clairvaux (1090–1153)*

5. "The most beneficial prayer will be the one which moves your heart in the most beneficial way."—*Blessed Jordan of Saxony (1190–1237)*

6. "Prayer unites the soul to God."—*Julian of Norwich (1342–1416)*

7. "Prayer is a strong wall and fortress."—*Martin Luther (1483–1546)*

8. "Aspire to God with short but frequent outpourings of the heart; admire His bounty; invoke His aid; cast yourself in spirit at the foot of His cross; adore His goodness; treat with Him of your salvation; give Him your whole soul a thousand times in the day."
   —*Saint Francis de Sales (1567–1622)*

9. "Pray often, for prayer is a shield to the soul."—*John Bunyan (1628–1688)*

10. "God does nothing but by prayer, but everything with it."
    —*John Wesley (1703–1791)*

11. "I used to ask God to help me. Then I asked if I might help Him. I ended up by asking Him to do His work through me."
    —*James Hudson Taylor, 1832–1905*

12. "Prayer is not a convenient device for imposing our will upon God, or for bending his will to ours, but the prescribed way of subordinating our will to his. It is by prayer that we seek God's will, embrace it and align ourselves with it. Every true prayer is a variation on the theme, 'Your will be done.' Our Master taught us to say this in the pattern prayer he gave us, and added the supreme example of it in Gethsemane."—*John Stott (1921–)*

A TOTALLY
DYSFUNCTIONAL FAMILY

The family of Herod the Great may qualify as the most totally dysfunctional family of all time! Herod married ten times. Nine of his wives were living in the royal household at the same time, viciously arguing over their position and trying to promote the interests of their children. Their plots and intrigue no doubt made Herod's life miserable, and he in turn made the lives of many of his courtiers miserable to the point of death. Herod's example may be one of the strongest arguments ever made against polygamy.

Herod's family tree is so complicated that very few have been able to chart it in a clear way. At least eight of his wives had children who inherited the king's wild passions for marriage and remarriage. With Herod's permission—and in some cases, Herod's suggestion—some of these children married other members of the family, including brothers, nephews, and nieces. Some of the family members married into the houses of "client kings," those who ruled at Herod's wish. His great-granddaughter Drusilla married Azizus the king of Emesa but then deserted him to marry Felix the Roman procurator. His great-grandson Tigranes became king of Armenia.

Several members of Herod's family changed partners, which was in direct violation of Jewish law. His granddaughter Herodias, the mother of the sensuous Salome, married Herod's son Philip but left him for another son, Antipas, the tetrarch of Galilee. His granddaughter Berenice married his grandson Herod king of Chalcis and then had an affair with Titus, the son of Vespasian.

A TOTALLY
DYSFUNCTIONAL FAMILY (CONT'D)

At times Herod's refusal to allow a family member to marry a would-be suitor turned out to be a serious political mistake.

For example, Salome fell in love with a man named Syllaeus, who was the prime minister of Herod's old enemies, the Nabataean Arabs. When Syllaeus asked for Salome's hand in marriage, Herod told him he would have to be circumcised and embrace the Jewish faith. Syllaeus withdrew from the area and returned to his native land.

In refusing Syllaeus permission to marry Salome, Herod created an enemy who eventually caused him great harm. A guerrilla war developed, and ultimately, when Herod sought to retaliate against Syllaeus, Syllaeus turned the Roman emperor Augustus against Herod. Augustus wrote a harsh letter to Herod, reducing him from a position of friend to that of "subject"—not a good position for the "king of the Jews" to find himself in!

Herod was notorious for his building programs. He built ten tremendous fortifications, including the temple mount in Jerusalem. What he failed to do, however, was to build a healthy family or a good reputation!

HE DIDN'T START THE FIRE

The Methodist Church likely would not exist today had it not been for a daring rescue of its founder. In 1709, at the age of five, John Wesley was asleep one night in the attic of his family's home. The house caught fire—it's unclear how it started—and the family rushed out. They forgot, however, about John. Fortunately, someone saw him standing at the window, and neighbors were able to help rescue him just in time.

Source: Stephen Tomkins, *John Wesley: A Biography* (Grand Rapids, MI: Eerdmans, 2003).

THE KEY TO GOOD WRITING

The first commercial version of the typewriter appeared in 1874. Not every writer, however, embraces technology. C. S. Lewis—born in 1898 and the author of more than fifty books— never learned to use a typewriter. He preferred to write in long- hand. To the consternation of those who like to study well-known writers' original manuscripts, he made a habit of throwing away his handwritten drafts.

Source: Michael Coren, *The Man Who Created Narnia: The Story of C. S. Lewis* (Grand Rapids, MI: Eerdmans, 1994).

WATER FROM THE SKY

The Garden of Eden was heaven on earth. Lush and green, full of trees and fruits, it was all that the first man and woman could ask for.

What was the average rainfall per month in this oasis? The answer is zero inches. Genesis 2:10 says a river watered the gar- den. In fact, there was no such thing as rain until Noah's time, when God used a flood to destroy all but Noah and his family.

AND THEN WHAT HAPPENED?

The Old Testament ends with the book of Malachi, written around 430 BC.

The New Testament begins with the book of Matthew, written about sixty-five years after Jesus' birth (6 or 5 BC).

Here's What Happened Between 430 BC and 6 BC

As Malachi ended, the Israelites were subject to the Persians, who allowed the Israelites to practice their religion. This situation lasted about 120 years.

Then Alexander the Great of Greece took charge. He, too, gave the Israelites religious freedom. He is the reason Greek became the universal language of his vast territories. This led to the translation of the Old Testament into Greek, making it more accessible to more people.

After Alexander died, a general named Ptolemy was in charge of Palestine (the "Promised Land" mentioned in the Old Testament), where most of the Israelites lived. He and the heirs who followed him treated the Israelites well, but this was not so with the kings of Syria, known as the Seleucids. One of these leaders, Antiochus IV, tried to force the Israelites to give up their religion, using torture and other means.

Hope arrived with the Maccabean revolt, initially led by a priest named Mattathias and carried on by his son Judas, a military genius.

For about one hundred years (roughly 167–63 BC), the Israelites were independent. Then the Roman general Pompey "annexed" Palestine, making it part of the Roman Empire. Eventually Herod the Great, a tyrant, came to power (38 BC). He was in charge when the New Testament story began.

THE NEW
GOOD SAMARITAN

When most people read or hear the biblical story of the good Samaritan, they have little trouble picturing themselves as the Samaritan who rescues the bleeding and beaten man at the side of the road. Yet few people bother to think what that act of kindness might actually require of them in real life . . . and what the outcome could be. One man was unexpectedly given the opportunity to make the choice first-hand. Later, he would wonder what his life would have been like had he chosen differently.

Walking down a dimly lit street late one evening, the man heard muffled screams coming from behind a clump of bushes. Alarmed, he slowed down to listen and panicked when he realized that what he was hearing was the unmistakable sounds of a struggle—heavy grunting, frantic scuffling, and tearing of fabric.

Only yards from where he stood, a woman was being attacked. He froze in his steps, hardly daring to breath lest the attacker should notice his presence. But then a strange thought occurred to him: Should he get involved?

Frightened for his own safety, he cursed himself for having suddenly decided to take a new route home that night. He had family responsibilities; what if he became another statistic? He instantly had the urge to run to a safe place and use his cell phone to call the police. But he could hear the struggle becoming more desperate.

An eternity seemed to pass as he argued with himself. The deliberations in his head had taken only seconds, but already the girl's cries were growing weaker. He had to decide—and fast. How could he sleep at night if he walked away from this?

THE NEW GOOD
SAMARITAN (CONT'D)

So he finally resolved that he could not turn his back on the fate of this unknown woman, even if it meant risking his life.

Known neither for his bravery nor for his athletic abilities, he nonetheless summoned up all the moral courage and physical strength he could muster. And once he had finally determined to help the girl, he became strangely transformed. He ran behind the bushes and pulled the assailant off the woman and wrestled with the attacker for a few minutes until the man fled.

Panting hard, he scrambled upright and approached the girl, who was crouched behind a tree, sobbing. In the darkness, he could barely see her outline, but he could certainly sense her trembling shock. Not wanting to frighten her further, he first spoke to her from a distance. "It's okay," he said soothingly. "The man ran away. You're safe now." There was a long pause, and then he heard the words, uttered in wonder, in amazement. "Dad, is that you?" Out from behind the tree stepped his youngest daughter.

JUST CAN'T TRUST ANYBODY

Time and again in the Bible, God proves he is trustworthy, and people prove they aren't. Even close relatives cannot be counted on—a lesson Abel learned the hard way. The betrayer, it's worth noting, usually scores a temporary win, but the tables can be turned on him later, as many of these Bible people discovered:

1. *Jacob and Rachel tricked Isaac,* convincing him that Jacob was the elder son, Esau; Jacob's father-in-law later deceived Jacob *(Genesis 27; 29:16–27).*

2. *Joseph's brothers thought they'd get rid of him* by selling him into Egyptian slavery; Joseph later rose to power and saved their lives *(Genesis 37:28; 45:4–7).*

3. *Korah, from the tribe of Levi, tried to overthrow Moses* and Aaron and take charge; God took his life *(Numbers 16:1–3, 28–32).*

4. *Delilah tricked Samson,* causing him to lose his strength; Samson got it back and destroyed the Philistines *(Judges 16:4–30).*

5. *Fearing the loss of his kingdom, Saul plotted to get rid of David;* Saul lost his life and David became king *(1 Samuel 18:8–9; 31:1–4).*

6. *Jezebel had Naboth killed to steal his vineyard;* she died and was devoured by dogs *(1 Kings 21:1–14; 2 Kings 9:30–37).*

7. *Several Chaldeans helped create a law they knew Daniel would violate,* resulting in his death; they died instead *(Daniel 6:4–16, 19–24).*

8. *Haman tried to wipe out the Persian Jews;* the Jews were spared and Haman wound up hanging *(Esther 3; 7).*

9. *Satan tried to destroy Job,* a man who loved God; God restored all that Satan stole from Job and then some *(Job 1–2; 42:10).*

10. *Herod the Great ordered the murder of all boys, ages two and under,* in his attempt to destroy the child Jesus; Jesus escaped *(Matthew 2:1–16).*

11. *Angry at John the Baptist, Herodias convinced her daughter to ask Herod Antipas for John's head on a platter;* John died but his influence lives on *(Mark 6:17–28).*

12. *Judas betrayed Jesus in exchange for thirty silver coins;* Judas later hanged himself *(Matthew 26:14–16; 27:3–5).*

13. *Members of the Synagogue of the Freedmen brought in false witnesses to condemn Stephen* because they didn't agree with his teaching; Stephen died but his story is still told *(Acts 6:8–14; 7:55–60).*

14. *In Damascus the Jews conspired to kill Paul* and stop him from preaching that Jesus is the Son of God; he escaped *(Acts 9:19–25).*

WEDDING
ANNOUNCEMENTS

B ible brides and grooms were married in many different settings and circumstances. Some were as smitten as any bride and groom should be; others barely knew each other. In most cases, a fabulous feast celebrated the nuptials. Wedding announcements of the best-known Bible brides and grooms might have read like this:

1. *Adam and Eve.* Eve, earth's first lady, became the bride of Adam this afternoon in a ceremony in the Garden of Eden. God the Father gave the bride away and blessed the union. The bride's wedding ensemble, also designed by God, was made of glowing skin—her own. (*Genesis 2:18–25*)

2. *Isaac and Rebekah.* Rebekah, daughter of Bethuel, was married to Isaac, son of Abraham, on the groom's family estate in Beersheba. The couple became engaged sight-unseen when Rebekah agreed to leave her family in Nahor and marry a distant cousin. Gifts from the groom's family included gold and silver jewelry. The bride's fashion-forward ensemble sparked a centuries-old tradition by including a veil. (*Genesis 24*)

3. *Jacob and Leah.* Leah, daughter of Laban of Nahor, secretly wed Jacob, son of Isaac, following a feast at Haran given by the bride's father. Unfortunately, the wedding was also a secret from the groom, who thought he was marrying the bride's sister. The couple honeymooned for a week. (*Genesis 29:18–28*)

4. *Jacob and Rachel.* Haran was once again the sight of nuptials as Jacob wed his first love, Rachel, one week after marrying her sister, Leah. The bride's father demanded a seven-year extension on his labor agreement with the groom in exchange for his daughter. (*Genesis 29:25–30*)

5. *Moses and Zipporah.* Zipporah, daughter of Reuel the priest, was married to Moses in the land of Midian. Prior to her marriage, the bride ran her father's sheep business along with her six sisters. Moses, the adopted son of Pharaoh's daughter, is wanted by the Egyptian authorities for murder. (*Exodus 2:11–21*)

WEDDING ANNOUNCEMENTS
(CONT'D)

6. *Boaz and Ruth.* Landowner and respected countryman Boaz has wed Ruth the Moabitess (widow of Naomi's son, Mahlon). Actually, Ruth was acquired in the purchase of land once belonging to Naomi's deceased husband and two sons. It seems, however, that true romance sparked the deal when Naomi engineered a blind date for Ruth and Boaz at a barley-threshing event. *(Ruth 3–4)*

7. *King of Persia and Esther.* The court of Ahasuerus, king of Persia, is pleased to announce his marriage to Esther, a Jewess, and her coronation as his queen. Esther replaces the deposed Vashti, who failed to fulfill her queenly obligations to entertain. Queen Esther is reputed to be a fine hostess and has already planned a special luncheon for the king and his highest noble, Haman, who is said to be near the end of his rope over the Jews' refusal to bow to him. *(Esther 1–2)*

8. *Joseph and Mary.* Mary, of the house of David, wed Joseph in Nazareth. Though there were rumors of a minor tiff just before the wedding that threatened to break them up, all seemed fine again after Joseph had a good night's sleep. He even claims to have dreamed the name of their firstborn child: Jesus. *(Matthew 1:18–25)*

9. *Cana wedding couple.* Though the bride and groom remain anonymous, Cana was the sight of a wedding of note. The excitement began when the host discovered a wine shortage halfway through the feast. The day was saved when a guest, Mary, asked her son, Jesus, to lend a hand in providing more. Servants brought jars full of water to Jesus, who miraculously sent them back full of a wine superior to what had already been served. *(John 2:1–11)*

10. *Christ and his bride.* You are cordially invited to the wedding of all eternity as the church, the bride of Christ, joins with him forever in heaven. Date to be announced by Gabriel at a moment's notice. Please be ready. *(Revelation 19:7–9)*

FAITH CONQUERS DEATH

Tom McGuinness didn't waste any time. As soon as he finished college, he entered the navy's Aviation Officer Candidate School and was well on his way to becoming a pilot. After Tom and his wife, Cheryl, had two children, Jennifer and Tommy, Tom transitioned from the military to a job with the airlines. It was a fateful decision. On September 11, 2001, Tom was the copilot on American Airlines Flight 11, the first plane to hit the World Trade Center.

The death of Tom McGuinness was a devastating blow to his family, but as Cheryl relates in her book *Beauty Beyond the Ashes*, she and her children were comforted by the knowledge that Tom, a mature Christian, was in heaven with his Savior and Lord. Tom's legacy, Cheryl wrote, is the "faith, love and obedience to God" that he modeled for his family, friends, and coworkers every day.

Source: Cheryl McGuinness with Lois Rabey, *Beauty Beyond the Ashes* (Los Angeles: Howard, 2004).

A CHANGE OF HEART THAT CHANGED HISTORY

In the Roman Empire believers were being tortured and killed, until a new emperor came along and made Christianity the state religion.

Constantine converted to Christianity when he had a vision concerning the monogram of Christ. (See page 179, number 4, for a picture of the Chi Rho monogram and an explanation of its meaning.) He felt compelled to put this emblem on his troops' shields before a big battle, and they won.

After his conversion, Constantine changed laws to benefit believers (for example, freeing clergy from taxes), abolished crucifixion as a punishment, issued the Edict of Milan (returning to believers property taken during their persecution), discouraged paganism, studied the Bible, and even preached. He had churches built, made more copies of the Bible available, and promoted Sabbath and Saints' Day observances.

Constantine saw himself as God's servant, sent to promote peace and purify the Christian faith. His influence brought new respect for believers and their Bible-based culture and enabled Christianity to spread across Europe and around the world.

THE SALTY PERSONALITY

Jesus referred to his followers as the "salt of the earth" (*Matthew 5:13*).

Ancient people were very familiar with the wonderful properties of salt:

Salt cleanses and heals. It especially guards wounds against infection. Jesus called his followers to promote physical, mental, and spiritual healing. Just as salt sometimes stings when it gets into a cut, so the truth sometimes stings those who need to hear it, even when the truth is spoken from a motive of love and genuine concern.

Salt nourishes the body. It is one of many nutrients required by our bodies to stay healthy. Too much salt, of course, can damage health. Just the right amount is required. In like manner, the followers of Jesus were admonished to bring balance and equilibrium to a world in need of spiritual nourishment.

Salt preserves. One of the main preservatives used in canning food is salt. In ancient times, many foods were wrapped in cakes of salt to preserve them. Jesus called his followers to preserve and safeguard the truths of God.

Salt flavors. Salt "brings out" the flavor in many foods, especially as they are cooked. In like manner, believers can help others discover and then share with the world their real God-given traits.

Jesus warned his followers not to lose their "saltiness," which can occur through dilution or pollution. If those who love God become so like those who do not, or if they allow themselves to become involved in wrongdoing, they lose their ability to impact the world.

INFINITE FREEDOM

Not a list of dos and don'ts, the life of faith is a life of freedom—"freedom to" and "freedom from." Romans 8 names twenty-five freedoms for those who follow Jesus.

Believers have the freedom to . . .

1. do what is right by the Spirit's help *(v. 4)*.
2. enjoy life and peace *(v. 6)*.
3. live forever by the Spirit's power *(v. 11)*.
4. live for God, not self *(vv. 12–13)*.
5. follow where God leads *(v. 14)*.
6. call God "Abba, Father" (the equivalent of "Daddy") *(v. 15)*.
7. share the present and future with Jesus *(v. 17)*.
8. long for what God longs for *(v. 23)*.
9. look forward to a perfected body *(v. 23)*.
10. be confidently hopeful and patient *(v. 25)*.
11. pray as a person needs to pray *(vv. 26–27)*.
12. expect good outcomes *(v. 28)*.
13. become like God's Son, Jesus *(v. 29)*.
14. expect to win *(vv. 31–39)*.
15. expect God to finish his work of salvation *(v. 32)*.
16. be loved in all situations *(vv. 35–39)*.
17. be more than conquerors *(v. 37)*.
18. face everything with confidence *(vv. 38–39)*.
19. be God's beloved in Christ *(vv. 38–39)*.

Believers have freedom from . . .

20. condemnation *(v. 1)*.
21. the law of sin and death *(v. 2)*.
22. slavery to fear *(v. 15)*.
23. bondage to decay *(v. 21)*.
24. the fear of not being good enough *(vv. 33–34)*.
25. the fear of not being strong enough *(vv. 35–39)*.

MASADA: FORTIFIED FOR SURVIVAL—AND LUXURY

Masada was a great fortress built by Herod the Great atop a virtually inaccessible plateau just west of the Dead Sea. The top of the plateau, which was the result of many years of natural erosion, was originally fortified by the Hasmonean kings in the two centuries before the birth of Jesus. Herod took over the fortified area as one of the fortresses he used to govern Judea.

After Antony married Cleopatra, Herod feared that Antony would seek to give Judea to Cleopatra. He fortified the Masada retreat just in case that happened. Masada's towers were nearly thirteen hundred feet above sea level. The summit was walled as an added fortification. A series of water cisterns and aqueducts were constructed west of the fortress in the Ben Yair ravine. These cisterns could hold forty thousand cubic meters of water. Water was hauled up a winding path and poured into vast cisterns on the summit.

Vast stores of food were also brought to the summit. These were taken up the steep slope on the eastern side of the fortress. The "snake path," a narrow and tortuous trail, had to be walked single file. The hike up to the summit on this path was more than twelve miles.

Two major palaces were built so all the amenities would be available to Herod should he need to live at Masada during a prolonged siege. Several smaller buildings were located near the palace on the summit, perhaps for use by Herod's many wives. A large building for servants included workshops, a kitchen, and servant sleeping quarters. A bathhouse and a synagogue were among the structures included in the compound at the summit. The bathhouse had a changing room, a warm room heated by clay pipes hidden in the walls, and a cold "plunge bath." Baths such as these were not common to the Jews—the bathhouse may have been built for Herod's foreign visitors.

MASADA: FORTIFIED FOR
SURVIVAL—AND LUXURY (CONT'D)

Perhaps the most amazing feature of Masada was the "Hanging Palace." This is the term used to describe several rooms built on the side of the precipitous plateau. The lowest room is 114 feet below the summit and can be reached only by a very steep staircase. It had a colonnaded courtyard with a small bathroom attached. It was decorated in a style very similar to ruins found at Pompeii. Colored panels were interspersed with panels painted to look like marble. Archaeologists believe this lowermost area of the Hanging Palace was exclusively for Herod the Great's personal use. It would have been very difficult for someone to kill Herod or rout him from that lowest room should Masada have been successfully overrun by enemy troops.

There is no evidence that Herod ever lived at Masada. He was never attacked there.

Masada was occupied much later by Jews revolting against Rome (AD 72–73). Unable to "starve out" the occupying Jews atop Masada, the Romans built a ramp with an incline of twenty degrees—a great engineering accomplishment in that day. They used an ironclad tower and battering ram to penetrate Masada's summit wall. After breaking through the wall, the Roman conquerors discovered the bodies of 960 Jews who had committed suicide rather than be taken prisoner. Traces of the Roman siege lines and remnants of the ramp remain in evidence today.

BITTER HERBS OR JUST SALAD?

Six specific plants in the Bible are identified as "bitter herbs" *(Exodus 12:8; Numbers 9:11)*. People today very likely would call these "salad greens"! The bitter herbs include:

Chicory. This was called "liver's friend" by the Egyptians, and the Egyptians consumed it in large amounts because it was thought to purify the blood and liver.

Dandelion. The root was used for medicinal purposes, and the leaves were eaten as a vegetable.

Endive. This tall leafy plant is related to chicory and is often used in salads. Endive indeed has a bitter taste.

Lettuce. Similar but not identical to the lettuce found in supermarkets today, this lettuce was weedy and had a bitter taste, with yellow flower heads.

Sorrel. This was known to the Israelites as "sheep's sorrel"—its greens were thought to combine well with other greens to improve their flavor. Sorrel also has a bitter taste.

Watercress. High in vitamins and iron, this plant is known for its pungent flavor and medicinal qualities.

All of these plants grew in ancient Egypt and were eaten by Moses and the Israelites during their celebration of the Passover Feast. In a number of places in the Bible, the word *herbs* refers in a general way to plants called "vegetables" today.

HOW THEY MET JESUS

Each of the people below has been a spokesperson for the gospel. Some were famous; others were infamous—at least before becoming believers. All have made significant contributions to the world through their lives and talents. Here's the way each first met Jesus:

1. *Chuck Colson.* Newly released from prison for his role in the Watergate affair, Colson made a simple confession of faith when an inner voice declared that Jesus was God. But not until he had spent the next week studying his Bible did he fully surrender to God and obtain an assurance of his faith.

2. *Amy Carmichael.* The well-known Irish missionary to India met Jesus when she heard Anna Bartlett Warner's simple hymn "Jesus Loves Me" while attending a children's mission in Yorkshire, England.

3. *Smokey Robinson.* The Motown legend said, "I've known God since I was a child, growing up in the ghetto section of Detroit. My mom was what I call a 'God lady.' She brought me up to know God . . . so I always knew that Jesus was the Son of God. Then in 1977, I made a personal decision; I decided for myself to accept Christ as my Savior."

4. *C. S. Lewis.* The beloved author and scholar had resisted all thoughts of God for as long as he could bear it, finally making his formal confession in 1929. Lewis claimed afterward that at the time, he was "the most dejected and reluctant convert in all England." He felt his conversion was quietly but miraculously completed during a sunny bus trip to the zoo, during which he finally accepted that Jesus was the Son of God.

5. *Billy Graham.* In the fall of 1934, at age sixteen, Billy Graham attended a meeting conducted by a traveling evangelist, Mordecai Ham, who visited Charlotte, North Carolina, for a series of revival meetings. It was in one of these meetings that Graham committed his life to Jesus.

HOW THEY MET JESUS (CONT'D)

6. *John Wesley.* In his own words: "In the evening I went very unwillingly to a society in Aldersgate Street, where one was reading Luther's preface to the Epistle to the Romans. About a quarter before nine, while he was describing the change which God works in the heart through faith in Christ, I felt my heart strangely warmed. I felt I did trust in Christ, Christ alone, for salvation: and an assurance was given me, that He had taken away my sins, even mine, and saved me from the law of sin and death."

7. *Charles Spurgeon.* Waylaid by a sudden Sunday morning snowstorm, Spurgeon ducked into a small Primitive Methodist church, where the pastor was absent due to the storm. At the last minute a layman took the pulpit. While telling the sparse congregation of their need for Jesus, he fixed his gaze on the only stranger present, Spurgeon, and challenged him directly to accept the Savior. Spurgeon did.

8. *David Berkowitz.* Better known as the "Son of Sam" murderer serving life in prison, David was confronted by another prisoner who told him that God loved him and had a plan for his life. Several weeks later, while he read the Bible given him by the other prisoner, which contained the New Testament and the Psalms, the love of Christ flooded into his life as he knelt in his cell. He says, "If God can save me . . . there's nobody who's beyond his outstretched hand of love."

9. *Martin Luther.* In his own words: "Night and day I pondered. . . . Then I grasped that the justice of God is that righteousness by which, through grace and sheer mercy, God justifies us through faith. Thereupon I felt myself to be reborn and to have gone through open doors into paradise. The whole of Scripture took on a new meaning."

10. *George W. Bush.* Although he already considered himself a "religious person," George Bush met Jesus in a personal way at age forty after visiting with the Reverend Billy Graham over the course of a weekend. His faith reached a new depth when he joined a men's Bible study group later that year.

SPECIAL RULES REGARDING
THE POOR

The poor were given special provisions in the Old Testament—including safeguards that in ancient times prevented them from automatically becoming slaves or being treated unjustly. Some of these provisions included:

1. The corners of fields were to be left unharvested so the poor might harvest them for personal use.

2. Gleanings of the harvests were to be left for the stranger, the fatherless, and the widow—in other words, if grain fell to the ground or a stalk of grain was not plucked, this grain was fair game for harvest by the poor.

3. If a sheaf of grain was forgotten and left in a field, the owner of the field was not to return for it but was to leave it for the poor. (A prime example of the laws related to gleaning and harvest is found in the book of Ruth. See also *Leviticus 19:9–10*.)

4. Every seventh year, when the land was set aside to rejuvenate, the poor were allowed to take food that grew naturally on the uncultivated land *(Exodus 23:11)*. The seventh year was called the sabbatical year.

5. Ownership of land returned to original owners every fiftieth year *(Leviticus 25:28)*. This was of great blessing to many poor people who had lost their land through bad business practices, drought, or death of owners.

6. Permanent slavery was prohibited. If a Jew needed to become the servant of another Jew during a difficult financial time, the "service" was reversed during sabbatical or Jubilee years (every seven or fifty years).

SPECIAL RULES REGARDING
THE POOR (CONT'D)

7. Interest was not to be charged on loans made to the poor *(Leviticus 25:35–37)*.

8. Garments were not to be permanently taken from the poor as a "pledge"; garments were required to be returned to their rightful owner by nightfall *(Deuteronomy 24:10–13)*.

9. The poor were to be given provision so they could participate fully in the feasts of Weeks (Pentecost) and Tabernacles.

10. Wages were to be paid daily to the poor so common workers might feed their families daily.

The poor were also given certain obligations. They were not allowed to take advantage of their position to obstruct the administration of justice or to unfairly gain favor. They were required to work and to glean if at all possible. Even though these laws were in place, the prophets often voiced God's complaint that the people had developed a hard heart toward the poor or were mistreating them in the courts. (See *Isaiah 10:1–2* and *Amos 2:6–7* as examples.)

The Bible says we will always have the poor among us—in other words, some will always earn or have more, and others will always earn or have less. Absolute financial equality is not taught in either the Old or New Testament, but compassion and generosity are greatly emphasized. Those who "have" are to be kind to and give freely to those who "have not."

THE TWENTY TALLEST CHURCHES IN THE WORLD

Even after God destroyed the Tower of Babel, people continued to build structures that reached heavenward, many of them places of worship. Whether erected to honor the majesty of God, emphasize the power of the church, or as a beacon to the lost, these structures stand out in the landscape. The height indicated for each building below is the distance from the ground to the tallest part of the structure, usually a spire or cross. The buildings are listed in descending order of height.

1. *Chicago Methodist Temple*—Chicago, Illinois, USA (568 ft.)

2. *Munster Cathedral*—Ulm, Germany (528 ft.)

3. *Lincoln Cathedral*—Lincolnshire, England (524 ft.)

4. *St. Olav Cathedral*—Tallinn, Estonia (520 ft.)

5. *Our Lady of Peace Basilica*—Yamoussoukro, Côte d'Ivoire (519 ft.)

6. *Cologne Cathedral*—Cologne, Germany (516 ft.)

7. *Saint-Pierre Cathedral*—Beauvais, France (502 ft.)

8. *Notre-Dame Cathedral*—Rouen, France (495 ft.)

9. *Old St. Paul's Cathedral*—London, England (493 ft.)

10. *St. Nicholas*—Hamburg, Germany (483 ft.)

11. *Notre-Dame Cathedral*—Strasbourg, France (465 ft.)

12. *Cathedral of Saint Stephan*—Vienna, Austria (449 ft.)

13. *St. Peter's Church*—Riga, Latvia (446 ft.)

14. *St. Peter's Basilica at the Vatican*—Italy (443 ft.)

15. *Neuer Dom*—Linz, Austria (440 ft.)

16. *Amiens Cathedral*—France (440 ft.)

17. *St. Petri Cathedral*—Hamburg, Germany (436 ft.)

18. *St. Michealis*—Hamburg, Germany (433 ft.)

19. *Malmesbury Abbey*—Malmesbury (Wiltshire), England (431 ft.)

20. *St. Marting*—Landshut, Germany (428 ft.)

THE ROAD TO HEAVEN WAS PAVED . . . WITH CONCRETE?

The Romans unintentionally gave Christianity a boost—by improving upon (some say inventing) concrete.

Roman roads were often paved with concrete. These roads made it relatively easy for Jesus' followers to travel and spread the gospel. Concrete was also used to construct the grand buildings that Roman emperors demanded. Such buildings needed big roofs, and until concrete came along, the walls of buildings weren't strong enough to support the vaults or domes that the style of the day called for, at least not without needing some sort of interior support beam, which was viewed as an eyesore.

Concrete made possible the construction of basilicas, which were designed for such uses as assembly halls. When the early believers were ready to graduate from meeting in private homes to gathering in larger buildings, they often chose the basilica design for their churches.

JUST WHAT THE DOCTOR ORDERED

Medical research studies conducted in the past fifteen years, such as the Stanford Forgiveness Project, have shown that forgiveness is about more than mending broken relationships. It is also good for a person's health.

Here are a few of the physical benefits that people who forgive may enjoy:

1. Less (up to 50 percent) stress and anxiety
2. Better sleep
3. Lowered risk of heart disease and heart attacks
4. A stronger nervous system
5. Lowered blood pressure
6. Fewer headaches and stomachaches
7. Improved circulation
8. Less depression

Holding on to anger and resentment—marks of unforgiveness—has been shown to have the opposite effects on the human body. Choosing forgiveness may be one of the smartest decisions a person can make for improving quality of health!

SMALL BUT IMPORTANT

The Bible describes the twenty-five things below as being "small." These things may have been diminutive, but they were of tremendous consequence, value, or importance!

1. *Manna (Exodus 16:14–15).* Manna was a "small round substance, as fine as frost on the ground" *(v. 14 NKJV)*. Nobody knows—then or now—what manna was. The word manna means "What is it?" Whatever manna may have been, it was highly nutritious, since it kept the Israelites fed for forty years!

2. *Matters of Judgment (Exodus 18:13–26).* Moses was advised to divide the responsibility for judging the people, so select rulers would decide "every small matter" *(v. 22 NKJV)*, leaving only the great matters for Moses to judge.

3. *Thing or Task (Numbers 16:9).* Moses asked the sons of Levi, "Is it a small thing to you that the God of Israel has separated you from the congregation of Israel, to bring you near to Himself, to do the work of the tabernacle of the LORD, and to stand before the congregation to serve them?" *(NKJV)*. What may seem like a small profession or task in our eyes can be great before God.

4. *Cloud (1 Kings 18:42–44).* Elijah's servant saw a cloud "as small as a man's hand" *(v. 44 NKJV)*, and Elijah knew immediately that this signaled the end of a long drought.

5. *Rain (Deuteronomy 32:2).* God told the Israelites through Moses that the words from his mouth would be as "small rain upon the tender herb" *(KJV)*. They would nourish without overwhelming.

6. *Weights and Measures (Deuteronomy 25:13–14).* God required exact weights and measures in honest transactions among his people. He commanded his people not to have different weights, "a great and a small" *(KJV)* to modify true value.

7. *Stones (1 Samuel 17:40).* The stones David chose for his sling in his battle against Goliath were small stones; many Bible experts believe they were less than an inch in diameter.

8. *A Small Petition (1 Kings 2:19–25).* Bathsheba said to her son, Solomon, "I desire one small petition of you; do not refuse me" *(v. 20 NKJV)*. Solomon not only refused her request, which was to give Abishag the Shunammite to his brother Adonijah, but he ordered that Adonijah be killed.

9. *Voice (1 Kings 19:11–13).* God did not speak to Elijah in an earthquake or fire but rather in a "still small voice" *(v. 12 NKJV)*.

SMALL BUT IMPORTANT (CONT'D)

10. *Fine Ashes (2 Kings 23:4–6).* King Josiah commanded the priest Hilkiah to take a false image out of the temple, burn it, and stamp the ashes "small to powder" *(v. 6 KJV)* and then scatter the ashes on the graves of the people as an act of cleansing God's house from false worship.

11. *Company of Troops (2 Chronicles 24:24).* It took only a "small company of men" from the army of Syria to defeat a great army of Israelites "because they had forsaken the LORD God of their fathers" and had killed the prophet Zechariah *(NKJV).*

12. *Beginning (Job 8:7).* The book of Job describes the Old Testament understanding of the way God blesses his people: "Though thy beginning was small, yet thy latter end should greatly increase" *(KJV).*

13. *Beasts (Psalm 104:25).* The psalmist praised God for his wonderful works, which included the wisdom of creating innumerable beasts "both small and great" *(NKJV).*

14. *Strength (Proverbs 24:10).* People who "faint in the day of adversity" are described in the Bible as those whose strength is "small" *(NKJV).*

15. *Remnant (Isaiah 1:9).* The prophets of Israel often saw the righteous Israelites as being "a very small remnant" *(NKJV).*

16. *Nation (Isaiah 60:22).* God promised the Israelites through the prophet Isaiah that the day would come when his glory would shine upon them and a "little one shall become a thousand, and a small one a strong nation" *(NKJV).*

17. *Band of Escapees (Jeremiah 44:28).* The prophet Jeremiah foretold that a "small number" of people would escape from persecution in Egypt and return to Judah as a witness that Jeremiah's prophecies were true *(NKJV).*

18. *Inner Circle (Daniel 11:21–23).* Daniel foresaw a day when a "vile person" *(v. 21 NKJV)* would arise in peace but seize a kingdom by intrigue— he would become very strong after he had won allegiance from others, and with a "small number of people" *(v. 23 NKJV)* he would arise to great power.

19. *Things or Daily Routines (Zechariah 4:10).* God said through the prophet Zechariah that we should never despise "the day of small things" *(NKJV).* In God's economy, little can always be multiplied into much!

20. *Boat (Mark 3:9).* Jesus asked his disciples to keep a "small boat" ready for him by the seashore in case the pressing crowds following him should "crush Him" as they came to him for healing *(NKJV).*

PHONE HOME!

Prayer is one of the most universal experiences for people of all cultures. Religious or not, people pray. Christianity teaches that prayer is rooted in a relationship with a good, loving, heavenly Father who longs for his children to know him, be close to him, and love him in return. The Bible gives these insights about prayer:

1. *Perspective.* Seek God's heart and mind *(Philippians 2:5).*

2. *Relationship.* Realize that God is a loving Father *(John 15:9).*

3. *Praise.* Commend God for who he is *(Psalm 150).*

4. *Thanksgiving.* Give thanks to God for all he has done *(Psalm 100).*

5. *Confession.* Admit mistakes and receive God's forgiveness *(1 John 1:8–9).*

6. *Petition.* Pray about everything (Philippians 4:6).

7. *Intercession.* "Stand in the gap" for others *(Ezekiel 22:30 NKJV).*

8. *Perseverance.* Keep on praying *(Luke 18:1–8).*

9. *Trust.* Have confidence in God *(Hebrews 11:6).*

10. *Submission.* Pray for God's will to be done *(Luke 22:41–42).*

AN OFFERING OF HERBS?

Jesus referred to herbs that were "tithed" by the religious Jews—in other words, given as an offering at the temple. He said, "Woe to you, scribes and Pharisees, hypocrites! For you pay tithe of mint and anise and cummin, and have neglected the weightier matters of the law: justice and mercy and faith" *(Matthew 23:23 NKJV)*.

Mint was often scattered in synagogues to reduce bad odors; it was also used in medicine and cooking.

The *anise* mentioned in the Bible is the dill of our day; it was used in Jesus' day for flavoring and medicine.

Cummin, also spelled cumin, was used in making unleavened bread and as a treatment for digestive disorders—it has been used in the Near East since the days of the prophet Isaiah.

Another herb, *rue*, has been called for centuries the "herb of grace" because it was scattered in public buildings as a protection against diseases—it has a strong, unusual taste and was used for medicinal purposes, not culinary.

Frankincense and *myrrh* produce gum resins that were highly prized in the Israelites' worship rituals. Both symbolized holiness to the Jews, and their gum resin was used to produce incense. Myrrh's gum resin was also valued as a perfume and for incense. Myrrh became in New Testament times a symbol of Jesus' suffering.

In the Old Testament, the herb *wormwood*—a silvery white plant—became a symbol for a bitter experience, sorrow, or calamity (see *Proverbs 5:3–4 NKJV*).

PHARAOH'S DAUGHTER

Who was the Egyptian princess who plucked baby Moses from the water, adopted him, and influenced his life for forty years? She was still alive and in some position of influence in the royal court when Moses fled from Egypt.

Some historians believe she was the daughter of Seti I, Queen Nefertari, whose mummy was among the treasures found in the Valley of the Queens. Others claim that Queen Hatshepsut—the first female pharaoh—was the foster mother of Moses.

BLESS THIS HORSE

Siena, Italy, is the site of an eight-hundred-year-old tradition called the Palio—a horse race, held twice a year, that pits the city's seventeen *contradas* (neighborhoods) against one another. Each contrada has its own flag, mascot, church, and colors. On the day of the Palio, each horse is marched up the aisle of the neighborhood church, where it is sprinkled with holy water and blessed by a priest, who urges the horse to win.

Sources: www.ilpalio.org/palioenglish.htm; www.2camels.com/destination366.php3; www.hiddentrails.com/europe/italy/palio.htm; www.kidlink.org/KIDPROJ/Recipe/paliodisiena.htm.

GOD IN EVERY STATE

The Declaration of Independence refers to "God" and "the Creator" once, but none of the names of God are found in the U.S. Constitution. Even so, the constitutions of all fifty states acknowledge the Almighty. Typical is this opening line from the Preamble to New York's Constitution, written in 1846: "We, the people of the State of New York, grateful to Almighty God for our freedom, in order to secure its blessings . . ."

WHAT TIME OF YEAR IS THAT IN HEBREW?

The length of the Hebrew month is based upon lunar cycles. In the Bible, months are usually identified by number—for example, the first month or the seventh month. They are sometimes identified by name. A month begins with the new moon—the first night in which no moon is visible in the sky. The fullness of a month is considered to be the fifteenth day of the month—the time when the moon is full. The Feast of Tabernacles, for example, always begins on the fifteenth day of Tishri—that is the fullness of the seventh month. Symbolically, seven refers to the perfection of wholeness, or God's perfect desire. The Feast of Tabernacles was established, therefore, at a time regarded as the fullness of God's wholeness. The Feast of Tabernacles is the major harvest feast of the Bible.

Below are the Hebrew months, with the corresponding time these months usually fall on a Western calendar:

1. Abib or Nisan	1. April
2. Ziv or Zif	2. May
3. Sivan	3. June
4. Tammuz	4. July
5. Ab	5. August
6. Elul	6. September
7. Tishri or Ethanim	7. October
8. Bul	8. November
9. Chislieu or Kislieu	9. December
10. Tebeth	10. January
11. Shebat	11. February
12. Adar	12. March

Do the Jews have a "leap year"? Seven times in nineteen years a thirteenth month, named Ve-Adar, is added to make up the difference between the Jewish year and the solar year.

WORTH A THOUSAND WORDS

Isaiah foretold that Jesus "had no beauty or majesty to attract us to him, nothing in his appearance that we should desire him" *(Isaiah 53:2 NIV)*. And what of his mother, Mary, and his disciples? No one knows for sure how they looked, but artists through the centuries have relied on their imaginations, and in some cases the faces of family members and friends, to create images that are for the most part respectful as well as inspirational. These eighteen paintings represent a small sampling of works that are drawn from New Testament events and stories:

1. *Annunciation.* Fra Angelico, San Marco Museum, Florence, Italy

2. *Madonna and Child.* Giotto, National Gallery of Art, Washington, D.C.

3. *The Adoration of the Magi.* Botticelli, National Gallery of Art, Washington, D.C.

4. *The Adoration of the Shepherds.* Giorgione, National Gallery of Art, Washington, D.C.

5. *The Holy Night.* Corregio, Dresde

6. *The Calling of St. Matthew.* Caravaggio, St. Maria del Popolo, Rome, Italy

7. *Christ in the House of Levi.* Veronese, Galleria dell'Accademia, Venice, Italy

8. *Apostles Peter and Paul.* El Greco, Hermitage Museum, St. Petersburg, Russia

9. *The Return of the Prodigal Son.* Rembrandt, Hermitage Museum, St. Petersburg, Russia

10. *Christ at the Sea of Galilee.* Tintoretto, National Gallery of Art, Washington, D.C.

11. *Christ Cleansing the Temple.* El Greco, National Gallery of Art, Washington, D.C.

12. *Christ Delivering the Keys of the Kingdom to St. Peter.* Perugino, Sistine Chapel, Rome, Italy

13. *The Transfiguration.* Raphael, Vatican Museum, Rome, Italy

14. *The Last Supper.* Leonardo da Vinci, Santa Maria delle Grazie, Milan, Italy

15. *Christ Before Pilate.* Tintoretto, Scuola di San Rocco, Venice, Italy

16. *Christ Crowned with Thorns.* Titian, Alte Pinakothek, Munich, Germany

17. *The Conversion of St. Paul.* Caravaggio, Santa Maria del Popolo, Rome, Italy

18. *The Last Judgment.* Michelangelo, Sistine Chapel, Rome, Italy

ESCHATOLOGY

The word *eschatology* comes from the Greek word *eskhatos*, which means "last things." It is the study of the end times—of what will happen in the earth's last days.

The primary event of the end times, according to believers, is the second coming of Jesus. Other eschatological concerns are what happens to a person's soul after he dies, who will be resurrected and how, and how the Last Judgment will work.

Many of Jesus' own prophecies about the end times have already come true (false Christs and false prophets rising up, wars and rumors of war, famines and earthquakes, persecution of believers). But exactly when will the world end? "This gospel . . . will be preached in the whole world . . . and then the end will come" *(Matthew 24:14 NIV).*

SHEKINAH

Shekinah is a Hebrew word (*shekhina*) meaning "dwelling" or "presence."

Exodus 40:34–35 says that after the tabernacle was completed, the glory of God filled this mobile house of worship—to the point that Moses could not go in. This radiance, or nearness of God, is a way to interpret the meaning of *shekhina*.

Such glory could also be seen in the burning bush, described in Exodus 3:1–6. God came to Moses in the form of fire and told him to take his shoes off because he was standing on "holy ground" *(v. 5 NKJV).* The overpowering presence of God was also evident on Mount Sinai when God relayed the Ten Commandments *(Exodus 19:16–18).* Again God came in the form of a fire, demonstrating his holiness and might.

WHO WERE THEY AND WHAT WERE THEY FOLLOWING?

The gospel of Matthew tells of how the wise men visited the child Jesus. Despite many scholarly investigations over the centuries, little is known about who these men really were, where they came from, or even what celestial sign they were following.

Clues are limited. The Greek word used to describe them in the original text, *basileios*, leaves doubt as to whether these men were actually rulers (kings), or simply powerful and highly placed men. Most scholars agree, however, that they were skilled astronomers.

The Bible doesn't say exactly how many wise men there were; early scholars probably inferred there were three because three different gifts were named. Neither do we know if all the visitors came from the same place in the East. Some scholars argue that the group probably came from Babylon, since Babylon is directly east of Jerusalem and the Babylonians were astute astronomers with records dating back to 2000 BC. Indeed, since the Jews were once captives in Babylon, the wise men would have had knowledge of the expected King and the Old Testament prophecies surrounding his arrival. They could even have been descendants of Jews who did not leave Babylon after their forced captivity.

Other scholars claim that the Magi were Persian, Arabian, or even Greek. Whoever they were, they must have had a good understanding of the Hebrew messianic prophecy. In the Old Testament book of Numbers, the prophet says, "A star will come out of Jacob; a scepter will rise out of Israel" *(24:17 NIV)*. At least some Jewish scholars would have interpreted this passage to say that at the birth of the Messiah there would be a celestial sign.

WHO WERE THEY AND WHAT
WERE THEY FOLLOWING? (CONT'D)

What was the celestial "star in the East" *(Matthew 2:2 NKJV)* that guided the wise men on their journey?

Using ancient astrological records and modern scientific knowledge to answer this question is complicated by the absence of an actual date for Jesus' birth. An error in the Christian calendar, which we now use, and the vagueness of clues given in the Bible make determining a date nearly impossible. The December 25 date, originally selected by the Roman emperor Constantine to replace a pagan celebration, is probably off by several months.

The favored theory is that the star may have been a nova or an extremely rare supernova—a white dwarf star that has blown off its upper layers in a violent explosion, making it as much as fifty thousand times brighter than our sun and viewable as a bright star in the night sky, lasting perhaps for several months to more than a year. If it occurs within our own galaxy, a supernova may be brighter than the moon and visible in full daylight.

The real importance of these visitors, however, lies not in their land of origin or even in the prophecy-fulfilling presence of the celestial sign that guided them. Had it not been for the wise men, Joseph would not have been warned of Herod's interest in the Messiah. In the end, the Magi brought more than just incense, frankincense, and myrrh (valuables that supported the family for the first years of Jesus' life); they also brought an opportunity for Joseph, Mary, and Jesus to escape to the safety of Egypt and away from Herod's slaughter of children in Bethlehem.

Sources: www.unmuseum.org/bstar.htm; astronomical enigmas: Mark Kidger, *Life on Mars, the Star of Bethlehem & Other Milky Way Mysteries* (Baltimore: Johns Hopkins University Press, 2005), chapter 3.

TYNDALE'S TRANSLATION

The Bible not only contains history but also has its own history as a written document. One of the heroes of that historical story is William Tyndale (1494–1536), a Bible scholar from England who was the first to translate the Scriptures from the original Hebrew and Greek into English.

At Tyndale's time, most Bibles were in Latin for use by clergy in the church. Tyndale wanted the common people to be able to read the Scriptures, but translating the Bible into the vernacular was illegal and considered heretical in England. He fled to Germany and worked in concealed places, hiding from authorities. Eventually Tyndale's Bible was printed—the first English New Testament to be printed on the Gutenberg press. Tyndale's location was betrayed by a friend, and he was arrested, imprisoned, and eventually put to death for his work. Three years later Tyndale's English Bible was printed officially by King Henry VIII in England.

JESUS IN THE SAND

Ocean City, Maryland, is the site of an unusual beach ministry. Randy Hofman, a minister, also happens to be a very talented artist.

During the summer months, Randy goes to the beach near the Ocean City boardwalk to dig in the sand with the other sand-castle builders. But instead of castles, Randy creates incredibly intricate sculptures depicting Jesus. His sculptures often portray religious scenes from well-known paintings and other artwork. Some of the sculptures depict other inspirational themes.

As visitors gather on the beach to view his art, Randy makes sure they receive literature explaining that his deep faith has inspired the sculptures. The literature also outlines the way for a person to come to know Jesus personally. Hofman estimates that he has distributed more than eight hundred thousand pieces of literature since he began his sand-sculpture ministry in the mid-1980s.

Sources: www.swapmeetdave.com/United/Beach.htm;
www.poptop.hypermart.net/testrh.html

WHY WORSHIP?

Worship means awareness and recognition of God, a topic that can never be exhausted. Worship has also been defined as serving God as God requests to be served—with thanksgiving, adoration, and praise.

1. "The great thing, and the only thing, is to adore and praise *God*."
   —*Thomas Merton*

2. "It is in the process of being worshipped that God communicates His presence to men."—*C. S. Lewis*

3. "Worship is celebration. All of life is a festival: being persuaded that God is everywhere present on all sides, we praise him as we till the ground, we sing hymns as we sow the seed, we feel his inspiration in all we do."—*Clement of Alexander*

4. "As worship begins in holy expectancy, it ends in holy obedience. Holy obedience saves worship from becoming an opiate, an escape from the pressing needs of modern life."—*Richard Foster*

5. "Worship is the opportunity for busy people to touch the eternal, for sinners to glimpse the holy, for broken people to be enfolded in his perfect love. Worship is moving beyond our self-centered lives to meet the one who created us for something better."—*Robert Frost*

6. "The heart of the issue in worship is this: My life needs God's presence to work God's purpose in my life."—*Jack Hayford*

7. "When we worship together as a community of living Christians, we do not worship alone, we worship 'with all the company of heaven.'"—*Marianne H. Micks*

8. "To be converted to faith in Jesus Christ is to return to the worship of the true God, and to dethrone all rivals to his authority."
   —*Graham Kendrick*

9. "True worship changes people. . . . The results of worship are that God is glorified, Christians are purified, the church is edified, the lost are evangelized"—*John MacArthur*

10. "To worship is to quicken the conscience by the holiness of God, to feed the mind with the truth of God, to purge the imagination by the beauty of God, to open the heart to the love of God, and to devote the will to the purpose of God."—*William Temple*

WHY DO GOOD PEOPLE SUFFER?

When people find themselves suffering, they often ask, "Why me?" Perhaps the better question to ask is, "Why now and for what purpose in my life?" There is much to be learned from suffering. Great character traits are often forged through suffering. The Bible gives ten specific reasons for affliction:

1. To work good in a person *(Psalm 119:71)*
2. To demonstrate God's faithfulness *(Psalm 119:75)*
3. To test a person's sincerity *(Job 1–2)*
4. To refine and purify a person and increase his fruitfulness *(John 15:2)*
5. To increase spiritual power *(Romans 5:1–8)*
6. To humble and correct *(Psalm 89:30–33)*
7. To provide an example for others *(1 Corinthians 10:6, 11)*
8. To manifest God's love *(Hebrews 12:5–10)*
9. To give an opportunity to earn reward *(2 Corinthians 4:17)*
10. To teach obedience and truth *(Hebrews 5:8)*

BIG BLESSINGS

Having an accurate worldview sometimes means seeing how blessed you are in comparison with most of the world!

You are truly blessed if you . . .

1. Woke up this morning with more health than illness (up to a billion people around the world are more sick than well).
2. Live out the week (millions around the world won't).
3. Do not live in danger of battle (people in more than fifty nations have war or conflict at their front door).
4. Aren't in prison (millions around the world are incarcerated, with estimates that at least 20 percent are innocent of the charges against them or are being held as political hostages).
5. Have enough to eat (twenty million people around the world don't).
6. Can attend church without fear of harassment, arrest, torture, or death (three billion people in the world cannot).
7. Have food in your cupboards or refrigerator, clothes on your back, a roof over your head, and a place to sleep (you are ahead of 75 percent of the world).
8. Have money in the bank or in your wallet, or even "spare change" (you are ahead of 92 percent of the world).
9. Can read (two billion people around the world cannot).
10. Have both parents alive and still married (most people in the United States are not as fortunate).

FAITHFUL TO THE FINISH LINE

Scotsman and Olympic champion Eric Liddell, whose life was immortalized in the movie *Chariots of Fire*, always loved to run, but he loved God even more. During the 1924 Paris Games, he refused to run on a Sunday because, he said, "It's the Lord's Day." Nonetheless, he won a gold medal in the 400-meter race a couple of days later.

After the Olympics, Eric returned to China, where he had been born to missionary parents, and took up the work he also loved: sharing God's love with others.

As a teacher, Eric strengthened minds and spirits through chemistry and Sunday school classes, but he did not neglect the body. At the Anglo-Chinese College in Tientsin, China, he got his pupils involved in sports and even spearheaded a drive to build a stadium so athletes would have better facilities.

Eric led devotions with his students each morning, teaching them about God and about living a life patterned after God's Son, Jesus. Affected by both Eric's words and his example, many students asked to be baptized.

The China of the 1930s became increasingly hostile to the British and the Americans, including missionaries. By 1941, Eric had sent his wife and children to Canada for safety; he remained behind. In March 1943, Eric was one of many forced into the Weihsien internment camp. Even there, Eric led worship, organized children's sports, and taught math.

Hard work, difficult conditions at the camp, and lack of medical care led to Eric Liddell's death in 1945. His story, thanks to the movie, lives on.

Source: Catherine Swift, *Eric Liddell* (Minneapolis, MN: Bethany House, 1990).

BETTER THAN LEGEND

Saint Patrick is surrounded by legend, his life celebrated almost worldwide. But the facts of his life alone are amazing enough without embellishment.

Born into a comfortable life in Roman Britain about 389, Patrick was kidnapped as a teenager, taken to Ireland, and sold into slavery. Forced to tend livestock, he endured severe hardship in isolated mountains. He had not embraced his family's Christian faith, but in desolation he clung to prayers of his childhood. After being held captive for six years, he escaped, made his way home, and was reunited with his family. Wounded and scarred from deprivation, but with a profound faith, Patrick entered the priesthood, convinced of a divine purpose for his sufferings.

In a series of dreams, he felt the Irish people call him to return to Ireland. By 432 his religious superiors agreed, and he returned to the site of his enslavement to plant seeds for their conversion. During his thirty years as a "wandering bishop," he wrote that he expected "daily to be killed, betrayed, or brought back into slavery." Within ten years he had established a network of churches and monasteries, which were placed in the hands of a native clergy. He personally baptized tens of thousands and ordained hundreds of priests.

Patrick was not the first Christian missionary to Ireland, but by the end of the fifth century either he or his disciples had traveled to every corner of the island, and what had been a nation of warring Celtic tribes was now a Christian nation.

Sources: "Follow in the Footsteps of Saint Patrick,"
www.storyofsaintpatrick.com; Robert Ellsberg, *All Saints* (New York: Crossroad, 1997), 121–23.

IS ENTHUSIASM GOOD OR BAD?

The word *enthusiasm* today means "great interest in" or "zeal for" something. The word comes from the Greek word *enthousiasmos*, meaning "to be inspired by a god."

In the fourth century, a group of Syrians became known as Enthusiasts because of their belief that through constant prayer, contemplation, and rigid habits, the Holy Spirit might displace the "unholy spirit" that resulted from humanity's "fall" in the Garden of Eden.

During the 1600s and 1700s, both in America and Europe, the word *enthusiasm* took on a negative meaning. It was used by nonchurchgoers and conservative churchgoers alike to describe an overemphasis on emotion and irrational religious behaviors. Those who were deemed to be "enthusiastic" spoke of receiving visions and divine messages, drawing scorn from less-zealous churchmen.

ATONEMENT = "AT-ONE-MENT"

This word *atonement*, while used frequently in the Old Testament, appears only once in the New Testament—and only in one version (*Romans 5:11 KJV*). Other New Testament passages use the word *reconciliation* in its place. The meaning of *atonement* is simply "at-one-ment"—or the state of being unified or reconciled. Believers frequently use the word as it is used in the Old Testament, to denote the way reconciliation is brought about. To make an *atonement* is to make payment for or correct one's offenses (*Exodus 32:30*). Jesus' act of dying was an atonement to God for the errors of humankind.

POMEGRANATES

The pomegranate—literally "grained apple"—was a common fruit in the Middle East during Bible times, used both as a food and in medicines.

The pomegranate is a brownish-red fruit about the size of a large orange, flat at the ends like an apple. Pomegranates come in varieties that are both sweet and sour. The inside of the pomegranate fruit is bright pink, juicy, and loaded with seeds, with membranes separating the fruit into sections.

The Israelites lamented the loss of pomegranates as they wandered in the wilderness of Zin *(Numbers 20:5)*. When Moses sent spies into Canaan, they brought pomegranates with them upon their return *(Numbers 13:23)*. An orchard of pomegranates is mentioned in Song of Solomon, which also refers to "spiced wine of the juice of my pomegranate" *(Song of Solomon 8:2 KJV)*. Pomegranate wine is still made in the Middle East. Pomegranates were carved into the pillars of Solomon's temple in Jerusalem *(1 Kings 7:18)*. Embroidered pomegranates—in blue, purple, and scarlet yarns—were worked into the hem of the high priest's ephod, a holy vestment worn while the high priest was on duty in the temple *(Exodus 28:33–34)*.

The pomegranate has been a major symbol for the Jewish people for thousands of years. The fruit's base has the shape of a crown, a symbol of the Jews' position as the "queen" of Jehovah, the almighty King. The many seeds of the fruit partitioned into sections came to symbolize the many people of Israel, separated into tribes but united as one nation.

A MOST VALUABLE BOOK

Throughout the ages and around the world, notable figures in a wide variety of fields—politics, journalism, the arts, and religion—have openly stated their high regard for the Bible, not only as great literature but as a life-influencing document:

1. "The Bible contains more true sublimity, more exquisite beauty, more pure morality, more important history, and finer strains of poetry and eloquence, than can be collected from all other books, in whatever age or language they may have been written."—*Sir William Jones (English cleric and naturalist, 1726–1800)*

2. "Bad men or devils would not have written the Bible, for it condemns them and their works—good men or angels could not have written it, for in saying it was from God when it was but their own invention, they would have been guilty of falsehood, and thus could not have been good. The only remaining being who could have written it, is God—its real author."—*John Flavel (Calvinist cleric in England, 1627–1691)*

3. "I believe the Bible is to be understood and received in the plain and obvious meaning of its passages; for I cannot persuade myself that a book intended for the instruction and conversion of the whole world should cover its true meaning in any such mystery and doubt that none but critics and philosophers can discover it."—*Daniel Webster (English theologian and American dictionary compiler, 1778–1858)*

4. "When you have read the Bible, you will know it is the word of God, because you will have found it the key to your own heart, your own happiness and your own duty."—*Thomas Woodrow Wilson (twenty-eighth president of the United States, 1856–1924)*

5. "Hold fast to the Bible as the sheet-anchor of your liberties; write its precepts in your hearts, and practice them in your lives. To the influence of this book we are indebted for all the progress made in true civilization, and to this we must look as our guide in the future."—*U. S. Grant (general and eighteenth president of the United States, 1822–1885)*

6. "It is impossible to mentally or socially enslave a Bible-reading people. The principles of the Bible are the groundwork of human freedom."—*Horace Greeley (American journalist and statesman, 1811–1872)*

A MOST VALUABLE BOOK (CONT'D)

7. "The most learned, acute, and diligent student cannot, in the longest life, obtain an entire knowledge of this one volume. The more deeply he works the mine, the richer and more abundant he finds the ore; new light continually beams from this source of heavenly knowledge, to direct the conduct, and illustrate the work of God and the ways of men; and he will at last leave the world confessing, that the more he studied the Scriptures, the fuller conviction he had of his own ignorance, and of their inestimable value."—*Walter Scott (Scottish novelist and poet, 1771–1832)*

8. "Holy Scripture is a stream of running water, where alike the elephant may swim, and the lamb walk without losing its feet."—*Gregory the Great (Italian pope, 560–604)*

9. "Nobody ever outgrows Scripture; the book widens and deepens with our years."—*Charles Haddon Spurgeon (English cleric, 1834–1892)*

10. "The Bible is to us what the star was to the wise men; but if we spend all our time in gazing upon it, observing its motions, and admiring its splendor, without our being led to Christ by it, the use of it will be lost to us."—*Thomas Adams (English cleric, circa 1640)*

11. "In what light soever we regard the Bible, whether with reference to revelation, to history, or to morality, it is an invaluable and inexhaustible mine of knowledge and virtue."—*John Quincy Adams (president of the United States, 1767–1848)*

12. "The Bible is the only cement of nations, and the only cement that can bind religious hearts together."—*Christian Karl Bunsen (Prussian scholar, 1791–1860)*

13. "It is a belief in the Bible, the fruit of deep meditation, which has served me as the guide of my moral and literary life." —*Johann Wolfgang von Goethe (German poet, dramatist, and philosopher, 1749–1832)*

A DEITY BY ANY OTHER NAME IS CALLED . . . ?

Belief in and worship of a Supreme Being is something that distinguishes humankind from the rest of the animal kingdom. Speak to a Jew, a Christian, or a Muslim, however, and out will come three very different definitions of *God*.

Christians believe in a Trinitarian God: God the Father, God the Son, and God the Holy Spirit; three in one. They believe God created the world and everything in it and wants to be personally involved with humans. Christians also believe God sent his Son, Jesus, to earth in human form so he could pay the price for humankind's wrongdoing by dying on the cross and being resurrected—thereby offering eternal life in heaven for those who believe in him.

Other religions also have other names for and definitions of their deities:

- In *Judaism*, there is one God with a singular personality. He created the world and is the Lord of the entire earth. Jews believe he chose them to help bring non-Jews into a covenant relationship with him, and that he will someday send a Messiah.

- *Muslims* call their deity Allah and consider him the creator and sustainer of the universe. He imparted revelation to his most notable prophet, Muhammad, to show people the right way to live. He requires absolute obedience in prayer, almsgiving, fasting at set times, and, if possible, a pilgrimage to Mecca.

- The *Hindus* have three main deities: Brahma (creator of the universe), Vishnu (preserver of the universe), and Shiva (destroyer of the universe). There are hundreds of other gods and goddesses—some good, some evil. The Hindu's goal is to break free from the cycle of reincarnation and merge his soul with Brahman (the supreme soul).

A DEITY BY ANY OTHER NAME IS CALLED . . . ? (CONT'D)

- In *Jainism*, an ancient Indian religion, there is no deity. There is Mahavira, the Great Hero, who has achieved full enlightenment and can guide others' souls from this life to the next.

- Ahura Mazda is the deity that *Zoroastrians* worship. They believe he created the world and everything in it. One day, believers say, a savior will come and cure all the world's ills. In the meantime, death brings judgment, with the good going to heaven.

- Buddha is not a god, but his teachings are considered scripture. *Buddhists* want to be enlightened like Buddha and get through the cycle of rebirth so they can achieve nirvana: the end of suffering, including even the awareness of suffering.

- *Sikhs* have one deity. They grow close to him by serving others.

- *Confucianism*—"way of life"—was founded by Confucius. It emphasizes good conduct and service to others and says, "Believe in any god, or in no god."

- Tao ("way" or "path") is a spiritual force. Living in harmony with an ever-present spiritual force is believed to free the soul. *Taoism* has no deity. A soul's fate hinges on one's good or evil actions.

- *Shintoists* believe there are spirits in everything. Amaterasu, a sun goddess, is the primary spirit. Earth, adherents say, was created by the god Izanagi and his wife, Izanami.

- In *Baha'ism*, there are many ways to get to God. All religions, adherents say, teach the same truths and are divine, and all prophets serve the same God. One goal of this faith is to unite all religions. The religion is named for its founder, Baha'u'llah.

Which religion? Which deity? The choice is up to the individual.

OLDEST CITY IN THE WORLD

Many archaeologists believe that Jericho is the world's oldest continually occupied city. Remains of houses built during the Stone Age have been found at the site. The site was originally an oasis with the benefit of a continuous spring. The many palm trees at the oasis give rise to Jericho's reputation as the "city of palms." The Old Testament Jericho was a little north of the New Testament city, which is the Jericho we know today.

Source: www.encyclopedia.thefreedictionary.com/Jericho.

SAINT LUKE'S LITTLE SUMMER

A spell of warm weather often occurs in October—usually after a period of cooler days that have caused people to think fall has arrived to stay. Sometimes this period of warmer days is called "Indian summer." In other circles, this spell of warm weather is called Saint Luke's Little Summer because the weather often occurs about the time of this saint's feast day on the church calendar, October 18.

BLIND OR DAZZLED?

The Bible words for blindness can refer to a permanent physical condition or to the temporary blindness of "being dazzled." This latter use of the word occurs only in cases when God causes loss of sight, such as Saul's road-to-Damascus experience (*Acts 9:3–8*), the loss of sight for the men who tried to break down Lot's door in Sodom (*Genesis 19:11*), and the blindness of the Syrian army seeking to capture Elisha (*2 Kings 6:18*).

GO YE, EVERYDAY EVANGELISTS

Jesus Christ's command was, "Go into all the world and preach the good news to all creation" *(Mark 16:15 NIV)*. Though it was a personal instruction to all of his followers, how literally are today's Christians taking that command, and how do they practice it in their everyday lives?

According to Barna Group research:

Parents are more likely than are nonparents to be sharing their faith in Christ with others (62% to 55%, respectively). (2002)

Eighty percent of evangelical Christians have shared their faith with a non-Christian in the past year. (2002)

Fifty-five percent of born-again Christians claim they have shared their faith with a non-Christian during 2004, compared with 58 percent in 1999.

Protestant non-mainline churchgoers (63%) are more likely than those attending mainline churches (52%) and Catholics (48%) to share their faith. (2002)

Forty-nine percent of born-again believers shared their faith in Jesus in the past year, taking a nonbelieving friend to church so they could hear the gospel. (2004)

Seventy-eight percent of born-again believers shared their faith in Jesus in the past year by offering to pray with a nonbeliever who was in need of encouragement or support. (2004)

Twenty-one percent of born-again people shared their faith in Jesus with a nonbeliever in the past year by sending letters or e-mails explaining aspects of their faith and encouraging him or her to consider it more closely. (2004)

Source: "Evangelism," The Barna Group, www.barna.org, Barna Update, n.d., accessed 1/22/05.

ONE SAINT'S LIFE

People sometimes assume that those canonized as saints are individuals who were called early in life to a church vocation or performed tremendous miracles. That, however, is not always the case. Many of those chosen by the Roman Catholic Church have lived seemingly "ordinary" lives—with ups and downs, hardship and struggle, purpose and peace.

Consider the story of Alphonsus Rodriguez, the third child of a well-to-do wool merchant in Segovia, Spain. When he was ten years old, Alphonsus spent a holiday with Jesuit missionaries at his family's country home, and during that time he had his first Communion. Five years later Alphonsus's father died, and Alphonsus left a Jesuit school and worked full-time with his mother in the family business. When he was twenty-three, he became sole proprietor of the business. At age twenty-six he married a girl named Maria.

Alphonsus, unfortunately, was not a very good business-man, and times were hard. Within a few years his wife died after a long illness. Alphonsus also lost a daughter and his mother to death from illness. This succession of losses made Alphonsus think very seriously about what God might want him to do. He sold his business, and he and his young son went to live with his two maiden sisters, Antonia and Juliana. They taught Alphonsus how to pray and meditate on the Scriptures. When his son died a few years later, Alphonsus sought to become one of the Jesuits at Segovia. Initially the Jesuits refused him—he was nearly forty years old by that time, his health was not good, and he did not have much education. Undaunted, Alphonsus enrolled in a school for little boys to learn Latin! He gave his money to his sisters and the poor in Segovia, and he determined to become a "servant"

ONE SAINT'S
LIFE (CONT'D)

until he was ordained. He finally was accepted by the Jesuits in 1571 and was given work as a hall porter at the College of Montesione on the island of Majorca. He did not become a full priest until he was fifty-four years old. He stayed in his position as hall porter until he was old and infirm, spending every minute when he was not at work in prayer. He gained a reputation with the Montesione students and visitors as a man who spoke and behaved "without reason for criticism." He often told his fellow Jesuits that he felt spiritually "dry" but he never despaired—at times he also experienced great personal outpourings of God's love.

In May 1617 the rector of Montesione, Father Julian, became very ill with rheumatic fever, and he asked for the prayers of Alphonsus, who spent the night interceding for him. In the morning Father Julian was well enough to lead a worship service. On October 29 of that same year, at the age of eighty-four, Alphonsus knew he was near death. He took holy Communion one last time, and for two days he rested in a state described as "quiet ecstasy," completely free of distress. Then suddenly he experienced a half hour of painful torment. When this subsided, he again was pain-free. He became very alert, looked around lovingly at those near him, kissed a crucifix, cried out the name of Jesus in a loud voice, and died. He was made a saint in 1888. He is remembered in Catholic church services every October 30.

A BIBLICAL ORCHESTRA?

It would be easy to form an orchestra if you had all the musical instruments popular in Bible times!

1. *Cornet.* In Hebrew it's called a "shofar," which means "brightness." Some were made from animal horns, others from a straight brass tube about eighteen inches long, with a clear, bright sound.

2. *Cymbal.* A pair of small bronze or brass disks struck against one another, much like today's finger cymbals. Larger cymbals such as might be seen in a modern orchestra were called "high-sounding cymbals."

3. *Dulcimer.* Unlike the more modern instrument, the biblical dulcimer was more of a bagpipe-like instrument usually having only two pipes. It's mentioned in Daniel 3:5, 15 *(AMP)*.

4. *Flute.* A pipe instrument that probably varied depending on the cultural influences. Made of wood, some would resemble today's single-pipe variety, while others probably had several pipes.

5. *Gittith.* A type of harp, it is the only stringed instrument named in the titles of the Psalms *(Psalms 8; 81; 84)*. The word means "on the harp which David brought from Gath."

6. *Harp and lyre.* Both were multistringed instruments. They were the first instruments mentioned in the Bible, and the instruments mentioned most often throughout the Bible. The most popular versions had three or ten strings and were plucked and strummed. Jubal invented the harp, David mastered it, and it was the forerunner of our modern harpsichord, clavier, and piano.

7. *Organ.* Unlike the modern keyboard instrument of the same name, this organ was a kind of wind instrument having seven or eight reeds of unequal length fastened together and played like a pipe.

8. *Pipe.* The Hebrew word for pipe means "bored through." It refers to various kinds of wind instruments (for example, the fife, flute, panpipe) and is mentioned in both the Old and New

A BIBLICAL ORCHESTRA? (CONT'D)

Testaments. Still used in Palestine today, it continues to be made of different materials such as reed, copper, and bronze.

9. *Psaltery.* Supposedly a harplike instrument with twelve strings, it no doubt required more skill and technique to play than smaller harps. It may have also been bowed like a violin.

10. *Sackbut.* Unlike the modern sackbut, which is a wind instrument, this strange harplike instrument was likely borrowed by the Israelites from the Syrians.

11. *Tabret.* A tambourine-like instrument incorporating timbrels, it was generally played during group dances. Playing the tabret for joyful occasions was considered a "women-only" activity.

12. *Timbrel.* Small cymbals (two brass disks) sometimes played by attaching them to the fingers of one hand or by holding them parallel to the floor (one in each hand) and striking one against the other.

13. *Trumpet.* Wind instruments that came in a variety of forms and materials including silver and ram's horn, they were used exclusively by the priests to announce the approach of festivals, herald the arrival of special seasons, and to give battle signals. "Trumpets" are among the symbols used in the book of Revelation.

14. *Viol.* A stringed instrument very similar to a lyre. It later developed into the modern guitar.

15. *Voice.* One of the most important musical instruments mentioned in the Bible! Among the more noted singers were Moses, David, and Deborah. Paul and Silas were credited with an earth-shaking duet in the New Testament, and all the Israelites were members of the Bible's biggest choir.

Source: www.paulsonmusic.com/MusicInstruments.html.

HE HAD A DREAM

Martin Luther King Jr. was pastor of Dexter Avenue Baptist Church in Montgomery, Alabama, when he was thrust into the national spotlight, leading the Civil Rights Movement of the 1960s. His work met opposition and he was jailed, his home bombed, and his life repeatedly threatened. That didn't deter him. When he prayed, he heard an inner voice saying, "Martin Luther, stand up for righteousness. Stand up for justice. Stand up for truth. And lo, I will be with you, even until the end of the world."

His famous speech "I Have a Dream," delivered on the steps of the Lincoln Memorial in 1963, mobilized support for desegregation and prompted passage of the Civil Rights Act of 1964. The next year, at age thirty-five, King became the youngest man to receive the Nobel Peace Prize. Four years later, in 1968, he died by an assassin's bullet.

Sources: Robert Ellsberg, *All Saints* (New York: Crossroad, 1997), 152–54; www.time.com/time/time100/leaders/profile/king.html.

ULTIMATE SURVIVORS

Perpetua was a new believer in Carthage, a prosperous noble-woman, married, and mother of an infant son. She was part of the thriving Christian community in second-century North Africa that fell under the rule of Roman emperor Septimus Severus. The emperor required all citizens to sacrifice to the Roman gods; for believers it effectively meant renouncing their faith.

At age twenty-two Perpetua was arrested with other believers preparing for baptism. Despite the pleading of her father, she declared to authorities, "I am a Christian." She and her servant, Felicitas, were condemned to face wild beasts in the arena.

Perpetua faced her sentence bravely, stating, "We are not left to ourselves, but are all in his [God's] power." She survived an attack by a wild heifer, but was put to death by the executioner's sword. Perpetua's prison diary, *The Passion of Sts. Perpetua and Felicitas*, encouraged the early church and survives to this day!

Sources: Robert Ellsberg, *All Saints* (New York: Crossroad, 1997), 105; Joanna Turpin, *Women in Church History* (Cincinnati: St. Anthony Messenger Press, 1989), 14–20; Mark Galli, Ted Olsen, eds., *131 Christians Everyone Should Know* (Nashville: Broadman, 2000), 362.

LIFE ON THE LINE

Wanted: *Men who will give up the comforts of home in exchange for low pay, sleeping on the ground in all kinds of weather, exposure to illness and intense suffering, inadequate nourishment, and threat of death. Might be called upon to assist with surgeries, and should be willing to bury the dead.*

Duties: *Preaching; teaching the Bible; praying for discouraged, terrified, sometimes-angry men; organizing hymn-singing; distributing religious literature; writing letters to families for men who are (1) illiterate or (2) dead; visiting the sick; and helping men prepare to meet their Maker.*

Ah, the job description of a Civil War chaplain!

Both the North and the South had chaplains assigned to their regiments, but there were never enough to go around.

There were other challenges too. Some chaplains weren't as qualified as they should have been or weren't up to the rigors of army life. In the South, Bibles were in short supply. The army was always on the move, and the weather was not always suitable for open-air preaching.

According to soldiers' comments, the positives outweighed the negatives. For the most part, the more than three thousand chaplains filled the roles of friend, spiritual adviser, and comforter. They sought to improve moral behavior and accompanied the men into battle. Some even fought.

Yes, it's true that some chaplains volunteered for the "adventure" of war, and some saw it as their patriotic duty. But many no doubt believed that soldiers facing danger and death would be especially open to hearing about God and making his acquaintance . . . before it was too late.

Source: John W. Brinsfield, William C. Davis, Benedict Maryniak, James I. Robertson Jr., eds., *Faith in the Fight: Civil War Chaplains* (Mechanicsburg, PA: Stackpole, 2003); Steven E. Woodworth, *While God Is Marching On* (Lawrence, KS: Univ. Press of Kansas, 2001).

LET'S PARTY!

In addition to the religious feasts established for the Israelites, folks in Bible times celebrated much like we do today—with lots of food and rip-roaring good times! The occasions varied from homecoming celebrations to marriages. Here are twenty-five of the most notable Bible hosts and guests of honor or occasions:

1. Abraham's banquet for angelic visitors *(Genesis 18:1–8)*

2. Lot's feast for angels who dropped in *(Genesis 19:3)*

3. Abraham's coming-of-age party for Isaac *(Genesis 21:8)*

4. Laban's wedding feast for Jacob *(Genesis 29:22)*

5. Joseph's reunion banquet for his brothers *(Genesis 43:16–34)*

6. Samson's wedding feast for his bride *(Judges 14:10–18)*

7. David's banquet for former enemy Abner *(2 Samuel 3:20)*

8. Israel's three-day feast for David's warriors *(1 Chronicles 12:39)*

9. Solomon's weeklong feast at the temple dedication in honor of God *(1 Kings 8:65)*

10. Elisha's ordination feast for the people *(1 Kings 19:21)*

11. King Ahasuerus's party for all his nobles and officials, which Queen Vashti refused to attend *(Esther 1:3–12)*

12. King Ahasuerus's feast for Esther's coronation *(Esther 2:17–18)*

13. Esther's banquet for the king and Haman *(Esther 7:1–10)*

14. Job's family feast given by his eldest son *(Job 1:13)*

15. Belshazzar's banquet for a thousand of his nobles *(Daniel 5)*

16. Herod's birthday party for himself *(Mark 6:21)*

17. Jesus' fish-and-loaves picnic for five thousand people *(Matthew 14:15–21)*

18. A king's son's wedding feast for unworthy guests *(Matthew 22:1–14)*

19. Simon's dinner for Jesus, where Jesus was anointed with expensive perfume *(Luke 7:36–50)*

20. The wedding feast in Cana for an unnamed couple, at which Jesus turned water into wine *(John 2:1–11)*

21. Levi's dinner party for Jesus with tax collectors and other diverse guests *(Luke 5:29)*

22. A father's homecoming gala for his prodigal son *(Luke 15:23–25)*

23. The Passover Feast hosted by Jesus for his disciples (the Last Supper) *(John 13)*

24. The Emmaus feast after Jesus' resurrection, at which his disciples finally recognized him *(Luke 24:30)*

25. The post-Calvary dinner, during which Jesus suddenly appeared to dine with his close disciples *(Luke 24:42–43)*

GO FIGURE!

Christian history is filled with a number of events, publications, words, phrases, and practices that can leave a person puzzled. Just consider:

- "Hair shirts" are garments woven of rough hair—usually goat hair—worn by ascetics to do penance or mortify the flesh. The irritation of itching is believed to lead to repentance.

- A Book of Sports? King James I of England issued a controversial declaration by this title in 1617–1618. In the book, he defined the kind of activities permitted in England on Sunday.

- "Gresaille" is a type of church window glass in which images have been painted in tints of gray. When stained glass of beautiful color is available, why gray? Some say the reason is that people look better and more timeless in black and white. Others claim that the gray tint is less distracting to those attending church services. Still others believe that the gray tint is chosen so as not to detract from the "full color" of divine and supernatural figures.

- In the Armenian tradition, bishops wear a flat lozenge-style disk of stiffened material suspended from the girdle around their waist. It is symbolic of a "sword of righteousness" and is called a "konker." To be konked by a bishop was an act of admonishment!

- Recycled holy bread? In the Assyrian church, holy leaven is kept in a chalice or small cupboard. It is mixed with flour and salt, and particles of previous consecrated bread, to make the bread that is consecrated for use in Communion. While the Jews typically consider unleavened bread appropriate for most holy rituals, Christians routinely add leaven.

GO FIGURE!
(CONT'D)

- Long before the invention of the computer, a collection of rules called "computus" was used to calculate the date of Easter each year.

- In old English religious writings, the word *conversation* had nothing to do with talking. It referred to "lifestyle" or "conduct." A person's conversation was not what he said but how he lived.

- The Coptic Christians have their own calendar. The starting date was 284, the year Diocletian became emperor of Rome. Diocletian ordered the destruction of churches and the burning of Christian books, issued edicts against clergy, and imposed a duty of sacrifice to pagan gods. Believers were especially persecuted from 303 to 305, a period called the Era of the Martyrs. The Coptic calendar has twelve months of thirty days each. In part, it is a calendar created in opposition to the Roman calendar established by Julius Caesar in 46 BC. Periodic adjustments are made to the calendar to accommodate the "extra" five to six days of modern calendars.

SKILLED WITH BOW AND ARROW

In ancient times, bows and arrows were used mainly for hunting, but by the time of the Old Testament, bows and arrows were common weapons of warfare. Archers were often trained from childhood and were deadly accurate. They were usually the first to contact the enemy, by shooting from a distance. Archers who rode in chariots added mobility to their firepower.

Old Testament archers used composite bows, made with a combination of wood and animal horn to give the bow flexibility and strength. A pull of about a hundred pounds was required to draw ancient war bows. Arrows were long, slender shafts of wood with tips of sharp stone or metal. They were crafted to pierce almost all types of armor. Each archer was equipped with a quiver—a deep, narrow basket constructed especially for arrows.

"Bowshot" was the term used to describe the distance an arrow could reach *(Genesis 21:16)*. In Old Testament times, that could be three hundred to four hundred yards.

The first person described in the Bible as an archer was Ishmael, Abraham's son *(Genesis 21:20)*.

Also in the Bible:

1. Jonathan purposefully shot arrows beyond a target as a warning for David to flee for his life *(1 Samuel 20)*.

2. In battling the Philistines, King Saul was "severely wounded by the archers" *(1 Samuel 31:3 NKJV)*. Rather than be taken captive, he fell on a sword to end his life.

3. Bathsheba's husband, Uriah, was killed by archers shooting from the walls of a city under siege by David's armies *(2 Samuel 11)*.

WHAT IS DEISM?

Unlike atheism, which teaches that there is no God, deism acknowledges God as the "Great Designer" but denies that God is concerned with the affairs of people. Deism casts God in an impersonal relationship to his creation and bases its understanding of God on reason and nature. Deists believe that all one needs is one's own common sense and the creation to contemplate. Faith of any kind is not acceptable to a deist, since faith is seen as the antithesis of reason.

While some sparse "congregations" of deists do exist across the U.S., there is no leader (such as a pastor or rabbi), no holy book (such as the Bible), and no prayers of supplication or praise, although some deists say they do offer prayers of thanks.

Sources: www.deism.org/frames.htm; www.religioustolerance.org/deism.htm.

THE END

A little girl ended her bedtime prayers by saying, "The end!" When her mother asked why, she said, "Because I'm tired of saying, 'Amen'!"

The little girl probably isn't alone in her misconception of the meaning of the word, since it's most frequently used at the conclusion of a prayer or hymn.

Amen is a Hebrew word meaning "trustworthy," "firm," "surely," "faithful." The Scriptures occasionally use it as a noun *(2 Corinthians 1:20)*, and once it is used as a title of Jesus *(Revelation 3:14)*. Jesus' New Testament teachings use the word frequently, but it has been translated in the King James Version as "verily."

Nowadays, however, in addition to concluding prayers and hymns, *amen* is often used as an interjection employed to express solemn ratification or hearty approval of words or actions.

GOD'S ASTRONOMY LESSON: AHEAD OF ITS TIME

In the Old Testament, Job asked God why good people suffer. Job seemed to imply in his questions of God that if he were God, he would handle things differently. God's lengthy reply reminded Job that he had little understanding of God and the mysteries of his creation. God especially seemed to point out to Job that he had created the universe and set the stars on their paths, and he therefore could handle Job's problems. God's answer also revealed a knowledge of the stars far beyond anything that technology could have shown the author of the book of Job at the time it was written.

In Job 38:31, God says to Job, "Can you bind the beautiful Pleiades? Can you loose the cords of Orion?" *(NIV)*. Thousands of years after this question was posed to Job, late-nineteenth-century astronomers finally possessed telescopes and other equipment strong and accurate enough to shed light on the question's full meaning.

They showed that Orion's band (around what would be considered the waist of figure in the constellation) consists of an almost perfectly straight line of second-magnitude stars about equally spaced and of the most striking beauty. Yet each of the stars is traveling in a different direction and at a different speed. In the course of time, the two right-hand stars, Mintaka and Alnilam, will approach each other and form what will be seen by the naked eye as a double star. The third, Alnitak, will drift away eastward so that the band will actually no longer exist. In fact, all the stars constituting the constellation of Orion are bound for different ports, and all are journeying to various corners of the universe, so that the bands are being dissolved—precisely as God said in his answer to Job.

GOD'S ASTRONOMY LESSON: AHEAD OF ITS TIME (CONT'D)

Since all stars are independent bodies, aren't all constellations destined for dissolution? And if that's true, what did God mean when he referred to the "binding" of the Pleiades?

The Pleiades is the brightest and most famous star cluster in the sky. It is popularly termed the Seven Sisters, since approximately seven stars are visible to the naked eye. Binoculars can bring dozens more stars into view. This open cluster is found in the constellation Taurus, about four hundred light-years from the solar system. Ancient astronomers would have most likely been limited to what they could observe of Taurus with their naked eyes. As technology progressed, however, it became more apparent that the grouping had many more stars than originally thought.

The twentieth century brought technology that allowed astronomers to view and photograph heavenly objects in greater detail and from greater distances than ever before. By 1956, astronomers at the University of California's Lick Observatory had identified more than twenty-five thousand individual measures of the Pleiades stars. Their study led to the discovery that the whole cluster is "moving in unison in a southeasterly direction like a swarm of birds flying together to a common destination." This leaves no doubt that the Pleiades are not a temporary or accidental agglomeration of stars but a system in which the stars are bound together by a close kinship—an exceedingly rare situation.

Scientists announcing these rare findings made no reference to the book of Job. Incredibly, however, there is no doubt that God's words, recorded thousands of years ago, have been proven absolutely true by the passage of time and by humanity's ability to observe creation in more depth.

Sources: sattre-press.com/serviss-curiosities-of-the-sky.html; www.bibletoday.com/archive/proof_text.htm; www.pleaseconvinceme.com/module_articleDetails.php?moduleName=Bible&moduleID=93&articleID=432.

JESUS AND THE PSALMS

Preachers today sometimes refer to the lyrics of a hymn in their sermons. Jesus also did so as he preached and at other times:

1. "Have you never read, 'Out of the mouth of babes and nursing infants You have perfected praise'?"
   (Psalm 8:2; Matthew 21:16 NKJV).

2. "Have you never read in the Scriptures: 'The stone which the builders rejected has become the chief cornerstone. This was the LORD's doing, and it is marvelous in our eyes'?"
   (Psalm 118:22–23; Matthew 21:42 NKJV).

3. "How then does David in the Spirit call Him 'Lord,' saying: 'The LORD said to my Lord, "Sit at My right hand, till I make Your enemies Your footstool"'?"
   (Psalm 110:1; Matthew 22:43–44 NKJV).

4. "I say to you, you shall see Me no more till you say, 'Blessed is He who comes in the name of the LORD!'"
   (Psalm 118:26; Matthew 23:39 NKJV).

5. "Is it not written in your law, 'I said, "You are gods"'? If He called them gods, to whom the word of God came (and the Scripture cannot be broken), do you say of Him whom the Father sanctified and sent into the world, 'You are blaspheming,' because I said, 'I am the Son of God'?"
   (Psalm 82:6; John 10:34–36 NKJV).

6. "I do not speak concerning all of you. I know whom I have chosen; but that the Scripture may be fulfilled, 'He who eats bread with Me has lifted up his heel against Me'"
   (Psalm 41:9; John 13:18 NKJV).

7. "This happened that the word might be fulfilled which is written in their law, 'They hated Me without a cause'"
   (Psalm 69:4; John 15:25 NKJV).

8. "My God, My God, why have You forsaken Me?"
   (Psalm 22:1; Matthew 27:46 NKJV).

9. "Father, 'into Your hands I commit My spirit'"
   (Psalm 31:5; Luke 23:46 NKJV).

COME AS A LITTLE CHILD

The most memorable conversion stories often involve people who've lived lives far from Jesus Christ, committed deeds that ordinary humans would find difficult to forgive, and then made a late-in-life decision to follow him. Research has shown, however, that most people who make a commitment to Christ do so at an early age.

According to the Barna Group, nearly half of all Americans who become believers do so before reaching the age of thirteen. About two out of three born-again Christians make a commitment to Christ before their eighteenth birthday, and one out of eight makes a profession of faith while eighteen to twenty-one years old.

While some observers have questioned the validity of childhood conversions, another Barna survey reveals that people who embrace Christ before the age of thirteen are more likely to remain absolutely committed to him in their adult years than are people who accept Christ in their teenage or adult years.

Sources: "Evangelism Is Most Effective Among Kids," The Barna Group, www.barna.org, Barna Update 12/24/04, accessed 9/5/05; "Barna's Annual Review of Significant Religious Findings Offers Encouragement and Challenges," The Barna Group, www.barna.org, Barna Update 12/24/04, accessed 3/17/06.

THE DEVIL KNEW HIS MUSIC

Many Christian parents today are concerned about the way in which popular music is sometimes used to mask malicious intent, or to incite the music's listeners to take action that is wrong in God's eyes. There's nothing new about that! When the devil came to tempt Jesus in the wilderness, he quoted a passage of Psalms—the songbook of Jesus' day. The devil said to Jesus, "If You are the Son of God, throw Yourself down from here [the pinnacle of the temple]. For it is written: 'He shall give His angels charge over you, to keep you,' and, 'In their hands they shall bear you up, lest you dash your foot against a stone'" *(Psalm 91:11–12; Luke 4:9–11 NKJV).*

Jesus wisely answered, "You shall not tempt the LORD your God" *(Luke 4:12 NKJV).* The devil may have known the lyrics (the psalm) . . . but Jesus knew what those lyrics were intended to mean! At no time did God ever intend for *anybody* to throw himself off a high ledge to prove he could miraculously escape harm!

Parents are wise today to know the lyrics of the songs popular with their children and to discuss what the lyrics really mean.

HER MAJESTY

The word *king* appears more than two thousand times in the Bible, but *queen* appears only about fifty times. Most biblical queens are unnamed and noted only briefly. Athaliah, who usurped the throne, is the only queen in the Old Testament who actually "reigned." Most of the Old Testament queens were known for their roles as queen mothers or the wives of ruling monarchs. Following are twenty-four of the queens mentioned in the Bible.

Queens of the Old Testament

1. *Abi (Abijah).* Daughter of Zecharia and mother of King Hezekiah of Judah *(2 Kings 18:2).*

2. *Athaliah.* Daughter of Jezebel and Ahab *(2 Kings 8:18, 26)*; granddaughter of King Omri *(2 Chronicles 22:2–3)*; and mother of King Ahaziah of Judah *(2 Kings 11:1–3).* Athaliah's son ruled for only one year, and the Bible tells us that he was an evil king, "for his mother advised him to do wickedly" *(2 Chronicles 22:3 NKJV).*

3. *Azubah.* Daughter of Shilhi and mother of King Jehoshaphat of Judah *(1 Kings 22:42).*

4. *Bathsheba.* Daughter of Aliam; wife of Uriah the Hittite; and later wife of King David *(2 Samuel 11:27)*; mother of King Solomon *(2 Samuel 12:24, 1 Kings 1:11).*

5. *Esther.* Daughter of Abihail *(Esther 2:15)*; wife of King Ahaseurus of Persia *(Esther 2:16–17).* She is credited with saving her people, the Jews, from destruction at the hands of Haman, adviser to the Persian king.

6. *Hamutal.* Daughter of Jeremiah of Libnah *(2 Kings 23:31)*; mother of King Jehoahaz and King Zedekiah of Judah *(2 Kings 23:31; 24:18).* She is the only woman identified as the mother of two kings.

7. *Hephzibah.* Mother of King Manasseh of Judah *(2 Kings 21:1).*

8. *Jecholiah.* Mother of King Azariah of Judah *(2 Kings 15:2).*

9. *Jedidah.* Daughter of Adaiah of Bozkath; mother of King Josiah of Judah *(2 Kings 22:1).*

10. *Jehoaddan.* Mother of King Amaziah of Judah *(2 Kings 14:2).*

11. *Jezebel.* Daughter of King Ethbaal of Sidon *(1 Kings 16:31)*; wife of King Ahab of Israel *(1 Kings 16:29–31).*

12. *Maachah (Michaiah).* Granddaughter of Abishalom and mother of King Abijam (Abijah) *(1 Kings 15:1–2)*; grandmother of King Asa of Judah *(1 Kings 15:9–10).*

HER MAJESTY (CONT'D)

13. **Meshullemeth.** Daughter of Haruz of Jotbah, and mother of King Amon of Judah *(2 Kings 21:19)*.

14. **Michal.** Daughter of King Saul *(1 Samuel 18:20–28)*; wife of King David *(2 Samuel 3:13–16; 6:20–23)*.

15. **Naamah.** Although an Ammonitess, one of the enemies of the Jews, she was mother of King Rehoboam of Judah *(1 Kings 14:21, 31)*.

16. **Nehushta.** Daughter of Elnathan of Jerusalem, and mother of King Jehoiachin (Jeconiah) of Judah *(2 Kings 24:8)*.

17. **Queen of Sheba (Queen of the South).** A visitor to the court of King Solomon *(1 Kings 10:1–13)*, she was identified by name as Nikauli by the Jewish historian Josephus. She is called the queen of the South in the New Testament, and her visit to Solomon was noted by Jesus *(Matthew 12:42; Luke 11:31)*.

18. **Tahpenes.** Wife of a weak pharaoh of the twenty-first dynasty who ruled at the end of David's reign and the beginning of Solomon's reign; foster mother to Hadad, a son of the king of Edom *(1 Kings 11:19–20)*.

19. **Vashti.** Wife of King Ahaseurus of Persia *(Esther 1:9, 16, 19; 2:17)*. She refused to follow a command of her husband and was subsequently replaced by Queen Esther.

20. **Zebudah.** Daughter of Pedaiah of Rumah, and mother of King Jehoiakim of Judah *(2 Kings 23:36)*.

Queens of the New Testament

21. **Bernice.** The elder daughter of Herod Agrippa I. She married her uncle, the king of Calcis, and was also a consort to her brother Herod Agrippa II. She visited Festus with Agrippa and listened to Paul's defense *(Acts 25:13, 23; 26:30)*. She was a mistress to the Roman emperors Vespasian and Titus.

22. **Candace.** This is actually the title of the queens of Ethiopia. A member of her royal staff accepted Jesus as his Savior and was baptized by the evangelist Philip *(Acts 8:27–28)*; tradition holds that this queen also became a Christian.

23. **Drusilla.** The younger daughter of Herod Agrippa I; wife of Aziz of Emes; and later wife of the Roman procurator Felix of Judea. She was present for Paul's second appearance before Felix *(Acts 24:24)*.

24. **Herodias.** The daughter of Aristobolus and Berenice; the granddaughter of Herod the Great. She was the mother of Salome, according to the Jewish historian Josephus. She is considered to be responsible for the death of John the Baptist *(Matthew 14:1–12; Mark 6:17)*.

COME SAIL AWAY

The church has many familiar symbols, including the cross. Lesser known is the symbol of the ship.

Some trace the origins of this symbol to Noah's ark, which saved a remnant of humankind, and two of every type of wildlife, from annihilation. Others point out the story in Matthew 8:23–26, where Jesus and his disciples were in a boat when a storm came up; Jesus calmed the seas and kept the boat from sinking.

The mast of a ship is in the shape of a cross, signifying that Jesus is on board. The sails must have wind; wind represents the power of the Holy Spirit. The church building itself has a "nave," which is where the people sit. *Nave* comes from the Latin word for ship.

Ships sail on turbulent seas, carrying passengers safely to shore. The church also weathers storms and ferries its people to a safe place: heaven.

ABSALOM: HANDSOME BUT TREACHEROUS

To say that Absalom, beloved son of Israel's King David, was a handsome man might be a royal understatement. Second Samuel 14:25–26 reveals that Absalom was physically almost perfect from head to toe. His hair was so thick that its sheer weight forced him to cut it regularly—removing about five pounds of hair each time.

Yet Absalom's beauty really was only skin-deep. His successful plot to murder his half brother because he raped Absalom's sister may have been more to avenge his honor than his sister's. His physical attractiveness served him well in his campaign to replace his father. Standing outside the king's gate, Absalom waylaid suppliants on their way to seek justice and convinced them that the king would not be interested but that he, Absalom, would take up their cause. In time he mounted a successful coup that sent King David and his loyal subjects fleeing into the desert and allowed Absalom to lay claim to the throne.

GOD'S TRADING POST

The Bible is often referred to as "God's Word," or simply "the Word." It has also been called "God's Trading Post"—a place to trade a secondhand religion for a firsthand relationship with God.

1. **Hear the Word.** Probably the easiest way to learn the Word is to hear it from a preacher or teacher. Hearing the Word increases faith *(Romans 10:17)*. Commit to regularly hearing the Word, not just when it is convenient.

2. **Read the Word.** Consistent daily reading of God's Word is one of the best ways to grow as a believer. Through Bible reading, your mind and heart are constantly informed as to who God is, and you are given wisdom to live the life God has planned for you.

3. **Trust the Word.** Eve gave in to temptation in the Garden of Eden when the serpent convinced her to doubt what God said. The Bible is worthy of trust—enough to stake your life on it for all eternity.

4. **Study the Word.** The difference between reading and studying the Word of God is simply having a pencil and paper on hand, recording observations and questions—and then doing further study on those. That's a good way to start studying; then you can advance to word and character studies and in-depth book studies. That's the way to grow in insight and wisdom and stature, as Jesus did *(Luke 2:52)*.

5. **Memorize the Word.** The psalmist wrote, "I have hidden your word in my heart that I might not sin against you" *(Psalm 119:11 NIV)*. Scripture stored in your mind is available for the Holy Spirit to bring to your memory whenever it's needed.

6. **Meditate on the Word.** When Jesus was born and the shepherds came to see him, Mary "treasured up all these things and pondered them in her heart" *(Luke 2:19 NIV)*. "Pondering," or meditation, brings the Word into the heart and spirit.

7. **Pray the Word.** The way to pray according to God's will and purpose is to pray God's Word. Pray the prayers of the Bible, and let the words of Scripture shape your prayers.

8. **Apply the Word.** Mark Twain said it wasn't the parts of the Bible he didn't understand that bothered him; it was the parts he did understand that bothered him! Applying the Word in everyday circumstances is where the Bible comes alive to bring its life to the believer.

9. **Respond to the Word.** When the angel told Mary she was going to give birth to Jesus, the Messiah, she responded, "Let it be to me according to your word" *(Luke 1:38 ESV)*. The Word invites personal response from everyone who hears it.

A 180-DEGREE CHANGE

Conversion is the act in which one turns from a life of wrong-doing to a life of right-doing. It involves (1) repentance, a genuine sorrow for wrongdoing and turning away from it, and (2) faith, a turning to Jesus as Savior and placing belief and trust in him. Conversion changes the direction of one's life. A person who is going along a road and realizes he is going the wrong way to get where he wants to go "converts" or "turns" to change the direction of his life. Conversion turns a person "from darkness to light, and from the power of Satan to God" *(Acts 26:18 NIV)*. Some notable conversions in Scripture are those of Paul *(Acts 9:1–22)*, the Philippian jailer *(Acts 16:19–34)*, and Lydia *(Acts 16:13–15)*. Not all conversions are dramatic, and each person's conversion is unique.

Source: *The Revell Bible Dictionary* (Old Tappan, NJ: Revell, 1990).

HOLY PARADOX

God alone is holy *(Revelation 15:4)*. He is completely pure. Things in the world are called "holy" because of their relationship to God. For example, days (Sabbath, *Exodus 20:8–11*), places (holy ground, *Exodus 3:5–6*), and objects (garments, *Exodus 28:2*) are holy because they are set apart to be used for God's purposes.

People can also be holy. God alone makes people holy, through Jesus and the Holy Spirit. Holy people reflect God's character, belong to God, and are dedicated to God alone. The paradox of holiness is that holy people are set apart to worship and serve God. Holiness also means sharing God's purpose—which is to love people with a pure, eternal, and lasting love and to bring them into relationship with him.

Source: *The Revell Bible Dictionary* (Old Tappan, NJ: Revell, 1990).

GIANT OR GIANT LIE?

For centuries, biblical historians and critics have debated the possibility that the story of David and Goliath, found in the Old Testament, is nothing more than a myth. A recent archaeological find has taken one *giant* step in the direction of confirming the Bible's account.

According to the Scriptures, the young Israelite lad David offered to kill the Philistine giant Goliath, who taunted the Israelite army on the battlefield with the challenge to send a single man to battle him. Rejecting all forms of armor, David brought down Goliath with a single well-placed stone to the forehead, launched from a simple shepherd's slingshot.

The story has inspired people of every age and background who aspire to surmount overwhelming odds—from Sunday school children and athletes to corporate underdogs. But was it true?

According to archaeologist Dr. Aren Maeir of Bar-Ilan University, his team has found convincing proof that Goliath existed at the time of the biblical account. A shard of pottery dating back to about 950 BC and bearing an inscription of Goliath's name was unearthed in the general area where Goliath purportedly lived in Philistine. According to Maeir, the pottery's age is consistent with the time that the battle would have occurred, and its condition supports the Bible's depiction of life in that part of the world at the time—assertions that help give credence to the Bible's account of the event as fact, not myth.

Source: uk.news.yahoo.com/13112005/80/goliath-s-name-found-archaeological-dig.html.

IT IS NO SECRET

In 1949 the Reverend Billy Graham agreed to be on a local Los Angeles radio program as a way to publicize his upcoming crusade in that city. The show's host, Stuart Hamblen, was also a singer and songwriter and had appeared in a number of western films with well-known movie stars. In the course of the show, Reverend Graham invited Stuart personally to attend his meeting, and Hamblen agreed.

Hamblen was not among those who went forward to receive Jesus at the end of the evening, but he later met with Mr. Graham at his hotel. Stuart's life was profoundly changed, and news of his new way of living spread quickly throughout Hollywood.

One day Stuart ran into his friend John Wayne. Wayne said, "Stuart, what's this I hear about you hitting the sawdust trail?" Stuart replied, "Oh, that's no secret, John. What God has done for me, he can do for you or anybody else." John replied, "That sounds like a song, Stuart." The inspiration led to one of the most successful gospel songs of the twentieth century, "It Is No Secret."

Hamblen, who went on to write many successful Christian songs, became well known for his opposition to alcohol consumption. His stand cost him his radio program over his refusal to do a commercial promoting alcohol. His principled stand even led the Prohibition Party to nominate him as its candidate for president of the United States in 1952. Hamblen racked up nearly seventy-three thousand votes and finished fourth in a field of twelve candidates, despite appearing on the ballot in only twenty-one states.

Sources: www.mymusicway.com/biography/hamblen.html;
truthminers.com/hoaxarticles/hamblin.htm.

THE PRESIDENTS SPEAK OF GOD

Every U.S. president since the beginning of the nation's history has invoked the name of God in his inaugural address. Many of those leaders left further evidence of their belief in God and the Scriptures well documented in other speeches and writings. Here is a sampling from earliest to most recent:

1. "It is impossible to rightly govern the world without God and the Bible."—*George Washington*

2. "The highest story of the American Revolution is this: it connected in one indissoluble bond the principles of civil government with the principles of Christianity."
   —*John Adams*

3. "I tremble for my country when I reflect that God is just."—*Thomas Jefferson*

4. "The reason that Christianity is the best friend of Government is because Christianity is the only religion that changes the heart."—*Thomas Jefferson*

5. "The liberty, prosperity, and the happiness of our country will always be the object of my most fervent prayers to the Supreme Author of All Good."—*James Monroe*

6. "We've staked the whole future of American civilization not on the power of government, far from it. We have staked the future of all our political institutions upon the capacity of each and all of us . . . to govern ourselves according to the commandments of God. The future and success of America is not in this Constitution, but in the laws of God upon which this Constitution is founded."
   —*James Madison*

7. "The Bible is the Rock on which this Republic rests."
   —*Andrew Jackson*

THE PRESIDENTS SPEAK OF GOD (CONT'D)

8. "It is no slight testimonial, both to the merit and worth of Christianity, that in all ages since its promulgation the great mass of those who have risen to eminence by their profound wisdom and integrity have recognized and reverenced Jesus of Nazareth as the Son of the living God."
—*John Quincy Adams*

9. "My great concern is not whether God is on our side, my great concern is to be on God's side."
—*Abraham Lincoln*

10. "A thorough knowledge of the Bible is worth more than a college education."—*Theodore Roosevelt*

11. "The study of the Bible is a post-graduate course in the richest library of human experience."
—*Herbert Hoover*

12. "America was born a Christian nation. America was born to exemplify that devotion to the elements of righteousness which are derived from the revelations of Holy Scriptures."—*Woodrow Wilson*

13. "The fundamental basis of this nation's law was given to Moses on the Mount. The fundamental basis of our Bill of Rights comes from the teaching we get from Exodus and St. Matthew, from Isaiah and St. Paul. I don't think we emphasize that enough these days. If we don't have the proper fundamental moral background, we will finally end up with a totalitarian government which does not believe in the right for anybody except the state."
—*Harry S. Truman*

14. "We should live our lives as though Christ was coming this afternoon."—*Jimmy Carter*

NO HORSING AROUND ABOUT GOD

"And they're off!" The Kentucky Derby, the Preakness Stakes, the Belmont Stakes—jockey Pat Day has seen them all and experienced great success at all three Triple Crown horse races. Ask him, though, about what really matters in his life, and he'll say it's his faith in God and his relationship with Jesus.

Day did not become a believer at an early age. He had been in thoroughbred racing for eleven years and was struggling with problems such as drug and alcohol addiction when he decided he needed God's help to turn his life around. Some of his colleagues scoffed at the "new" Pat Day, but Day has continued to take a strong stand for what he believes. This Racing Hall of Fame jockey speaks at events hosted by Race Track Chaplaincy of America, Inc., telling all who will listen about the difference God has made in his life.

Few can argue with Day as he gives all the credit to God for his nearly nine thousand first-place finishes.

Source: www.charismamag.com/display.php?id=10083.

HAVING A BALL AND HELPING OTHERS

David Robinson never intended to play professional basketball. His interests ran to music, math, and computers. He also had an interest in the military; his father was a submarine sonar/radar technician with the U.S. Navy. Robinson played some basketball before entering the U.S. Naval Academy, but it wasn't a burning passion.

That changed once he got to Annapolis. He joined the basketball team and earned All-American honors. Drafted by the San Antonio Spurs, he had a stellar NBA career that included All-Star and MVP accolades and two championships.

Shortly after entering the NBA, Robinson realized he was unhappy with his life. A talk with the Spurs' chaplain led him to read the Bible, be baptized, and become a believer. This changed his personal life—and the lives of others. He and his wife started a foundation and a school, the Carver Academy, for underserved children.

Why the foundation and school? The stated purpose is to jump-start leaders whose integrity and faith will make them world-class . . . like Robinson himself.

Sources: Nathan Aaseng, *Sports Great David Robinson* (Springfield, NJ: Enslow, 1998); Ambrose and Freda Robinson with Steve Hubbard, *How to Raise an MVP—Most Valuable Person* (Grand Rapids, MI: Zondervan, 1996); www.philanthropyintexas.com/03MarchApril/david-robinson-print.htm.

THE ROSETTA STONE AND THE BIBLE

The Rosetta stone is an ancient, irregularly shaped stone slab covered with carved inscriptions. It was obviously broken off of a larger stone tablet. Discovered in Egypt in 1799, the stone was a life-altering discovery for archaeologists and biblical scholars. It provided the missing link between known languages and the lost language of Ancient Egypt, which slowly vanished when Greeks, successors to conqueror Alexander the Great, became rulers of Egypt upon his death. They made Greek the official language of Egypt.

The Rosetta stone's inscriptions are of two identical records written in two languages (Egyptian and Greek) and three alphabets. Since two of the alphabets were already known when the stone was discovered, deciphering the third was made possible.

Thomas Young of England and Jean-Francois Champollion of France did the arduous work of deciphering what was written on the stone. As a result, the entire world of ancient Egypt has been opened to archaeologists, historians, and biblical scholars, providing a previously unavailable view into life and culture during Old Testament times. Egyptian hieroglyphic inscriptions on buildings and objects throughout the ancient world suddenly took on new meaning, each opening a new window to the Old Testament world.

Most significantly for biblical scholars, part of what has emerged are records that provide solid confirmation of biblical records and descriptions of culture and rulers of the time.

A SHORT LIFE, WELL SPENT

John was born in England in 1607 into a fairly well-to-do family. A man of faith, John earned two degrees at Emmanuel College and was ordained. He and his wife, Anne, immigrated in 1637 to Massachusetts, where John's excellent education and Puritan sensibilities secured him a post as teacher and assistant pastor at the First Church of Charlestown.

The year before John arrived in the New World, the Massachusetts Bay Colony had begun building a college. John died the year after he arrived in Massachusetts, and he left the school half of his estate (about £800) and his library (about four hundred volumes—substantial for that time). The following year, the school was given John's name: Harvard College.

Study of the Bible was a significant part of the curriculum, and a lifestyle of faith was emphasized at Harvard College, now known as Harvard University. All but two of the school's first fifteen presidents were clergymen.

A RUSSIAN GRANDMOTHER'S BIBLE

Under orders from Soviet dictator Stalin, authorities in Stavropol, Russia, confiscated thousands of Bibles and sent Christians to prisons, where most of them died as "enemies of the state."

Sixty years later, in 1994, a Co-Mission ministry team arrived in Stavropol. The team was told about a warehouse where the confiscated Bibles were still stored. After much prayer by the team, officials granted permission to distribute the Bibles. Local Russians were hired to go to the warehouse and load their trucks with the books.

One of the men hired, a hostile agnostic, disappeared from the group, hoping to steal a Bible. He later was found in a corner of the warehouse, weeping with one of them in his hands. He had picked up a Bible only to find it had been his own grandmother's! Her signature was on the inside. Today that man continues to read the very Bible his grandmother was persecuted for owning.

Source: www.bible.org.

WHAT'S GOD LIKE?

Many people seem to think of God as being judgmental. The Bible presents insight that gives a more complete and balanced overview of him. According to the Scriptures, God is

1. Faithful
   (Lamentations 3:22–23)

2. Good *(Psalm 34:8)*

3. Gracious *(Psalm 111:4)*

4. Holy *(Isaiah 6:3)*

5. Immutable (unchanging)
   (Malachi 3:6)

6. Longsuffering *(Psalm 86:15)*

7. Loving *(1 John 4:8)*

8. Merciful *(1 Peter 1:3)*

9. Omnipotent (all-powerful)
   (Isaiah 46:9–11)

10. Omnipresent (ever-present)
    (Ephesians 4:6)

11. Omniscient (all-knowing)
    (Matthew 10:29–30)

12. Personal *(Philippians 4:19)*

13. Righteous *(Psalm 116:5)*

14. Sovereign *(Deuteronomy 4:39)*

15. Truthful *(Hebrews 6:18)*

QUESTIONS GOD ASKS US!

Why do the innocent suffer? Did God create evil? Is there only one way to heaven? Is there a hell? These are just some of the questions people want to ask God. But there's another side to the story—God has his own questions! Consider these questions God asks in the Bible:

1. "Where are you?"
   (Genesis 3:9 NIV)

2. "Who told you?"
   (Genesis 3:11 NIV)

3. "Why are you angry?"
   (Genesis 4:6 NIV)

4. "Where is your brother?"
   (Genesis 4:9 NIV)

5. "What have you done?"
   (Genesis 4:10 NIV)

6. "Whom shall I send?"
   (Isaiah 6:8 NIV)

7. "Who is my equal?"
   (Isaiah 40:25 NIV)

8. "Is anything too hard for me?"
   (Jeremiah 32:27 NIV)

9. "Who gives speech to mortals?" *(Exodus 4:11 NRSV)*

10. "Are you as strong as [me]?"
    (Job 40:9 NLT)

11. "How long will these people reject Me?"
    (Numbers 14:11 NKJV)

12. "Have I not commanded you?" *(Joshua 1:9 NIV)*

13. "Does the clay say to the potter, 'What are you making?'"
    (Isaiah 45:9 NIV)

14. "Should people cheat [me]?"
    (Malachi 3:8 NLT)

GET REAL!

Psalms is a favorite book of the Bible. The 150 songs and prayers honestly and candidly express the gamut of human emotion— joy, praise, reassurance, anger, sadness, desperation, fear, desire. It's been said that every emotion except one—apathy—can be found in the Psalms!

Look up these psalms as examples of the wide range of emotion and expression found in the book of Psalms:

- *Psalm 6* speaks of languishing, terror, weariness, grief, and weakness.
- *Psalm 10* is a cry for God's presence in hard times.
- *Psalm 22* expresses abandonment and startling isolation.
- *Psalm 27* expresses David's confidence in God.
- *Psalm 33* is a song of praise to God.
- *Psalm 44* is a cry for help after defeat.
- *Psalm 51* is a prayer for forgiveness.
- *Psalm 56* expresses fear yet ultimate trust in God.
- *Psalm 63* is a prayer of longing and desire for God.
- *Psalm 91* is praise to God for the security he gives to those who trust him.
- *Psalm 102* is a prayer of anguish in a time of distress.
- *Psalm 109* is a prayer for God to vindicate a person who has been betrayed and falsely accused.
- *Psalm 129* is a prayer for enemies to "wither."
- *Psalm 137* laments the wasted years of Babylonian exile.
- *Psalm 139* is an account of God's intimate knowledge of his people.

Many people through the centuries have reported that reading and praying the Psalms aloud has helped them express their deepest emotions.

BIBLICAL SUPPORT FOR THE ANTICHRIST

What or who is the Antichrist? While the definition means anyone who is "against Christ," most Bible scholars, as well as the popular media, have assumed that the prophetical biblical references denote a particular person.

The word *Antichrist* is only found in four Bible passages and, surprisingly to many people, does not appear at all in the book of Revelation. All references to the Antichrist were penned by the apostle John, and all are found within the books of 1 and 2 John.

LORD OF THE FLIES

William Golding's well-known novel *Lord of the Flies* tells the story of children lost on an island and pitted against an evil beast who is the title character. The beast's name was not a whim of fancy for the author, however, but a literal translation from the Greek for the name Beelzebub, another name for the devil, found in the King James Version of the New Testament.

THE CARPENTER'S CALLING CARD

Tradesmen during Jesus' life in Palestine would have been instantly recognizable by the symbols they wore. Carpenters stuck wood chips behind their ears, tailors stuck needles in their tunics, and dyers wore colored rags. On the Sabbath these symbols were left at home. Carpenters in Jesus' time would have created mainly farm tools (carts, plows, winnowing forks, and yokes), house parts (doors, frames, posts, and beams), furniture, and kitchen utensils.

Source: catalog.lexpublib.org/TLCScripts/interpac.dll?SearchForm&Directions=1&
Config=pac&Branch=,0,&FormId=0,.

MEGAHIT CHRONICLED

The C. S. Lewis fantasy that won the hearts of children worldwide in print made it big in the box office as it came to the silver screen in December 2005. What is turning out to be the first installment in the Chronicles of Narnia series, *The Lion, the Witch and the Wardrobe*, was a megahit for Disney and Walden Media, who teamed up to make the classic children's story into a feature film. In its first three months, the movie grossed more than $670 million. A sequel, *Prince Caspian*, is set for release in December 2007.

The Lion, the Witch and the Wardrobe is the story of four siblings: Peter, Susan, Edmund, and Lucy Pevensie. They discover that a professor's wardrobe leads them into the kingdom of Narnia, and they help to save Narnia from the curse of the evil White Witch. The popular series incorporates biblical themes such as temptation, betrayal, and Jesus' death and resurrection.

"*The Lion, the Witch and the Wardrobe* has many fantasy elements," Walden Media CEO Cary Granat said. "It is a film that has unbelievably great scenes for families, with four kids who leave a world consumed by war that they have no control over only to enter a world where a war is raging in which their actions are crucial to the outcome."

C. S. Lewis launched the famous Chronicles of Narnia series with *The Lion, the Witch and the Wardrobe* in 1950 and followed it up with six more titles: *The Magician's Nephew, The Horse and His Boy, Prince Caspian, The Voyage of the Dawn Treader, The Silver Chair,* and *The Last Battle*. The books have sold 95 million copies in forty-one languages since they were first published.

Source: "'Chronicles of Narnia' to Be Film," *The Hollywood Reporter: www.hollywoodreporter.com* (March 2, 2004).

WHAT A WOMAN!

The mother-in-law of King Lemuel (whom many believe to be King Solomon) described for her son the ideal wife, and perhaps the ideal daughter-in-law. Her advice in Proverbs 31 lists very specific attributes for the "virtuous woman"—which literally means "woman of strength." According to this chapter of Proverbs, the virtuous woman:

1. Is trustworthy *(v. 11)*

2. Is a good steward of her husband's goods and money *(v. 11)*

3. Treats her husband well *(v. 12)*

4. Seeks out quality goods that have long-lasting value *(v. 13)*

5. Willingly works with her hands *(v. 13)*

6. Provides nourishing food for her family, even if it means extra effort *(v. 14)*

7. Is diligent in everything she does *(v. 15)*

8. Is nurturing in preparing what her family members need *(v. 15)*

9. Gives her family's employees fair wages *(v. 15)*

10. Wisely considers investments before purchasing them *(v. 16)*

11. Is profitable in business *(v. 16)*

12. Seeks to extend the value of what she has *(v. 16)*

13. Does what will make and keep her strong physically *(v. 17)*

14. Examines merchandise carefully before buying it *(v. 18)*

15. Is willing to make the extra effort, go the extra mile *(v. 18)*

16. Is willing to take personal responsibility for what she does with her talents, money, and time *(v. 19)*

17. Is generous to the poor *(v. 20)*

18. Seeks to help those in need *(v. 20)*

19. Plans ahead *(v. 21)*

20. Seeks the best for her family *(v. 21)*

21. Takes excellent care of herself and seeks to maintain a good appearance *(v. 22)*

22. Deals honorably in what she sells and buys *(v. 24)*

23. Brings honor to herself and her family *(vv. 25, 28)*

24. Speaks wisely and kindly *(v. 26)*

25. Stands in awe of God *(v. 30)*

DO YOU *BELIEVE* IT?

Can a book reflecting the moral codes of societies thousands of years old significantly influence the decisions made by Americans today? According to research conducted by the respected Barna Group, the Bible unquestionably does just that.

Their survey showed that about half of all adults (54%) claim to make moral choices on the basis of a specific set of beliefs—not all of them biblical. About one of every six adults (16%) says he or she makes moral choices based on the content of the Bible.

The extent to which people within that group of 16% rely on Scripture as a basis for moral decisions also varies. Sixty percent of those describing themselves as "evangelicals" rely on the principles contained in the Bible as their *main source* of moral counsel. This contrasts with 20% of those considering themselves to be "non-evangelical born-again" adults, 6% of those simply describing themselves as "Christian," and 2% of people aligned with non-Christian faiths. Protestants were three times more likely than Catholics to base their morals on biblical teaching (23% versus 7%).

The research also revealed a disparity between people of differing educational backgrounds, with college graduates twice as likely as other adults to have a biblical view of life (9% versus 4%, respectively). An even more intriguing discovery was that African- American adults, who generally emerge as the ethnic segment most deeply committed to the Christian faith, were substantially less likely than either whites or Hispanics to have a biblical worldview (1% of black adults compared with 6% among whites and 8% among Hispanics, and less than 0.1% of Asians).

Source: "Most Adults Feel Accepted by God, but Lack a Biblical Worldview," The Barna Group, www.barna.org, Barna Update 8/9/05, accessed on 12/19/05.

FIRST PRINTING

From earliest days, God's people have used the book of Psalms for worship. When compiled as a separate book set for singing or chanting, the book of Psalms is called a Psalter.

The first book to be printed in the American Colonies was a Psalter, known as the Bay Psalm Book. The title page of the first edition of 1640 reads, "The Whole Booke of Psalmes *Faithfully* TRANSLATED *into* ENGLISH *Metre.* Whereunto is prefixed a discourse declaring not only the lawfulness, but also the necessity of the heavenly Ordinance of singing Scripture Psalmes in the Churches of God. Cambridge, Mass. Stephen Day. *Imprinted,* 1640."

Early residents of the Massachusetts Bay Colony brought several Psalters with them to the colonies, but they hired "thirty pious and learned Ministers" to provide this new translation that would be in use for more than one hundred years. Copies of this historic book still exist, including one in the Library of Congress.

Sources: www.redeemer.on.ca/academics/polisci/psalter_intro.html; www.cgmusic.com/workshop/baypsalm_frame.htm.

SAVE OUR SEA

The Dead Sea is shrinking rapidly. In the last forty years, the water level has dropped seventy-five feet. The sea recedes at the rate of about three feet per year. About one-third of the sea's surface area has been lost, reducing the Dead Sea to its current fifty-mile length and ten-mile width.

The Jordan River is the primary water source flowing into the Dead Sea. Increasing demands for the river water divert the water supply for large-scale irrigation, industrial uses, tourism, and urban development, reducing the once-full river to a comparative trickle by the time the river empties into the sea. Generally low rainfall in recent years has failed to produce runoff water from creeks—formed in the Judean hills west of the sea—that in previous times helped to replenish the water supply.

From antiquity, the Dead Sea has been significant to the region. Within a couple hours' drive southeast of Jerusalem, the Dead Sea forms the east border between Israel and Jordan and is bounded by the Judean Mountains to the west. The Dead Sea is never expected to disappear entirely; the evaporation rate slows as surface area decreases and saltiness increases. International efforts are at work to save the Dead Sea.

Sources: www.desert-voice.net/dead_sea.htm; www.jordanembassy.de/saving_the_dead_sea.htm; news.bbc.co.uk/1/hi/world/middle_east/392442.stm.

TALK ABOUT CHURCH!

Is a church a building, a group of people, or an idea? Here are twelve opinions:

1. "The church was not merely a thermometer that recorded the ideas and principles of popular opinion; it was a thermostat that transformed the mores of society."—*Martin Luther King Jr.*

2. "Going to church doesn't make you a Christian any more than standing in a garage makes you a car."—*Anonymous*

3. "Baseball is like church. Many attend, few understand."—*Leo Durocher*

4. "Church attendance is as vital to a disciple as a transfusion of rich, healthy blood to a sick man."—*D. L. Moody*

5. "One hundred religious persons knit into a unity by careful organization do not constitute a church any more than eleven dead men make a football team. The first requisite is life, always."—*A. W. Tozer*

6. "The Church is the one institution that exists for those outside it." —*William Tyndale*

7. "America has begun a spiritual reawakening. Faith and hope are being restored. Americans are turning back to God. Church attendance is up. Audiences for religious books and broadcasts are growing. And I do believe that he has begun to heal our blessed land." —*President Ronald Reagan*

8. "The Churches must learn humility as well as teach it." —*George Bernard Shaw*

9. "A church without youth is a church without a future. Moreover, youth without a church is youth without a future." —*Pope Shenouda III, Pope and Patriarch of Alexandria*

10. "Now I understand why Henry VIII started his own church." —*President John F. Kennedy* (Comment after the Vatican scolded him for supporting separation of church and state during his campaign, 1960)

11. "The Church is not a gallery for the exhibition of eminent Christians, but a school for the education of imperfect ones." —*Henry Ward Beecher*

12. "An instinctive taste teaches men to build their churches with spire steeples, which point as with a silent finger to the sky and stars." —*Samuel Taylor Coleridge*

THE REST, THEY SAY . . .

At age fifty, Jan Karon decided it was time to leave a successful advertising career to pursue her lifelong dream of becoming an author. When she did, she found she had absolutely nothing to say. Weeks stretched into months of a long, anxious season with no money and lots of bills. She later recognized that during that time God was drawing her closer to himself, strengthening her faith, and encouraging her trust.

One night while lying in bed, she got an image of an ordinary-looking minister in her mind. In her imagination she followed him around a village, meeting a dog named Barnabas and a boy named Dooley. She got out of bed, went to her computer, and began to write. That was the beginning of the successful Mitford series of books, which feature the heartwarming protagonist Father Tim Kavanagh. Sales of the eight books in the series have topped twenty million volumes.

Source: www.cbn.com/700club/guests/bios/jan_karon_120204.asp.

SOUL SURFER

Amateur surfing champion Bethany Hamilton was already a local hero, but after she lost her left arm to a shark in 2003, her courage became known worldwide.

At age thirteen Bethany was surfing on Kauai's north beach when the shark attacked. She lost 70 percent of her blood, but within a month Bethany was back riding the waves.

Her comeback courage has brought invitations for interviews and tours to talk with military amputees and inspire victims of the 2004 Indian Ocean tsunami. On a trip to New York City, she took off her ski jacket and gave it to a homeless girl. Wearing only a tank top, Hamilton canceled a shopping spree, saying she already had too many things.

Bethany sees the loss of her arm as a blessing in disguise, an opportunity to be noticed so she might tell others about her faith in Jesus. "This was God's plan for my life, and I'm going to go with it. He definitely got me through this."

Sources: the.honoluluadvertiser.com/article/2004/Apr/05/il/il01a.html;
cnn.com/2005/US/05/09/cnn25.tan.hamilton;
www.beliefnet.com/story/137/story_13707_1.html.

A FOLDED NAPKIN

In Bible times, people generally used pieces of bread in the way we use a table napkin—to wipe fingers or sop up spills. Occasionally, however, pieces of cloth were used for religious feast meals, and especially in the homes of the wealthy.

If a napkin was left unfolded at a meal's end, the person was sending a signal that he had thoroughly enjoyed the meal and hoped to return soon. The unfolded napkin was taken as a sign that the person had left "only temporarily" and might be back soon to resume eating. (In a very similar fashion, people today often unfold napkins in restaurants before they make a trip to a salad or food bar, to send a signal that they are occupying the table and plan to return to it.) A napkin left folded was a sign that the diner had completely finished the meal and did not intend to return to that particular dining experience again. In some cases, it was a sign regarded as an insult: "I ate, but I did not enjoy."

At the time of the Resurrection, Jesus' disciples entered the empty tomb to find the cloth that had covered Jesus' face neatly folded in a corner. They immediately took this as a sign that Jesus had fully accomplished all he came to earth to do, and that he never intended to return again to the experience of death and burial. He meant what he said on the cross: "It is finished!" *(John 19:30 NKJV)*.

BROTHER TO ALL

Roger Louis Schutz-Marsauche was born in Switzerland in 1915, the youngest of nine children. He quickly learned from his parents a charitable tolerance for diverse Christian traditions. In the 1940s, he acquired a small farm in Taize, France, where he could offer a way of "assisting some of those most discouraged, those deprived of a livelihood: and it could be a place of silence and work." Brother Roger worked the farm and prayed that God would send him coworkers who shared his vision.

An ecumenical monastic community came into being and grew, eventually becoming a pilgrimage destination for believers from around the world. Each year tens of thousands of believing youth travel to Taize for intense weeklong sessions of prayer and meditation.

Although Brother Roger was killed in 2005, he left a living legacy in the Taize community that continues to thrive.

Sources: www.timesonline.co.uk/article/0,,60-1739368,00.html;
news.bbc.co.uk/1/hi/world/Europe/4158886.htm; www.taize.fr.

EACH ONE TEACH ONE

Known as "the Apostle to the Illiterates," Dr. Frank Laubach (1884–1970) was a missionary whose literacy program has been used to teach millions worldwide to read in their own language. Laubach became aware of the importance of literacy while serving as a missionary in the Philippines. Many of those he served suffered greatly from poverty and injustice. Laubach saw literacy as a means of improving their economic and political standing. He designed reading primers and charts to teach reading and also began the Each One Teach One literacy program, which called upon the newly literate to teach their neighbors and friends.

Laubach also believed that the most mediocre mind, praising Jesus, could do more for humankind than the most brilliant mind that dismissed Jesus. Laubach routinely prayed, "Think Thy thoughts in my mind. What is on Thy mind for me to do now?" Laubach believed that such a prayer could help people open themselves up to receiving the creative and beneficial ideas that Jesus desired to pour into their minds.

Sources: Chi.gospelcom.net/DAILYF/2002/06/daily-06-11-2002;
Experts.abouc.com/e/f/fr/Frank_Laubach.htm.

LAKE OR SEA?

The word *sea* is usually reserved for bodies of salt water. It's also used for a freshwater lake called the Sea of Galilee.

This sea plays a prominent role in Bible stories. Jesus met Peter, Andrew, James, and John along its shores—these four men became the first of his inner circle of twelve disciples *(Matthew 4:18–22)*. Also on this sea, the disciples learned how powerful Jesus was; during a terrible storm, which the Sea of Galilee is known for, Jesus calmed the wind and waves *(Matthew 8:23–27)*.

The Sea of Galilee is known by other names in the Bible, including Gennesaret and Tiberias. Modern-day Israelis call the harp-shaped Sea of Galilee "Kinneret," from a Hebrew word meaning "harp."

Fed by the Jordan River, the Sea of Galilee is thirteen miles long and eight miles wide. In Bible times, it was a great place to fish, and the fertile land surrounding it was a good place to live and work. Several cities sprang up on its shores, including Capernaum, Bethsaida, and Tiberias. Capernaum appears to have been the headquarters city for Jesus' ministry.

Today, the Sea of Galilee is a popular tourist destination— there is even talk of building a Bible theme park along its shoreline. The sea is also vitally important as a source of drinking water for the state of Israel.

In 1986, when the sea's water level dropped as the result of a severe drought, an interesting discovery was made. Two men found a wooden boat in the mud. Once excavated and tested, the boat was found to be quite old, built and used between 100 BC and AD 70. It became known as "the Jesus Boat" because it was typical of the style of fishing vessels on the Sea of Galilee at the time of Jesus. The preserved remains of the boat can be seen by tourists visiting Nof Ginosar, a kibbutz (a collective farm, or commune) on the north shore of the Sea of Galilee.

TIME IS EVERYTHING

Sundials are great for telling time—when the sun is out. But after dark? No good.

It is unknown exactly who developed the first mechanical clock, but it is known that prior to the thirteenth century, monasteries used mechanical bells to call the monks to prayer. In monasteries, time was everything. Part of serving God was being aware of him at all times, praying at set times for those outside the monastery's walls, and being disciplined in the use of all resources—including time. In the monks' eyes, there truly was no time to waste!

It appears that mechanical clocks were first built in monasteries, with a mechanism originally designed to ring "call to prayer" bells at a set time.

The word for "bell," interestingly, is *clokke* in Middle English, *clocke* in Old French, and *clocca* in Medieval Latin.

Sources: Franklyn M. Branley, *Keeping Time* (Boston: Houghton Mifflin, 1993), 23; David Christianson, *Timepieces: Masterpieces of Chronometry* (Buffalo, NY: Firefly, 2002), 19, 25.

A LAYER CAKE MADE OF DIRT

History books help us understand "what happened when." Some of the history books' information comes from people who literally dug up history: archaeologists. Where did they dig? Many dug in the Middle East, in mounds called "tells."

Picture this: people build a city. Then comes an earthquake, or disease, or famine, or an enemy invasion. People leave. Years later they return to the abandoned city, tear down the ruined buildings and cover them with dirt, and build on top. And they do this for centuries. Why return? Because the city was near a water source or had fertile soil nearby or was near a major road or caravan route. The higher the city (as tells rose with the addition of layers), the easier it was to spot approaching enemies.

In Bible lands, archaeologists have dug through layers of dirt to make a number of important discoveries that verify the exact location of places mentioned in the Scriptures.

Some cities in Israel have "Tel" as part of their name, most notably Tel Aviv.

What will you find when you start digging in the Middle East? You never can tell. . . .

WHO ARE THE MORAVIANS?

Visitors to any number of Moravian villages in the eastern part of the United States might assume that the Moravians were simply immigrants who built whole communities wherever they settled. But that's only part of the story.

Moravians were originally members of a Protestant church formed in the late 1400s after philosophy professor John Hus, a priest and rector of the university in Prague, was burned at the stake for heresy. Hus advocated that the church needed to reform. He pushed for the Bible to be made available in the language of the people, for laypeople to receive holy Communion (as opposed to priests only), and for all people in the church to follow Jesus more fully.

His followers organized a church called the Unitas Fratrum (Unity of Brethren)—now the Moravian Church. The name Moravian identifies the fact that the church was begun in ancient Bohemia and Moravia, in what is the present-day Czech Republic.

The first Moravians in America settled in Pennsylvania to share the gospel with Native Americans. Their work spread into the Carolinas, and today the Moravian Church has congregations in twenty states or provinces of the United States and Canada. The Moravian Church in America became established as a distinct church body in 1848.

Moravians point to the Bible as the only source of Christian doctrine, and pattern all acts of worship on models laid out in the Scriptures. Emphasis is placed on a godly life as the essential evidence of a faith that brings salvation. The basic Moravian motto in accepting the creeds of other denominations (such as the Apostles' Creed, the Nicene Creed, and the Augsburg Confession) is "In essentials, unity; in nonessentials, liberty; and in all things, love."

Sources: www.mcsp.org/who.htm;
www.moravianseminary.edu/general/moravians.htm.

"GOD'S FRIEND"

Teresa of Avila is one of the great figures in the history of faith. By her own account, she was halfhearted in her devotion until a vision of Jesus changed her forever.

Teresa was born in 1515 in Avila, Spain. She joined the Carmelite Order in 1535. The convent was lax, resembling a boardinghouse. She suffered a serious illness with a painful convalescence of three years. Her spiritual life was average and superficial until one day she glanced at an image of the suffering Jesus on the cross and it became "real" to her. Immediately she was filled with disgust for the mediocrity of her spiritual life and devoted herself to prayer. She began to undergo profound mystical raptures and experiences related to God's transforming love. For the rest of her days, she gave herself to the spiritual life and the renewal of the Carmelite monasteries.

Teresa won approval from the Roman Catholic Church to form the Discalced (shoeless) Carmelites in 1562. Strict poverty was a feature of the order, and the sisters in the order followed a rigorous schedule of prayer. In all, she established sixteen convents in Spain.

Teresa had a sense of humor. Once when praying in the midst of much suffering, she thought she heard God say, "But this is how I treat my friends." Teresa replied, "No wonder you have so few of them." She wrote *The Way of Perfection* and *The Interior Castle*. For Teresa, spiritual progress was measured not by penance but by growth in constant love for others and in the desire to find and live out the will of God. Prayer was vital to all of life. She died in 1582.

Sources: www.newadvent.org/cathen/14515b; www.ccel.org/t/teresa/teresa; www.domestic-church.com/CONTENT.DCC/19980901/SAINTS/ST_THERESA.

THE CRYSTAL QUARTZ CROSS

While excavating the floor of an ancient mission church in Tallahassee, Florida, archaeologists expected to find only the bodies of the people believed buried beneath the church floor from 1656 to 1704. That's when Mission San Luis was home to Apalachee Indians and Spanish friars, soldiers, and families.

According to one scientist, they were "blindsided" by the discovery of an intricately decorated cross, about three inches tall and carved from a single piece of crystal quartz. The cross is now an icon of the Catholic Church.

The cross's significance lies in the fact that it appears to have been carved by an Apalachee Indian using Spanish tools. Experts say that makes it one of the earliest symbols of a merger between American Indian and European Christian cultures.

Archaeologists find the cross to be exceedingly rare for two other reasons. First, quartz crystal held special properties for Native Americans. To have a material that was traditionally sacred to the Apalachee tribe fashioned into a cross is highly unusual.

Second, the marks on the cross indicate that it was created with a variety of tools. When the cross was discovered, archaeologists assumed it was a European-made artifact given to an Apalachee Indian. But in 1996, a Florida State biophysicist examined it under a high-powered microscope and discovered marks made by both European tools (such as a round metal file) and the more primitive boring tools used by the Apalachees.

Source: *Tallahassee Democrat*, 3/7/06.

COURAGE! IT'S COMMANDED!

It isn't enough to know what God wants you to do. It takes courage to actually do what God calls you to do. These were people or groups of people God *commanded* to have courage:

1. The ten spies sent to Canaan by Moses *(Numbers 13:20)*

2. Joshua *(Joshua 1:6–9, 18)*

3. Israel under Joshua *(Deuteronomy 31:6–7; Joshua 10:25)*

4. Israel under David *(2 Samuel 10:12; 1 Chronicles 19:13)*

5. Solomon *(1 Chronicles 22:13; 28:20)*

6. Hezekiah *(2 Chronicles 32:7)*

7. Israel under Ezra *(Ezra 10:4)*

8. All people *(Psalms 27:14; 31:24)*

9. Neighbors—God not only commanded his people to have courage but also expected them to encourage one another to have courage! *(Isaiah 41:6)*

AUTHOR! AUTHOR!

Some of the most beautiful literature ever written appears in the Old Testament books of Psalms and Proverbs. Yet few people can name most of the authors identified in various chapter headings, and little is known about most of them. Here's a list of some of the authors of the Psalms and Proverbs:

1. David, king of Israel, is assumed to have written most of the psalms, although he is given direct credit for only seventy-three of them.

2. The sons of Korah wrote Psalms 42; 44–49; 84–85; and 87.

3. Asaph wrote Psalms 50 and 73–83.

4. Heman wrote Psalm 88.

5. Ethan wrote Psalm 89.

6. Hezekiah is believed to have written Psalms 120–123; 128–130; 132; and 134–136.

7. Solomon wrote Psalms 72; 127; and Proverbs 1–29.

8. Agur wrote Proverbs 30.

9. Lemuel wrote Proverbs 31.

10. Moses wrote Psalm 90.

11. "Anonymous" is credited with writing forty-eight psalms.

EVEN THE WAVE OBEYS

Situated two hundred yards off the beach at Navalady, Sri Lanka, the Samaritan Children's Home provided a home for twenty-eight children. Sunday, December 26, 2004, began quietly. It was a happy time. On Christmas Eve the children sang and danced at the Christmas Eve pageant. The next day, 250 people gathered for Christmas dinner.

The morning calm quickly turned to chaos. Staff shouted an alert—a "thirty-foot wall of water" was about to crash on the orphanage. Dayalan Sanders, the pastor who founded and directed the orphanage, called for the children. They came running, piled into the boat, and the overloaded craft took off. Sanders said they were "eyeball-to-eyeball" with the towering tsunami.

Sanders stood up and lifted both his hands and said, "I command you in the name of Jesus Christ, on the strength of the Scriptures, that when the enemy comes in like a flood, the spirit of the Lord shall raise up a standard against him. I command you in the name of Jesus Christ to stand still." And the wave— a massive wall of water—stood still. Villagers who survived the tsunami by climbing to the tops of the trees confirmed what Sanders said—they saw the wave literally stop as it reached the orphanage property, giving the children in the boat the split seconds they needed to get out of its way to safety.

Though the orphanage structure was destroyed, all the children survived.

> So shall they fear
> The name of the LORD from the west,
> And His glory from the rising of the sun;
> When the enemy comes in like a flood,
> The Spirit of the LORD will lift up a standard against him.
> —Isaiah 59:19 NKJV

Sources: http://www.worldvision.org/worldvision/radio.nsf/stable/53A5906A6A9FA 79688256F86008265F1?OpenDocument; www.markcahill.org; www.cbn.com.; http://goodnewschristianministry.org/orphanage.htm.

A WOMAN OF SUBSTANCE

Elizabeth's marriage to respected Paris physician Felix Leseur in 1887 brought this already-affluent woman wealth and social standing. Elizabeth was a Bible student with a firm faith from childhood, and her faith drove the good works she fostered across Paris.

Felix, an avowed atheist, had agreed not to interfere with his new wife's faith, but he did everything in his power to help her see its "foolishness." So, cherishing marital harmony, Elizabeth tried to minimize the opportunities for Felix to criticize her.

In 1903 Elizabeth came to know Jesus in a far more personal way, her hunger to study the Bible increased, and the understanding of what it meant to be a godly wife to an unbelieving husband began to take new shape. Elizabeth loved her husband desperately and grieved the possibility that he would not join her in heaven. Sadly, Elizabeth's new zeal was the object of constant ridicule from Felix and his friends. So she quietly endured the taunts, relentlessly lived her faith, and believed he would someday know and serve God. Felix, however, was not swayed, and when Elizabeth died of cancer in 1914, Felix still rejected God's existence.

Months later Felix discovered Elizabeth's secret diary. It chronicled her journey of faith, her love for her heavenly Father, and the belief that her husband would someday know God's love. Elizabeth's words moved Felix in a powerful way. He repented, was baptized in the church, and ultimately became a priest. He ministered avidly for Jesus the rest of his life.

Sources: www.catholic.net/rcc/Periodicals/Faith/0102-97/bio.html;
www.op.org/DomCentral/study/aumann/cs/cs10.htm.

NO APOLOGY FOR APOLOGETICS

Apologetics is the branch of theology concerned with defending faith in a way that is based on reason. Christian apologetics deals with answering critics who oppose or question the validity of Christianity. The word *apologetics* comes from a Greek word meaning "verbal defense." Believers are specifically instructed to engage in apologetics: "In your hearts set apart Christ as Lord. Always be prepared to give an answer to everyone who asks you to give the reason for the hope that you have" *(1 Peter 3:15 NIV)*. The apostle Paul was a highly skilled apologist, able to reason with both Jews and Gentiles.

Apologetics can involve studying biblical manuscript transmission, philosophy, biology, mathematics, evolution, logic, history, and other subjects. It also involves simply responding thoughtfully and logically to a question about Jesus or a Bible passage.

Sources: www.carm.org/apologetics/intro.htm; www.cs.uni-potsdam.de/ti/kreitz/Christian/Apologetics/all.html.

WHO QUALIFIES FOR SAINTHOOD?

The Roman Catholic Church canonizes certain individuals as saints after their deaths. Recognized not only for their exemplary lives and association with visions and miracles, saints, Catholics believe, are intermediaries between God and humans, and prayers for specific concerns associated with each saint are common.

The Eastern Orthodox Church defines a saint as anyone who is currently in heaven. The church makes no true distinction between the righteous living and the dead—saints are alive in heaven—so the Orthodox treat the saints as if they were still here. They honor and respect them as though they possess divine power, and ask for their prayers.

In most Protestant churches, the word *saint* generally refers to anyone who is a Christian.

SWEEPING FOR A LOST COIN

Jesus told a parable in which a woman who had lost a coin lit a lamp, swept her house, and searched diligently until she found it. Jesus said when she found the coin, she called her friends and neighbors to say, "Rejoice with me, for I have found the piece which I lost!" *(Luke 15:9 NKJV)*. Jesus concluded, "I say to you, there is joy in the presence of the angels of God over one sinner who repents" *(v. 10 NKJV)*.

In Jesus' time, unmarried women wore headbands to hold their scarves in place. A scarf could be pulled over the face if modesty was required, or pulled back up over the hair if work was being done. The headband of an unmarried woman had nine coins, part of the woman's dowry. At the time of marriage, a tenth coin was stitched to the band. This was a sign to the world that the woman was married—it was a custom similar to adding a wedding band to an engagement ring. A woman who "lost a coin" had, in essence, lost her identity as a married woman.

In Hebrew, the number ten commonly refers to the Law and to the relationship between the Jews and God. In his parable, Jesus was telling the Scribes and Pharisees that they had "lost" part of their identity when it came to their relationship with God. They needed to find again God's compassion and love for people, and to rekindle a joy when people were restored to right relationship with God.

COMMANDED BUT HARD TO DO

*F*orgiveness is an easy word to say, a challenging word to define and practice, and the most precious gift ever given humankind.

1. "Forgiveness is an act of the will, and the will can function regardless of the temperature of the heart."
   —*Corrie ten Boom*

2. "Forgiveness is the fragrance from the violet beneath the heel which has crushed it."—*Mark Twain*

3. "If you do not forgive men their trespasses, neither will your Father forgive your trespasses."—*Matthew 6:15 NKJV*

4. "Forgiveness is God's command."—*Martin Luther*

5. "God wants to bring peace, forgiveness, and joy to your life—and He will if you will allow Him."—*Billy Graham*

6. "To err is human, to forgive is divine."—*Alexander Pope*

7. "It is in pardoning that we are pardoned."
   —*Saint Francis of Assisi*

8. "There is no sin nor wrong that gives a man such a foretaste of hell in this life as anger and impatience."
   —*Saint Catherine of Siena*

9. "Thou must be emptied of that wherewith thou art full, that thou mayest be filled with that whereof thou art empty."
   —*Saint Augustine*

10. "Be kind to one another, tender-hearted, forgiving each other, just as God in Christ also has forgiven you."
    —*Ephesians 4:32 NASB*

11. "God so loved the world that He gave His only begotten Son, that whoever believes in Him should not perish but have everlasting life."—*John 3:16 NKJV*

12. "To be a Christian means to forgive the inexcusable, because God has forgiven the inexcusable in you."—*C. S. Lewis*

EXCEEDINGLY BEAUTIFUL WOMEN

Only four women in the Old Testament are described in Hebrew as being exceedingly beautiful in physical countenance: Rachel, wife of Jacob *(Genesis 29:17)*; Abigail, wife of David *(1 Samuel 25:3)*; Bathsheba, wife of David *(2 Samuel 11:2)*; and Esther, wife of the Persian king Ahasuerus *(Esther 2:7)*. It's interesting to note that none of these women were the "first wife" of the men who found them exceedingly beautiful and claimed them as their spouse.

WHICH LAWS DID THEY BREAK?

The gospel of Matthew tells that Jesus and his disciples were hungry one Sabbath and began to pluck and eat heads of grain. The Pharisees denounced them for breaking the Sabbath laws. (See Matthew 12:1–2.) The laws were *not* in the Bible, but rather they were laws that various religious leaders had added through the centuries: no reaping (picking), no threshing (rubbing grain from husk), no winnowing (removing husks), and no preparing food (with the intent of eating).

THEIR FEES WERE TOO HIGH

Who were the money changers Jesus drove from the temple? When Jews came from various Gentile nations to make sacrifices at the temple, they needed to exchange their "unclean" Gentile money for the acceptable "shekels of the sanctuary." Temple shekels were required for making cash donations, as well as for purchasing sacrificial animals and birds. The money changers Jesus evicted were guilty of charging exorbitant "exchange fees" as they provided this service. *(See Matthew 21:12.)*

IT'S A DEAL!

The Bible reflects an unusual manner of sealing a deal, especially one involving the land of a deceased relative. In order to make every matter legal, a man would take off his sandal and give it to the other party in the agreement. This was the way a contract was publicly approved in ancient Israel.

Removing a shoe also was used to attest to the ending of an obligation. When a man died, his nearest kin had the right to inherit or purchase his land, but the land came with the deceased's wife and family. The added responsibility of the new family was often off-putting to people struggling to survive and work their own land. According to Deuteronomy 25:7–10, a widow whose in-law refused to assume responsibility could call him before a counsel, remove one of his sandals, and spit in his face. This freed him from obligations to her, but, as outlined in Deuteronomy, his house was then somewhat disgraced. Still, the removal of the sandal made the way clear for others to purchase the land and ready-made family.

When Boaz sought to marry the widowed Ruth, he first had to obtain the right to purchase her land from a relative more closely related to Ruth than he was. According to Ruth 4, the relative declined his right to buy, because he didn't want the added responsibility of the widow and her mother-in-law. To signal his willingness to step aside in favor of Boaz, he removed his shoe (and presumably gave it to Boaz).

SHE USED EVERY VESSEL
SHE COULD FIND

The Bible tells the story of an unnamed woman who faced the most serious crisis of her life. This woman was the widow of one of the "sons of the prophets" *(2 Kings 4:1 NKJV)*, which meant that he was being trained in the Law by Elisha, the most notable prophet in Israel at the time. The man died and left bills that his widow could not pay.

As if it weren't enough that this woman had lost her husband and her livelihood, she also faced the loss of her two sons.

At that time, a child could be sold into slavery to meet a debt *(see Leviticus 25:39–41)*. This woman faced the imminent prospect of losing her two sons to her husband's creditors. She did the only thing she knew to do—she went to the prophet Elisha and told him her problem.

Elisha responded by asking her, "What do you have in the house?" *(2 Kings 4:2 NKJV)*. She replied that the only thing she had was a jar of olive oil. Elisha said, "Go, borrow vessels from everywhere, from all your neighbors—empty vessels; do not gather just a few" *(v. 3 NKJV)*. Then he advised her to go into her house, shut the door behind her and her two sons, and begin to pour oil out of her jar into the empty vessels. She did as he said. Oil continued to pour from her little jar until she had filled every empty vessel in the house. It was only when one of her sons told her there were no more vessels left that the oil ceased to flow.

The widow returned to Elisha and asked him what she should do next. He told her, "Go, sell the oil and pay your debt" *(v. 7 NKJV)*.

SHE USED EVERY VESSEL
SHE COULD FIND (CONT'D)

The oil sold for an amount sufficient to pay off all her bills—and more! She had enough money left over to raise her sons until they became wage earners.

This woman's story is the first of five told about the miraculous power of God at work on behalf of his people who lived in the Northern Kingdom of Israel. At the time, the Northern Kingdom had no functioning priesthood. The spiritual leaders of the people were prophets raised up by God to proclaim God's message and teach the Law. In each of the five stories, the power of God to provide or to heal comes about because people followed the detailed instructions of the prophet. The emphasis is twofold: the goodness of God is coupled with the obedience of God's people. The obedience required in each of these five miracles is "blind trust"; what the people are told to do makes no "sense." In every case, the goodness of God is "overflowing"; it goes beyond what might be expected.

The miracles conveyed a great message to God's people at that time: God had not forgotten them. God still cared for them and would meet their needs. But the miracles also bore the message that the people needed to trust in God and obey him completely to experience his protection and provision.

IF TREES COULD TALK

If the trees below—all mentioned in the Bible—could talk, what a tale they could tell!

1. Green Poplar, Almond, and Chestnut Rods *(Genesis 30:37 NKJV)*. When Jacob peeled rods from these three trees and put the rods in the watering troughs of his flocks, the flocks produced streaked, speckled, and spotted offspring, all of which became Jacob's possession.

2. A Withering Fig *(Mark 11:13–14, 20–21)*. When Jesus saw an unproductive fig tree, he said, "Let no one eat fruit from you ever again" *(v. 14 NKJV)*. The tree immediately dried up from the roots and died.

3. Forests Instead of Wilderness *(Isaiah 41:19–20 NKJV)*. The prophet Isaiah foretold a day when the wilderness would become a forest with cedar, acacia, myrtle, oil, cypress, pine, and box trees. Isaiah said the people would know the forest had been created by God.

4. Dinner Under a Broom Tree— also Called Juniper *(1 Kings 19:4–8)*. An angel of God prepared a picnic for Elijah under a broom tree that was a day's journey away from Beersheba. The angel fed Elijah a cake baked on coals and gave him water to drink. Elijah went on his way, traveling forty more days on the strength of that meal.

5. A Water-Purifying Tree at Marah *(Exodus 15:25)*. The Bible doesn't say what type of tree this was, but we do know that God showed Moses the tree and when Moses cast it into the bitter, undrinkable waters at Marah, the waters became sweet and drinkable.

6. A Mulberry Cast into the Sea— Also Called Sycamine *(Luke 17:6)*. When the disciples asked Jesus to increase their faith, he replied, "If you have faith as a mustard seed, you can say to this mulberry tree, 'Be pulled up by the roots and be planted in the sea,' and it would obey you" *(NKJV)*. In other words, faith the size of a grain of cayenne pepper, which is the size of mustard seed in the Middle East, could uproot a tree twelve to fifteen feet high.

7. Up in a Sycamore *(Luke 19:1–10)*. Jesus saw that Zacchaeus had climbed a sycamore tree to see him as he passed through Jericho. Jesus saw him there and invited himself to Zacchaeus's house for a meal, during which he gave Zacchaeus an opportunity to repent of overcharging the people in his role as a tax collector. Zacchaeus vowed to give his ill-gained wealth to the poor.

8. A Tree Used to Make Iron Float *(2 Kings 6:1–7)*. While helping to cut down some trees along the Jordan River, one of Elisha's students lost a borrowed ax head in the water. Elisha threw a stick into the water where the iron ax head had disappeared, and the ax head floated to the surface!

9. Clapping Forest *(Isaiah 55:12)*. Isaiah foretold a day of abundance and joy in Israel when the hills would sing and "the trees of the field shall clap their hands" *(NKJV)*.

IF TREES COULD TALK (CONT'D)

10. A Parable of Trees and a Bramble Bush *(Judges 9:1–15 NKJV)*. A rare parable in the Old Testament tells how the trees invited the olive and fig trees—as well as the vine—to rule over them, but all declined. The trees then invited the bramble to be their king and the bramble agreed, which led, of course, to the demise of the forest.

11. A Sound in the Treetops *(2 Samuel 5:22–25)*. When the Philistines sought to engage in battle against David and the armies of Israel in the valley of Rephaim, God gave David a divine battle plan: "Circle around behind them, and come upon them in front of the mulberry trees" *(v. 23 NKJV)*. The troops were to advance only when they heard the sound of marching in the tops of the trees. The result? The Philistines were driven back.

12. Rare Wood for a King *(2 Chronicles 9:10–11)*. Solomon made walkways for his palace, as well as harps and other stringed instruments, from the very rare wood of the algum trees. Nobody in Judah had ever seen the beauty of this wood before. (The word is spelled "aglum" in some versions of the Bible.)

13. Capturing a Would-Be King *(2 Samuel 18:9–15)*. As the trea- sonous Absalom sought to escape David's troops, his mule passed under the boughs of a terebinth tree. Absalom's hair became caught in the tree's branches, and he was pulled from his mule and left hanging from the tree, where he was an easy target for Joab to kill.

14. A Miraculous Walking Stick *(Exodus 4:2–4)*. It was not uncommon for people in Bible times to make personal walking sticks from small tree limbs. These sticks, or rods, were very useful, especially to shepherds, who used the rods to protect their flocks from predators. When God encountered Moses by a burning bush, he bestowed miraculous powers to Moses' walking stick, turning it into a serpent on occasion and also using it to part a sea and bring water from a rock.

15. A Rod That Budded *(Numbers 17:8)*. One day when Moses went into the tabernacle, he found that the walking stick of Aaron, Moses' brother, had miraculously sprouted and put forth buds, blossoms, and ripe almonds! It was a sign to the Israelites of God's favor on Aaron as high priest.

GOD BLESS YOU!

Aaaaah-*choo!* is very often followed by the words "God bless you!" in Western cultures. But it's a lovely phrase to offer in any language. Here is the phrase in fifteen different languages, along with an approximate phonetic pronunciation for each. Since many of these languages use non-Latin character sets, the words have been written in phonetic English equivalents.

1. *German: Gott segnen Sie* (Got-seeg-nen-zee)

2. *Dutch: De god zegent u* (Deh goot zeh-gent oo)

3. *French: Dieu vous bénissent* (Day-oo voo bay-nee-sah)

4. *Italian: Il dio li benedice* (Eel dee-oh lee beh-neh-dee-chee)

5. *Portuguese: O deus bless o* (Oh day-oos bless oh)

6. *Spanish: El dios le bendice* (Ell dee-ohs leh ben-dee-seh)

7. *Russian: Da blagoslovit vas Gospod'* (Dah blog-ohs-loh-vit vahs Gahspoh-d)

8. *Swedish: Gud välsignar dig* (Guud vel-signar day)

9. *Norwegian: Gud velsigner dig* (Guud vel-signer die)

10. *Korean: Hanahnim oonheh chooshegeh seumnida* (pronounced more or less as it looks)

11. *Estonian: Jumal õnnistagu sind* (You-mal enn-eestagu sin-d)

12. *Hebrew: Elo'im yevarheha* (Eh-loh-em veh-var-heh-hah) or *Elo'im yevareh otha* (Eh-loh-em veh-var-reh o-tha)

13. *Latin: Deus beatus vos* (Day-oos bee-ah-toos vohs)

14. *Danish: God velsigne jer* (Goht vehl-sig-neh yur)

15. *Finnish: Jumala siunatkoon sinua* (You-ma-la see-you-nat-cone see-nu-ah)

AN UNLIKELY PARTICIPANT

He was a habitual drunkard and was rumored to be addicted to other vices that could not be mentioned in the polite society of his day. He drained the royal treasury to pay for his extravagant expenses associated with women and wine. He married off his children like pawns to suit his foreign policy. He was described by J. R. Green as a man with a "big head . . . slobbering tongue . . . quilted clothes . . . rickety legs . . . goggle eyes." When people compared him with King Henry or Queen Elizabeth, he seemed woefully lacking in dignity. He was highly criticized for his drunkenness and silly behavior. Some labeled him a coward. Even so, God used this man to assemble scholars and establish the "Authorized Translation of the Bible" in 1611. This man's name became linked with the most influential Bible of all time. His name was King James I.

THREE GENERATIONS OF PROLIFIC WRITERS

Does a desire to write run in families? That seems to have been the case in the Mather family!

One of the most prolific authors of Christian books in the history of the United States was Cotton Mather, a Puritan minister who served as pastor of the Second Church of Boston for many years. In all, he wrote 469 books. Cotton was both a third-generation clergyman and a third-generation author. Cotton's father was Increase Mather, who was a noted American Congregational minister and the president of Harvard College for sixteen years (1685–1701). He wrote many volumes on history and theology. Cotton's grandfather was Richard Mather, a Puritan who immigrated to the New World in 1635 and wrote many publications about a specific doctrine called the "Half-Way Covenant."

Many of Cotton's books were very popular in his day, particularly *Wonders of the Invisible World* (1692), *Essays to Do Good* (1710), and *Christian Philosopher* (1721).

What Makes a Monk a Trappist?

The word *trappist* is often linked to the word *monk* in literature, but what makes a monk a trappist? Trappists are actually an order of monks founded by a Frenchman, Armand Jean Le Bouthillier de Rance, the abbot of La Trappe, which was an abbey near Soligny, France, in the late 1700s. Although the monks are known as Trappists, the Catholic order for these monks is technically known as either the Order of Reformed Cistercians or Cistercians of Strict Observance. The order is strict indeed! In addition to vows of chastity and poverty, Trappist monks take a vow of silence, and they abstain from meat, eggs, and fish. The Trappist habit is white with a black hood (cowl) and yoke (scapular)—a strip of cloth that drapes the shoulders and hangs to the floor.

The order of nuns who take similar vows was founded in 1796 in Tart, France, and is the Cistercian Nuns of the Strict Observance.

The most famous Trappist monastery is Tre Fontane, south of Rome. It is the traditional site of Saint Paul's martyrdom.

Bringing in the Sheaves

Grain in Bible times was harvested by cutting the stalks with a sickle. Flax was harvested by pulling up the entire stalks. Reaping was considered very hard labor. Workers generally reaped grain by bending over, grasping a handful of stalks, and cutting them off near the ground.

The Bible uses reaping as a metaphor to illustrate the truth that every act has consequences *(2 Corinthians 9:6)*. Galatians 6:7–9 says, "Whatever a man sows, that he will also reap. . . . Let us not grow weary while doing good, for in due season we shall reap if we do not lose heart" *(NKJV)*.

When Jesus sent his disciples out to preach, he spoke of fields ready for harvest *(Luke 10:1–2)*. These fields represented people ready to respond to the gospel, the "good news" about Jesus.

Harvesting was a year-round activity in Israel: olives in October, almonds in January, flax in February, citrus crops in March, barley in April, wheat in May, first figs in June, grapes and dates from June to August, and summer figs in August.

JUST ADD WATER

A number of miracles in the Bible involve water, which is a symbol through-out the Bible for purity and redemption. Here are twenty-five Bible miracles associated with water:

1. God created the waters *(Job 38:8–30)*.

2. Moses parted the Red Sea *(Exodus 14:21–22)*.

3. Moses caused the parted Red Sea to return to its normal state after the Israelites crossed it *(Exodus 14:26–31)*.

4. Jesus turned water into wine *(John 2:1–11)*.

5. Elijah purified polluted waters *(2 Kings 2:19–22)*.

6. Moses struck a rock and water gushed forth—first time *(Exodus 17:1–6)*.

7. Moses struck a rock and water gushed forth—but he was supposed to speak to the rock this time *(Numbers 20:1–13)*.

8. An angel provided water for Hagar *(Genesis 21:14–19)*.

9. God caused water to turn to blood as a plague against Egypt *(Exodus 7:17–24)*.

10. Moses caused bitter waters to become sweet *(Exodus 15:23–25)*.

11. The Israelites crossed the Jordan River on dry ground to enter Canaan *(Joshua 3:17)*.

12. Samson was given a divine supply of water *(Judges 15:19)*.

13. Jesus walked on water—and helped Peter to walk on water too *(Matthew 14:22–33)*.

14. Elijah offered a sacrifice that was consumed by fire even though he had drenched the wood and sacrifice with water *(1 Kings 18:32–38)*.

15. Elijah struck the Jordan River and it dried up so he could cross it *(2 Kings 2:8)*.

16. Elisha struck the Jordan River and it dried up so he could cross it *(2 Kings 2:14)*.

17. The army of Israel was given a divine supply of water *(2 Kings 3:16–20)*.

18. God caused water to appear as blood to the Moabites *(2 Kings 3:21–24)*.

19. Naaman was healed in the waters of the Jordan *(2 Kings 5:1–14)*.

20. Elisha caused an iron ax head to float *(2 Kings 6:1–7)*.

21. Jesus calmed the storm on the Sea of Galilee *(Mark 4:35–41)*.

22. An angel stirred up the waters of the Pool of Bethesda to cause healing *(John 5:1–4)*.

23. Jesus caused waters to yield a miraculous catch of fish *(Luke 5:1–11)*.

24. Jesus caused a boat he was in to reach its destination immediately *(John 6:21)*.

25. Jesus caused a miraculous catch of fish after the Resurrection *(John 21:3–11)*.

THE BEAUTIFUL IRISH BOOKS

Some of the most beautifully written and illustrated books in church history are associated with Ireland. The original texts of the six early Irish books are considered highly prized by the institutions in which they are housed. If on display, they are viewed only under black light and are guarded carefully.

The books are popular, in part, because of their beautiful illumination or decoration. "Decoration" refers to illustrations of the text, graphic designs in the margins, or the highlighting of specific words or phrases with special lettering. "Illumination" refers more specifically to the decorating of a particular letter, often the first letter of a chapter, book of the Bible, or story. The letter is usually colored brightly and is often embellished with a design that may include embedded illustrations or symbols.

Book of Armagh. This book comes from the ninth century. It was written on vellum (made from animal skins), with loose pages bound together in book form. It was written partly in Latin, partly in Irish. It includes the non-Vulgate text of the Latin New Testament, the Pauline Epistles, the Catholic Epistles and Acts, a Life of Saint Martin of Tours, and documents about Saint Patrick. It is currently in the Trinity College Library in Dublin.

Book of Cerne. This was a ninth-century collection of non-liturgical Celtic prayers. It is in the Cambridge University Library.

Book of Deer. This ninth-century Irish manuscript has the four Gospels written in Gaelic, but the text is considered to have errors made in the copying of the Bible text. The name

THE BEAUTIFUL
IRISH BOOKS (CONT'D)

of the book comes from notes in the manuscript that describe the foundation of and grants of land made to the Monastery of Deer in Aberdeenshire in Scotland. It is now in the Cambridge University Library.

Book of Durrow. This was the first Irish manuscript with elaborate decoration or illumination. It is dated 675. Scholars believe it was written in Northumbria and then preserved at Columba's monastery at Durrow. It is now in the Trinity College Library in Dublin.

Book of Kells. This ornamented and illuminated Latin manuscript of the Gospels came originally from the monastery at Kells in Ireland. The book has 340 leaves, each 9.5 inches by 13 inches. The leaves are made of thick glazed parchment with brownish-black ink. The work was probably begun at Iona and finished at Kells. The illumination is very intricate and detailed. The book is now at the Trinity College Library in Dublin.

Book of Lismore. This book about the lives of saints is written in "middle Irish." The fifteenth-century manuscript was found in Lismore Castle and is now at Chatsworth House.

IS THE STABLE A FABLE?

W as Jesus born in a barn? A cave? A stable?

Most likely, Mary and Joseph arrived in Bethlehem well ahead of Mary's due date, giving them plenty of time to find appropriate accommodations. The Bible says that "while they were there [in Bethlehem], the days were accomplished that she should be delivered" *(Luke 2:6 KJV).*

It is also likely that Jesus' family stayed with relatives rather than in any part of a public house. Scripture makes no mention of an innkeeper, and the Greek word *kataluma*, translated as "inn" in Luke 2:7 *(KJV)*, can mean "guest chamber." It is used elsewhere in the New Testament to reference a large, furnished upper room in a private home (see *Mark 14:14–15)*. According to biblical archaeology experts, Jesus was most likely born in an area of the home that was outside the normal guest and living quarters—perhaps a room with a hay ledge or "manger" at one end—where animals could be moved out of the elements.

CHURCH: AN INOCULATION AGAINST DIVORCE?

W ill regularly attending church help lower a couple's chances of divorce?

Statistics obtained by a variety of government and research groups indicate that the general divorce rate among Americans in 2001 was at about 41% per capita. In the same year, the Barna Group surveyed people who regularly attended churches of various denominations. When compared with the government statistics, their findings seem to point to the possibility that people who regularly attend church lower their chances of getting divorced.

They also found that the likelihood that someone will have gone through a divorce varies by the type of church attended. Divorce rates were found to be highest among Baptists (29%) and those attending nondenominational churches (34%). The lowest divorce rates were among Lutherans (21%) and Catholics (21%). Denominations falling in between were Pentecostals (28%), Episcopalians (28%), Methodists (26%), and Presbyterians (23%).

Sadly, Barna research also indicates that more than 90% of the born-again adults who have been divorced experienced that divorce after they accepted Jesus Christ, not before.

Sources: "Denominations," The Barna Group, www.barna.org, Barna Update 9/8/04, accessed 12/11/05; "Born Again Adults Less Likely to Co-Habit, Just as Likely to Divorce," The Barna Group, www.barna.org, Barna Update 9/8/04, accessed 3/17/06; www.divorcestatistics.org.

Jesus and Deuteronomy

Many people find the book of Deuteronomy in the Old Testament to be a little boring—there are lots of rules and regulations but not much action. This book, however, was one Jesus quoted in critical moments and taught as part of the Sermon on the Mount! Below are some of the things Jesus said that are straight out of the book of Deuteronomy. The first three of these are statements Jesus made to the devil, who came to tempt him in the wilderness:

1. "It is written, 'Man shall not live by bread alone, but by every word that proceeds from the mouth of God'" *(Deuteronomy 8:3; Matthew 4:4 NKJV).*

2. "It is written again, 'You shall not tempt the Lord your God'" *(Deuteronomy 6:16; Matthew 4:7 NKJV).*

3. "Away with you, Satan! For it is written, 'You shall worship the Lord your God, and Him only you shall serve'" *(Deuteronomy 6:13; Matthew 4:10 NKJV).*

4. "If your brother sins against you, go and tell him his fault between you and him alone. If he hears you, you have gained your brother. But if he will not hear, take with you one or two more, that 'by the mouth of two or three witnesses every word may be established'" *(Deuteronomy 19:15; Matthew 18:15–16 NKJV).*

5. [Among the commandments Jesus cited after a man came to him asking which commandments he should keep:] "'Honor your father and your mother'" *(Deuteronomy 5:16; Matthew 19:19 NKJV).*

6. [To a lawyer who asked which was the greatest commandment of the law:] "'You shall love the Lord your God with all your heart, with all your soul, and with all your mind'" *(Deuteronomy 6:5; Matthew 22:37 NKJV).*

7. "You have heard that it was said to those of old, 'You shall not murder, and whoever murders will be in danger of the judgment.' But I say to you that whoever is angry with his brother without a cause shall be in danger of the judgment" *(Deuteronomy 5:17; Matthew 5:21–22 NKJV).*

8. "You have heard that it was said to those of old, 'You shall not commit adultery.' But I say to you that whoever looks at a woman to lust for her has already committed adultery with her in his heart" *(Deuteronomy 5:18; Matthew 5:27–28 NKJV).*

9. "You have heard that it was said, 'An eye for an eye and a tooth for a tooth.' But I tell you not to resist an evil person. But whoever slaps you on your right cheek, turn the other to him also" *(Deuteronomy 19:21; Matthew 5:38–39 NKJV).*

PROVE IT!

Is it possible to prove that God exists? People of every generation have attempted to prove God's existence. Reason, philosophy, and logic have produced similar lines of argument over hundreds and thousands of years. Five main "arguments" in favor of God have emerged:

The Cosmological Argument. This argument comes from the Greek word *kosmos*, meaning "world, order, or universe." It states that there is a First Cause of everything. Nothing caused itself to exist by its own cause; everything known has a cause outside itself and before itself. Causes, however, cannot go back infinitely; there must be a First Cause that ultimately caused everything else. Without it, the whole process of causation would never have started. The First Cause is called God.

The Teleological Argument. Known today as Intelligent Design, this argument comes from the Greek word *telos*, which means "goal or purpose." This argument states that the evidence of design and purpose in the universe points toward an intelligent Creator. It is reasonable to conclude that the existence of a watch indicates a watchmaker. In the same way, the existence of a purposeful universe points to a purposeful Creator.

The Ontological Argument. This argument comes from the Greek word *on*, which means "being," and is based on reason alone. One ontological argument was devised by Anselm of the eleventh century. He argued that there has to be a being greater than anything else that can be conceived. Anselm said that being is God.

The Moral Argument. This argument poses the question, What is the source of moral values? Where does the idea of right and wrong come from? Moral obligation, the obligation

PROVE IT! (CONT'D)

to do good and avoid evil, is a reality. Matter does not have morality; it simply is. In a purely materialistic world, people's actions cannot be evaluated as right or wrong. Even atheists and agnostics appeal to right and wrong, to justice and fair play. Moral relativism is a popular thought today. People often say there is no moral duty that is true for everyone; people must follow their own private conscience. However, even the existence of a personal conscience points to the existence of a personal, moral Creator. That Creator has made people with a sense of morality and obligation.

The Fulfillment Argument. Yet another argument states that the existence of desire within each person points toward something outside of the person to satisfy the desire. Each person has desires—such as the desire for food, sex, sleep, friendship, and understanding. These desires can be satisfied. However, creatures also desire meaning and purpose. These desires cannot be satisfied fully by anything that exists naturally. Even after achieving fortune, fame, and success, the question eventually arises, Is that all there is? Fulfilled natural desires do not fulfill the desire for purpose and meaning. C. S. Lewis, the twentieth-century apologist, makes the statement in his book *Mere Christianity*, "If I find in myself a desire which no experience in this world can satisfy, the most probable explanation is that I was made for another world."

The Bible never tries to prove that God exists; it presupposes the existence of God. Arguments for God's existence do not finally prove the God of Christian faith. Ultimately that is not possible by rational argument. But such arguments do point to the fact that humans are not self-sufficient. In truth, humans are dependent creatures, created to need other people . . . and God.

A PARTRIDGE IN A PEAR TREE?

Nobody really knows with certainty about the origin—and original intent—of the song "The Twelve Days of Christmas." It appears to have been used in the nineteenth century as a memory game for children. In recent years, some have speculated that the song might have been used to teach children basic facts about the Bible and the church. Whether that was the original intent of the song or not, each element of the song *may* be linked to a basic tenet of faith, with the "true love" who gives the gifts being God.

The partridge in a pear tree = Jesus

Two turtledoves = Old and New Testaments

Three French hens = faith, hope, and love

Four calling birds = the four Gospels of Matthew, Mark, Luke, and John

Five golden rings = the first five books of the Old Testament, called the Torah or Law

Six geese a-laying = the six days of creation

Seven swans a-swimming = the sevenfold gifts of the Holy Spirit: prophesying, serving, teaching, exhorting, contributing, leading, and showing mercy

Eight maids a-milking = the eight "blessed are you" statements of Jesus in Matthew 5:3–10

Nine ladies dancing = the ninefold fruit of the Holy Spirit: "love, joy, peace, patience, kindness, goodness, faithfulness, gentleness and self-control" *(Galatians 5:22–23 NIV)*

Ten lords a-leaping = the Ten Commandments

Eleven pipers piping = the eleven faithful disciples

Twelve drummers drumming = the twelve points of belief in the Apostles' Creed

REV UP!

A revival is a supernatural work of God that awakens people to obeying him. In Scripture, revivals followed a time of idolatry and wrongdoing. At various times in history, the people of God worshipped other gods. God then raised up leaders who called the people back to himself. These are some of the revivals mentioned in the Bible:

1. *Under Samuel (1 Samuel 7:3–6).* Samuel, a prophet, called the people of Israel to get rid of their foreign gods, return to God with all their hearts, commit themselves to God, and serve him only. The people heard Samuel, and they fasted and confessed their wrongdoing. Samuel cried out to God, and God answered him.

2. *Under David (1 Chronicles 15:25–28).* When the ark of the covenant was brought into Jerusalem for the first time, there was shouting and the sound of rams' horns and trumpets, cymbals, and lyres and harps.

3. *Under Elijah (1 Kings 18:31–39).* In the contest between Elijah and the worshippers of the false god Baal, God sent fire to consume the water-drenched sacrifice. The people fell on their faces and said, "The LORD— he is God!" *(v. 39 NIV).*

4. *Under Hezekiah (2 Chronicles 29).* King Hezekiah "did right in the sight of the Lord" *(v. 2 AMP).* Hezekiah removed idols from God's temple and purified it with burnt offerings. The king and the whole assembly bowed in worship, and the service of God's temple was reestablished.

5. *Under Nehemiah (Nehemiah 8–9).* After the wall around Jerusalem was rebuilt, Ezra read from the Book of the Law. And when he did, the people lifted their hands and said, "Amen!" and then bowed down and worshipped God with their faces to the ground. Later they fasted and confessed their wrongdoing and spent more time worshipping God.

6. *Under Jesus (John 4:39–42).* When a Samaritan woman who had spoken with Jesus told the townspeople about what he said, many believed in Jesus. The Samaritans asked Jesus to spend time with them, so he stayed in their town two days. Because he did, "many more became believers" *(v. 41 NIV).*

7. *Under Peter (Acts 2).* At Pentecost, after Peter gave a great sermon, the people repented, were baptized, received forgiveness for their wrongdoing, and received the Holy Spirit. That day three thousand people accepted Peter's message and were baptized.

8. *Under Philip (Acts 8:4–8).* After the persecution in Jerusalem that dispersed the believers to other parts of Israel, Philip the Evangelist proclaimed the good news about Jesus in Samaria. When the crowds heard him and saw the miraculous signs that accompanied his message, they paid attention to what he said! People were delivered of evil spirits, and many paralytics and disabled people were healed. There was great joy in the city.

A MONUMENTAL
CHARITABLE GIFT

George Frideric Handel (1685–1759) was born in Germany and became a naturalized citizen of England in 1712. After nearly thirty years of great success as a composer and producer of Italian operas in London, Handel's fortune began to change. A rival Italian opera company in London seriously compromised his income—the music world seemed to be shifting to oratorio-type works. About that time a wealthy English country gentleman and huge fan of Handel, Charles Jennens, approached Handel to commission him to write an oratorio, "the subject of which would be the Messiah."

At that same time, Handel was unexpectedly approached by the lord lieutenant of Ireland, William Cavendish. At this time, 1741, Dublin was considered to be in its golden age—a great center of the arts. Cavendish invited Handel to Dublin to perform his works for charity as well as profit. The prospect of a new public, a charitable cause, and a series of concerts ignited Handel's creativity, and he feverishly planned a series of "entertainments" for the Irish city. He decided that *Messiah* would be the main work in a public concert for charity, and he immediately set Jennens's libretto to music, composing *Messiah* in only twenty-four days.

Handel shared the proceeds of the first performance of *Messiah* with three Dublin charities: the Society for Relieving Prisoners, the Charitable Infirmary, and Mercer's Hospital. The public eagerness for the first concert in 1742 was so great, and the anticipated audiences so large, that the charities issued an announcement in the Dublin newspaper that women "should not wear hooped dresses" and men "should not wear their swords" to make more room for audience members in

A MONUMENTAL
CHARITABLE GIFT (CONT'D)

the seven-hundred-seat music hall. Released from the demands of Italian opera, Handel chose primarily "singing actors" for the *Messiah* premiere in Dublin. One of the singers, Susannah Cibber, was so emotional and powerful in singing her aria, "He Was Despised," that one male audience member rose from his seat and cried out during the performance, "Woman, for this, be all thy sins forgiven."

The London premiere of *Messiah* during Holy Week the next year (1743) generated controversy. The piece was advertised as a "New Sacred Oratorio," but it was performed at the Covent Garden Theatre, a notoriously nonreligious venue. To further complicate matters, Handel chose singing actors, not necessarily known for their piety, to sing the oratorio.

From the year 1750 until Handel's death in 1759, *Messiah* was performed annually for the benefit of London's Foundling Hospital, a charity for the "maintenance and education of exposed and deserted young children." One music critic and historian of that era noted that Handel's *Messiah* "fed the hungry, clothed the naked, fostered the orphan . . . more than any single musical production in this or any country."

PULLING IN THE SAME DIRECTION

A "yoke" is most commonly associated with oxen and other animals that are harnessed together with this wooden contraption so they can help farmers plow.

In the Bible, the yoke has additional meanings. It is a symbol of slavery in the Old Testament. Jeremiah talks about the Israelites' being "under Babylon's yoke," forced to submit to King Nebuchadnezzar (*Jeremiah 27:8 NLT*).

The apostle Paul said in 2 Corinthians 6:14 that followers of Jesus should not marry those who don't believe in him, because the two spouses would wind up pulling in opposite directions, causing friction in the relationship.

On the other hand, being yoked together with other believers—working for a common cause like sharing the gospel—is good (*Philippians 4:3*). And being yoked with Jesus—serving and loving him—is a positive experience (*Matthew 11:29–30*).

ANOTHER WORD FOR "WORD"

L*ogos* is a Greek word that sums up a simple idea: there is order to the universe; life has meaning. As such, *logos*, which means "word," has real power.

The members of the church that formed after the death and resurrection of Jesus agreed. One of Jesus' disciples, John, wrote in his gospel that Jesus himself was "the Word"—the logos. Jesus, he said, has been around forever. He is God. He was at Creation; he caused it. It was the spoken word (for example, "Let there be light" in *Genesis 1:3*) that launched life on earth and the entire universe.

As *logos* connotes order and meaning, church leaders said, Jesus—the Word—came to bring meaning and creative power to a human being's life.

BOOT CAMP FOR GOD'S ARMY

Nobody's perfect. Neither are any of the world's institutions—including the church. Still, as these comments make clear, the church has a mission that only it can fulfill:

1. "The Christian church is a society of sinners. It is the only society in the world in which membership is based upon the single qualification that the candidate shall be unworthy of membership."
    —*Charles Clayton Morrison (American magazine editor, 1874–1966)*

2. "The church is the only thing that is going to make the terrible world we are coming to endurable; the only thing that makes the church endurable is that it is somehow the body of Christ and that on this we are fed. It seems to be a fact that you have to suffer as much from the church as for it, but if you believe in the divinity of Christ, you endure it."
    —*Flannery O'Connor (American author, 1925–1964)*

3. "The holiest moment of the church service is the moment when God's people—strengthened by preaching and sacrament—go out of the church door into the world to be the church. We don't go to church; we are the church."—*Ernest Southcott (British churchman)*

4. "When the church transcends culture, it can transform culture. In the Dark Ages, reform did not arise from the state but from communities of those who remained uncompromising in a compromising age."
    —*Charles Colson (American speaker and author, 1931–)*

5. "The church is not a gallery for the exhibition of eminent Christians, but a school for the education of imperfect ones."
    —*Henry Ward Beecher (American clergyman, 1813–1887)*

6. "The Church exists for the sake of those outside it."
    —*William Temple (British churchman, 1881–1944)*

7. "There is no salvation outside the church."
    —*Saint Augustine (bishop of Hippo, 354–430)*

8. "The Church after all is not a club of saints; it is a hospital for sinners."
    —*George Craig Stewart (bishop of Chicago, 1879–1940)*

9. "Man is a being born to believe. And if no Church comes forward with its title-deeds of truth . . . to guide him, he will find altars and idols in his own heart and his own imagination."
    —*Benjamin Disraeli (British prime minister, 1804–1881)*

Sources: Edythe Draper, *Draper's Book of Quotations for the Christian World* (Wheaton, IL: Tyndale, 1992); *The Macmillan Dictionary of Quotations* (New York: Macmillan, 1987, 1989); Robert Andrews, *The Concise Columbia Dictionary of Quotations* (New York: Avon, 1987, 1989).

THE WEDDING PLANNER

Some of the most stirring imagery in the Bible compares a believer's relationship to God with a joyful marriage.

In the ancient Middle East, the wedding engagement was almost as binding as the marriage itself. The engaged man and woman were called "husband" and "wife" and were to meet the same standards of fidelity as when they married.

The choice of a spouse was the parents' prerogative. Usually it was the young man's parents who selected a bride for him. The bride ultimately became a member of the bridegroom's family. Sometimes the young man chose his bride, with the parents negotiating the dowry. Once a bride was chosen, negotiations began. Each family had a "deputy" who acted on behalf of the family's interests.

A marriage dowry was paid to the bride's family to compensate for the loss of her contribution to her family. An unmarried daughter generally tended flocks or worked in the field; upon her marriage, she was no longer available to help. It was customary for the bride to receive part of the dowry, which belonged to her permanently, protecting her in the event of a divorce. It was also customary for the father to give his daughter a special marriage dowry as a "parting gift" from her family.

Among the ancient Hebrews, the betrothal was a spoken covenant with a ceremony attended by the families of the bride and groom. The young man then presented his bride-to-be with jewelry or other valuable articles, or a document saying he promised to marry her. At least one year elapsed between the betrothal and the wedding.

For the wedding ceremony, the groom was dressed as a "king," complete with a crown if he could afford it, or a gar-

THE WEDDING PLANNER (CONT'D)

land of fresh flowers as a headpiece. His clothes were scented with frankincense and myrrh. The bride was adorned as a "queen" with a crown of her own. Brides sometimes wore embroidered garments, along with stones and jewels that belonged to the family from previous generations.

Most often, the bridegroom went in person—accompanied by his friends—to bring his bride to his home for the wedding festivities. Before leaving her home, the bride received the blessing of her relatives. A grand procession followed the couple all the way back to the groom's house, and along the way there was singing, music, and dancing.

The marriage feast in the groom's house was attended by many relatives and friends. Each guest was required to wear a wedding garment. A steward or friend supervised the feast and instructed the servants to be attentive to the guests and carry out all the necessary details. Parents and friends then blessed the couple and wished them well.

A canopy or tent was prepared for the bride and bridegroom. They stood or sat under the canopy during the wedding ceremony. The bride and groom were then escorted to a room for the consummation of their marriage. A blood-stained cloth was exhibited after consummation as proof that the bride was a virgin.

Wedding festivities continued for a week or longer. The celebration was marked with music praising the new couple.

Sources: www.bibletexts.com/glossary/wedding.htm;
www.bible-history.com/isbe/M/MARRIAGE.

HOLD STILL! DON'T MOVE THOSE DATES!

The church traditionally celebrates a number of feasts and celebrations every year. Some fall on the same date every year, while others don't. Those that don't are called "moveable feasts." Which are which? See below . . .

Movable Feasts

1. *Ash Wednesday*, the beginning of Lent (forty-six days before Easter)

2. *Easter*, celebrating the resurrection of Jesus (between March 22 and April 25)

3. *Ascension Day*, marking forty days after Jesus' resurrection, when he ascended into heaven *(Acts 1:9)* (forty days after Easter)

4. *Whitsunday*, celebrated by the Church of England, which marks Pentecost, the day the Holy Spirit "came to rest" on the apostles *(Acts 2:3 NIV)* (seventh Sunday after Easter)

5. *Trinity Sunday*, on which Christians celebrate the triune nature of God: God the Father, God the Son, and God the Holy Spirit (eighth Sunday after Easter)

6. *Advent*, which announces that Christmas is approaching (the Sunday closest to November 30)

Fixed or Immovable Feasts

1. *Epiphany*, marking the visit of the Magi to the child Jesus (January 6)

2. *Transfiguration Day*, a feast day commemorating the day that Jesus went to Mount Tabor with Peter, James, and John, and his appearance changed before their eyes (Matthew 17:2) (August 6)

3. *All Saints' Day*, celebrating the lives of the saints (November 1)

4. *Christmas Day* (Jesus' true birth date is unknown, but in AD 325 Constantine the Great chose December 25, and so it remains.)

NOW, THAT'S A
NICE NEIGHBORHOOD

Fred Rogers was an unlikely icon. As a child, he was fat, which made him the target of bullies. Instead of becoming bitter, however, he developed compassion and used this deep concern for others to change children's television forever.

Rogers began working in television in 1951 in New York, then moved to Pittsburgh, where he worked on his first children's program. During his lunch break, he attended seminary classes. He was ordained by the United Presbyterian Church in 1963, charged "to serve children and families through the mass media." He hosted a children's show in Canada, called *Mister Rogers*. Then came *Mister Rogers' Neighborhood* in 1968, the longest-running show on PBS.

Mister Rogers earned countless awards for his work, including the Presidential Medal of Freedom. To generations of children, however, he was just "the man in the sweater" who made them feel safe, smart, and of great value to the world.

Sources: Amy Hollingsworth, *The Simple Faith of Mister Rogers* (Brentwood, TN: Integrity, 2005); www.misterrogers.org/mister_rogers_neighborhood/biography.asp.

ONE-OF-A-KIND
TEACHER

Susanna Wesley (1669–1742) never preached a sermon, published a book, or founded a church. Even so, she is known as the Mother of Methodism because of her profound influence on two of her sons, Methodism founders John and Charles Wesley.

Susanna was a strict but loving mother who taught her children self-discipline from an early age. Susanna also had a unique approach to teaching her children. She did not attempt to begin teaching them the letters of the alphabet until their fifth birthday, at which time she put all her usual household duties aside for the day. No one was allowed to come into the room where she and her little pupil were, from 9:00 till 12:00 and from 2:00 till 5:00. During these six designated hours for individual tutoring, Susanna taught her five-year-old the alphabet and the basics of reading. Eleven of her thirteen children successfully learned the letters of the alphabet and how to read on their fifth birthdays. The most important book for the Wesley children to read, of course, was the Bible.

A window in the Lady Chapel of Liverpool Cathedral is dedicated "to Susanna Wesley and all devoted mothers."

NOTHING TO SNIFF AT

Like gold and jewels, fragrances were a measure of wealth in Bible times. Ancient clay tablets testify to the fact that colossal fortunes were paid to perfume makers who provided essences to the rich and famous. Nearly every royal court counted jars of frankincense, cinnamon, aromatic resins, and oils of nard and myrrh among its treasures.

Fragrance played a recurring and important role in many scenes from the Bible.

In Exodus 30:34–38, God gave Moses a very specific recipe for combining spices, incense (frankincense), galbanum, onycha, and storax to make holy anointing oil and incense to be burned as a testimony in the tabernacle (a sanctuary or place of worship). So proprietary was this blend that God decreed that anyone making the substance for his own use or pleasure must be exiled from his people.

The title of Christ (from the Greek *Christos*), which means "the Anointed One," has indirect reference to the fragrant holy oils used to anoint for service to God. Appropriately, then, the three wise men who came to worship the child Jesus brought precious gifts for him, including frankincense and myrrh.

Jesus was again touched by fragrance when a woman poured an entire bottle of expensive perfume over his head shortly before he was betrayed and crucified. His disciples bemoaned the extravagant waste. But Jesus declared that her preparation of him for death would be remembered wherever the story of his life, death, and resurrection was preached. (See *Mark 14:1–11*.)

Today fragrances are still a part of worship in many Christian and Jewish services.

THE CROSS AND THE HURRICANES

When Dean and Ruth Lindsey furnished their winter home on the Florida Gulf Coast, they included a foot-high cross as a symbol of their faith to those who rented their condo. The cross was a personal item they didn't pack away when they left to go north every spring, so it, like furniture and other objects used by renters, was marked with their condo number (1E).

In 2004, Hurricane Ivan destroyed their beachside home, smashing through the windows and doors and washing everything it could out to sea. The resort area was still under repair in June 2005 when Hurricane Arlene swept into the same area. Walking the beach after this second hurricane, the Lindseys' condo manager noticed something that had washed ashore during the storm—a cross with 1E etched on the bottom. Mrs. Lindsey called the cross's return "amazing . . . a miracle!"

Source: *Tallahassee Democrat*, 6/21/05.

WHO STARTED CHRISTMAS?

A woman had spent hours Christmas shopping with her two young children, who seemed to ask for everything they saw. As she got on a very full department store elevator to go home, she suddenly felt overwhelmed—not only by the shopping experience but also by the fact that she felt she had to go to every party, every open house, and every program being held that year. In addition, she felt pressure to bake traditional holiday treats, get her Christmas cards out on time, and find the perfect gift for every person on her list.

As the elevator doors closed, she just couldn't take it anymore. She said with a big sigh, "Whoever started this whole Christmas thing should be found, strung up, and shot."

From the back of the car a quiet, calm voice responded, "Don't worry, we already crucified him."

Nobody on the elevator said another word.

JERUSALEM BY ANY OTHER NAME

The city that for centuries has been the capital city of the Jews is mentioned by the name "Jerusalem" 810 times in the Bible. It is also known by these names:

1. **Jebusi** *(Joshua 18:28 KJV)* or **Jebus** *(1 Chronicles 11:4 KJV)*
2. **Zion** *(1 Kings 8:1 NIV)*
3. **City of David** *(2 Samuel 5:6–7 NIV)*
4. **Salem** *(Psalm 76:1–2 NIV)*
5. **Ariel** *(Isaiah 29:1 NIV)*
6. **city of God** *(Psalm 46:4 NIV)*
7. **city of the Great King** *(Psalm 48:2 NIV)*
8. **City of Judah** *(2 Chronicles 25:28 NIV)*
9. **The Throne of the Lord** *(Jeremiah 3:17 NIV)*
10. **holy mountain** *(Daniel 9:16 NKJV)*
11. **the holy city** *(Nehemiah 11:1 NIV)*
12. **city of our solemnities** *(Isaiah 33:20 KJV)*
13. **City of Truth** *(Zechariah 8:3 NIV)*
14. **Oholibah** *(Ezekiel 23:4 NIV)*
15. **THE LORD IS THERE** *(Ezekiel 48:35 NIV)*

POSITIVE COMMANDS

Most people know the Ten Commandments as mostly a set of "Thou shalt *not*" commands. In two chapters of the book of Deuteronomy in the Old Testament, God also gave positive commands about what the Israelites were to *do*:

1. Fear God *(Deuteronomy 6:2)*
2. Keep his statutes and commandments *(vv. 2–3)*
3. Love God with all their heart, soul, and strength *(v. 5)*
4. Keep the words of the Law in their heart *(v. 6)*
5. Teach the Law diligently to their children *(v. 7)*
6. Keep God's commandments posted as a reminder to think about them and do them *(v. 8)*
7. Let others in the neighborhood know that they (the Israelites) seek to keep God's commandments *(v. 9)*
8. Do what is right and good in the sight of God *(v. 18)*
9. Utterly destroy their enemies who practice wrongdoing *(Deuteronomy 7:2)*
10. Make no covenant with their enemies *(v. 2)*
11. Destroy their enemies' places of worship *(v. 5)*
12. Destroy all signs of false gods in their community *(v. 5)*
13. Burn the idols (statues of false gods) that people might be keeping individually or in their homes *(v. 5)*
14. Listen to and keep all of God's judgments *(v. 12)*

DEAD SEA VITALITY

Inability to sustain sea or plant life is what gives the Dead Sea its name. The "dead" sea, however, is a "living" treasure. It is rich in minerals, health benefits, and cultural heritage. Located on the border between Israel and Jordan, the salt-saturated sea is a natural wonder. The shoreline is the lowest place on the surface of the earth at 1,310 feet below sea level. It is the world's saltiest body of water, with salt concentrations nearly ten times that of the oceans and three times that of Utah's Great Salt Lake.

Mineral-rich waters of the Dead Sea contain potash, magnesium, bromine, and potassium and are mined for use in fertilizer, plastics, and cosmetics. Dead Sea minerals are used in the making of cosmetics and bath products. The mineral-rich mud stimulates blood circulation, deep-cleans pores, and exfoliates dead skin cells. The Sea also attracts the "curative health trade." Thousands of people travel to the Dead Sea each year for "spa" treatments, including mud packs and bathing in nearby natural springs. Magnesium, essential for cell metabolism, provides relief for psoriasis sufferers. Bromide enhances relaxation. Bitumen, a natural tar, is an anti-inflammatory agent. Potassium improves oxidation that benefits asthma patients. King Solomon, Queen Cleopatra, and Herod the Great are among the historical figures in the Bible who visited the Dead Sea for health reasons.

The Dead Sea region is also a destination for tourists exploring archaeological and historical treasures such as the Masada fortress, the Qumran caves where the famous Dead Sea Scrolls were found, and Ein Gedi, the refuge of David as he fled from King Saul.

Far from "dead," the Dead Sea is a world treasure and very much alive.

Sources: www.extreme science.com; www.bibleplaces.com.

TOYS FOR LITTLE JESUS

Children of every age have possessed their special toys. As a child, Jesus probably played games common to children of that time, similar to hopscotch and jacks. Whistles, rattles, toy animals on wheels, hoops, and spinning tops have been found by archaeologists. Older children and adults found time to play too, mainly with board games. Archaeologists have also found one notable exception to the commandment banning "graven images"—in the tolerance of dolls for children.

Source: catalog.lexpublib.org/TLCScripts/interpac.dll?SearchForm&Directions=1&Config=pac&Branch=,0,&FormId=0.

THE SNAKES OF IRELAND

Saint Patrick was a priest credited with converting the population of Ireland to Christianity. He is also said to have driven all the snakes off the island, although no snakes were known to exist on post-glacial Ireland.

So were the snakes he banished reptiles or those of another kind?

The pagan Druids were a powerful influence in Ireland at the time of Patrick. Their symbol was the Snake of Wisdom. Patrick's missionary work ended the Druids' religious influence in Ireland, thus driving out the Druids.

LONGEST PRESS RUN

In 1534, England's King Henry VIII granted the University of Cambridge the right to print and sell "all manner of book." The Cambridge University Press has printed and published continuously since 1584. The Press's first Bible was printed in 1591. It was an edition of the Geneva Version of the Bible, the translation that crossed to America with the Pilgrim Fathers. Today the Press still produces high-quality Bibles.

Sources: www.cambridge.org/aus/information/introduction.htm;
www.cambridge.org/uk/bibles/info/about.htm;.

SPEED-READING BIBLES

Bible reading isn't exactly a national pastime. On a *Tonight Show* broadcast, Jay Leno asked the audience to name one of the Ten Commandments. One audience member suggested, "God helps those who help themselves." No one in the audience could name any of the twelve disciples, but crowd members correctly named all four members of the Beatles rock-and-roll group.

Now there is help. British publishers last year released *The 100-Minute Bible*, which summarizes the Bible into fifty readings of about four hundred words each. Each section takes about two minutes to read. Over half of the readings are given to the life of Jesus; there are seventeen devoted to the Old Testament, and seven to the latter part of the New Testament. The book can be read in just one hundred minutes. Author Michael Hinton intended this "Bible" to get people interested in reading the whole Bible, not as a substitute.

Some other "quick read" Bible versions can help those who are on the go. *The Bible in 90 Days*, published by Zondervan, invites people to read twelve pages of the Bible every day and supplement the Bible reading with church or small-group study classes. Another version, The *HCSB Light Speed Bible*, takes just twenty-four hours to read. Based on the Holman Christian Standard Bible, this version utilizes a speed-reading technique with the text. Headings, subheadings, and underlinings have been added to help the reader focus on important people and facts. *Bible to Go*, published by FaithWords, covers the entire Bible from Genesis to Revelation and can be read in an hour.

None of these speed-reading versions, however, are intended to be a substitute for regular Bible reading, study, and memorization for in-depth understanding.

Sources: www.christiantoday.com/news/missions/light.speed.bible.released.as.
answer.to.busy.lives;www.csmonitor.cm/2005/0927/p01s04woeu;www.biblein90d
ays.com/about.

WILL THE REAL MESSIAH PLEASE STAND UP?

There have been many false messiahs in history, but only one true Messiah. The coming of a Messiah was foretold in Scripture, and Jesus perfectly fulfilled the prophecies when he came.

1. He would be born of a woman *(Genesis 3:15; Galatians 4:4)*.
2. He would be a descendant of Abraham *(Genesis 12:3; Matthew 1:1)*.
3. He would be from the tribe of Judah *(Genesis 49:10; Luke 3:23–33)*.
4. He would be a descendant of David *(2 Samuel 7:12–13; Romans 1:3)*.
5. He would be born of a virgin *(Isaiah 7:14; Matthew 1:18–21)*.
6. He would be born in Bethlehem *(Micah 5:2; Matthew 2:1)*.
7. He would be called Immanuel *(Isaiah 7:14; Matthew 1:22–23)*.
8. He would be visited by kings *(Isaiah 60:3; Matthew 2:1–12)*.
9. He would be in Egypt *(Hosea 11:1; Matthew 2:14–15)*.
10. He would be called a Nazarene *(Matthew 2:19–23)*.
11. He would be filled with God's Spirit *(Isaiah 11:2; 61:1; Luke 4:17–21)*.
12. He would bring good news to the poor, and freedom for prisoners *(Isaiah 61:1; Luke 4:17–21)*.
13. He would heal many *(Isaiah 53:4; Matthew 8:16–17)*.
14. He would be rejected by his own *(Isaiah 53:3; John 1:11)*.
15. He would make a triumphal entry into Jerusalem on a donkey's colt *(Zechariah 9:9; John 12:13–15)*.
16. He would be praised by little children *(Psalm 8:2; Matthew 21:15–16)*.
17. He would be betrayed for thirty pieces of silver *(Zechariah 11:12–13; Matthew 26:14–16)*.
18. He would be accused by false witnesses *(Psalm 27:12; Matthew 26:59–61)*.
19. His miracles would not be believed *(Isaiah 53:1; John 12:37–38)*.
20. He would be silent before his accusers *(Isaiah 53:7; Matthew 26:62–63)*.
21. He would be spit on and struck *(Isaiah 50:6; Matthew 26:67)*.
22. People would cast lots for his clothing *(Psalm 22:18; Matthew 27:35)*.
23. He would be crucified with thieves *(Isaiah 53:9, 12; Matthew 27:38)*.
24. His flesh would be pierced *(Zechariah 12:10; John 19:34)*.
25. His bones would not be broken *(Psalm 34:20; John 19:32–36)*.
26. He would be resurrected *(Psalm 16:10; Luke 24:1–7)*.
27. He would ascend into heaven *(Psalm 68:18; Acts 1:9–11)*.

GNOT SO SMART

It was heresy in the apostle Paul's day, and it is still heresy today—gnosticism. That's a Greek word (the *g* is silent) which means "knowledge." People who buy into gnosticism as a religion believe that eternal life is attainable by the enlightened few who have secret knowledge. Ignorance, not wrongdoing, they claim, is the downfall of humanity.

Gnosticism is a path to saving oneself through the evolving divinity of the spirit; there is no need for God, because the enlightened Gnostic will eventually become divine. Gnosticism claims it's the spirit that is all-important; the material world and the body are evil. That thinking meant a person could live however he or she chose to live, and that led to all sorts of debauchery. It also led to the denial of (1) the divinity of Jesus, who came in a human body, and (2) the sufficiency of his physical death as a sacrifice for wrongs—two basic beliefs of Christianity.

A COSTLY MISPRONUNCIATION

In Hebrew, the word *shibboleth* literally means an "ear of wheat." Through usage, however, *shibboleth* has come to be a word used to distinguish members of a group from outsiders. The scenario is found in Judges 12, when the Gileadites defeated the Ephraimites in battle. To detect any Ephraimites who might attempt to escape captivity, the Gileadites required every man desiring to cross the Jordan River to say the word *shibboleth*. The Ephraimite dialect did not have the "sh" sound, and the Ephraimites attempting to escape said "sibboleth" instead. Some forty-two thousand Ephraimites were detected—and killed—because they couldn't say the word properly.

Source: *Mysteries of the Bible* (Reader's Digest Association, Inc., 1988), 112.

INFALLIBLE?

Bibles are expected to be letter-perfect. But that doesn't always happen, which has made for some interesting Bible manuscripts:

The "Wicked Bible." In 1631, a version of the King James Bible was printed that left out the word *not* in the seventh commandment. Exodus 20:14 read, "Thou shalt commit adultery." King Charles I was not amused and ordered the "Wicked Bible" destroyed immediately. There are, however, eleven copies remaining. One is on display in the Bible Museum in Branson, Missouri.

The "Unrighteous Bible." In a later 1653 edition, the word *not* was also missing, which seriously skewed 1 Corinthians 6:9, which read, "Know ye not that the unrighteous shall inherit the kingdom of God?" The proper reading is, "Know ye not that the unrighteous shall not inherit the kingdom of God?" That edition was recalled and is known as the "Unrighteous Bible."

The "Wife-Hater Bible." Printed in 1810, the "Wife-Hater Bible" reads, "If any man come to me, and hate not his father . . . and his own wife also . . ." The correct reading should be, "and his own life also" *(Luke 14:26)*.

The "Fool Bible." In 1763, a misprint in the "Fool Bible" caused Psalm 14:1 to read, "The fool hath said in his heart, there is a God." The correct reading would be, "there is no God."

The "Idle Shepherd Bible." In an 1809 King James Bible, the "idol shepherd" of Zechariah 11:17 became a lazy sheep-herder—"the idle shepherd."

"Rebekah's Camels Bible." Instead of "damsels," it was Rebekah's "camels" that rose with her in the "Rebekah's Camels Bible" of 1823: "Rebekah arose, and her camels" *(Genesis 24:61)*.

The "Sting Bible." The 1746 "Sting Bible" noted that after Jesus healed a man with a speech impediment, "the sting of his tongue was loosed, and he spake plain." What Jesus actually loosed was the "string" of his tongue *(Mark 7:35)*.

INFALLIBLE (CONT'D)

The "Murderer's Bible." The "Murderer's Bible," printed in 1801, declared, "these are murderers" instead of "murmurers" *(Jude 16)*. Of the Syrophenician woman who sought help for her daughter with an unclean spirit, the Bible stated that Jesus said, "Let the children first be killed." What Jesus really said was, "Let the children first be filled" *(Mark 7:27)*.

The "Large Family Bible." The "Large Family Bible" printed in 1820 reads, "Shall I bring to birth, and not cease to bring forth?" instead of "cause to bring forth" *(Isaiah 66:9)*.

The "Lions Bible." The 1804 "Lions Bible" states, "The murderer shall surely be put together" instead of "put to death" (Numbers 35:18). And also, "thy son that shall come forth out of thy lions," instead of "out of thy loins" *(1 Kings 8:19)*.

The "More Sea Bible." The "More Sea Bible" of 1641 reads in Revelation 21:1, "the first heaven and the first earth were passed away; and there was more sea." The correct reading is, "there was no more sea."

The "Blessed Placemakers Bible." An error in the 1562 Geneva Bible read, "Blessed are the placemakers" instead of "peacemakers" in the Sermon on the Mount *(Matthew 5:9)*.

The "Parable of the Vinegar Bible." A mistake in a heading in a 1717 King James Bible referred to the "Parable of the Vinegar," rather than the "Parable of the Vineyard."

The "Sin On Bible." A mistake in the "Sin On Bible," printed in 1716, completely changed what Jesus said to a man he healed. John 5:14 read, "sin on more," instead of "sin no more."

The "Printers Bible." Perhaps the error in the 1702 "Printers Bible" provides the best summary for this article: "Printers have persecuted me without a cause," instead of "princes" *(Psalm 119:161)*.

Sources: www.catholicapologetics.net/0002kjv.htm; www.biblecollectors.org/bible_misprints.

How Old *Is* That Scroll?

The number of ancient Bible manuscripts discovered by archaeologists is far greater than the number of manuscripts of any other single book from the ancient world. Even more astonishing is that they are considered by experts to be in far better condition than other manuscripts recording ancient history.

More than twenty-five thousand manuscripts or portions of the Old and New Testaments have been discovered, many of them found in a cave in 1945 by a shepherd boy looking for his sheep. Carbon dating and other verification techniques have confirmed that these manuscripts, known as the Dead Sea Scrolls, were written from the third century BC to AD 68.

The sheer number of manuscripts that confirm Bible events is even more astonishing when compared with other historic records. For example, there are only ten manuscripts referring to Julius Caesar's invasion of Britain, all of them written eight hundred years or more after the event.

Some of the Dead Sea Scrolls are nearly one thousand years older than the oldest copies of the Hebrew Old Testament previously discovered.

Sources: chi.gospelcom.net/GLIMPSEF/Glimpses/glmps055.shtml;
alpha.reltech.org:8080/; www.asia.si.edu/collections/biblicalHome.htm.

Dowry Veils

In Bible times, a young woman's dowry was often a set of coins and semiprecious stones stitched in strands on the front of her wedding veil and headpiece. These items were considered to be the bride's possession throughout her life. Should her husband be killed in battle or die before she did, the bride could use these items to provide for herself and her children. The veil and headpiece were very heavy, but they were worn only at the time of the wedding. A woman guarded these possessions very carefully; they were her personal "savings account."

Even today in the Middle East, women among the Bedouins—nomadic wanderers and many of the shepherds who live in the desert areas of the Middle East nations—have dowry veils. Some have as many as a hundred antique coins or pieces of semiprecious stones stitched into them. The stones include lapis, turquoise, coral, and onyx.

FOR THE SAKE OF OTHERS

It's the same through all history: What counts in life is what we do for others.

1. "The sole meaning of life is to serve humanity."
   —*Leo Tolstoy (Russian novelist, 1828–1910)*

2. "You must give time to your fellow man—even if it's a little thing, do something for others—something for which you get no pay but the privilege of doing it."—*Albert Schweitzer (physician, humanitarian, 1875–1965)*

3. "Everybody can be great. Because anybody can serve. You don't have to have a college degree to serve. You don't have to make your subject and your verb agree to serve. . . . You only need a heart full of grace. A soul generated by love."—*Martin Luther King Jr. (civil rights leader, 1929–1968)*

4. "We serve God by serving others. The world defines greatness in terms of power, possessions, prestige, and position. If you can demand service from others, you've arrived. In our self-serving culture with its me-first mentality, acting like a servant is not a popular concept."
   —*Rick Warren (pastor, author, 1954–)*

5. "When we honestly ask ourselves which person in our lives means the most to us, we often find that it is those who, instead of giving advice, solutions, or cures, have chosen rather to share our pain and touch our wounds with a warm and tender hand."
   —*Henri Nouwen (Dutch Christian writer, 1932–1996)*

6. "The high destiny of the individual is to serve rather than to rule."
   —*Albert Einstein (German-born American physicist, 1879–1955)*

7. "In this life we cannot do great things. We can only do small things with great love."—*Mother Teresa (humanitarian, 1910–1997)*

8. "How wonderful it is that nobody need wait a single moment before starting to improve the world."—*Anne Frank (author, Holocaust victim, 1929–1945)*

9. "The most eloquent prayer is the prayer through hands that heal and bless. The highest form of worship is the worship of unselfish Christian service. The greatest form of praise is the sound of consecrated feet seeking out the lost and helpless."—*Billy Graham (Christian evangelist, 1918–)*

10. "Christ has no body now on earth but yours; yours are the only hands with which he can do his work, yours are the only feet with which he can go about the world, yours are the only eyes through which his compassion can shine forth upon a troubled world. Christ has no body now on earth but yours."
    —*Teresa of Avila (Spanish Catholic mystic, 1515–1582)*

11. "As long as I see any thing to be done for God, life is worth having; but O how vain and unworthy it is to live for any lower end!"
    —*David Brainerd (missionary to American Indians, 1718–1747)*

12. "What we do during our working hours determines what we have; what we do in our leisure hours determines what we are."
    —*George Eastman (inventor, philanthropist, 1854–1932)*

THE FORTIES

Numbers in the Bible often have a special meaning or theme. After the number seven, forty is the number that appears most frequently in the Bible. Forty has significance in both weights and measures as well as in the lives of biblical people. The number forty has been associated with cleansing, testing, or trial:

1. It rained forty days and nights during Noah's flood *(Genesis 7:4)*.

2. Isaac was forty years old when Rebekah became his wife *(Genesis 25:20)*.

3. Moses lived in the desert for forty years before freeing the Israelites *(Acts 7:29–36)*.

4. Moses spent forty days on Mount Sinai with God *(Exodus 24:18)*.

5. Israel spied out the land of Canaan for forty days *(Numbers 13:25)*.

6. Israel wandered forty years in the desert *(Numbers 14:33)*.

7. Goliath taunted Israel for forty days *(1 Samuel 17:16)*.

8. Jonah reluctantly warned Nineveh that judgment would come in forty days *(Jonah 3:4)*.

9. Jesus spent forty days in the wilderness before being tempted by Satan *(Matthew 4:2)*.

10. There were forty days between the resurrection and ascension of Jesus *(Acts 1:3)*.

FOUNDING FATHERS YOU'D HAVE SEEN IN CHURCH

Fifty-two of the fifty-five framers of the U.S. Constitution were members of established churches in the colonies. Personal beliefs notwithstanding, church membership provided an important connection to the community in the young nation. Some either changed church affiliation in their lifetimes or had dual membership. The religious affiliation of the framers was as follows:

1. Congregationalist: seven, including John Hancock

2. Dutch Reformed: two (better known as Huguenots at the time)

3. Episcopalian: twenty-six, including George Washington and Benjamin Franklin, who was also a deist

4. Lutheran: one founder, Thomas Mifflin, who was also a Quaker

5. Methodist: two, Richard Basset and William Few

6. Presbyterian: eleven founders, including William Samuel Johnson

7. Quaker: three founders, including cartographer Jacob Broom

8. Roman Catholic: two, including Daniel Carroll, whose brother, John, was the first Catholic bishop in the U.S.

9. Deist: one, Thomas Jefferson (and Benjamin Franklin—see Episcopalian above)

10. Unknown: three

"YOU WILL GO FORTH"

At age sixteen, So Young Kim was one of South Korea's top gymnasts preparing for the 1988 Olympics in Seoul. Three weeks before a major competition, So Young was paralyzed attempting a difficult routine on the uneven bars.

Her aunt visited her in the intensive-care-unit and left her a note with the Bible verse, "For you who fear My name, the sun of righteousness will rise with healing in its wings; and you will go forth and skip about like calves from the stall" (Malachi 4:2 NASB). Reading that, So Young said, "I felt peace flood my soul. For the first time in my life, I sensed that there was a God who cared for me and wanted to heal me. Then, after that moment, I accepted Jesus Christ as my Lord and Savior."

There were more hard times: So Young's boyfriend left her; her father died suddenly of a heart attack; she struggled with being quadriplegic. She expected God to heal her body, but "he didn't; he healed me in a totally different way." She said, "When I found his purpose for my disability, it became no longer a disability, but the gift of understanding those who are in the same situation." So Young organizes ski camps for disabled Koreans and works to provide wheelchairs for disabled people. She is praying for an open door into North Korea. "I don't know how God will use me, but I'm just excited to see his plan for me."

Source: American Bible Society, retrieved August 13, 2005.

REBEL WITH A CAUSE!

Quakers are often perceived as very conventional, quiet pacifists. George Fox, however, the founder of the Society of Friends (Quakers), was anything but quiet, conventional, or quick to make peace!

Fox had an intense spiritual experience when he was nineteen and began wandering in solitude throughout England. He stopped attending the "conventional" church and eventually called himself an "itinerant religious reformer."

In 1649, at the age of twenty-seven, he attracted widespread attention by standing up during the sermon at the main church in Nottingham. He rebuked the preacher for declaring the Bible to be the source of divine truth. "No!" Fox cried. "It is not the Scriptures; it is the Spirit of God." He believed strongly that the Spirit of God inspired all Scripture. He was immediately imprisoned. On his release, he repeated his protests elsewhere. Many were attracted to his message, but he frequently was put in prison as a "disturber of the peace," the longest imprisonment lasting three years. In 1655 he was called to London for examination before Cromwell, who pronounced his doctrines and character irreproachable. Ironically, Fox's following increased in large numbers.

While the convention of his day was often older men marrying younger women, Fox again defied convention. He married his wife, Margaret, when he was nearly forty and she was fifty. And rather than stay quietly at home and be the administrator of the Quaker movement he had founded, Fox did the opposite. He was rarely at home. He went on extensive preaching campaigns throughout England, to Holland, North America, and the Caribbean.

INSIGHT INTO "TRUTH"

The Hebrew word for *truth* is pronounced "ameth," but in the Hebrew script the word only has three letters: *aleph*, the first letter of the Hebrew alphabet; *min*, the middle letter of the alphabet; and *tau*, the last letter of the alphabet. The Jewish people believed that these letters conveyed the meaning that God's truth was from the beginning, is applicable in every moment, and will last until the end of the ages.

When Jesus stated that he was "the way, the truth, and the life" (*John 14:6* NKJV), he was building on this concept. The truth of God—which included all of God's commandments, plans, and purpose—was embodied in Jesus, not only in that moment but from the beginning of time and throughout eternity.

EYE OF A NEEDLE

City gates in the time of Jesus were as high as a city's walls and wide enough for loaded carts to pass through. The gates were opened at dawn and closed at dusk. A smaller entryway, similar to a small doorway in a home, was sometimes cut into a city gate so people might come and go from the city even if the larger gate was closed. This smaller opening was called "the eye of the needle." For an animal such as a camel to get through it, the beast had to crawl on its knees, without any baggage—not an impossible task but very difficult! (See *Matthew 19:24*.)

DON'T TELL

Several times in his ministry, Jesus admonished those he healed or delivered to "not tell" about what had been done to them. Certainly those who knew the people who had been set free of their ailments saw a very clear before-and-after picture of healing and spiritual deliverance. Why did Jesus say, "Tell no one"?

The foremost reason is likely that Jesus didn't want the people to conclude that there was a particular "Jesus formula" for healing or delivering the sick, possessed, and oppressed. His healing methods varied from person to person. There was no "this set of words" or "that specific ritual practice" in Jesus' healing ministry. The focus was never upon a ritual or methodology. The focus was always on the creativity, sensitivity, and sovereignty of Jesus as the Son of God as he dealt with people individually. In the one case where Jesus did *not* say, "Tell no one," the people did draw conclusions about methodology. A woman with an issue of blood that had lasted twelve years touched the hem of Jesus' garment and was made well *(Matthew 9:20–22)*. A short while after this, the New Testament says, "And when the men of that place recognized Him, they sent out into all that surrounding region, brought to Him all who were sick, and begged Him that they might only touch the hem of His garment. And as many as touched it were made perfectly well" *(Matthew 14:35–36 NKJV)*.

KINDNESS

Kindness is one of the foremost character traits associated with the Holy Spirit. It is listed among the "fruit of the Spirit" *(Galatians 5:22–23).*

1. "Life is made up, not of great sacrifices or duties, but of little things, in which smiles, and kindnesses, and small obligations, given habitually, are what win and preserve the heart and secure comfort."
—*Sir Humphrey Davy (English chemist, 1778–1829)*

2. "Kindness is the golden chain by which society is bound together."
—*Johann Wolfgang von Goethe (German poet, dramatist, and philosopher, 1749–1832)*

3. "Kindness in women, not their beauteous looks, shall win my love."
—*William Shakespeare (English poet and dramatist, 1564–1616)*

4. "I expect to pass through life but once. . . . If therefore, there be any kindness I can show, or any good thing I can do to any fellow-being, let me do it now, and not defer or neglect it, as I shall not pass this way again."—*William Penn (English Quaker, American colonist, and founder of Pennsylvania, 1644–1718)*

5. "Kind looks, kind words, kind acts, and warm handshakes—these are secondary means of grace when men are in trouble and are fighting their unseen battles."—*John Hall (Irish-American Presbyterian clergyman and author, 1829–1848)*

6. "A kind heart is a fountain of gladness, making everything in its vicinity freshen into smiles."—*Washington Irving (American author, 1783–1834)*

7. "Kindness is a language the dumb can speak, and the deaf can hear and understand."
—*Christian Nestell Bovee (American author and editor, 1820–1904)*

8. "The true and noble way to kill a foe, is not to kill him; you, with kindness, may so change him that he shall cease to be a foe, and then he's slain."—*Charles Aleyn (English historical poet, 1590–1640)*

9. "Kindness in ourselves is the honey that blunts the sting of unkindness in another."—*Walter Savage Landor (English author, 1775–1864)*

10. "The one who will be found in trial capable of great acts of love is ever the one who is always doing considerate small ones."
—*Frederick William Robertson (English clergyman, 1816–1853)*

11. "Half the misery of human life might be extinguished if men would alleviate the general curse they lie under by mutual offices of compassion, benevolence, and humanity."
—*Joseph Addison (English essayist, 1672–1719)*

12. "It is one of the beautiful compensations of life that no man can sincerely try to help another, without helping himself. Both man and womankind belie their nature when they are not kind."
—*Gamaliel Bailey (American journalist and abolitionist, 1807–1859)*

THE DREADED PHILISTINES

The name *Philistines* was first used by the Egyptians to describe a sea people defeated by Rameses III in a naval battle about 1188 BC. This people is said to have come from Caphtor, generally identified as the island of Crete *(Genesis 10:14)*. The Philistines occupied part of southwest Palestine, an area known today as the Gaza Strip, from about 1200 to 600 BC.

Crete was also the supposed home of the Cherethites, sometimes associated with the Philistines *(Ezekiel 25:16)*. Philistine territory was considered Cherethite in 1 Samuel 30:14. The Hebrew word for the Philistines was *pelishti*, which is the basis for the name Palestine.

Some archaeologists believe there were two different groups that bore the name *Philistines.* The early group, the Philistines of Gerar, was a rather peaceful group led by Abimelech, who befriended both Abraham and Isaac *(Genesis 20–21)*. This group built and fortified five major cities: Ashkelon, Ashdod, Ekron, Gath, and Gaza. This group may have been conquered by sea people from Crete, who possessed iron weapons and were more aggressive. Each city had its own independence and leader, but the five leaders banded together to form a ruling council and to serve as military leaders of a joint force in times of war *(Judges 16:5, 8; 1 Samuel 29:1–7)*.

Although Philistia was within the territorial boundaries of the Promised Land assigned by Moses to Judah and Dan, no unified attempt was ever made to conquer the area. Most of the tribe of Dan moved north of the Gaza Strip, and territorial feuds with the Philistines began and never really ended.

The Philistines were the primary enemy of the Israelites in the time of Samson.

THE DREADED PHILISTINES (CONT'D)

It was the threat of the Philistines that prompted the Israelites to demand a king. The first Israelite king, Saul, was killed by the Philistines. David's slaying of Goliath, a giant from Gath, was a key factor in his rise to fame. By the end of David's reign, Philistine power had declined significantly. The Bible states that by the mid eighth century BC, the Philistines were offering tribute to King Jehoshaphat of Judah *(2 Chronicles 17:11)*.

No Philistine literature has survived, making it difficult for historians to reconstruct their exact religious beliefs and rituals. The Old Testament states that they worshipped three gods—Ashtoreth, Dagon (symbolized by a fish), and Baal-Zebub (symbolized by a fly), each of which had major shrines *(Judges 10:6; 16:23; 1 Samuel 5:1–7; 2 Kings 1:2)*. The Philistine soldiers appear to have carried images of their gods into battle, perhaps as standards *(2 Samuel 5:21)*. The soldiers are depicted in Egyptian artifacts as wearing short tunics, being clean-shaven, with crested or decorated helmets. They carried round shields and fought with spears and swords.

The Philistines appear to have adopted the manufacture and distribution of iron implements and weapons from the Hittites, another ancient people living north of Canaan. They were also skilled goldsmiths *(1 Samuel 6:4–5)*. The pottery of the Philistines reflected Greek as well as Egyptian and Canaanite styles.

The Philistines loved beer. Archaeological digs have unearthed large beer mugs decorated with red and black geometric designs, as well as cups, beakers, and bowls.

The Philistines were taken into captivity by Nebuchadnezzar, and nothing more was heard about them after Alexander the Great. The area was incorporated into the Roman province of Syria in 62 BC by Pompey.

PASS THE CURDS, PLEASE

The word *curds* in the Bible does not refer to cottage cheese, as some people think, but rather it was a word used to describe cheese or a type of thick yogurt eaten in Bible times. Curds were made from fermented cow, goat, camel, or sheep milk. Curds were often flavored with garlic, dill, thyme, olive oil, or parsley.

HER HONOR, CANDACE

In Bible times, *Candace* was Ethiopia's monarch. The Bible tells a story about a eunuch who served as head of the Candace's treasury. While on the way home from Jerusalem, he met Philip, who told him about Jesus and baptized him. According to tradition, this eunuch was instrumental in taking the gospel to Ethiopia, and from there, believers took it to other African nations. (See *Acts 8:26–39*.)

LOW BUT NOT LOWLY

Jericho is the lowest town in the world—250 meters below sea level. It has a very mild climate in the winter. This made it a very popular winter resort for the wealthy in Bible times. (Today the city is governed by the Palestinian Authority, and travel to and from it is limited.) At the time of Jesus, the town was also populated by hundreds of priests and their families who traveled to Jerusalem periodically to take their turn in temple service.

WHAT DID JESUS
REALLY LOOK LIKE?

We can never know for certain how Jesus might have looked as he walked the earth. The Bible, however, does give some clues.

We know that Jesus must have looked much like other Jews of his time and country. The Gospel writers tell of Jesus' ability to avoid an angry mob simply by mingling with the crowd. He was physically enough like his compatriots that Judas was compelled to identify him with a kiss of betrayal.

So what does that tell us? Archaeologists have firmly established that the average Semitic male at the time of Jesus was just over five feet tall with an average weight of 110 pounds, deep olive complexion, and dark eyes. Since Jesus worked outdoors as a carpenter until he was about thirty years old, it is reasonable to assume he was tanned and more muscular and physically fit than Westernized portraits suggest.

Popular depictions of Jesus with long hair are also likely inaccurate. This notion is probably based on a popular misconception that Jesus was a "Nazirite," a man who had taken a religious vow that included refraining from cutting one's hair either permanently or temporarily. The confusion comes from the fact that Jesus was a "Nazarene"—from the Galilean region of Nazareth—and *not* a permanent Nazirite. This is confirmed by the fact that Jesus did not observe other Nazirite vows. Also, as a priest after the order of Melchizedek *(Hebrews 5:5–6)*, it's far more likely that Jesus kept his hair fairly well trimmed.

AN OFFERING OF
FIFTY-SEVEN CENTS

A little girl was found sobbing near a small church. The pastor of the church stopped to ask her why she was crying. She replied that she had been turned away from attending Sunday school because the church was "too crowded."

The pastor observed her shabby, unkempt appearance and silently bemoaned the likelihood that one of his own flock had been so prejudiced and unkind. He took her by the hand, led her inside, and found a place for her in the Sunday school class most appropriate for her age. The happiness she registered on her face was overwhelming to the pastor.

Some two years later the parents of this child asked the kind-hearted pastor to come to their poor tenement building. Their daughter had died, and in going through her belongings, they had discovered a crumpled red purse that she had no doubt rummaged from a nearby trash Dumpster. Inside the purse the parents had found fifty-seven cents and a note scribbled in her childish handwriting. It read, "This is to help build the little church bigger so more children can go to Sunday school."

The parents told the pastor that their daughter had saved for two years to make this offering of love. As the pastor tearfully read the note, he knew instantly what he would do. Carrying this note and the cracked red pocketbook to the pulpit, he told the story of the little girl's unselfish love and devotion. He challenged his parishioners to get busy and raise enough money for a larger building.

As it turned out, the city newspaper learned of the story and published it. The article was read by a wealthy Realtor who offered the church a parcel of land worth many thousands of dollars. When told that the church could not pay so much, he offered to sell the land to the church leaders for fifty-seven cents.

An Offering of
Fifty-Seven Cents (cont'd)

Church members made sacrificial donations to build on the new property. Their giving and the sacrificial gift from the little girl inspired other contributors, many of whom did not even live in the area. Within five years the little girl's gift had inspired contributions that topped $250,000—a very large sum of money in the early 1900s.

The church that stands today on the property purchased for fifty-seven cents is Temple Baptist Church. It seats 3,300. Nearby is Temple University, where thousands of students are educated each year. Also located nearby is the Good Samaritan Hospital and a Sunday school building for hundreds of children—both of which were established by Temple Baptist Church. In one of the rooms of the Sunday school building hangs a photograph of the sweet-faced little girl whose offering of fifty-seven cents inspired such a remarkable outcome over the years. Alongside her photo is a portrait of the pastor who loved her, Dr. Russ H. Conwell, author of the international best-seller *Acres of Diamonds*.

Source: "An Offering of Fifty-Seven Cents" is drawn from a sermon preached by Russell H. Conwell on December 1, 1912, titled "The History of Fifty-Seven Cents." The sermon was delivered to Grace Baptist (Temple) church.

REAL REST STOPS

Stopping for a moment of contemplation or prayer can be a restoring treat whether navigating through a busy city or touring scenic mountaintops. The fifteen beautiful little chapels listed below, located across the U.S., offer the visitor a few moments' quiet inspiration and the occasional breathtaking view. Some have a steady stream of visitors, while others are little jewels just waiting to be found. All are open to the public.

1. *Begley Chapel*. Situated on the campus of Lindsey Wilson College in Columbia, Kentucky, this tiny chapel's hard-to-miss double-silo shape is a stylized nod to the rural countryside surrounding the campus. The quiet, intimate interior is contemporary in design.

2. *Chapel by the Sea*. Located on Captiva Island in Florida, this chapel was built in 1901 as the island's one-room schoolhouse that doubled as a church on Sundays. This charming chapel now serves as a seaside meditation site and place for weekly worship.

3. *Chapel of Transfiguration*. This tiny, rustic log structure sits on a rise just within the southern entrance of Grand Teton National Park in Wyoming. A large window behind its altar frames the magnificent beauty of the mountains.

4. *Guardian Angel Roadside Chapel*. A private family built this chapel for travelers in 1991 in memory of a family member who believed her life was once saved by a guardian angel. Located just off Interstate 35 at Clear Lake, Iowa, exit 193, the large stained-glass cross at the altar of the church was designed to serve as a beacon to interstate travelers. The chapel is open dawn to dusk.

5. *The Little Blue Church (St. Peter's Catholic Church)*. Located on Ali'i Drive in West Hawaii (on the island of Hawaii), this tiny church sits next to the ocean and is surrounded by colorful floral bushes. There are only a dozen pews and a pulpit, but the setting is very serene. A beautiful etched-glass window casts soft light over the entire church, especially at sunset.

6. *The Little Chapel of Silence*. Located on the University of Southern California campus in Los Angeles, California, this quiet, dignified chapel provides a place for contemplation for students and other visitors.

7. *Loretto Chapel*. This lovely little church in Santa Fe, New Mexico, is perhaps best known as the site of the "miracle" spiral staircase that ascends, unsupported, to a second-story choir loft.

8. *Memory Park Christ Chapel*. This chapel is found in South Newport, Georgia. Built in 1950 by grocer Agnes Harper (who wrote the deed in the name of Jesus) it measures ten feet by fifteen feet, has space for thirteen people, a wee pulpit, pews, and a stained-glass window with just enough space for Jesus. It is open twenty-four hours a day, seven days a week.

9. *Ramona Chapel*. This historic chapel was moved twice before landing in its current home in Heritage Junction Historic Park inside William S. Hart Regional County Park in

REAL REST STOPS (CONT'D)

Santa Clarita, California. The chapel has recently been refurbished to welcome visitors.

10. *St. Anthony of Padua Chapel.* Located in Festina, Iowa, this chapel was dedicated in 1886 and claimed to be "the Smallest Church in the World" for many years. With its twelve-foot-by-sixteen-foot interior, normal-sized doorway and pews, forty-foot steeple, and room for eight people, it is nonetheless a charming spot to seek solace.

11. *St. Paul's Chapel at Trinity Church.* Found across the street from Ground Zero in New York City, this is the city's oldest public building in continuous use and the site of refuge for rescue workers during the 9/11 crisis.

12. *Thorncrown Chapel.* Situated deep in the Ozark woodlands just north of Eureka Springs, Arkansas, Thorncrown's redwood arches and glass walls make it seem like part of the forest that surrounds it. Designed by noted architect E. Fay Jones, it is regarded as one of the most beautiful chapels in America.

13. *Traveler's Chapel.* Nashville, Illinois, is the site of this Lincoln Log version of a church oddly standing next to a convenience store parking lot. The inside walls are covered with Bible verses scrawled on bits of plywood. Instead of pews there is a padded piece of wood for kneeling in front of a floor-to-ceiling cross.

14. *Wayfarers Chapel.* Located at 5755 Palos Verdes Drive South in Rancho Palos Verdes, California, this soaring structure's glass walls allow the visitor to enjoy the lush landscape while worshipping or meditating.

15. *Unnamed Chapel.* Near Yuma, Arizona, this tiny structure was built by a farmer on the edge of his fields, in honor of his wife. A sign on the dirt road that leads to the church reads, "Stop, Rest, Worship." Find it about ten miles outside town on Highway 95.

GLOWING WITH GOODNESS

When Monica on the TV show *Touched by an Angel* revealed her true identity near the end of an episode, the glowing light that suddenly surrounded her was a dead giveaway: she was an angel.

In centuries past, artists had a similar way of portraying divine beings (such as Jesus and the angels) and other revered individuals (such as the Virgin Mary, the disciples, and saints of the church): with a halo—a circle or disk of light around their heads.

A plain, round halo is used for angels and saints. A round halo with a cross or monogram is used for Jesus. Another word for halo is *nimbus.* A nimbus also is sometimes used to describe a "cloud of light" more than a well-defined disk around the head of a holy being.

In some Christian art, halos are oval. These are called "mandoria," based on the Italian word for almond. The halos nevertheless symbolize divinity and holiness.

An "aura or "aureole"—from the Latin word for "golden" —is a glorious radiance or luminous cloud surrounding the whole figure of an angel, saint, or divine being in Christian art. A halo surrounds only the head.

Whether on canvas or on film, and whatever shape it takes, a "circle of light" continues to tip off the observer: this is someone special!

THINGS GOD WON'T DO

Although God is *capable* of doing all things—he is omnipotent, or all-powerful—there are certain things that God has said in the Bible he *won't* do:

1. God will not break his own law *(Psalm 119:89)*.

2. God will not lie *(Hebrews 6:17–19)*.

3. God will not apologize for or fail to display any of his attributes at any time *(2 Timothy 2:13)*.

4. God will not forgive wrongdoing unless a person believes in Jesus as Savior *(Romans 3:26)*.

5. God will not show preference for one person over another *(Romans 2:11)*.

6. God will not turn away any person who comes to him for forgiveness and believes in Jesus as Savior *(John 6:37)*.

7. God will not make mistakes in judgment *(Romans 9:14)*.

8. God will not answer prayer unless a person *believes* his prayer will be answered *(Hebrews 11:6)*.

9. God will not curse people who come to him admitting their mistakes *(1 John 1:9)*.

10. God will not change his eternal plan *(Numbers 23:19)*.

11. God will not overlook the acts or words of people who are rebellious against him *(Proverbs 1:22–33)*.

12. God will not give in to temptation or do what is evil *(James 1:13–14)*.

13. God will not tolerate hypocrisy *(Isaiah 1:13)*.

14. God will not forget or fail to answer prayers made with faith *(Mark 11:22–24)*.

15. God will not overrule a person's free will to make choices about who he is *(Romans 8:1–14)*.

16. God will not make any person equal to himself or to Jesus *(Isaiah 46:9)*.

17. God will not withhold a harvest from the good seeds a person sows *(Galatians 6:7–8)*.

18. God will not force a person to stop doing wrong *(Romans 6:16–23)*.

19. God will not judge people who hate him by the same standards that he judges the deeds of people who love him and have asked for his forgiveness *(Revelation 20:11–15)*.

20. God will not forgive wrongdoing unless a person asks to be forgiven *(Luke 13:5)*.

21. God will not force a person to mature spiritually *(Hebrews 5:13–6:2)*.

22. God will not give a "free pass" to believers who choose to do wrong *(Romans 6:15)*.

23. God will not call a person his "child" if that person chooses to serve the devil *(1 John 3:9–10)*.

IS IT A HYMN OR A
GOSPEL SONG?

The terms *hymn*, *gospel hymn*, and *gospel song* are often used interchangeably, but they actually have very different meanings.

Hymn is a general term for a song of praise or worship. Traditional hymns usually have a strong poetic rhythm or "meter," with a set pattern of rhyme. Hymns generally have a message about Jesus or are based on a concept or text from the Bible, either New Testament or Old Testament.

A gospel hymn is based specifically on the first four books of the New Testament or uses words borrowed from the Gospels.

Gospel songs came out of the revival movements early in the twentieth century—especially the revivals of the Salvation Army and D. L. Moody. Gospel songs borrowed musically from Sunday school hymns and spirituals. They tended to be easily sung, unsophisticated in melody and harmony, and they generally focused on personal salvation messages and Bible texts.

The foremost characteristic of a gospel song is a "refrain"—sometimes called the "chorus"—which is sung at the end of each verse. While hymns sometimes have lyrics that carry from verse to verse in their concept and phrasing, gospel songs generally have verses that are complete statements. Therefore it is possible for a person or group to sing selected verses of a gospel song—such as verses 1 and 4—without any loss in the overall message of the song.

Some of the most popular gospel songs through the years have been "The Old Rugged Cross" and "Blessed Assurance." Gospel songs are still sung widely in many evangelical churches.

IS IT A HYMN OR A
GOSPEL SONG? (CONT'D)

In black churches, gospel music incorporates elements of jazz and ragtime. The songs are known for an interaction between lead singers and the congregation.

Handclapping and dancing often accompany the singing of gospel songs, in both white churches and black churches. Gospel music can usually be sung with or without instrumental accompaniment.

And what about the term "chorus"? Originally the word referred to portions of a hymn or song that were sung by an entire choir or an entire congregation. The word was originally used in ancient Greek theater to refer to a group of people voicing a particular segment of a play in unison; later it referred to the segments of operas sung by a large group of actors in support of or in response to a soloist. Today the word refers to an entire song that is usually sung in unison by both song leader and those gathered for a religious service.

Church music today, at least in some evangelical and charismatic churches, seems to be evolving out of the gospel song into "only the chorus." Songs are more like the refrains of old gospel songs than hymns—still focused on Jesus or Bible themes and definitely intended for praise but simple in structure and readily sung by the average layperson. The choruses tend to be repeated, as refrains are repeated in gospel songs, but with only one or even no verses.

HOW WERE YOUR GODPARENTS INVOLVED?

For countless centuries, believing parents have chosen "godparents" for their children—a man and a woman, often a married couple, to serve as role models and spiritual mentors for their children from birth to adulthood.

One of the foremost roles for a godparent is to be present at the child's baptism. Many traditional denominations baptize infants, but the exact procedures and roles for the godparents vary widely.

In the Czech tradition, the baptism of a baby is the occasion for a major celebration, similar to a wedding. The parents of the baby do not attend the baptism service, but the godparents do. While the godparents and child are at church, the parents wait and pray at home. In Czech families, godparents are generally considered to be the legal guardians of the child should the parents die. It is customary therefore for all of the children in a family to have the same godparents so the children can remain as a unit in the event of their parents' deaths.

Spanish traditions related to baptism call for godparents to be the main guests at a dinner party held at the home of a newly baptized child. The godmother carries the child into the house after the baptism service and formally introduces the child to every person present, beginning with the child's own mother and father, then its siblings, then other relatives and guests.

In many traditions, a baby being baptized is held by its godmother during the baptism ceremony. The godparents assume responsibility, along with the parents, for raising the child to fully embrace the faith, to know key church traditions and Bible verses, and to attend church regularly.

THE TEN LARGEST PROTESTANT
CONGREGATIONS IN THE U.S.

As you read through this list of the ten largest Protestant congregations in the United States, you may be surprised to note that none of these churches is in America's three largest cities: New York City, Chicago, and Los Angeles.

1. *Lakewood Church.* Located in Houston, Texas, this is a nondenominational charismatic congregation. Joel Osteen is the church's pastor. Average Sunday attendance: 25,060.

2. *World Changers Christian Center.* Located in College Park, Georgia, this nondenominational church was founded in 1986 by Creflo Dollar. Average Sunday attendance: 23,093.

3. *Calvary Chapel of Costa Mesa.* Located in Santa Ana, California, this church was founded in 1965 by Chuck Smith, a leading figure in the Jesus Movement. Average Sunday attendance: 20,000.

4. *The Potter's House.* In 1996 T. D. Jakes moved the congregation of fifty families to Dallas, Texas, where it quickly grew to its present size. Average Sunday attendance: 18,500.

5. *Second Baptist Church.* Located in Houston, Texas, this church was founded in the Southern Baptist tradition in 1928 and is led by Pastor Ed Young. Average Sunday attendance: 18,000.

6. *Southeast Christian Church.* Located in Louisville, Kentucky, this church was founded in 1962 and belongs to the Christian Church denomination. The pastor is Bob Russell. Average Sunday attendance: 17,863.

7. *First Assembly of God.* Located in Phoenix, Arizona, this church's average attendance was 250 in 1979 when pastor Tommy Barnett arrived; that number grew to more than 2,700 in just three weeks. Average Sunday attendance is 17,532.

8. *Willow Creek Community Church.* This church is located in South Barrington, Illinois. Bill Hybels has been the senior pastor of this nondenominational church since its founding in 1975. Average Sunday attendance is 17,115.

9. *Calvary Chapel of Ft. Lauderdale.* Located in Fort Lauderdale, Florida, this nondenominational congregation's pastor is Bob Coy, and its average Sunday attendance is 17,000.

10. *Saddleback Valley Community Church.* Two hundred and five people, most of whom had never been to church before, attended Saddleback's very first service on Easter Sunday 1980 in Lake Forest, California. Rick Warren is pastor. Current average Sunday attendance is 15,030.

Sources: www.forbes.com/2003/09/17/cz_lk_0917megachurch.html; source for church attendance averages: Dr. John N. Vaughan, Church Growth Today as quoted by *Forbes* magazine 9/17/03.

WHAT'S *THAT* MEAN?

*H*ermeneutics is from the Greek word *hermeneuo*, meaning "I interpret, explain, or translate." Hermeneutics is the science of interpretation—the principles and procedures for understanding something. Biblical hermeneutics concerns how to interpret the Bible. (Don't confuse this with "homiletics," the procedures for preparing and presenting sermons!)

The most basic principle for interpretation is to consider the context. Taking words out of context misrepresents a speaker's or writer's intention. Statements in the Bible need to be interpreted in light of their context—in the passage or paragraph, in the biblical book being read, and ultimately in the context of all Scripture. This is the literary context.

A single word without a context has no certain meaning. The word *tract*, for example, could refer to anatomy, real estate, or publishing. A doctor, realtor, or proofreader might say, "I examined the tract." That brief sentence does not communicate clearly unless a context is indicated: who said it and to what was he referring?

Context recognizes how words work together to express thoughts. Context also involves the world referred to by the words—the connection of the words to the thing or event described. This is the historical context.

To assure the fullest and most accurate understanding, interpreters of Scripture take into account the historical and cultural setting as well as the literary context. Readers seeking to respond to God's Word apply the meaning of the text in their own lives. Every person's historical and cultural context is different, but overall, human needs and God's provisions remain the same.

WHAT'S *THAT* MEAN? (CONT'D)

Combining the literary and historical contexts produces a definition of the task of hermeneutics: (1) to understand what the text meant to the first people who heard or read it, and (2) to state what it means in our context and be able to apply it. Doing the first step well means being able to do the second step better.

In the task of interpretation, other things may have to be considered beyond historical and literary context. A reader can ask: (1) What kind of material is being studied—history, prophecy, poetry? (2) What is the main idea in this passage? (3) How is the message communicated? Who is speaking to whom? How? Why? Is the message based on comparisons and contrasts? Are questions being asked and answered? Are illustrations used? Are commands given or promises made? Is certain information repeated? Careful observation makes for more accurate and beneficial interpretation.

The task of interpretation is not an end in itself. The task is to understand the text, but the goal is to know God and to be his people. The Bible says that is why God revealed his words and his mighty acts in Scripture: to make people his very own and provide guidance for their lives *(Jeremiah 31:31–34)*.

TO BELIEVE OR
NOT TO BELIEVE

It's easy to be a believer after a miracle has happened, but how easy is it before the fact? In Bible times, as in these days, the faith of the people could be strong or weak.

Strong in Faith

1. A man with leprosy believed that Jesus had the power to heal him *(Matthew 8:2)*.

2. John the Baptist believed that Jesus was coming as the prophets had said he would *(Matthew 3:11–12)*.

3. Peter believed he could walk on water *(Matthew 14:28–29)*.

4. Jesus' disciples trusted him to feed four thousand people with seven loaves of bread and a few fish *(Matthew 15:32–38)*.

5. A Roman officer believed Jesus could heal his servant with just a word *(Luke 7:1–10)*.

Weak in Faith

1. People in Jesus' hometown couldn't believe he was special *(Matthew 13:54–58)*.

2. The disciples lacked faith needed to help a demon-possessed boy *(Matthew 17:14–21)*.

3. The disciples feared a storm—though Jesus was right there with them *(Mark 4:35–40)*.

4. The disciples worried about things like food and clothing *(Luke 12:27–31)*.

5. The disciples couldn't believe their eyes when a fig tree withered *(Matthew 21:18–22)*.

HOLY HIEROGLYPHICS?

Why do believers use visual symbols? Do they come from the Bible?

Symbols are images of easily recognized objects that immediately and clearly convey the message intended. While some symbols have their origins in biblical passages, others are drawn from the culture that existed at the time they evolved. Symbols have been used to help speak the common language of Jesus' church among people of different backgrounds, cultures, and languages.

In the early church, believers used symbols to help communicate with one another at a time when they were under great persecution from the Romans. If two strangers met, it would have been risky for either of them to ask the other if he was a believer. So one would draw an arc in the sand or dirt. If the other was a Christian, he would complete the symbol with a reverse arc touching the first arc at one end and overlapping it on the other, forming the outline of a fish. The fish outline was a logical symbol for the early church to adopt, since fish play a major role in the Gospels (for instance, Jesus bade his followers to be "fishers of men") and many of Jesus' followers were fishermen by profession.

LET IT SNOW!

Snow is mentioned only once in the historical books of the Bible as actually *falling (2 Samuel 23:20)*. The allusions to snow, however, are so numerous in the poetical books of the Bible that there is little doubt that a great deal of snow fell in ancient Israel in winter months. The first-century Roman historian Josephus noted that it was a peculiarity of the low plain of Jericho that the climate remained warm there even when snow was prevalent in the remainder of the region. Snow is considered a sign of God's creative power *(Psalm 147:16)* and is said to be of great benefit to the soil *(Isaiah 55:10)*. It has been ascribed to images of brilliance *(Matthew 28:3)* and to purity *(Isaiah 1:18)*. Job spoke of the cleansing effects of snow water *(Job 9:30)*, the rapid melting of snow under the sun's rays *(Job 24:19)*, and the consequent flooding of brooks *(Job 6:16)*.

"SIGNS" OF THE TIMES

A number of symbols are used in churches, often at particular times of year, to depict both the spiritual and historical significance of various events or rites. Not all symbols are common to all denominations, and some denominations shy away from use of historical symbols (except for the cross) altogether.

1. *Advent Wreath.* Used during the last four weeks before Christmas, this symbol features one pink and three purple candles stationed around a circle of entwined evergreens representing eternity. One candle is lit each Sunday in Advent—first the three purple candles representing watchfulness, then the pink candle on the last Sunday before Christmas to represent joy. Sometimes a fifth candle (white) is added to the center and lit on Christmas Day.

2. *Standing Lamb.* The image of a haloed lamb standing with a banner grasped in his foreleg is frequently used during the Easter season. Its symbolism is drawn from John 1:29, where John refers to Jesus as "the Lamb of God." Called "Agnus Dei" in some traditions, the figure represents Jesus' triumph over death when he rose from the dead.

3. *Angel.* As messengers of God, angels often appear in the context of a message from God. For instance, an angel told Mary that she would bear the baby Jesus, announced Jesus' birth to shepherds in the fields, and greeted mourners at Jesus' empty tomb with news of his resurrection. Angels are also often used to represent God's protection.

4. *Chi Rho.* This ancient symbol is often seen in such places as altar cloths or the stoles of ministers' robes. Early believers used this monogram (from the first two letters of the Greek word translated as "Christ"— XPICTOC) as a sign of their faith. There are several slight variations in the way the symbol may be displayed—all using X and P.

"SIGNS" OF THE TIMES (CONT'D)

5. *Linking Circles.* The three circles represent the members of the Trinity—God the Father, God the Son, and God the Holy Spirit—and the Trinity's eternal nature. The interlinking feature symbolizes that God is one God although he reveals himself in three persons.

6. *Shepherd's Staff.* The shepherd's staff is used as a reminder that Jesus is the "Good Shepherd." While the emblem may be found pictorially anywhere in the church, it is most often noticed when a member of the clergy carries an actual staff into a worship service as a symbol of ecclesiastical authority and reminder of Jesus' presence.

7. *Cross.* Nearly thirty different variations of the cross exist around the world as a symbol of Jesus' sacrificial death and resurrection. The one most often seen on altars and Communion tables in the U.S. is the "Calvary Cross," which sits on a three-tiered base representing the hill of Calvary. The three steps have also been interpreted as standing for faith, hope, and love.

8. *Crown and Scepter.* The scepter, a symbol of authority, together with the crown, creates this symbol of Jesus' triumphant reign over all creation. The emblem is often found on clothes or ornaments used at Christmas, on Ascension Sunday, and on Christ the King Sunday.

9. *Crown of Thorns.* The crown of thorns is a symbol of Jesus' suffering and Pilate's ascription of him as King of the Jews *(Matthew 27:27–29)*. The emblem is most often seen during Lent (the forty days leading up to Easter) and especially during Holy Week—the week leading to Easter.

"SIGNS" OF THE TIMES (CONT'D)

10. *Descending Dove.* Most often seen during the season of Pentecost, this symbol of the Holy Spirit is derived from the account of Jesus' baptism, when the Spirit descended on him in the form of a dove. The halo around its head identifies the Spirit as a member of the Trinity. A dove shown without the halo is usually a symbol of peace.

11. *Harp.* The harp is used as a symbol of praise to God, and the use of musical instruments to enhance praise. The harp is also used as a symbol of King David and the Psalms.

12. *IHS or IHC Monogram.* This sacred monogram is formed of the first three letters of the Greek word translated as "Jesus" (IHCOYC). The horizontal line that forms a cross on the H signifies an abbreviation. One variation of the monogram is often mistaken for a dollar sign ($); it may sometimes be found on tombstones in old cemeteries.

13. *Keys.* Though used throughout the church to denote salvation (the keys to the kingdom of heaven), keys are also used by Catholic and Orthodox traditions to represent the authority of the church to forgive wrongs in Jesus' name. Two keys represent dual authority: to open heaven to the repentant and to lock heaven to the unrepentant.

14. *Lion.* The lion as a symbol of Jesus, the Lion of Judah, is rooted in Revelation 5:4–5. Early believers were also influenced by a mythological tale that compares Jesus to a lion. Biblical reference also uses the lion to represent the treachery and stealth of Satan *(1 Peter 5:8)*. The lion is now seen more in displays that have roots in the Crusades, when it was widely used on heraldic standards.

15. *Oil.* Oil was used in the Old Testament as a sign of consecration to God. It was symbolic of God's call and empowerment of individuals for specific tasks. In a New Testament setting, oil further represents the presence of the Holy Spirit in individual lives.

"SIGNS" OF THE TIMES (CONT'D)

16. *Olive Branch.* The first account of an olive branch as a symbol occurs in the story of Noah, when the released dove returned bearing an olive branch. It marked the end of the great flood. The olive branch has since been widely used as a symbol of peace.

17. *Palm Branch.* Palm branches are often waved as part of Palm Sunday pageantry to recall Jesus' triumphal entry into Jerusalem, when the people strewed the branches in his path as a sign of adulation. A Roman symbol of victory, they have been used by the church as a symbol of Jesus' ultimate victory over sin and death. Church martyrs are sometimes portrayed holding palm branches.

18. *Pearl.* The pearl is symbolic of the kingdom of heaven, and is taken from Jesus' parable of the "pearl of great price" in Matthew 13:45–46 *(NKJV)*. Matthew's gospel also uses the pearl as a symbol of the Holy Scriptures. Imitation pearls are sometimes incorporated as decorations on liturgical vestments or in decorations for the Advent and Christmas seasons.

19. *Quatrefoil.* The quatrefoil is a four-lobbed symbol, which, when used in liturgical settings, stands for the four evangelists of the New Testament: Matthew, Mark, Luke, and John. The pattern is frequently seen—often in a set of four— as part of church architecture and especially in windows.

20. *Rainbow.* Taken from the story of Noah and the great flood, when God placed his rainbow in the sky as a seal of his promise never to destroy the earth again with a flood, the rainbow is sometimes used in art as Jesus' throne, where it is symbolic of glory and final judgment.

21. *Shamrock.* The shamrock is a symbol of the Trinity and of Saint Patrick, who used it to explain to unbelievers how God is one God in three Persons. Patrick would hold up a shamrock and challenge his hearers: "Is it one leaf or three?" "It is both one leaf and three," they would inevitably reply. "And so it is with God," he would conclude.

"SIGNS" OF THE TIMES (CONT'D)

22. *Shell.* The scallop or cockle shell is sometimes portrayed with three water drops (to represent the Trinity) and is a symbol of baptism. Some churches use a shell to pour water during infant baptism rites and then present the shell to the child's family. It is also used to represent pilgrimage or travel and is thus often seen during the season of Epiphany during which the Christ child's family would have been fleeing to Egypt.

23. *Four-pointed Star.* A four-pointed star resembles a cross and is used as the "star of Bethlehem" or "natal star." Seen most frequently during the Christmas season, the cross shape is a reminder both of Jesus' birth and of the purpose for which he was born.

24. *Trefoil.* The trefoil is a single design composed of three joined circles, which represent eternity, signifying one God in three Persons. It is derived from the shamrock, which Saint Patrick used to illustrate the doctrine of the Trinity. It is seen in many forms in churches, especially as part of windows or architecture.

25. *Triquetra.* The triquetra is a triple-arc symbol composed of three interlocked pieces marking the intersection of three circles. It is most commonly a symbol of the Holy Trinity (God the Father, God the Son, God the Holy Spirit) and is seen primarily in churches in Great Britain. First adopted by the Celtic Christian Church, it is sometimes stylized as three interlaced fish.

Source: Original graphics created by Walter E. Gast, home.att.net/~wegast/symbols/symbols.htm, by permission as granted on that site.

PRINTER, PHRASEMAKER, AND COMMENTATOR

Theologian and scholar William Tyndale is perhaps best known for translating the Bible into an early form of Modern English. He was also the first person to use Gutenberg's movable-type press to print the Scriptures in English.

Born near Gloucester, England, in 1494, Tyndale earned degrees from both Oxford and Cambridge and was the captain and spiritual leader of the Army of Reformers. His fluency in eight languages secured his place as one of the major architects of the English language—even more so than Shakespeare—since so many of the phrases Tyndale coined are still in our language today.

Besides translating the Bible, Tyndale also held and published views that were then considered heretical by both the Catholic Church and the Church of England. A clergyman once taunted Tyndale with the statement, "We are better to be without God's laws than the Pope's." Tyndale, infuriated by such heresies, replied, "I defy the Pope and all his laws. If God spare my life ere many years, I will cause the boy that drives the plow to know more of the Scriptures than you!"

Tyndale's Bible translation, containing notes and commentary promoting these views, was banned by the authorities, and Tyndale himself was burned at the stake in 1536 by agents of Henry VIII.

Source: www.greatsite.com/timeline-english-bible-history/william-tyndale.html.

VOICE OF PRAISE AND RESCUE

On June 7, 1663, while the men were away working in the fields, a group of outlaw Indians entered Catherine DuBois' village in upstate New York under the pretext of selling vegetables. They began murdering the unarmed villagers and then took about forty-five women and children captives, among them Catherine and her baby daughter, Sarah.

Would-be rescuers, led by Catherine's husband, searched the Catskills for three months with no success. Then a friendly Indian gave a clue to the location of the captives. Meanwhile, food was becoming scarce for the Indians, and winter was not far off. The outlaws decided to burn some of their captives. Catherine and Sarah were selected to be first.

As the torch was about to be put to her pyre, Catherine began singing the words of Psalm 137. Enchanted by her voice, the Indians demanded that she continue to sing. The approaching rescuers heard her, were guided to the spot, attacked the kidnappers, and released all the prisoners.

NOT THAT GUY

World War II–era big-band leader Tommy Dorsey is often credited with composing one of the most beloved gospel songs of all time. But the attribution is a case of mistaken identity.

"Precious Lord, Take My Hand" was indeed penned by Tommy Dorsey, but this Tommy was a jazz musician who later in life dedicated himself to gospel music. He served as choir director of Chicago's Pilgrim Baptist Church for more than forty years and wrote more than two hundred songs during his ninety-six years.

"Precious Lord" was written after his wife, Nettie, died while giving birth to a child. Uneasy about his wife's condition, Dorsey had nevertheless left on a trip that morning; both Nettie and the child died before he could return.

Heartbroken, Dorsey composed the song on the spur of the moment, and it gave him some peace. The song's popularity grew quickly after he sang it for his friend, gospel singer Theodore Frye, and Frye's choir sang it the next Sunday at the Ebenezer Baptist Church.

Read more about Tommy Dorsey's life on page 267.

Source: www.christianitytoday.com/tc/2003/004/16.16.html.

CLERICAL FASHION SHOW

Both Catholic and Protestant ministers may wear a variety of robelike garments in religious services. Many Protestant ministers wear a flowing, full-sleeved robe similar to that worn for a graduation ceremony, and a stole (a narrow decorative band that drapes around the neck and hangs down the front).

Priests in both the Catholic and Episcopal/Anglican traditions usually wear an alb (a high-necked, full-length, robelike garment with a front placket and long, coatlike sleeves) and a stole or some other vestment. The alb is usually made of white linen and is often gathered at the waist with a ropelike "belt."

A cassock resembles a slim-fitting, full-length topcoat with buttons down the front and is sometimes worn alone for daily work. A surplice (a full-bodied, hip-length garment with wide sleeves) is worn on top of the cassock in the sanctuary.

A minister who usually wears vestments of some type may be said to be in "mufti" if he is wearing regular street clothes.

TEN OLD TESTAMENT CHEATERS AND LIARS

Lying and cheating were or will be dead-end, unproductive paths for all of the Bible figures below!

1. *Satan (Genesis 3).* The father of lies began his deceit of humankind when he said that God didn't really mean that Adam and Eve would die literally if they ate fruit from the forbidden tree in the Garden of Eden.

2. *Cain (Genesis 4).* Adam and Eve's son resented the favor that his brother, Abel, had found in the sight of God. Luring Abel into a field, Cain murdered him, and the murder was compounded by a lie: "Then the LORD said to Cain, 'Where is your brother Abel?' 'I don't know,' he replied. 'Am I my brother's keeper?'" *(v. 9 NIV).*

3. *Abraham (Genesis 20).* While he was living in Gerar, Abraham began to worry that King Abimelech would be attracted to his wife, Sarah, and would kill Abraham to marry her. To save his own skin, Abraham told Abimelech that Sarah was his sister, so Abimelech added Sarah to his harem. Abraham's lie was revealed to the king when God visited him in a dream and threatened his life for the illicit marriage.

4. *Jacob (Genesis 25–27).* Jacob conspired with his mother to deceive his dying father so he, instead of his slightly older twin, Esau, could inherit everything. First, he tricked Esau into giving up the inheritance. Then, disguised as Esau, he went to see his nearly blind father and received the official inheritance blessing.

5. *Rebekah (Genesis 25–27).* In a way, Jacob's mother, Rebekah, was the mastermind behind Jacob's scheme to cheat Esau. She spied on her husband, cooked the tasty meal of lamb Jacob passed off as wild game to his father, and even fashioned the disguise Jacob wore.

6. *Laban (Genesis 29).* After seven years of working for Laban, Jacob was tricked by his would-be father-in-law into marrying the man's older daughter, Leah, instead of her sister, Jacob's beloved Rebekah. Laban eventually allowed Jacob to wed Rebekah as well, but it cost Jacob seven more years of labor.

TEN OLD TESTAMENT CHEATERS AND LIARS (CONT'D)

7. *Potiphar's Wife (Genesis 39).* When handsome young Joseph rebuffed the advances of his boss's wife, she accused him of attacking her. While the accusation landed Joseph in prison, it placed him in a position for his talent of dream interpretation to be discovered by Pharaoh, who ultimately elevated Joseph to a position of power in Egypt.

8. *Aaron (Exodus 32).* Moses' brother Aaron was left in charge while Moses was on the mountain receiving the Ten Commandments from God. Moses' long absence unnerved the frightened Israelites, and they demanded that Aaron give them a god they could see. Aaron fashioned a golden calf for them to worship. When a furious Moses questioned Aaron, he denied making the idol, claiming it emerged from the molten gold all on its own!

9. *The Old Prophet (1 Kings 13).* Instructed by God to accomplish his task, then return home by a different route before eating or drinking, a young prophet was accosted by an old prophet who invited him to dinner. The old man lied that an angel instructed him to feed the young man. At dinner the old man confessed his lie, and the younger prophet paid for his disobedience to God with his life.

10. *Gehazi (2 Kings 5).* Elisha's servant, Gehazi, greedily sought the gifts Elisha had refused after telling Naaman how to be healed of leprosy. Pretending to be on an errand for Elisha, Gehazi solicited and received the gifts from a grateful Naaman. Elisha discerned his servant's deceit and pronounced that, for his lie and greed, Gehazi would be stricken with Naaman's leprosy.

LEARN, STUDY, AND PASS IT ON

It's a little confusing. The New Testament has three names for those who were close to Jesus: *apostles*, *disciples*, and *followers*. In essence, they mean the same thing.

Apostle is from the Greek word *apostolos*, meaning "one who is sent." Jesus "sent" his apostles when he told them to share the gospel with all nations *(Matthew 28:19–20)*.

Disciple also comes from the Greek and refers to one who studies under a certain teacher, absorbing lessons that he or she then passes on to others. Jesus' first twelve followers are usually called the disciples.

A *follower* is . . . one who follows. Jesus drew many followers, people who agreed with his teachings and grew to love him for his honesty, compassion, and healing power.

MEGACHURCH

A megachurch is a large church, frequently defined as having more than two thousand worshippers for a typical weekly service. It is seen as a relatively new phenomenon in Protestant Christianity in the United States. Most megachurches are independent from organized denominations, although a growing number are part of mainline churches. They tend to be evangelical in their theology but avoid unusual or unconventional doctrinal positions. They also avoid the use of tobacco and alcohol and often rebuff lifestyles that value physical possessions as symbols of success.

While the phenomenon is mainly American (typically found in exurban areas of the Sun Belt in the southern United States), megachurches are found around the globe. Examples are Yoido Full Gospel Church in Seoul, South Korea (with 780,000 members in 2003, making it the largest church in the world), and Hillsong Church in Sydney, Australia (with 15,000 attending each Sunday).

THE WEIGHTY SOUL

D r. Duncan MacDougall of Haverhill, Massachusetts, postulated that if the soul were material and therefore had mass, a measurable drop in the weight of the deceased would be noted at the moment the soul left the body. The belief that the soul of a human being has a detectable physical presence was around well before the twentieth century, but the claim that a soul has measurable mass is traced directly to experiments conducted by MacDougall in 1907.

MacDougall constructed a special bed in his office "arranged on a light framework built upon very delicately balanced platform beam scales," which were sensitive to two-tenths of an ounce. He placed a succession of six patients in the end stages of terminal illnesses on the bed, observing them before, during, and after the process of death, and measuring any corresponding changes in weight. He attempted to control for as many physiological explanations for the observed results as he could conceive.

His findings, published in the *New York Times* and the medical journal *American Medicine*, included a description of the methods he used and the results. Two of the six cases could not be used because of technical problems. Of the remaining four, all showed a drop in weight of varying small amounts at the moment of death. He concluded, "Is it the soul substance? How other shall we explain it?"

MacDougall's critics have found multiple ways to question his work and noted that the doctor later attempted to photograph the soul as it exited the body, without apparent success.

Sources: Duncan MacDougall, "The Soul: Hypothesis Concerning Soul Substance Together with Experimental Evidence of the Existence of Such Substance," *American Medicine* (April 1907); "He Weighed Human Soul," *New York Times* (October 16, 1920), 13.

THE TEARS OF THE RUSSIAN

On a recent visit to the United States, an official of The United Methodist Church in Estonia spoke of his gratitude for the freedom to worship openly in his nation—a freedom reestablished after the demise of Communism in 1991. The newfound freedom had made it possible for leaders of varying religious groups to begin meeting openly and to develop ecumenical ties. These ties, in turn, had helped foster the reemergence of personal faith as an accepted practice in the former USSR and its satellite nations.

The depth of this gratitude was illustrated, he said, by a rabbi from Russia who visited this ecumenical group one December. The group met at a Chinese restaurant for dinner. Since it was a special occasion, the Chinese restaurateur brought each person a small, brass Christmas tree ornament at the end of the meal. The back of each ornament was stamped with the words "Made in India."

They chuckled at the irony of receiving a gift made in India from a Chinese restaurant. But laughing ceased when they noticed tears rolling down the rabbi's cheeks. Concerned that they might have offended him in some way, they asked what had made him sad.

"*Nyet*—not sad," the rabbi said, smiling. "These are tears of joy because I am now in a nation where a Buddhist can give a Jew a Christmas gift made by a Hindu."

LIFE IN A NUTSHELL

One of the smartest questions a person can ask about life is this: "What's it all about, God?" The writers, philosophers, and theologians below may very well have consulted the Creator and his instruction manual (the Bible) before drawing their thoughtful conclusions about life.

1. "And why should mortals fear to tread the pathway to their future home?"—*Emily Brontë (English novelist, 1818–1848)*

2. "Be such a man, and live such a life, that if every man were such as you, and every life a life like yours, this earth would be God's Paradise."
—*Phillips Brooks (U.S. Episcopal bishop, 1835–1893)*

3. "Every man's life is a plan of God."
—*Horace Bushnell (American Congregational minister, 1802–1876)*

4. "God has given to man a short time here upon earth, and yet upon this short time eternity depends."—*Jeremy Taylor (English churchman, 1613–1667)*

5. "I count that part of my life lost which I spent not in communion with God, or in doing good."—*John Donne (English poet, 1572–1631)*

6. "It is with life as with a play; what matters is not how long it is, but how good it is."—*Lucius Seneca (Roman philosopher, 4 BC–AD 65)*

7. "Life can only be understood backwards; but it must be lived forwards."—*Søren Kierkegaard (Danish philosopher, 1813–1855)*

8. "No man has a right to lead such a life of contemplation as to forget in his own ease the service due to his neighbor; nor has any man a right to be so immersed in active life as to neglect the contemplation of God."
—*Saint Augustine (bishop of Hippo, 354–430)*

9. "The glory of God, and, as our only means to glorifying him, the salvation of human souls, is the real business of life."
—*C. S. Lewis (British author, 1898–1963)*

10. "The rule that governs my life is this: Anything that dims my vision of Christ, or takes away my taste for Bible study, or cramps my prayer life, or makes Christian work difficult, is wrong for me, and I must, as a Christian, turn away from it."
—*J. Wilbur Chapman (American evangelist, 1859–1918)*

11. "The most important thing in life is to live your life for something more important than your life."—*William James (American psychologist, 1842–1910)*

12. "You can't do anything about the length of your life, but you can do something about its width and depth."—*Evan Esar (American humorist, 1899–1995)*

Source: Edythe Draper, *Draper's Book of Quotations for the Christian World* (Wheaton, IL: Tyndale, 1992).

FAITH AND WORK

For some it's a necessary evil. For others it could be an escape from home pressures. For still others it's a place of challenge and fulfillment. It's the workplace!

Millions of people spend forty hours a week—and more—on the job. Besides providing a paycheck, the workplace is also assuming something of a family or community atmosphere for many employees.

Another change is permeating the workplace—faith. Faith-based workplace programs have been around for decades but exploded in popularity in the 1990s. Work pressures and job dissatisfaction make the workplace fertile ground for spiritual soul-searching. In several recent national studies, only about 50 percent of all employees reported that they are happy with their jobs. People who can bring their spiritual values to work are happier, more productive, stay longer, and help the company more than people who don't feel they can bring their values to work.

Amy Baker, author of *Succeed at Work Without Sidetracking Your Faith*, says, "We're seeing more organizations like prayer groups and Bible studies. They're not all that different than the company bowling league or dining-out club." On-the-job prayer groups and Bible studies are growing; an estimated three thousand to four thousand chaplains actively serve American businesses. Os Hillman, president of the International Coalition of Workplace Ministries, said, "Religion is important to many people's lives, and they want to at least be able to talk about that part of their life and not feel like they have to hide around a corner."

FAITH AND WORK (CONT'D)

In the wake of high-profile "ethics failures" in corporate America, more and more employers are realizing the need for increased integrity in the workplace. The business world is increasingly receptive to efforts that encourage creation of an ethical workplace. Workers who bring their faith to work generally bring their integrity with them. A secular study in the February 2001 issue of *Sales and Marketing* magazine reported that 58% of employees cheated on an expense report, 50% worked a second job on company time, 22% listed a "strip bar" as a restaurant on an expense report, and 19% gave kickbacks to customers. Employers are eager to see a decline in those statistics!

Religious leaders in America recognize the workplace as a place where God is at work. Dr. Billy Graham said, "I believe one of the next great moves of God is going to be through the believers in the workplace." Chad Hammond, the director of New Venture, a division of the Billy Graham Evangelistic Association, reported, "We reviewed fifty-two movements in the body of Christ. We narrowed it down to twenty-eight, then twelve, then four to invest our resources in the coming years. The workplace is one of those because this is an area where we see God working."

Statistics confirm that. Ten years ago there was one conference on spirituality and the workplace; today there are literally hundreds. Publishers are releasing dozens of books on faith and work annually. Corporate chaplains now number in the thousands.

Source: www.businessweek.com/1999/99_44/b3653001.htm.

FACING SUFFERING THE "BIBLE" WAY

The Bible states that both good and bad times come into the life of every person. God's promise is that he will be with his people *in* their times of suffering and that ultimately he will use suffering for good outcomes. The ultimate benefit may come in eternity, not on earth.

The Bible gives directions about how people are to face and endure times of persecution and suffering.

Here are things not to do:

1. Demand to know why.
2. Withdraw from God and other people.
3. Become impatient with God.
4. Seek your own remedies.
5. Give in to despair or depression.
6. Delude yourself about the underlying cause of the suffering, trying to second-guess the purpose of your suffering, or exalting yourself for experiencing suffering.
7. Indulge yourself or give in to temptations as a means of compensating for suffering.
8. Become angry.

In contrast, here are things *to do*:

9. Choose to trust that God can turn even suffering to good *(Romans 8:28)*.
10. Pray *(1 Peter 5:6–7)*.
11. Acknowledge that God is present with you in suffering *(Hebrews 13:5)*.
12. Stay in fellowship with other believers *(Hebrews 10:24–25)*.
13. Remember that God sets and knows your limits of endurance *(1 Corinthians 10:13)*.
14. Be patient and wait for God's perfect timing *(Psalm 31:14–15)*.
15. Trust in God for guidance *(Proverbs 3:5–6)*.
16. Seek the truth *(John 8:32)*.
17. Stay pure; refuse to give in to temptations to do wrong *(1 Peter 2:11–12)*.
18. Stay hopeful in God *(Job 13:15)*.

HARDSHIP AND HEROISM

One of the first missionaries from the United States was Adoniram Judson (1788–1850). He took Christianity to Burma and while there, had every reason to quit and return home . . . but didn't. When war with England broke out in Burma, Judson was imprisoned because he looked like the light-skinned enemy. For twenty-one months he was held in the most squalid conditions. He was suspended upside down at night, preventing sleep and causing fierce cramping as blood rushed to his head. His devoted wife brought food for him daily, and she pleaded with the guards for better treatment as well as for his release.

Within months of his release, Mrs. Judson and their young daughter died. Judson nearly had a breakdown. Daily he knelt by her grave. He dug his own grave in case it might be necessary.

Much of Judson's work involved translating the Bible into the Burmese language. In all, he worked thirty-four years in Burma, and because of his faithfulness more than a million Burmese believers trace their spiritual heritage back to his ministry there.

Sources: www.wholesomewords.org/missions/judson; www.reformedreader.org/rbb/judson.

SHARE THE HEALING

Joyce Meyer is one of the most popular ministers today. She has a daily television program with audience potential of 2.5 billion people. She teaches on emotional healing, overcoming the past, and freedom from condemnation. The ministry of this worldwide speaker, author, and conference teacher began in the basement of her home.

Born in 1943, Joyce began her life in a dysfunctional family. Her father abused her for eighteen years. She divorced her first husband, who abused her, and walked away with her son and only what she could carry. In the months that followed, she met a man named David Meyer, who specifically prayed for God to send him a wife. After five dates he asked Joyce to marry him. Slowly God began to heal Joyce, and she began to share her painful story to help others. In addition to a vast television outreach, Joyce has written seventy-five books.

Source: www.joycemeyer.org/bio.

WAS JESUS A REAL PERSON?

The Bible is not the only ancient manuscript to mention Jesus; two first-century historians also wrote about him.

Historian Flavius Josephus (AD 38–100) described Jesus as "a wise man, if indeed one should call him a man. For he was a doer of startling deeds, a teacher of the people who receive the truth with pleasure. And he gained a following both among many Jews and among many of Greek origin. He was the Messiah. And when Pilate, because of an accusation made by the leading men among us, condemned him to the cross, those who had loved him previously did not cease to do so. For he appeared to them on the third day, living again, just as the divine prophets had spoken of these and countless other wondrous things about him. And up until this very day the tribe of Christians, named after him, has not died out."

Cornelius Tacitus (AD 55–120) is considered the greatest historian of ancient Rome. His history confirms the existence of Jesus, saying that the Roman emperor Nero tortured "the persons commonly called Christians, who were hated for their enormities. Christus [Christ], the founder of the name, was put to death by Pontius Pilate, procurator of Judea in the reign of Tiberius: but the pernicious superstition [about Jesus' resurrection], repressed for a time, broke out again, not only through Judea, where the mischief originated, but through the city of Rome also."

Sources: *Jewish Antiquities*, 18.63–64; *Annals* XV, 44.

FOR GOD AND FOR COUNTRY

Who were the Four Chaplains? Why were they honored with a postage stamp in 1948 and a Senate resolution establishing Four Chaplains Day in 1998?

George Fox, Alexander Goode, Clark Poling, and John Washington—Methodist, Jewish, Dutch Reformed, and Catholic, respectively—decided, in the wake of Pearl Harbor, to apply for the Chaplains Corps.

All four men wanted to be near the front but instead were sent to Greenland.

Heading for Greenland on the decrepit *Dorchester*, a former luxury liner, the chaplains and nine hundred troops met disaster when a torpedo hit the ship. As the ship was sinking, the chaplains gave away their life jackets and gloves to help save more men. They convinced many others who were paralyzed by fear to get into the lifeboats.

Throughout the short voyage and the tragedy, the chaplains worked as a team, bolstering the faith of the troops and ultimately sacrificing their own lives for others.

Source: Dan Kurzman, *No Greater Glory* (New York: Random House, 2004).

A CODED MESSAGE

Samuel F. B. Morse, artist and inventor, is best remembered for creating a system for sending messages instantly over long distances. He sent the first telegraphic message on May 24, 1844, over an experimental line from Washington, D.C., to Baltimore, Maryland. The message said, "What hath God wrought?" Taken from the Bible (*Numbers 23:23 KJV*) and recorded on a paper tape by the receiver, the phrase had been suggested to Morse by Annie Ellworth, the young daughter of a friend. The message, however, was not without meaning to Morse.

Seven days after his great success with the first telegraph message, Morse wrote to his brother, Sidney, in a humble and cautious tone. Twice he quoted the famous message, expressing his deep appreciation to God for inspiring his success. He then quoted a former opponent, now won over, as saying, "It is an astonishing invention."

RELIGION ROCKS

Gospel music was nothing new in the 1960s. What was new, however, was hearing God and Jesus mentioned—in a positive way—in songs being put out by rock-and-roll singers. Not every song on the list below was a Top 20 hit, but what they all had in common was an ability to cause listeners to perceive God in a new light.

1. "Oh Happy Day" *(Edwin Hawkins Singers)*
2. "Put Your Hand in the Hand" *(Ocean)*
3. "Spirit in the Sky" *(Norman Greenbaum)*
4. "Jesus Is Just Alright" *(Doobie Brothers)*
5. "Day by Day" *(from* Godspell*)*
6. "Jesus Christ Superstar" *(from* Jesus Christ Superstar*)*
7. "I Don't Know How to Love Him" *(Yvonne Elliman, from* Jesus Christ Superstar*)*
8. "Have a Talk with God" *(Stevie Wonder)*
9. "Property of Jesus" *(Bob Dylan)*
10. "Jesus Is Love" *(Commodores)*
11. "Mighty Clouds of Joy" *(B. J. Thomas)*
12. "When I Look at the World" *(U2)*

SHAKESPEARE OR THE BIBLE?

Shakespeare and other writers often get credit for coining certain phrases, but many of those phrases, idioms, and proverbs come straight from the Bible:

1. "There is nothing new under the sun" *(Ecclesiastes 1:9 NIV)*.
2. "Am I my brother's keeper?" *(Genesis 4:9 NIV)*.
3. An eye for an eye *(Exodus 21:24)*.
4. The prodigal son *(Luke 15:11–32)*.
5. "The truth will set you free" *(John 8:31–32 NIV)*.
6. "It is more blessed to give than to receive" *(Acts 20:35 NIV)*.
7. Doubting Thomas *(John 20:24–25)*.
8. A house divided against itself cannot stand *(Matthew 12:25)*.
9. The good Samaritan *(Luke 10:30–37)*.
10. Go the extra mile *(Matthew 5:41)*.
11. See the handwriting on the wall *(Daniel 5:1–8)*.
12. Have his head on a platter *(Matthew 14:6–11)*.
13. I wash my hands of it *(Matthew 27:24)*.
14. "The love of money is the root of all evil" *(1 Timothy 6:10 KJV)*.
15. You can't take it with you *(1 Timothy 6:7)*.

THE LONG AND
SHORT OF IT

In ancient Israel, both men and women had long hair, although women tended to have longer hair than men did. Samson and Absalom in the Old Testament were noted for their hair. Samson's uncut hair was a sign of his dedication to God and an indication of his strength *(Judges 13:5)*. Absalom, son of David, was known for his long, thick hair, which got so heavy that he had to have it trimmed *(2 Samuel 14:26)*. The deaths of both men directly involved their hair. Philistines captured Samson after his hair was cut; Absalom's hair got caught in a tree during a battle.

Hair had religious significance in Bible times. Well-dressed hair indicated joy and general welfare. Unkempt hair was a sign of mourning or shame. Shaving all of a man's hair—from either his face or his head—signaled grief or suffering *(Job 1:20; Jeremiah 48:37)*. Jewish men were not to cut the hair at the sides of the head or the beard *(Leviticus 19:27)*. Ordinarily, shaving the head and beard was not allowed except for ritual shaving for purification ceremonies. The mutilation of a man's beard was an insult to the ancient Israelites. A Nazirite was a person who vowed, among other things, to let his hair grow; after the vow was fulfilled, the hair was shaved and offered as a burnt sacrifice to God.

By New Testament times, men were wearing short hairstyles. Different lengths of hair between men and women distinguished the sexes. Paul said in 1 Corinthians 11:14–15 that long hair was degrading to a man but a tribute to a woman.

Source: www.keyway.ca/htm2000/20001205.htm.

THSLTTLLGHTFMN

If the song title "This Little Light of Mine" were written as it would have been in Old Testament Hebrew, the result would be "Thslttllghtfmn." The Old Testament was originally written without vowels, word division, or punctuation. The Hebrew alphabet contains no vowels. A system of dots and dashes, called points, are written above, below, or inside the letter to aid in pronunciation.

Source: www.jewfaq.org/alephbet.htm.

FIRST WAVES

The first-ever vocal radio broadcast on December 24, 1906, in Brant Rock, Massachusetts, included a Bible reading. Canadian-born Reginald Fessenden, who had worked for Thomas Edison, was both inventor and broadcaster. Fessenden was the first person to prove that voices and music could be heard over airwaves without wires. On that first broadcast he played "O Holy Night" on the violin, read the Christmas story from the Gospel of Luke, and played a phonograph record of Handel's "Largo."

Source: inventors.about.com/gi/dynamic/offsite.htm?site=http://www.wfn.org/story.html.

WHAT'S THE TANAKH?

The name of the Hebrew Bible is *Tanakh* (pronounced ta-KNOCK). The word is an acronym based on the three sections of the Bible: Torah (the Law), Nevi'im (the Prophets), and Kethuvim (the Writings). The Tanakh contains the same books as the Christian Old Testament, but in a slightly different order and with other minor differences. The first letters of these three words are T-N-K. Combined, these letters form the word *Tanakh*.

DO NOT PASS GO

Religious education doesn't have to be boring. And religious family entertainment doesn't have to be expensive. Board games provide both—a family alternative to entertainment, with religious themes and content.

Some games are Christian takeoffs of best sellers, such as Bible editions of favorites like Scattergories, Outburst, and Guesstures. Other popular, Christian-focused family games are Settlers of Canaan, in which each player represents a tribe of Israel as they seek to settle the land of Canaan and build Jerusalem; Ark of the Covenant; Journeys of Paul, a historical strategy game; Bible Trivia; and Bibleopoly. For Roman Catholics, Divinity is a game that teaches the Catechism.

Board games are also available for non-Christian faiths. The Jewish game Kosherland is based on the enduring favorite Candyland. Exodus and Torah Slides and Ladders are popular Jewish children's games. A Muslim bingo-style game, Know Islam Know Peace, teaches basic Islamic tenets and history. Race to the Kabah resembles Trivial Pursuit as players make their way to the sacred Mecca building known as the Kabah. Leela, a Hindu game described as a "metaphysical Chutes and Ladders," is for adults. It comes with 133 pages of instruction. Girls playing the pagan game Go Goddess Girl! learn about ancient goddesses, supposedly to help them get in touch with their "girl power."

Toy industry experts say board games are a one-time purchase providing budget-friendly family entertainment. They also provide opportunity for family interaction that doesn't happen with videos or computer games.

Sources: www.acfnewsource.org/religion/gods_gameboard.html;
www.pbs.org/wnet/religionandethics/week612/feature.html.

BROADCASTING THE GOOD NEWS

Many people don't realize that Christian broadcasting is only about a hundred years old. Below are some milestones in its first century:

- *December 24, 1906*—First vocal radio broadcast of any kind features a reading from Luke 2.
- *1921*—First Christian radio broadcast airs on KDKA Pittsburgh, Pennsylvania.
- *1921*—First purely Christian radio station is established in Washington, D.C.
- *1921*—First radio church broadcast airs in Pittsburgh from Calvary Episcopal Church.
- *1931*—First missionary radio station, HCJB, hits the air in Quito, Ecuador.
- *1939*—First *Back to the Bible* program airs from Lincoln, Nebraska (the program still airs nationwide).
- *1940*—In New York, RCA's experimental television station W2XBS broadcasts the first Christian television program.
- *1950*—Pacific Garden Mission in Chicago airs the first Christian radio drama, *Unshackled*, on WGN (*Unshackled* is still in production, making it the longest-running radio drama of all time).
- *1954–1960*—First Christian broadcasting networks begin taking shape.
- *1957*—First Television Crusade with Billy Graham airs on the ABC network.
- *1960*—The FCC rules that television stations have the right to sell airtime for religious broadcasts.
- *1960*—Pat Robertson forms the Christian Broadcast Network.
- *1961*—First Christian TV station (WYAH/CBN) goes on the air in Portsmouth, Virginia.
- *1968*—First of several prime-time Christian specials airs on network television (NBC), featuring major entertainment figures and hosted by Oral Roberts.
- *1971*—First Christian cable-TV channel is established.
- *1971*—First Christian satellite broadcast is made.
- *1977*—First twenty-four-hour Christian TV station goes on the air (KTBN/Trinity Broadcasting Network).
- *1985*—First Christian news network is formed.
- *1993*—CBN lawsuit ends seventy-year ban on all Christian broadcasting in Canada.
- *1993*—First Christian radio station in Russia, TEOS, begins broadcasting.

Note: Some items appear on the Web site www.cdu.jesusanswers.com/photo.html.

RAISE YOUR EBENEZER!

A verse in the hymn "Come, Thou Fount of Every Blessing" contains the line "Here I raise my Ebenezer." One might think of the Charles Dickens character Ebenezer Scrooge.

In 1 Samuel 7:12 the prophet and priest Samuel placed a large stone marking the spot where the people of Israel repented of disobedience and recommitted themselves to the Lord. Samuel called this stone Ebenezer, which means "the stone of help," and said, "Up to this point the Lord has helped us." The stone marks the place where the restoration of the people began. It was dedicated as a monument to God's help. Figuratively, "Ebenezer stones" are sometimes set up to help a person remember something specific God has done on his or her behalf.

Sources: www/housetohouse.com; www.revneal.org.

NOT ROCKET SCIENCE

N eighbor. Sounds like a simple, straightforward word—one who lives near or next to another. If it's so obvious, why did the "expert in the law" (Luke 10:25–37 NIV) ask, "Who is my neighbor?" after Jesus said, "Love your neighbor as yourself"? Jesus explained his answer with the parable of the good Samaritan. The expert got the point: a neighbor is one who shows mercy on one who needs mercy.

From this perspective, the concept of "good neighbor" is very challenging. It puts a personal face on faith, to keep faith from becoming merely abstract or theoretical. Is there a person with a need? The good neighbor is the one who does whatever he or she can to meet that need.

ALONE TOGETHER

Spending time alone in the desert or wasteland has a powerful attraction for people seeking solitude. God spoke to Moses in the desert, calling him to lead the Israelites out of Egypt. It was in the desert that the Lord spoke "face to face" with Moses after he fulfilled that calling *(Exodus 33:11 NIV)*. Jesus took time alone in a wilderness to pray before beginning public ministry.

In the history of the church, the tradition of "Desert Fathers" in the third and fourth centuries eventually became the beginning of the monastic movement. During this period of about two hundred years, countless men and some women moved from their villages to live in caves in desert areas. They lived in regions with sparse vegetation and water, and an abundance of snakes, lizards, and vultures. The absence of personal comfort was just what appealed to these solitaries seeking to overcome the temptation to worldliness. They went not to "escape," but to confront the enemies of the soul. Such people were known as hermits and came to be regarded as holy.

Antony of Egypt (251–356) was one of the first in this tradition. Born in Egypt to wealthy parents, Antony was left in charge of their estate upon their deaths when he was about eighteen years of age. Soon after, he heard the gospel read in church: "Sell all that you have and give it to the poor." Antony immediately sold his possessions, gave the proceeds to the poor, and made provision for his sister at a convent. He sought training and guidance from holy men on the life of a hermit and moved out to the desert.

The desert was a place of temptation and testing, not unlike Jesus' forty days in the wilderness when he confronted Satan.

ALONE TOGETHER (CONT'D)

Antony lived in caves and huts, dividing his days between prayer, study, and work. Pilgrims came to him seeking spiritual advice. He contended with great deprivation and the harsh desert environment to become a lover of God. He spent twenty years in isolation, emerging to share the wisdom of solitude with others. He organized a community for laypeople to live together bound by vows of poverty and prayer. When he received a letter from the Roman emperor Constantine, Antony was not impressed. He told his followers, "Marvel, instead, that God wrote the law for mankind and has spoken to us through his own Son."

An Egyptian named Pachomius (290–346) is considered the founder of communal monasticism. He introduced aspects of community living by sharing meals and common prayer within the desert tradition. He also organized the monks to produce their own food and clothing so they were not dependent upon public charity.

In the next century, Benedict of Nursia (480–543) founded the monastery of Monte Cassino, where he wrote his "Holy Rule," the monastic code that forms the basis of the Benedictine religious order of today. Benedict's monastery treated all monks equally, and all were expected to work. This equality appealed to the Western mind, and the Benedictines eventually became the standard for Western monasteries.

Sources: www.cin.org/dsrft17.html; www.ctlibrary.com/ch/1999/Issue64/64h038.html; www.ctlibrary.com/ch/1999/Issue64/64h042.htlm.

FAMILY RESEMBLANCE

Human beings uniquely share God's nature. The Latin term is *imago dei* (pronounced ee-*mah*-go *day*-ee)—"the image of God." In Genesis 1:26 God said, "Let us make man in our image, in our likeness" *(NIV)*.

This resemblance means that (1) people are moral creatures able to know right and wrong, (2) humans have intellect to use to understand the world, (3) God made people to be in relationship with him, (4) God created people for eternal life, to live forever with him, and (5) humanity was given dominion as stewards and caretakers over the rest of creation.

Because Adam and Eve disobeyed God, and because everyone since has also in one way or another, the image of God is distorted in humankind. The story of the Bible is the story of God reconciling and restoring individuals to be all that God created them to be. The "new self . . . is being renewed in knowledge in the image of its Creator" *(Colossians 3:10 NIV)*.

AWE-FULL BLESSING

On the surface, the phrase "the fear of the LORD," found repeatedly in the Bible, sounds scary: a paralyzing dread of a powerful, terrifying God. In fact, that phrase means a profound and healthy respect due God because of who he is. It is a respect one gives to a superior, not a colleague or friend. The fear of God is an awe that inspires one to obedience, submission, and worship.

Solomon wrote, "The fear of the LORD is the beginning of wisdom" *(Proverbs 9:10 NIV)*. This reverence keeps a right perspective on an infinite, holy, all-powerful God and finite, flawed, weak people. This is good news, not bad news, because people need a God who is greater than they are.

God pronounces blessing on those who fear him: fulfillment, deliverance, descendants, God's goodness, God's mercy, salvation, blessing, confidence, life, and satisfaction.

ONE-LINERS TO SOAK UP

MOVERS AND SHAKERS

Living the life of faith is the evidence that a person believes the truth. In the parable of the wise and foolish builders, Jesus said that the person who hears his words and puts them into practice is like a man who builds his house on the rock. The person who hears the words of Jesus but does not put them into practice is like a foolish builder who builds his house on sand. (See *Matthew 7:24–27.*) A number of people through the ages have also addressed the idea that it is important not only to talk the talk but also to walk the walk:

1. "Talk doesn't cook rice."—*Chinese proverb*

2. "To dispose a soul to action we must upset its equilibrium."
   —*Eric Hoffer (social writer, 1902–1983)*

3. "I have always thought the actions of men the best interpreters of their thoughts."—*John Locke (British philosopher, 1632–1704)*

4. "First say to yourself what you would be; and then do what you have to do."—*Epictetus (Greek philosopher, 55–135)*

5. "A thought which does not result in an action is nothing much, and an action which does not proceed from a thought is nothing at all."
   —*Georges Bernanos (French writer, 1888–1948)*

6. "I do not believe in fate that falls on men however they act; but I do believe in fate that falls on them unless they act."
   —*G. K. Chesterton (English writer, 1874–1936)*

7. "Don't do nothing just because you can't do everything."
   —*Bob Pierce (World Vision founder, 1914–1978)*

8. "Do what you can, with what you have, where you are."
   —*Theodore Roosevelt (twenty-sixth U.S. president, 1858–1919)*

9. "One does what one is; one becomes what one does."
   —*Robert von Musil (Austrian novelist, 1880–1942)*

10. "Knowing is not enough; we must apply. Willing is not enough; we must do."—*Johann von Goethe (German novelist, 1749–1832)*

11. "Determine never to be idle. No person will have occasion to complain of the want of time who never loses any. It is wonderful how much may be done if we are always doing."
    —*Thomas Jefferson (third U.S. president, 1743–1826)*

12. "It is time for us all to stand and cheer for the doer, the achiever—the one who recognizes the challenge and does something about it."
    —*Vincent Lombardi (football coach, 1913–1970)*

"COLORFUL" THEOLOGY

Color has long played an important part in Christian traditions and practices. As worn or displayed throughout the church at different seasons of the liturgical year (a calendar of holy days and feasts of the church), colors are used to symbolize aspects of the season being celebrated. Specific colors are often associated with specific seasons:

1. *Black.* Physical or spiritual death; used for Good Friday
2. *Blue.* Heaven, truth, and Advent
3. *Brown.* Spiritual death and degradation
4. *Gray.* Repentance, especially during Lent
5. *Green.* Triumph of life over death; liturgical color for Trinity and Epiphany seasons
6. *Purple (violet).* Penitence and mourning; also royalty; liturgical color for Advent and Lent
7. *Red.* Martyred saints; liturgical color for Pentecost
8. *White.* Purity, innocence, and holiness; liturgical color for Christmas and Easter seasons
9. *Gold.* Joy at Jesus' birth (Christmas season); hope inspired by his resurrection (Easter season)
10. *Silver.* Sometimes in place of white for purity, innocence, and holiness, especially at Christmas

Sources: www.ucc.org/worship/colors.htm; www.networks-now.net/litresswraoc /TNLitColor.htm; www.fisheaters.com/colors.html.

MURMUR, MURMUR, COMPLAIN, COMPLAIN

The Israelites were known for their murmuring and complaining as they wandered in the wilderness. Below are things the Israelites might have said as they wandered for forty years between Egypt and the Promised Land:

1. "What, manna again?"
2. "My feet hurt!"
3. "What do you mean there are no bazaars in the wilderness?"
4. "Move again? But we just got here!"
5. "Did he say wondering or wandering?"
6. "Are you sure we shouldn't stop and ask somebody for directions?"
7. "Next time we set up camp, I am *not* living next door to your mother!"
8. "I'm tired of wearing the same old thing!"
9. "This gives a whole new meaning to 'camping trip.'"
10. "Are we there yet?"

AN UNLIKELY BUT
EFFECTIVE EVANGELIST

Bible scholars don't know very much about who he was or how he came to be in the wilderness of the Gerasenes. What they do know from the Bible account of his life is that he came from the Decapolis—the name given to ten Romanized cities in an area that stretches from Damascus to the Dead Sea. He was possessed and tormented by unclean spirits that gave him great physical strength but also caused him to rip his clothes from his body and dwell in caves used as tombs. He roamed among a vast herd of swine intended for Roman sacrifices. Few people in the Bible are described as being in such torment or anguish.

When Jesus encountered this man, he cast out the demons that controlled him. Within moments observers saw the man "sitting at the feet of Jesus, clothed and in his right mind" *(Luke 8:35 NKJV)*. The transformation was instantaneous and complete! The man begged Jesus that he might go with him, but Jesus commanded instead, "Return to your own house, and tell what great things God has done for you" *(v. 39 NKJV)*. The Bible says he "went his way and proclaimed throughout the whole city what great things Jesus had done for him" *(v. 39 NKJV)*. A few months later four thousand families from the Gentile world gathered to hear Jesus and to be miraculously fed by him. Many of these people were from the Decapolis! *(See Matthew 15:29–38.)* How had they heard about Jesus? Very likely from this first "missionary," who freely proclaimed Jesus' miracle-working power over all manner of evil.

THE "FANTASTIC" VOYAGE
OF GEORGE MACDONALD

Could it be that God did not love everyone the same, and that he decided long ago whom he would and would not admit into heaven?

Scotsman George MacDonald grew up in a legalistic Congregational church where he was taught that his future was decided before he was born. MacDonald couldn't reconcile that portrayal of God with the God of love he had read about in the Bible. Surely God loved everyone! And so, after graduating from Aberdeen University, MacDonald studied for the ministry and became the pastor of Trinity Congregational Church. Almost no one there agreed with his beliefs, however, and he was forced to resign his pulpit.

Employment-wise, it was all downhill from there. He taught, and lectured in the U.S., preached now and then, and edited a children's magazine. Mostly, however, he pursued his passion for writing.

Today MacDonald is best known and remembered as a writer of fantasy and children's literature. *At the Back of the North Wind*, now a classic, reflects his gift for infusing his faith into a story that children both enjoy and learn from. MacDonald is also famous for writing *Phantastes, The Princess and the Goblin, Lilith*, and *The Light Princess*, some of his fifty-plus books.

For all his talent, MacDonald did not make much money from his work and had trouble supporting his wife and eleven children. In poor health for much of his life, he had a stroke when he was seventy-four that caused a final decline, and he died in 1905.

BEING A WITNESS

The Greek word for witness has a double-sided meaning. One side means "to tell." A witness is someone who relays what he has personally experienced. The truth, according to the Bible, is established by the agreement of two or more witnesses. The other side of the word's meaning conveys the concept "willing to die" or "dying to tell." A person who is a witness has a sense of urgency and responsibility that he *must* tell what he knows, even to the point of being willing to die for the privilege of telling.

MARANATHA!

Maranatha was an Aramaic or Syriac expression used by the apostle Paul *(1 Corinthians 16:22)*. It subsequently became a word that was used frequently as first-century believers greeted each other or parted from one another. The word literally means "Our Lord comes." It was spoken in reference to Jesus, whose return to this earth was perceived as imminent. The early believers longed to see Jesus again and to welcome him back to this earth as their sovereign King. The expression was one that inspired hope and a compelling urgency to share the gospel with as many people as possible before Jesus arrived.

WHO GETS THE GLORY?

Honor, majesty, splendor, grandeur are synonyms for *glory*. To define the glory of God is to attempt to express God's perfection. Every attribute of God—his love, wisdom, mercy, justice, goodness, character—is perfect. The glory of God is the fullness of all that God is. As God makes himself known, his glory is revealed *(Psalm 111:3)*.

1. Creation displays God's glory *(Psalm 19:1)*.
2. Jesus' role on earth was to glorify God *(John 17:1–4)*.
3. God made people for his glory *(Isaiah 43:7)*.
4. Wrongdoing causes people to "fall short of the glory of God" *(Romans 3:23 NIV)*.
5. Through faith, a person can bring glory to God *(2 Corinthians 3:18)*.

EXCHANGING GIFTS

It was customary in Bible times, as it is today, for national rulers to exchange gifts. When the queen of Sheba came to visit King Solomon, she brought a gift that has been estimated to be worth $15 million! She gave to Solomon 120 talents of gold, spices in great quantity, and precious stones. The gold alone was worth about $7 million. The Bible says that "never again came such abundance of spices as the queen of Sheba gave to King Solomon" *(1 Kings 10:10 NKJV)*. The spices and precious stones were likely worth $7 million to $8 million.

In return, this queen was given "all she desired, whatever she asked" *(v. 13 NKJV)*. The Bible is silent on just what that was! Solomon certainly gave her "according to the royal generosity" *(v. 13 NKJV)*, which meant that he gave her items valued at more than what she gave him. Some Bible scholars also believe that the queen of Sheba went back to her nation with a child that Solomon fathered.

One thing seems certain. The queen of Sheba came to Solomon as a godless skeptic with many questions. She left saying, "It was a true report which I heard. . . . Your wisdom and prosperity exceed the fame of which I heard. Happy are your men and happy are these your servants, who stand continually before you and hear your wisdom! Blessed be the LORD your God, who delighted in you, setting you on the throne of Israel!" *(1 Kings 10:6–9 NKJV)*.

HUMILITY

Pride is considered by many to be the worst of all wrongs. Humility, in contrast, is considered by many to be the most noble of all virtues!

1. "The casting down of our spirits in true humility is but like throwing a ball to the ground, which makes it rebound the higher toward heaven."
   —*John Mason (English cleric, 1706–1763)*

2. "True humility is not an abject, groveling, self-despising spirit; it is but a right estimate of ourselves as God sees us."—*Tryon Edwards (American theologian and great-grandson of Jonathan Edwards, 1809–1894)*

3. "It is easy to look down on others; to look down on ourselves is the difficulty."—*Lord Peterborough (aka Charles Mordaunt, English general, 1658–1735)*

4. "It was pride that changed angels into devils; it is humility that makes men as angels."—*Saint Augustine (bishop of Hippo, 354–430)*

5. "They that know God will be humble; they that know themselves cannot be proud."—*John Flavel (English cleric, 1627–1691)*

6. "Humility is the root, mother, nurse, foundation, and bond of all virtue."—*Saint John Chrysostom (German archbishop, 347–407)*

7. "The Christian is like the ripening corn; the riper he grows the more lowly he bends his head."
   —*Thomas Guthrie (Scottish cleric, 1803–1873)*

8. "Trees that, like the poplar, lift upward all their boughs, give no shade and no shelter whatever their height. Trees the most lovingly shelter and shade us when, like the willow, the higher soar their summits, the lowlier droop their boughs."
   —*Edward George Bulwer (English novelist, 1803–1873)*

9. "It is no great thing to be humble when you are brought low; but to be humble when you are praised is a great and rare attainment."
   —*Saint Bernard of Clairvaux (French clergy, 1091–1153)*

10. "God walks with the humble; he reveals himself to the lowly; he gives understanding to the little ones; he discloses his meaning to pure minds, but hides his grace from the curious and the proud."
    —*Thomas à Kempis (German scholar, 1380–1471)*

11. "After crosses and losses, men grow humbler and wiser."—*Benjamin Franklin (American statesman, inventor, and author, 1706–1790)*

12. "If thou desire the love of God and man, be humble, for the proud heart, as it loves none but itself, is beloved of none but itself."
    —*Francis Quarles (English author, 1592–1644)*

13. "Nothing sets a person so much out of the devil's reach as humility."
    —*Jonathan Edwards (American theologian, 1703–1758)*

14. "Humility is to have a right estimate of one's self—not to think less of himself than he ought."— *Charles H. Spurgeon (English cleric, 1834–1892)*

NOTHING ON HIS OWN

Jesus never claimed to do *any* miracle, sign, or wonder in his own strength, ability, power, or intelligence. He said of himself, "The Son can do nothing by himself; he can do only what he sees his Father doing, because whatever the Father does the Son also does" *(John 5:19 NIV)*. The word for "nothing" in the original Greek language means exactly what it does in English: *nothing!* Jesus chose to live with the same limitations as all men. He performed his miracles as a man totally dependent upon God.

TWO TYPES OF COINS

The Jews' King Herod was allowed by Rome to mint bronze coins but not gold or silver ones. He never put a human head or animal image on his coins—to do so would have offended the Jews. The Roman governors, however, put on their coins images of caesars and symbols associated with their gods. Pontius Pilate, who ordered Jesus' crucifixion, issued a coin with a Roman religious symbol, greatly upsetting the Jews he governed.

FASTEN YOUR BIBLE BELT!

Newspaperman H. L. Mencken was the one who came up with the phrase "Bible Belt." The term first appeared in 1926 in an article in *American Mercury*, a magazine Mencken cofounded and edited. Since that time, it has referred to a part of the U.S. (primarily Southern and Midwestern states) where fundamentalist, conservative Protestant believers who take the Bible literally, reside. Some cities (Nashville, Tulsa, Dallas) are referred to as the "Buckle" of the Belt.

THE MYSTERY OF THE STAIRCASE

Santa Fe, New Mexico, is the site of a special chapel built in the late nineteenth century. When the Loretto Chapel was completed in 1878, it lacked access to the choir loft twenty-two feet above the floor of the nave. Carpenters called in to remedy the problem concluded that access to the loft would have to be by ladder, as there was no room for a staircase in the small chapel. Hoping for a better solution, the nuns of the chapel prayed and asked for the special help of Saint Joseph, the patron saint of carpenters. Legend says that on the ninth day of prayer, a man showed up at the chapel with a donkey and a toolbox, looking for work. Months later an elegant circular staircase was completed, and the carpenter disappeared without pay or thanks. A thorough search for the man yielded no trace.

The stairwell he constructed was innovative for the time, and some of the design considerations still perplex experts today. It has two 360-degree turns, no visible means of support, and was apparently built with wooden pegs instead of nails. Questions also surround the number of stair risers compared with the height of the choir loft, and about the types of wood and other materials used. Over the years many have flocked to Loretto Chapel to see the miraculous staircase, and it has been the subject of many articles, television specials, and movies. To this day the identity of the carpenter remains unknown.

Source: www.lorettochapel.com/.

A PROMISE IS A PROMISE

The Ford Escort made its way down the interstate at a reasonable rate of speed. It was the day before Thanksgiving 1993. Newlywed Kim Carpenter and his wife, Krickitt, were on their way to her parents' house in Phoenix.

The weather was clear. There was nothing to indicate that this would be anything but an uneventful trip.

Everything changed in a matter of seconds. A truck ahead of them suddenly slowed, forcing Krickitt to swerve to avoid an accident.

Too late. The car made contact with a piece of the truck. Then real disaster struck: a truck behind them broadsided their car, sending it flying and turning it upside down.

The Carpenters had been married only ten weeks. Theirs was a slowly built relationship that started with phone calls; she was a telephone sales rep for a sportswear company, and he was a college baseball coach. He placed a lot of orders, he liked her voice, she became interested in him, and soon calls became letters, and photos, and a face-to-face meeting, and finally a proposal and a wedding.

Both Kim and Krickitt are devout believers. It was important to each of them to marry someone who had faith in Jesus. Little did they know how their faith would be tested.

In the accident, Kim suffered some serious injuries, but Krickitt was worse off. She had a head injury that caused swelling in her brain. When the doctors first saw her, they held out little hope for her survival.

Family and friends streamed into the hospital to offer support. Believing that God was the only One who could heal his wife, Kim went to the hospital chapel on two occasions and prayed that God would reduce the swelling in her brain and raise her low blood pressure. Both of these things were critical to her survival. And both situations began to improve right after Kim prayed.

In the following days, Krickitt was moved out of ICU and began to do simple things, such as sitting up and talking. It was clear, though, that it would take a long time for her to get back to normal.

A PROMISE IS A PROMISE (CONT'D)

The road was a lot longer than Kim could ever have imagined. As Krickitt went through occupational, speech, and physical therapy, it became obvious that she'd changed. The friendly, outgoing, bubbly personality was gone, replaced by frustration, anger, and childish behavior. Kim had a hard time coping with these changes, but they weren't the worst result of the accident. Krickitt had the kind of amnesia that erases recent events—in her case, her entire relationship with Kim. He was a stranger.

Fortunately, Krickitt remembered her relationship with God, and it became a life raft that made her situation more endurable.

When Krickitt finally finished with therapy and returned to their home in Las Vegas, New Mexico, Kim hoped for the best. Instead the couple continued to struggle.

Kim spoke one day with Krickitt's therapist, who reminded him that God was still on the case. It was the encouragement he needed.

Some said Kim should divorce Krickitt, but he wouldn't consider it. "I made a vow," he said.

And despite her amnesia, Krickitt was as committed to staying together as he was. The two had a second wedding ceremony—a rededication—in 1996.

Kim and Krickitt Carpenter continue to reside in Las Vegas, New Mexico. Both a book (*The Vow*, published in 2000) and a movie about their experiences are still widely used as examples of how to make a good marriage. Their story has been featured in *People, Reader's Digest, Christian Digest, Dobson's Family News and Focus*, the *New York Times*, the *Los Angeles Times*, and such television programs as *The Oprah Winfrey Show, Dateline, Inside Edition, The Leeza Gibbons Show, The Sally Jesse Rafael Show, The Maury Povich Show, CNN News*, the *700 Club*, CBS's *Day and Date*, the Family Channel, and even MTV.

Source: Kim and Krickitt Carpenter with John Perry, *The Vow* (Nashville: Broadman, 2000). Story update from the Author Review at http://www.amazon.com/Vow-Kim-Krickitt-Carpenter-Story/dp/0805421300.

IF YOU CAN'T STAND THE HEAT . . .

Fire can burn away what's unnecessary and spark new, healthy growth. In the Bible, it also signifies that God is on the scene:

1. God used a pillar of fire to help the Israelites find their way through the wilderness at night *(Exodus 13:21)*.

2. The fire on the altar in the tabernacle (the Israelites' house of worship) had to be kept burning at all times; it was a reminder that God was always with his people *(Leviticus 6:12)*.

3. God's tongue is described as "a consuming fire." This expresses his anger with the disobedient Israelites *(Isaiah 30:27 NIV)*.

4. God's word is "like fire." It burned with anger at prophets who lied to his people *(Jeremiah 23:29 NIV)*.

5. Jesus came to earth to baptize people with the Holy Spirit (who helps humans deal with life) and with fire; this symbolizes that God is always around—he never goes AWOL *(Matthew 3:11)*.

6. God appeared to Moses in a bush that burned without being destroyed. This showed Moses God's power, which he would need to lead the Israelites out of slavery *(Exodus 3:2–5)*.

7. When God came to Mount Sinai to meet with the Israelites, he came "in fire"; the people knew to stand back because this was a holy place *(Exodus 19:16–18 NIV)*.

8. When God sent angels to rescue the prophet Elisha, they looked like chariots of fire *(2 Kings 6:17)*.

9. The "tongues of fire" that landed on people during the day of Pentecost (the celebration of the end of grain harvest) were a sign of the Holy Spirit *(Acts 2:3–4 NIV)*.

10. People who turn away from God are like chaff (seed covering); they'll get burned up with "unquenchable fire" *(Matthew 3:12 NIV)*.

11. People who love God will be put through a fire that will "refine them like silver" and "test them like gold" *(Zechariah 13:9 NIV)*.

12. People who don't want to serve God are like a worthless field that eventually is burned *(Hebrews 6:7–8)*.

13. A person's tongue can say kind things or be like a fire that destroys others—for example, through gossip *(James 3:5–6)*.

14. When the end of the world comes, everything will be destroyed by fire *(2 Peter 3:10)*.

15. When God said he would serve as "a wall of fire" around the city of Jerusalem, he meant he would protect it *(Zechariah 2:4–5 NIV)*.

A POET AGAINST ALL ODDS

Born in Senegal, Africa, in 1753, Phillis was sold into slavery at age seven to John and Susannah Wheatley of Boston. Although originally brought into the Wheatley household as a servant, Phillis was soon accepted as a member of the family. She was raised and educated with the Wheatleys' children. Phillis was a baptized member of the Old South Meeting House (a national landmark in Boston that was a Puritan meetinghouse at the time), a remarkable thing for an African-American of her day.

Phillis quickly learned to read and write English and was reading the Greek and Latin classics and passages from the Bible at age twelve. At thirteen she wrote her first poem. She became a Boston sensation after she wrote a poem on the death of the evangelical preacher George Whitefield.

Most of Phillis's poems reflect her love for God, and stress the theme of Christian salvation. In 1773 a book of thirty-nine of her poems was published in London—the first book to be published by a black American.

Sources: www.lib.udel.edu/ud/spec/exhibits/ treasures/american/wheatley.html; womenshistory.about.com/library/bio/blbio_phillis_wheatley.htm; www.earlyamerica.com/review/winter96/wheatley.html.

ONE FOR THE BOOK

Surveys show that Americans generally believe religion is losing its influence in American culture. But American book-buying habits cast doubt on that belief.

A 2003 survey conducted by the Barna Group reported that nearly half of all adults, and slightly more than half of all teens, had read at least one Christian book the previous year. Many had actually purchased those books. The leading purchasers were Protestant ministers, who bought an average of twenty Christian books in the year covered by the survey.

Source: "Half of All Americans Read Christian Books and One-Third Buy Them," The Barna Group, www.barna.org, Barna Update, 1/27/2003, accessed on 2/25/06.

AN OVERLOOKED CENTER OF CHRISTIANITY

People tend to think of Rome, Jerusalem, and even Canterbury or Constantinople as major centers of Christianity . . . but Kiev?

Many know Kiev as the capital of Ukraine, a nation that was part of the former Soviet Union. A great majority of people today, especially those born after the creation of the Soviet Union or after its downfall, tend to think of the various nations that were once in it as having been not only communistic but also atheistic for centuries. Kiev, however, was the birthplace of the Russian Orthodox Church and was the center of Russian orthodoxy for more than three hundred years. Moscow did not become the headquarters of the Russian Orthodox Church until Metropolitan Peter of Kiev took up residence there in 1326.

Perhaps Kiev's most famous structure is the Pechyorska Lavra, known by most as the Cave Monastery. It is Russia's oldest monastery—founded about 1050 by Antonii Feodosii, a Russian from Lyubetch who had been a monk in Greece. The monastery complex covers fifty-four acres and is located on the banks of the Dnieper River. The Hagia Sophia—a shrine to "Holy Wisdom"—was built in 1040. It had thirteen cupolas, symbolizing Jesus and the twelve apostles, and it stood as a testament to the Christian roots of the city for hundreds of years.

The main church associated with the Cave Monastery, the Cathedral of the Dormition, was built between 1073 and 1078. It was heavily bombed by the German air force in 1941. Several other churches were built on the monastery grounds between the twelfth and the eighteenth centuries, and they continue to attract not only faithful pilgrims but also students of architecture and art.

WHAT'S A WISE PERSON TO DO?

The book of Proverbs has a great deal to say about wisdom and the attributes of the wise person. Below are the foremost characteristics of a person who is steeped in God's wisdom.

1. Hears and increases learning—he will acquire and add to knowledge of what is wise *(Proverbs 1:5)*

2. Hears and heeds wise counsel *(Proverbs 1:5)*

3. Appreciates correction *(Proverbs 9:8)*

4. Quickly receives instruction *(Proverbs 9:9)*

5. Provides for the future *(Proverbs 21:20)*

6. Controls his tongue *(Proverbs 29:11)*

7. Helps others believe in Jesus so they will receive eternal life *(Proverbs 11:30)*

8. Speaks of things that promote health and well-being *(Proverbs 12:18)*

9. Obeys parents *(Proverbs 13:1)*

10. Chooses to associate with those who are wise *(Proverbs 13:20)*

11. Stays out of trouble—departs from evil *(Proverbs 14:16)*

12. Appreciates and rightly uses riches *(Proverbs 13:11)*

13. Uses knowledge rightly *(Proverbs 15:2)*

14. Seeks eternal life *(Proverbs 15:24)*

15. Pacifies the anger of others *(Proverbs 29:8)*

16. Holds his peace in times of strife *(Proverbs 17:28)*

17. Does not overindulge in intoxicating beverages *(Proverbs 20:1)*

18. Puts down crime *(Proverbs 20:26)*

19. Obeys the law *(Proverbs 28:7)*

20. Brings happiness to parents *(Proverbs 10:1)*

21. Eventually rules over those who are foolish *(Proverbs 11:29)*

22. Enjoys favor from those who have authority over him *(Proverbs 14:35)*

23. Speaks only what is true and wise *(Proverbs 16:23)*

24. Has inner strength and confidence *(Proverbs 24:5)*

25. Knows how to defeat spiritual and natural enemies *(Proverbs 21:22)*

RAISE THE FLAG, SALUTE THE FAITH

It is not known who created the first flag, but it is believed that flags originated in India or China. Many of the earliest flags from these countries had images embroidered on them, such as tigers or birds.

Sometime in the Middle Ages, the concept of a national flag took hold in Europe. Many of the leaders of the nations, searching for emblems to adorn these flags, chose the symbol of their patron saints.

In later centuries, and beyond Europe, nations frequently chose to put symbols of religious faith on their flags as well.

During the Crusades, a cross adorned many flags. The cross found its way onto the flags of Great Britain, Denmark, Finland, Greece, Norway, and Sweden.

The flag of the United Kingdom, adopted in 1801 and best known as the Union Jack, incorporates into its design the cross of Saint George (England), the cross of Saint Andrew (Scotland), and the cross of Saint Patrick (Ireland).

Scotland and Ireland have their own flags. Scotland uses an X-shaped cross (for Saint Andrew). The Republic of Ireland has a tricolor flag: a green band for Catholics, an orange band for Protestants, and a white band down the center to signify union between the two.

The flags of the Scandinavian countries—Sweden, Denmark, Finland, Iceland, Norway—sport the Scandinavian cross, a symbol of Christianity. Denmark's flag (1625), called the Dannebrog ("Cloth of the Danes"), is believed to be the oldest national flag in the world.

The Dominican Republic's flag (1844) has a cross at its center, a symbol of faith added by the leader of this nation's inde-

RAISE THE FLAG, SALUTE THE FAITH (CONT'D)

pendence movement. The republic's coat of arms features a Bible opened to the Gospel of Saint John, and in Spanish, "God, Country, Freedom."

Greece has a flag (1822) with a cross prominently featured as well. It represents the nation's Greek Orthodox faith.

Lebanon, a nation that is 30% Christian, has a cedar tree at the center of its flag (1943). The tree, told of in the Bible because its wood was used in the construction of King Solomon's temple, stands for holiness.

Tuvalu, formerly known as the Ellice Islands, adopted a flag in 1978 that incorporates Britain's Union Jack with its three crosses. The young nation's coat of arms includes its motto: "Tuvalu for God."

Moldova, once a part of Romania, gained independence in 1991. Its flag has the nation's coat of arms at the center; pictured is an eagle in whose beak is an Orthodox Christian cross.

Tonga was strongly influenced by Christian missionaries in the nineteenth century. When it was time to design the nation's first flag, leaders placed a cross on it. King George Tupou I later developed a new design: a red background (representing the blood of Jesus when he died on the cross) with a red cross on a square of white in the upper left-hand corner. Tonga law states that no one can ever change the flag's design.

Vatican City has a flag (1929) with expressions of faith all over it. It contains the papal (pope's) colors, yellow and white, which represent the color of Saint Peter's Keys (the "keys" to the kingdom of heaven that Jesus gave to Peter). The emblem on the flag shows the papal crown being supported by the keys.

WOULD YOU HAVE GONE TO KESWICK?

Few Christians know today of the Keswick Conventions, but in the late nineteenth century nearly all evangelicals were eager to hear the latest from Keswick.

Keswick was an annual summer convention held by evangelical believers at Keswick in the Lake District of England. It was founded in 1875 by the vicar of Keswick in the aftermath of massive revivals held by D. L. Moody and his well-known song leader Ira David Sankey. Keswick had as its motto "All one in Christ Jesus," and the keynote speakers each summer became well known for presenting major teachings on prayer, the deeper life of faith, Bible study, and asking the Holy Spirit to be present in a special way in the life of a person. These four things were regarded as important means of helping a person deal with everyday life the way Jesus would. The participants had a zeal for foreign missions and personal holiness. Later, Keswick conferences were held annually in the United States and Canada.

In addition to being an annual event, Keswick became known as a theological system. It rejected the possibility of moral perfection after salvation—popular in many circles in the late nineteenth century—and advocated instead a believer's need to rely on the Holy Spirit and personal expressions of faith to overcome ongoing temptation. The Keswick conventions had a lasting impression on well-known preachers at the turn of the twentieth century, especially A. B. Simpson, R. A. Torrey, and H. A. Ironside. One of the phrases made popular at Keswick was repeated often throughout the twentieth century: "Let go and let God."

IS IT GOOD OR BAD TO BE A PILLAR?

Most people think of "pillars" as being strong support structures—both literally in buildings and figuratively in organizations. Pillars in ancient times, however, were not always associated with buildings, nor were they always good:

1. *Hilltops.* The Hebrew word for hilltop, *matsuq*, refers to something high and narrow—columnlike or pillarlike. The high priest Samuel stated that all the "pillars of the earth" are God's and that he has set the world upon them (*1 Samuel 2:8 NKJV*).

2. *Asherah poles.* The Law of Moses commanded the Israelites to utterly destroy the "groves" (*Deuteronomy 12:3 KJV*) of the heathen, which were not trees but rather carved wooden pillars, similar to totem poles, erected as idols for worship ceremonies.

3. *Salt.* Lot's wife became a pillar of salt during the destruction of Sodom and Gomorrah. Apparently, the fire and brimstone from the sky fell upon her and "froze" her in place so she appeared pillarlike (*Genesis 19:26*).

4. *Stone pillow.* Jacob took the stone he had used as a pillow and set it upright as a small "pillar"—a monument to the vision of his dream—and then poured oil on top of the stone in dedication (*Genesis 28:18 NIV*).

5. *Cloud and fire.* God led the Israelites through the wilderness by means of a pillar of cloud during the day and a pillar of fire at night (*Exodus 13:21–22*). The high column of cloud or fire apparently could be seen by all the Israelites.

6. *Platform for a coronation.* An oak "pillar" was made in Shechem—it likely was a high wooden platform constructed on the flat top of a hill—and used as the place where Abimelech was made king (*Judges 9:6*).

7. *A lasting memorial.* Absalom built a pillar in the King's Valley. His reason? He had no son and saw the monument as the way he would be remembered. He gave the monument his name (*2 Samuel 18:18*).

8. *Pillars with names.* In building the temple, Solomon set two pillars on the porch of the temple and named them Jachin and Boaz. The names literally mean "God has established" and "In God is strength" (*1 Kings 7:21*).

9. *A sign of deliverance.* The prophet Isaiah foretold a day when a pillar, or monument, will be constructed in Egypt to commemorate the deliverance and salvation of the Egyptians (*Isaiah 19:19–22*).

10. *Nebuchadnezzar's image.* A nine-story-high and twelve-feet-wide image, perhaps an obelisk-style pillar, was built in the plains of Dura outside Babylon to show the power of the Babylonians. Nebuchadnezzar required all of his governors to bow to the image, but Shadrach, Meshach, and Abednego refused (*Daniel 3:12*).

ANCIENT WORDS, EVER NEW

The original languages of the Bible are Hebrew, Aramaic, and Greek.

Biblical Hebrew

Most of the Old Testament was originally written in Hebrew. Biblical Hebrew is one of the Semitic languages. (The word *Semite* comes from the name of Noah's oldest son, Shem.) Both Hebrew and Aramaic are part of a language group found mainly in ancient Syria, Lebanon, and Israel. It is believed that Hebrew came from the Canaanite language.

Around AD 200, Hebrew ceased as a living language when the Judean Jews were defeated in battle and survivors were forced to leave Israel. The language was nearly extinct but survived throughout the years, primarily in Jewish religious communities and academic settings. It was revived as the mother tongue of the Jews in the late nineteenth century. Today about 4.6 million people speak "modern" Hebrew.

A few words in the English language are derived from biblical Hebrew, such as *amen, hallelujah*, and *hosanna*. Many names originated in this language, including Adam, Daniel, David, Deborah, Joseph, Rebecca, and Jacob.

Biblical Aramaic

A second language of the original Scriptures, Aramaic, is also a Semitic language. Several Old Testament passages are written in Aramaic (for example, *Daniel 2:4–7:28; Ezra 4:8–6:18; 7:12–26; Jeremiah 10:10–11; Genesis 31:47)*. Several New Testament words and phrases are Aramaic—for example, *Talitha, cumi* ("Little girl, I say to you, arise") in Mark 5:41 *(NKJV)*, *Maranatha* ("O Lord, come!") in 1 Corinthians 16:22 *(KJV)*, and *Golgotha* ("Place of a Skull") in Matthew 27:33 *(NKJV)*. Aramaic has been spoken throughout parts of Syria-Palestine from as early as the ninth century BC to the

ANCIENT WORDS, EVER NEW (CONT'D)

present day in modern dialects. Several dialects of Aramaic are still in use today in parts of Syria near Damascus, southeastern Turkey, western Iran, and southern Iraq.

At one time, Aramaic was considered a universal language. It was the second-most-used diplomatic language for the Persian Empire from the eighth to the fourth centuries BC. It was also one of the most common languages spoken during the emergence of Christianity. Jesus probably spoke a dialect of Aramaic. In the first century AD, Aramaic, in one dialect or another, was the common daily tongue of the Palestinian Jews, though it is probable that many Jews also spoke Hebrew and Greek.

Biblical Greek

The original language of all the New Testament books, biblical Greek is classified as Koine Greek, a common dialect used in the everyday language from the fourth century BC to the sixth century AD. It differs slightly due to the influence of both Hebrew and Aramaic.

The significance of Greek for the study of the Bible is invaluable. Not only was the entire New Testament written in Greek, but a major translation of the Old Testament was done in Greek. It is known as the Septuagint, which was compiled in the third to second centuries BC for Jews living in Alexandria, Egypt, who spoke only Greek. In addition, several manuscripts found among the Dead Sea Scrolls are in Greek. New Testament scholar Gleason Archer has noted that Greek was the ideal language for the gospel: "Accurate in expression, beautiful in sound, and capable of great rhetorical force, it furnished an ideal vehicle for the proclamation of God's message to man, transcending Semitic barriers and reaching out to all the Gentile races."

Source: Gleason Archer quote from Merrill C. Tenney, ed., *Zondervan Pictorial Encyclopedia of the Bible*, vol. 3 (Grand Rapids, MI: Zondervan, 1975), 870.

THE CHAIN GANG

Imprisonment has sometimes been a means of persecuting righteous people for serving God. False accusations, jealous authorities, and betrayals have led to false charges and arrests. But rarely is that the end of the story—imprisonments of godly people often are a stepping-stone to a higher purpose.

1. *Joseph.* Falsely accused by Potiphar's wife, Joseph was sent to prison but from there was promoted to prime minister (*Genesis 39:20*).

2. *Pharaoh's cupbearer.* This servant was put in prison with Joseph but later was restored to his position and was instrumental in bringing about Joseph's release from prison (*Genesis 40:2–3*).

3. *Samson.* Betrayed by Delilah, Samson ground grain in prison but later, as a prisoner, killed more enemy Philistines in one day than he had in his entire life to that point (*Judges 16:21*).

4. *Jeremiah.* Accused of deserting to the Babylonians, Jeremiah was put in prison but was later released and ultimately was allowed to escape to Egypt (*Jeremiah 37:11–15*).

5. *John the Baptist.* Herod had him imprisoned for criticizing his marriage to Herodias, but while in prison he received a personal message of encouragement sent by Jesus (*Matthew 14:3–4*).

6. *Jesus.* Betrayed by Judas, Jesus was imprisoned for several hours before his crucifixion, but his imprisonment allowed him an opportunity to proclaim his identity in face-to-face encounters with the high priest Caiaphas, the Roman procurator Pilate, and King Herod (*Matthew 26–27*).

7. *The apostles.* Jealous religious authorities jailed the apostles, but as a result, they had an opportunity to declare Jesus openly to high-ranking officials (*Acts 5:17–19*).

8. *Peter.* Imprisoned by King Herod, Peter was freed by an angel as believers prayed (*Acts 12:3–14*).

9. *Paul.* He was imprisoned several times for telling others about Jesus, but it was while in prison that Paul wrote many of the letters that are now part of the New Testament (*Acts 21–26*).

10. *Silas.* Put in prison with Paul, he helped lead the jailer and his family to faith in Jesus (*Acts 16:19–33*).

THEY RECEIVED PAUL'S LETTERS

The apostle Paul is credited with writing at least thirteen of the twenty-seven books of the New Testament. Here are the places and people to whom his letters were addressed:

1. *Rome.* The book of Romans was written to believers living in Rome.

2. *Corinth.* Two letters, 1 and 2 Corinthians, were written to the church in Corinth, Greece. Some scholars believe that 2 Corinthians is actually two letters linked together as one in the New Testament.

THEY RECEIVED PAUL'S LETTERS (CONT'D)

3. *Galatia.* The book of Galatians was written to several churches in the region of Galatia, which is now northern Turkey.

4. *Ephesus.* Paul taught for at least two years in Ephesus, on the western coast of what is now Turkey. He no doubt had many faithful friends among those reading the book of Ephesians.

5. *Philippi.* The book of Philippians was written to the church at Philippi, Greece.

6. *Colossae.* The book of Colossians was written to believers in Colossae, Greece.

7. *Thessalonica.* Two letters, 1 and 2 Thessalonians, were written to the first-century church in Thessalonica, Greece.

8. *Timothy.* The New Testament has two letters, 1 and 2 Timothy, written from Paul to his faithful coworker Timothy.

9. *Titus.* Paul wrote one letter, the book of Titus, to his coworker Titus.

10. *Philemon.* One of the shortest books in the entire Bible, the book of Philemon is Paul's letter on behalf of a slave named Onesimus to his owner, a man named Philemon.

IT JUST TAKES TWO

The Bible is full of numbers, and most are significant. These verses show that only two people or things, a seemingly insignificant amount, are more than sufficient in the eyes of God:

1. God created two lights for Earth's benefit: the sun and the moon (*Genesis 1:16*).

2. When Mary and Joseph presented Jesus in the temple for the first time, they were required to bring two doves or two young pigeons to sacrifice (*Luke 2:22–24*).

3. Jesus sent out his disciples two by two, giving them authority over evil spirits (*Mark 6:7*).

4. When one person won't admit an infraction against another, the wronged party takes two witnesses to confront the wrongdoer (*Matthew 18:15–17*).

5. When two people agree on something and pray, God will act (*Matthew 18:19*).

6. When at least two of Jesus' followers come together, Jesus is right there too (*Matthew 18:20*).

7. There are two unchangeable things: God's promises and his vows (*Hebrews 6:17–18*).

8. All of God's requirements hinge on two things: loving him and loving your neighbor (*Matthew 22:34–40*).

9. The widow's seemingly small offering of two copper coins was actually a great gift (*Luke 21:1–4*).

COUNT YOUR BLESSINGS!

An old gospel song says, "Count your blessings, name them one by one." Below are twenty-five things the Bible says are among God's blessings:

1. *Dominion.* God alone has all dominion *(Psalm 22:28)*, and he shares that with humans to rule over creation. With that comes the responsibility to take care of the gifts of creation. God also gives people authority over other people, with the responsibility to provide loving care.

2. *Assurance.* God is a personal God, and he can be known with certainty and confidence. Scripture says, "Draw near to God . . . in full assurance of faith" *(Hebrews 10:22 NIV)*. God is there for each individual— and that's a fact to count on!

3. *Eternal life.* The gift of God is eternal life to all who believe in Jesus *(1 John 5:12–13)*. Eternal life is more than "forever after"; it is also "here and now." Eternal life is about quality of life, not just quantity.

4. *Fellowship with God.* Adam and Eve had perfect fellowship with God until they disobeyed him. And when they did, they hid. But God came looking for them. God still seeks out each person and provides everything needed to have the gift of a relationship with him.

5. *Fellowship with others.* The community of believers is close-knit and caring. In the early church, believers devoted themselves to having fellowship with one other, breaking bread, and praying *(Acts 2:42)*. God intends for believers to share life with others. That way, good things get better, and the hard things aren't quite as hard.

6. *Power.* God knows that life is difficult and that people need help. His power is available to believers; it's the same power that brought Jesus back to life *(Romans 8:11)*. God's power provides spiritual strength and the ability to know his love *(Ephesians 3:16–21)*.

7. *Grace.* God took the initiative to meet the human need for salvation. By God's grace, what was dead has been made alive, what was old has been made new, and what was lost has been found. God's grace is offered only as a gift. Those who want God's grace must receive it from him *(Ephesians 2:8)*.

8. *Understanding.* Without Jesus, humanity stumbles in darkness, unable to know what is good. With Jesus, humans can understand ultimate truth and make wise choices. Solomon realized that his task to govern the people was more than he could do on his own, so he asked God for an "understanding heart"—and he is considered the wisest person of all time *(1 Kings 3:9)*.

COUNT YOUR BLESSINGS! (CONT'D)

9. *Joy.* Joy is lasting; happiness is temporary. Joy comes from the Holy Spirit *(Romans 14:17)*, not from situations or circumstances. Because of that, a person can have joy even when things are going badly *(1 Peter 1:6–9)*.

10. *Justice.* To live in a just society is a blessing. To work to make the right thing happen for others is a blessing—the hungry get fed, a child in poverty has opportunity, the homeless have a place to sleep, a person who is beat down has someone to help him up *(Jeremiah 31:23)*.

11. *Power.* God is all-powerful and all good. He created the earth by his power and rules by power. God uses his power to help people *(2 Chronicles 25:8)*. He even shares his power with people *(Psalm 68:35)*. Power is both a blessing and a responsibility.

12. *Longevity.* Life is a blessing. Long life is an even greater blessing. Wisdom is one of the fruits of long life; respect is due to those who live long. Long life is not guaranteed, but those who reach old age are blessed *(Psalm 91:16)*.

13. *Rest.* God rested after his work of creation *(Genesis 2:2)*. The "rest" that comes when work is complete is a sense of peace, knowing that it takes more than personal effort to be fruitful; it takes trusting in God to do his part, to do what only he can do.

14. *Perseverance.* Life isn't easier for believers than for anyone else; in fact, it may be harder. Believers need perseverance—also called endurance—to keep going in spite of disappointment and difficulty. God blesses his people with the ability to persevere and remain hopeful *(Matthew 10:22)*.

15. *Family.* God made families to provide for the most basic of human needs—mutual love and caring, protection and nurture, food and shelter. He even sets the "solitary" in families *(Psalm 68:5–6 NKJV)*. The church is a type of family, recognizing God as the Head and other people as "brothers and sisters." In the family of God, each person shares the responsibility to love one another.

16. *Favor.* In a very real sense, knowing God is like being a child of the King of the universe. God hears the appeals of each person and lovingly responds with all the resources of the universe at his command *(Philippians 4:19)*.

17. *Love.* "The greatest of these is love" *(1 Corinthians 13:13 NIV)*. Of all the gifts of God, love is the greatest. Love reveals best what God is like. It is how he wants to make himself known to other people. When people love others, they show them what God is like.

COUNT YOUR BLESSINGS! (CONT'D)

18. *Provision.* Wealth is indeed a blessing. The question is, "What is the wealth being used for?" The greatest blessing is in using wealth to bless other people. That's what God does with his wealth *(Psalm 132:15)*.

19. *Healing.* God's plan is for perfect health for everyone forever *(Exodus 15:26; Revelation 22:2)*. People's disobedience corrupted God's perfection, making the human being finite and subject to injury and illness. God's redemption covers everything, bringing health and healing to body, mind, and spirit.

20. *Holy Spirit.* The Holy Spirit is God's presence with his people on earth. The Holy Spirit is a blessing and brings blessing—filling God's people with the character and power of Jesus *(Acts 1:8)*.

21. *Salvation.* God has provided everything needed to know him and have a relationship with him, and that is salvation. The one condition is that salvation is offered as a gift and has to be received as a gift *(Ephesians 2:8)*.

22. *Strength.* Strength for the believer is a paradox. The apostle Paul said that when he was weak, then he was strong *(2 Corinthians 12:9–10)*! Paul even boasted in his weakness so he could know Jesus' strength. Human weakness is the ideal opportunity for the display of divine power.

23. *Freedom.* Disobeying God keeps people from living the life he had in mind for them from before creation. Jesus' sacrifice on the cross frees people from wrongdoing, selfishness, and fear. Living the life God intended is freedom to be who God created you to be. It's the best life possible *(John 8:36)*.

24. *Intercession.* Praying for others is an opportunity to bless them, even before they know they need—or want—a blessing! People have many kinds of needs, and God invites us to bring all those needs and requests—whatever they are—to him. God hears and answers prayer *(James 5:16)*!

25. *Opportunity to bless.* The greatest reason to seek God's blessing is to be a blessing to others *(Genesis 12:2)*!

CHRISTMAS DATING

In the early years of Christianity, Easter, not Christmas, was the main holiday. The celebration of Jesus' birth was observed at different times throughout the year, and it wasn't until the fourth century that a specific date was set for it.

No one knows exactly on what day Jesus was born, or even exactly in what year, but both Pope Julius I (in AD 336) and, as mentioned earlier, Roman emperor Constantine (in AD 360) have been credited with choosing December 25 to celebrate his birthday. The date coincided with the pagan winter solstice rituals (December 21–22) celebrated in many cultures. Pope Julius saw this as an opportunity to replace the popular pagan festivals with a Christian observance. The word *Christmas* is a contraction of "Christ's Mass"; this liturgical mass began shortly after Jesus died as an observance honoring his birth.

First called the Feast of the Nativity, the custom of Christmas observance spread to Egypt by 432 and to England by the end of the sixth century. By the end of the eighth century, the celebration of Christmas had spread all the way to Scandinavia. Today Christmas is observed around the world. An enormous number of customs—with secular, religious, or national dimensions—surround Christmas, and these customs vary from nation to nation. Some Orthodox churches observe Christmas on January 6–7, holding to the old Julian calendar named after Julius Caesar.

Sources: www.twopaths.com; www.historychannel.com/exhibits/holidays/christmas/real2.html; www.tartanplace.com/christmas/xmashistory/constantineconverts.html.

CAVE YEN?

Spelunkers and other cave lovers find Israel to be exactly their kind of place. The Holy Land is a land of porous sandstone, limestone, and chalk. The result? Many natural caves. They were used as dwelling places (*Genesis 19:30*), hiding places (*1 Samuel 22:1*), and burial places (*John 11:38*). Caves were also used as stables, so it's possible that Jesus was born in a cave. They were dry and ideal for storage—the Dead Sea Scrolls survived in caves nearly two thousand years without much deterioration.

STAR POWER

The six-sided Star of David, the Magen David, is the official symbol of the Jewish people. Where it came from is not certain, but legend says it represents King David's shield or an emblem on his shield. The six points of the hexagram point north, east, south, west, up, and down—a symbol of the almighty power of God. The Star of David was adopted as the official emblem for the Jewish people by the Zionist Congress in 1897.

Sources: www.menorah.org/starofdavid.html;
www.aish.com/literacy/concepts/Star_of_David.asp.

THE BEST BIBLE

Authenticity and readability are two factors to consider when choosing a Bible to purchase or give. One factor in selecting a Bible is whether the version is a translation or a paraphrase. A Bible translation provides authentic, precise interpretation from the Bible's original texts. A paraphrase is a "retelling" of the Bible in modern language. It isn't as true to the original languages, but it can be more readable. The best Bible version to choose, however, is the translation that will be read!

SACRED SITES

Adherents of most of the world's major religions have this in common: a specified place to gather for prayer and other communal activities.

A synagogue is a Jewish house of prayer and study; it is the equivalent of a Christian church or Muslim mosque. People gather for prayer in the sanctuary, the main room of the synagogue. Jewish people can pray anywhere to satisfy the obligations of daily prayer. There are certain Jewish prayers, however, that can only be said in the presence of a minyan, a quorum of ten adult men. Torah readings are also part of the synagogue service. The Torah scrolls are held in the ark, the most important feature of the sanctuary. People stand whenever the ark is open and when the Torah is carried to or from the ark. A synagogue is also a place of religious education for children, and a place to gather for social events.

The Islamic center of worship is called a mosque. The mosque is an important part of a Muslim's life. It is where Muslims gather to pray, and it is also used as a community center for social activities. It is considered a virtue to go to a mosque to say prayers. Muslims are expected to be in a state of purity of body, mind, and soul before entering a mosque, and to perform purification rituals in the fountains provided for washing before prayers. Worshippers must remove their shoes before entering the carpeted prayer hall. Muslims lie prostrate in their prayer; therefore the mosque must be clean. In most mosques around the world, men and women pray in separate areas.

Sources: www.jewfaq.org/shul.htm#Items; www.religionfacts.com/judaism/practices/synagogue.htm; Lexicorient.com/e.o/mosque.htm.

SIGNS OF THE END

There's been a lot of talk about the end of the world since the Left Behind series of books was published. Through the centuries, Jesus' followers have believed that he will return to earth a second time. Jesus said in Matthew 24 that in the days leading up to his arrival, there will be trouble the likes of which the world has never seen. Throughout the Bible, there are vivid descriptions of what will happen during this time of trouble:

1. There will be horrible wars (*Matthew 24:6–7*).
2. There will be lots of "carrying on" (*Luke 17:28 MSG*).
3. Many false messiahs will prowl around (*Matthew 24:5*).
4. Jesus' followers will be persecuted (*Matthew 24:9*).
5. Food will be scarce (*Revelation 6:5–6*).
6. Beasts will kill many humans (*Revelation 6:8*).
7. There will be powerful earthquakes (*Revelation 6:12*).
8. "Strange events" in the skies, and "strange tides" at sea, will occur (*Luke 21:25 NLT*).
9. The moon will turn to blood (*Joel 2:31*).
10. Trees and grass will burn (*Revelation 8:7*).
11. "Fiery mountains" will pelt the earth (*Revelation 8:8–11 CEV*).
12. Water will be poisoned (*Revelation 8:10–11*).
13. The dark day of judgment will arrive (*Joel 2:2*).
14. God will track down wrongdoers (*Amos 9:2–3*).
15. Idol worship will run rampant (*Revelation 9:20*).
16. The sun will scorch people like fire (*Revelation 16:8–9*).
17. "Babylon," the power base of the Antichrist (the beast), will burn (*Revelation 18:2–9*).
18. "Stinking sores" will afflict millions (*Revelation 16:2 MSG*).
19. Saints (God's people) will be martyred (*Revelation 17:6*).
20. The Antichrist will rule the world (*Revelation 13:1–8*).
21. The dead will remain unburied (*Isaiah 34:3*).
22. The earth will be wasted (*Isaiah 24:1*).
23. People will die "on their feet" (*Zechariah 14:12 MSG*).
24. The good news: followers of Jesus will be rewarded with eternal life in heaven (*Luke 18:29–30*).

YA GOTTA HAVE IT

What is it that a person most needs, according to a popular show tune? Ya gotta have heart!

In Scripture, the heart refers to a person's inner self. It's what's at a person's deepest center—his being, his moral choices, who he is when no one else is around. It is with the heart that a person seeks and responds to God. A "hard" heart keeps a person from God.

The heart determines the outcome of a person's life. Just as the physical heart determines physical life and well-being, so the spiritual heart determines spiritual life and well-being. How does one maintain a vital, healthy spiritual heart? Read the Word of God *(Psalm 119:11)*, love God *(Deuteronomy 6:5)*, and ask God for a "new" heart *(Ezekiel 36:26)*.

LIVE THE PASSION

A vocation is what a person is created to do. Not all vocations are careers, jobs, or produce income. Vocations have another purpose—fulfilling God's calling on a person's life. The word comes from the Latin *vocare*, meaning "to call." For many, a vocation is a call to full-time religious life. But for most people, a vocation is what they most "need" to do. It's that activity that energizes heart, mind, and soul. It's what makes their hearts race with enthusiasm.

A vocation is a discernment, not a decision. It takes listening to determine one's vocation—listening to one's own heart and listening to God's voice. According to author Frederick Buechner, a vocation is the "place where your deep gladness and the world's deep hunger meet."

Source: Frederick Buechner, *Wishful Thinking: A Theological ABC* (Harper San Francisco, 1973), 95.

THE BIG PICTURE

It comes from the German word *Weltanschauung*, and everyone has one whether they know it or not. It's a worldview, a perspective on life and reality. A worldview is like a pair of lenses through which a person understands life and the world around him.

Everyone believes something. Whether the belief is about society, marriage, or education, each belief element becomes part of a total belief system. Beliefs are shaped by personal reflection and thinking and by the whole context of people and events surrounding each individual from birth. Factors such as heredity, culture, social structures, childhood experiences, family, coworkers, and neighbors all influence personal belief.

Understanding what shapes a person's belief system can help that person—or a therapist or counselor—better understand the person's behavior. Understanding a belief system can also help answer questions such as these: How well does the person function in the world? How does he impact other people? What gives the person a valid purpose for life?

According to Brian Walsh and Richard Middleton, authors of *The Transforming Vision: Shaping a Christian Worldview*, a worldview addresses the ultimate questions:

Who am I? What is the nature and significance of human beings?

Where am I? What is the origin and nature of the world in which we live?

What's wrong? How do we account for the brokenness in the world?

THE BIG PICTURE (CONT'D)

What's the remedy? How can the brokenness be remedied?

A worldview is either undermined or confirmed by one's daily experience of life. For example, if a person believes that money buys happiness, yet finds himself less happy attempting to acquire more stuff, he might begin to question the validity of his worldview. An individual who understands life from a totally scientific point of view yet is unable to come to terms with mortality might experience a "crisis" related to his worldview.

Believers in Jesus begin with the basic principle that God as Creator gives meaning to life and reveals himself to humanity. Humanists think there is no revelation, that religion is a rational construct. Atheists deny God's existence, claiming it cannot be scientifically verified. Agnostics say humanity cannot know whether God exists, the scientific process is the key to understanding life, and religion is irrelevant.

A believer's worldview is grounded in the belief that God is a personal, moral God. He is both Creator and Sustainer of the universe. Humanity is God's unique creation, made in his image with the capacity to have a relationship with him. For a believer's worldview to be genuine, it ultimately must be biblical.

SO MUCH FOCUS ON A PLACE SO SMALL

Israel is so small that a soaring eagle can see almost all of it at once on a clear day. From north to south, Israel is little more than 150 miles in length. The distance east to west is 100 miles at its widest point. The nation is only a little larger than the state of New Jersey. Square foot for square foot, no other part of the world has played such a historic role in human history. Israel is positioned at the crossroads of three continents—Africa, Asia, and Europe.

Its highest point is the snow-topped Mount Hermon at 9,400 feet. The lowest point, the Dead Sea, has a tropical climate and is the lowest place on the land surface of the earth. The Great Rift that extends four thousand miles from Turkey into Africa runs through Israel and forms the Jordan River, the Sea of Galilee, and the Dead Sea.

GOD BLOGGERS

A "blog" (contraction of "Web log") is a Web site where comments and journals are posted on a regular basis and displayed in reverse chronological order. Blogs are intended for the general public and usually focus on a particular subject. First appearing in 1995, blogs have become a popular means of communicating and creating Internet communities. According to the Pew Internet and American Life Project, at the end of 2004 eight million U.S. adults reported having created a blog.

Believers are among the growing millions participating in the blogging movement. Blogs are used for influencing public opinion, engaging in theological dialogue, and allowing for pastoral discussion. The first-ever Christian bloggers convention, GodBlogCon, was held at Biola University in 2005. Some Christian bloggers are forming and joining cyberchurches and using pod-cast technology (audio computer files distributed over the Internet) for evangelistic purposes around the world. Futurists predict that the Internet will continue to aid the spread of Christianity, but that cyberchurches will never replace "brick-and-mortar" churches.

Source: www.christiantoday.com/news/life/internets.biggest.year.of.growth.impacting.christianity/280.htm.

THE ESSENCE OF FRIENDSHIP

Friends are without question one of life's greatest joys, and making friends is an art to be cultivated.

1. "To have a good friend is one of the highest delights of life; to be a good friend is one of the noblest and most difficult undertakings."—*Author Unknown*

2. "Friendship is born at that moment when one person says to another: 'What? You, too? I thought I was the only one.'"
—*C. S. Lewis (author, 1898–1963)*

3. "As a ship is tried in the furnace, so friends are tried in adversity."
—*Menander (Greek playwright, 342–291 BC)*

4. "It's so much more friendly with two."—*A. A. Milne, in words given to the character Piglet (British author, 1882–1956)*

5. "The best mirror is an old friend."
—*George Herbert (British poet, 1593–1633)*

6. "A real friend is one who walks in when the rest of the world walks out."—*Walter Winchell (commentator, 1897–1972)*

7. "A friend is someone who knows the song in your heart and sings it back to you when you have forgotten how it goes."
—*Author Unknown*

8. "A friend is a present you give yourself."
—*Robert Louis Stevenson (Scottish novelist, 1850–1894)*

9. "Hold a true friend with both your hands."—*Nigerian proverb*

10. "The best way to destroy an enemy is to make him a friend."
—*Abraham Lincoln (sixteenth U.S. president, 1809–1865)*

11. "One who looks for a friend without faults will have none."
—*Hasidic saying*

12. "My friends are my estate."
—*Emily Dickinson (American poet, 1830–1886)*

A PENNY'S WORTH OF WISDOM

A woman and her husband were once entertained at a very posh restaurant by the husband's wealthy boss. As they entered the restaurant together that evening, the boss stopped suddenly, stared at the sidewalk, then retrieved a darkened penny from the pavement and smiled as though he'd found a fortune.

As the evening wore on, the woman could no longer contain her curiosity as to what made the penny so valuable to him.

"On it are the words 'In God We Trust,'" he said. "If I trust in God, the name of God is holy, even on a coin. God drops a message right in front of me telling me to trust him? Who am I to pass it by? I pick the coin up as a response to God that I do trust in him. For a short time, at least, I cherish it as if it were gold. I think of it as God's way of starting a conversation with me."

Then the man added, "Lucky for me, God is patient and pennies are plentiful!"

FOUR LINES WORTH SINGING . . .
OVER AND OVER AGAIN

Thomas Ken (1637–1711) did not seem destined for greatness. His parents died when he was a child. Raised by other family members, he followed a path that was typical for a number of English boys without family occupations to pursue or a family estate to manage. He attended Oxford University and somewhere along the way decided that the life of the church was for him. And so he was ordained in 1662.

Ken had a passion for the ministry, but he was also brutally honest. If he saw sin in others, he pointed it out. That included monarchs. His honesty earned him a prison term at one point.

In the midst of his ups and downs, Ken wrote hymns. Protestant churchgoers of the past three hundred years have since become very familiar with the last four lines of three of his hymns; those lines are now called the Doxology, which begins, "Praise God from whom all blessings flow . . ." (A doxology is a short hymn of praise and thanksgiving.)

Source: Kenneth W. Osbeck, *101 Hymn Stories* (Grand Rapids, MI: Kregel, 1982), 66–68.

IS THERE A PASTOR IN THE HOUSE (AND SENATE)?

The year was 1774. Fed up with Great Britain, American colonists created the Continental Congress, which met for the first time in Philadelphia. There were plenty of issues to discuss, including one with far-reaching ramifications. Jacob Duche, an Episcopal priest, was selected to serve as chaplain.

Thus began a tradition that has seen only one brief interruption since.

After America became the United States in 1789, the Senate and the House of Representatives each appointed its own chaplain. The Senate chose an Episcopalian, Samuel Provoost of New York. The House chose a Presbyterian, William Lynn of Pennsylvania.

How is it that these legislative bodies were allowed to make these appointments, given concerns over the separation of church and state?

That question was settled in 1983. The Supreme Court pointed out that the House and the Senate have the right, granted by the Constitution, to appoint their own officers, with no restrictions.

About that "brief interruption": It occurred from 1855 to 1861. The House brought in local clergymen, because appointments were becoming popularity contests. The Senate followed suit from 1857 to 1859. When volunteers turned out to be unreliable, both chambers went back to appointing chaplains.

Chaplains' responsibilities resemble those of any pastor: offering spiritual counsel, holding Bible studies, performing weddings and funerals, and visiting the sick in the hospital. There is one big difference: the chaplains open legislative sessions with prayer.

Probably the best-known Senate chaplain was Peter Marshall, who served from 1947 to 1949. His life story became a movie, *A Man Called Peter*.

FEARLESS AND FAITH-FULL

An ordinary Dutch woman, Corrie ten Boom (1892–1983) worked with her father in the family watch repair business. When World War II broke out in Europe, her "ordinary" life ended and her faith was tested. The ten Boom family either had to play it safe and ignore what was happening to their Jewish neighbors or risk their lives and stand by their convictions. The family chose to open their home as a hiding place for Jews seeking refuge. In 1944, the Gestapo raided their home. Corrie, her sister Betsy, and their father were sent to concentration camps. Only Corrie survived.

Corrie committed to carry on the struggle against injustice and anti-Semitism after World War II. She traveled to sixty-four countries in thirty-three years of public ministry. Her autobiography, *The Hiding Place*, told the story of her family and her faith. The book was made into a major motion picture by the same title. Her message—always conveyed in very simple, down-to-earth language and illustrations—was consistently a message of God's mercy, love, and forgiveness.

Sources: www.intouch.org/myintouch/mighty/portraits/corrie_ten_boom_19770; www.usoe.k12.ut.us/curr/char_ed/stories/sketches/tenboom.html.

A UNIFIED SNEEZE

The graduates walked into the crowded auditorium, their maroon gowns flowing and the traditional caps tilted at various angles. Dads swallowed hard behind broad smiles, and moms freely brushed away tears. It was May 20, 2001—graduation day at Washington Community High School in Washington, Illinois.

This class would not pray during the commencement ceremony— not by choice but because a recent court ruling prohibited it. The principal and student speakers carefully stayed within the legal guidelines. Their speeches were inspirational, but no one asked for divine guidance or recognized God.

The ceremony was nearly over when a student walked to the microphone, stood in silence for a moment, and then . . . every one of his classmates sneezed! The "speaker" looked at his audience and said, "*God bless you*—each and every one of you!" And he walked offstage.

The audience exploded into standing-ovation applause.

IT'S A GOOD DAY TO PRAY

When did America observe its first National Day of Prayer?

Some might assume that it's a modern innovation, something that came out of the Jesus Movement of the late 1960s and early 1970s. Or perhaps it goes back as far as World War I or World War II, when the nation was suffering through times marked by a great loss of life.

Actually, the first National Day of Prayer was declared before the official founding of the United States of America.

It happened in 1775. America was on the verge of standing on its own. Members of the Continental Congress looked around and said in effect, "We're about to do something big here: start a new nation. We need all the help we can get!" And so they asked the people to pray.

President Abraham Lincoln also felt a need to call the nation to its knees. His 1863 proclamation, in the midst of the Civil War, declared a day of "humiliation, fasting, and prayer."

The National Day of Prayer became "official" in 1952, thanks to a joint resolution by Congress and President Harry Truman. It was President Ronald Reagan, in 1988, who approved an amendment that set a specific date for prayer: the first Thursday in May.

According to the National Day of Prayer Web site, the day is now treated like many other holidays, having earned a place on Hallmark calendars. It is observed, the site says, across the nation at state capitols, in schools and businesses, and in churches and homes.

Source: www.ndptf.org.

THE NAME ABOVE ALL OTHERS

Believers call God by many names—Father, Creator, and Lord, among others. The Israelites in Old Testament times were much more circumspect when speaking God's name.

The original Hebrew text of the Old Testament records God's name as "YHWH," translated as "Yahweh" or "Jehovah," both meaning "Lord." The Hebrew language has no vowels; readers "fill in the blanks" as they're reading.

One reason the Israelites had such great respect for God's name was that he commanded them to do so, as in Exodus 20:7: "You shall not misuse the name of the LORD your God" (NIV). Assuming that merely speaking his name would invoke his anger, they instead called him "Adonai" (another Hebrew word meaning "Lord").

Yahweh is also translated as "I AM WHO I AM" *(Exodus 3:14 NIV)*. "I AM" denoted absolute supremacy and omnipresence.

THEY CAN GO HOME AGAIN

Israel is considered the homeland of the Jews once again, but for centuries the Jews had no designated political "home."

In 721 BC and 586 BC, the Assyrians and the Babylonians, respectively, drove large numbers of Jews out of Israel. A second widespread dispersion of Jews to other parts of the world occurred after Rome destroyed the second temple in Jerusalem in AD 70. Together, these dispersions of Jews are known as the "Diaspora."

Since the Diaspora began, Jews have chosen or been forced to make new homes for themselves on nearly every continent.

In 1948 Israel became a nation once again. The Jews believe that Israel has always belonged to them. In Genesis 15:18, God promised them the land "from the river of Egypt to the great river, the Euphrates" *(NIV)*.

Many Jews have returned to their homeland in the past sixty or so years. Israel has a law, called the "Law of Return," which says that any Jew currently living elsewhere can move to Israel and be granted citizenship.

OYE!

Is Yiddish a real language? Did Old Testament or New Testament people speak it?

Yiddish was the vernacular language of most Jews in Eastern and Central Europe before World War II. Today it is spoken by descendants of those Jews living in the United States, Israel, and other parts of the world.

Yiddish in Yiddish means "Jewish." While the grammar and vocabulary are basically Germanic, Yiddish is written using the right-to-left letters of the Hebrew alphabet (some of them used differently than for writing Hebrew). Yiddish has been described as German with a lot of "schmaltz" reflecting the turbulent journey of the Jewish people through the centuries.

Yiddish most likely developed somewhere between the ninth and twelfth centuries as Jews from France and Italy migrated to Germany and began to incorporate language elements of French, Italian, and German with Hebrew. As Jews settled in Eastern Europe during the late Middle Ages, Slavic elements were incorporated into Yiddish.

English words and phrases have entered Yiddish and become an integral part of the language as it is spoken in the United States and other English-speaking countries.

Today Yiddish is spoken by about four million Jews around the world, especially those in Israel, Europe, and the United States. But not every Jew who speaks Yiddish can communicate with every other Yiddish speaker in the world. There are two Yiddish dialects, one of which is further subdivided. Yiddish is especially popular among the Orthodox Jewish communities of the greater New York area and in modern-day Israel.

Sources: www.yivo.org/archive/yiddish/yiddish.htm; www.du.edu/dumagazine/ summer2006/academic.html; www.jewishgen.org/databases/GivenNames/ yiddish.htm.

RETIREMENT HOME BECOMES
TOURIST ATTRACTION

Arkansas' Ozark hills are a beauty to behold. That's what Jim Reed, a native Arkansan, thought as he was selecting a place to retire. What better place to build a home than smack-dab in the middle of some wooded acres, far from the congestion of a big city and close to nature? That was the plan, anyway.

Plans have a way of changing.

As more and more people began dropping by the future home site, admiring the view, Reed came up with a better idea: he would build a chapel that others could visit and enjoy.

And not just any chapel—a chapel made of glass, so visitors could see the woods and the hills and reflect on God and the beautiful world he created.

Building projects are rarely easy, and what became known as Thorncrown Chapel was no exception. Finding an architect— E. Fay Jones—was easy. It wasn't so easy to come up with funds. Halfway through the project, the money was gone, and Reed was driven to his knees to pray for help. Within a matter of days money came in, and the chapel was completed. It opened on July 10, 1980, and has since received millions of visitors. Thorncrown Chapel has been featured on *NBC Nightly News* and in *Time* magazine, and it won the American Institute of Architecture's Design of the Year Award for 1981 and AIA's Design of the Decade Award for the 1980s.

Source: www.thorncrown.com.

BAPTIZING THE BABY

Why do some churches baptize infants, while others dedicate them—and what's the difference?

The intent of both ceremonies is to initiate the child into the family of Jesus. Both services place emphasis on pledges by the parents and the religious community to nurture the child in the faith.

Catholic, Episcopal, Lutheran, Presbyterian, and most Methodist churches typically conduct a rite during which the minister or priest uses water from either his hand or a pitcher to anoint the top of the child's head. This ritual is usually called infant baptism. While each denomination's statement regarding the rite's purpose and intent varies slightly, they generally all agree that it signals the child's official induction into the church.

When a child reaches eight to ten years of age (considered the age of personal responsibility for believing) he is likely to go through another service called confirmation, during which he affirms his faith in Jesus and is accepted as a full member of the congregation.

Evangelical, independent, Pentecostal, and Baptist denominations usually dedicate babies. Again, the intent is to make their religious upbringing the responsibility of the church at large. When the child reaches an age at which he can decide for himself to accept Jesus as his Savior, he will be invited to make a public confession of his faith and subsequently be baptized as a sign of his conversion.

DR. LIVINGSTON, I PRESUME

I have sometimes seen, in the morning sun, the smoke of a thousand villages where no missionary has ever been." These words by missionary Robert Moffatt ignited a fire in the heart of a man who is remembered as one of the world's greatest explorers.

Born in 1813, David Livingston was a young Scotsman who had just completed his medical training when he heard Moffatt speak. Moffatt's ministry placed him on the edge of known African civilization. Livingston determined that he would go beyond Moffatt's boundary to search out the thousand villages where no missionary had ever gone.

Livingston's ability to glean and assimilate information about people and things was a valuable asset as he moved through territories where no outsider had ever ventured before. In addition to preaching and practicing medicine, Livingston taught the people the value of irrigation and helped them in many other practical ways.

Once, in an effort to end a siege on a village by marauding lions, Livingston was critically injured by a lion. While healing, he returned to Moffatt's compound, where he met and married Moffatt's daughter, Mary. Some years later, one of Livingston's sons died during the family's failed attempt to cross the desert. He subsequently sent his family back to England while he continued his work in Africa.

Livingston was horrified by slave trade and especially by the Zanzibar slave market. Drawing worldwide attention to this abomination was a prime focus of his trips back to England and Scotland.

Though he suffered greatly physically and emotionally, Livingston's faith remained unmovable. He died in 1856 in a Chitambo village while on his knees in prayer.

Source: www.wholesomewords.org/missions/giants/biolivingstone.html.

A KNIGHT'S SON AND THE CATHEDRAL

Lincoln Cathedral, located in the northeastern part of England, was first constructed between 1072 and 1092. On Palm Sunday in 1141, a major fire followed by an earthquake destroyed much of the building. During its reconstruction, King Henry appointed Hugh, the son of a knight, to be bishop of Lincoln.

Hugh was equally at home with kings and commoners. He reminded each of the three kings under whom he served that he actually served the King of kings (Jesus). Hugh was known for his compassion, humility, and common touch among the poor and sick, especially the lepers. Hugh's leadership and dedication were critical to the restoration of the decimated cathedral—he was often seen working alongside the common laborers who were rebuilding the structure.

Bishop Hugh died before restorations were completed in 1220, but he was so highly regarded by those whom he had served that it is said the king helped carry his coffin to its final resting place within the cathedral. He was later made a saint of the church.

Only a few years later, in 1237, the cathedral's central tower, which had survived the Palm Sunday devastation, collapsed due to faulty construction of the original structure by the Normans. Even so, Lincoln Cathedral remained the second-most-visited destination for pilgrims until Henry VIII destroyed the structure during his reign (1491–1547).

Today the only part of the original building that remains is its facade.

Sources: www.sacred-destinations.com/england/lincoln-cathedral.htm;
www.sacred-destinations.com/england/lincoln-cathedral.htm.

TERMS OF ENDEARMENT

"Darling." "Sweetheart." "Love of my life." How encouraging those words sound to a man or woman!

In the New Testament, the apostle Paul had some special ways of referring to members of the young churches he worked with. His descriptions of the people told them how precious they (and all those who love God) are to God:

1. "Life-giving perfume" (*2 Corinthians 2:16 NLT*)
2. God's "own" (*2 Corinthians 1:22 NLT*)
3. Temple of the living God (*2 Corinthians 6:16*)
4. "God's masterpiece" (*Ephesians 2:10 NLT*)
5. God's children (*Romans 8:16*)
6. "Citizens of heaven" (*Philippians 3:20 NLT*)
7. God's "choice possession" (*James 1:18 NLT*)
8. "A chosen people" (*1 Peter 2:9 NIV*)
9. "God's instruments to do his work" (*1 Peter 2:9 MSG*)
10. "Friends of God" (*Romans 5:11 NLT*)

ANGELS FROM ALL ANGLES

Angels are not to be confused with humans, Jesus, or God. Angels, however, are important members of God's heavenly team. They do what God tells them to do.

1. God created them (*Nehemiah 9:6*).
2. God is their boss (*Hebrews 1:7*).
3. They make important announcements, such as telling the shepherds that Jesus had been born (*Luke 2:10–14*).
4. They don't marry (*Matthew 22:30*).
5. They are not human; they are spirits (*Hebrews 1:14*).
6. They shouted for joy when God created the world (*Job 38:4–7*).
7. Jesus ranks higher than they do (*1 Peter 3:21–22*).
8. They are referred to by several names: cherubim (*Genesis 3:24*), seraphim (*Isaiah 6:2*), servants (*Psalm 103:21 NIV*), chariots (*2 Kings 6:17*), and messengers (*Daniel 4:13 NIV*).
9. They share knowledge with humans (*Daniel 9:21–22*).
10. They share prophecies concerning the future (*Acts 1:10–11*).

THE RIGHT FRAME OF MIND

B eing a believer, and being the owner of a chain of popular craft stores, David Green has a good life, but there was something bothering him back in 1997.

It was beginning to look a lot less like Christmas, and a lot more like "Happy Holidays" and "Season's Greetings."

He decided to do something about it. He decided that his stores, Hobby Lobby and Mardel's Christian Office and Supply, would run full-page ads in major U.S. city newspapers at Christmastime to promote what Christmas is really about: the birth of Jesus. The December 2005 ad, for example, created by a Grand Rapids, Michigan, marketing and communications firm called the Jager Group, proclaimed, "It's a Boy!"

Green didn't stop with Christmas. He decided to run ads at Easter to remind the country that Jesus rose from the dead on Easter Sunday.

None of these actions came as a surprise to those who know Green, whose path to success began in 1970. People who were into arts and crafts were gobbling up small wooden picture frames, so David and his wife, Barbara, decided to start a manufacturing business.

Slowly the business grew and became Hobby Lobby, which has spread to most of the fifty states. Green, meanwhile, has made *Forbes* magazine's list of the world's richest people.

What do the Greens do with their earnings? One thing they do is help pay for the printing and worldwide distribution of literature that tells the story of Jesus.

For the Greens, it's all about changing lives for eternity.

REST ASSURED, THIS WOMAN COULD WRITE

Fanny Crosby didn't let a little thing like blindness get in her way. Encouraged by a devoted grandmother and other loving family members, she grabbed hold of life at an early age and determined that she would make her mark in the world.

As she grew up, others read to her from the Bible and instilled in her a love of poetry. It's no wonder, then, that at church she was deeply impressed by the hymns. She was only eight when she wrote her first poem.

Through the years, Fanny received further encouragement to study and excel from well-read religious acquaintances and from her grandfather, to whom she sent many of her poems. Biographers say that she had a wonderful ability to memorize Scripture.

At age fourteen, Fanny had an opportunity to enroll at a new school, the New York Institute for the Blind. She continued to indulge her love of literature, which strengthened her writing skills. At twenty-two, she became a teacher at the Institute, and then its poet laureate. Her writing talent caught the attention of many famous individuals, including Presidents Martin Van Buren and John Polk, who became her friends. She met a future president, Grover Cleveland, when they were both working at the Institute, and he became a close friend as well.

In 1864 Fanny wrote her first hymn—the first of thousands that she attributed to divine inspiration.

Fanny lived to be ninety-five. Her headstone bears the first two lines of one of her best-known hymns, "Blessed Assurance."

A TO *Z*

Jesus is quoted in the book of Revelation as saying, "I am the Alpha and the Omega" *(Revelation 22:13 NIV)*. In the Greek language, *alpha* is the first letter of the alphabet, and *omega* is the last letter. In the English language, Jesus' statement is tantamount to saying, "I am the *A* to *Z*." Jesus made a bold claim that everything needed for life—not only on this earth but for all eternity—was resident in and flowed from himself. (See *John 3:16; 10:10.*)

YOUR FUTURE HOME?

Are you anticipating a vast mansion in heaven? Many Christians believe that a fabulous multiroom manor awaits them, because Jesus is quoted as saying in the King James Version of the Bible, "In my Father's house are many mansions: if it were not so, I would have told you. I go to prepare a place for you" *(John 14:2)*. The word that has been translated "mansions" is perhaps more correctly translated as "rooms," "resting places," or "dwellings." Those in right standing with God will assuredly have a *place* in heaven that will be glorious, but the *size* of the dwelling place was not considered important to Bible writers.

YOU DON'T WANT TO GO THERE

Talk about polar opposites—heaven and hell are as different as night and day. And while heaven sounds wonderful, the Bible's descriptions of hell sound, well, awful:

1. It's a fire that never goes out *(Mark 9:43)*.
2. It contains "gloomy dungeons" *(2 Peter 2:4 NIV)*.
3. It's where the body and soul are destroyed *(Matthew 10:28)*.
4. People there will weep and gnash their teeth *(Matthew 13:40–42)*.
5. It's a place of darkness *(Matthew 25:30)*.
6. Its inhabitants will suffer everlasting punishment *(Matthew 25:46)*.
7. No one there can get into heaven, and vice versa *(Luke 16:19–26)*.

DINNER AT SOLOMON'S HOUSE

King Solomon has been called the wisest man who ever lived—certainly he was one of the wisest kings who ever ruled Israel. Even a wise king, however, can require of his people an amount of support that may be regarded as unwise. The Bible tells us that the *daily* provision in King Solomon's court included "thirty measures of fine flour, and threescore measures of meal, ten fat oxen, and twenty oxen out of the pastures, and an hundred sheep, beside harts, and roebucks, and fallowdeer, and fatted fowl" *(1 Kings 4:22–23 KJV)*. Multiply this daily amount by the days of a year, and the amount of food required was astounding. Bible scholars have estimated that this quantity of food would cost in excess of $20 million a year, not counting the costs of hunting and slaughtering, butchering, dressing, and preparing the flour and meat into edible fare. There may have been as many as thirty thousand people eating at the extended "table of the king"—especially given the number of Solomon's wives and concubines—but even so, this amount of food was considered excessive. Vast acres of pasture were required for grazing such animals, and overall the supply of food contributed to the king was regarded as an extremely oppressive form of taxation.

In addition to providing food for Solomon and his court, the people of Israel supplied barley and straw for the king's horses and steeds—no small feat. Solomon had forty thousand stalls for horses for his chariots, and twelve thousand horsemen! (See *1 Kings 4:26 NKJV*.)

OBEDIENCE

Obedience is always a response to authority—a person obeys those who are "over him" and who command, compel, invite, or require his obedience, usually in exchange for their protection, provision, and affiliation. To obey is ultimately required of all people to some degree, but obedience "to whom" and "with what motives" are often questioned.

1. "Let thy child's first lesson be obedience, and the second may be what thou wilt."—*Thomas Fuller (English clergyman, 1608–1661)*

2. "The first law that ever God gave to man, was a law of obedience; it was a commandment pure and simple, wherein man had nothing to inquire after or to dispute. . . . From obedience and submission spring all other virtues, as all sin does from self-opinion and self-will."
—*Michael de Montaigne (French essayist, 1533–1592)*

3. "Thirty years of our Lord's life are hidden in these words of the gospel: 'He was subject unto them.'"
—*Jacques Bossuet (French bishop, 1627–1704)*

4. "Obedience to God is the most infallible evidence of sincere and supreme love to him."
—*Nathaniel Emmons (American theologian, 1745–1840)*

5. "We are born subjects, and to obey God is perfect liberty. He that does this shall be free, safe, and happy."
—*Lucius Seneca (Roman philosopher, 4 BC–AD 65)*

6. "Doing the will of God leaves me no time for disputing about his plans."—*George MacDonald (Scottish novelist, 1824–1905)*

7. "One very common error misleads the opinion of mankind, that authority is pleasant, and submission painful. In the general course of human affairs the very reverse of this is nearer to the truth—command is anxiety; obedience is ease."
—*William Paley (English theologian, 1743–1805)*

8. "No principle is more noble, as there is none more holy, than that of true obedience."—*Henry Giles (American clergyman, 1809–1882)*

9. "True obedience neither procrastinates nor questions."
—*Francis Quarles (English author, 1592–1644)*

THE SIGN OF
THE CROSS

The symbol of a cross has been associated with faith in Jesus from the day of his crucifixion—a cross atop a building or in a window conveys a message virtually all people recognize: "Jesus is welcome here . . . this is a Christian place." The symbol is so quickly acknowledged that many religious denominations and organizations have included the symbol of a cross in their logos, and people have been quick to wear crosses and even sport them on bumper stickers as a means of sending a message to others: "I am a believer."

But what about the tracing of the shape of a cross with one's hand—a practice known simply as making the "sign of the cross"?

This gesture has also been a traditional sign of Christianity since the first century. Early believers made the sign of a "full cross"—using two or three fingers to touch the top of the head, then the toes, and then the tip of one horizontally extended hand to the tip of the other horizontally extended hand, returning finally to the center of the chest. In this way, the believers "put on" total identity with what Jesus accomplished on the cross for every person who accepts him as Savior.

Traditional churches now take the right hand from the forehead to the center of the chest, then from shoulder to shoulder, and then back to the center of the chest. In the West, the chest is crossed left to right, and in the East from right to left. Some churches use three fingers to make the sign of the cross, others use two fingers.

At the reading of the gospel in many mainline churches, laypeople sometimes make a triple sign of the cross with their

THE SIGN OF
THE CROSS (CONT'D)

thumb—on their forehead, on their lips, and over their heart. The sign is intended to symbolize their desire that the gospel message be applied to their mind, to their speech, and to their heart—so the gospel teachings will be foremost in their thoughts, they will speak only words in alignment with the gospel truth, and they will be wholeheartedly committed to living out the gospel message.

In all cases, the person making the sign of the cross on his or her body has been admonished by the church through the ages to see the gesture as a means of identifying with Jesus. When a priest or bishop makes the sign of the cross on the forehead of a baby or an adult believer—or makes the sign in the air toward a person or a congregation—the cleric is bestowing the identity of Jesus on those who are perceived as willing and qualified to receive it. Making the sign of the cross is sometimes an act associated with prayer or healing and sometimes a means of sealing baptism or confirmation vows. It is made as an expression of God's forgiveness, and it often is made as a part of the rituals associated with anointing a person for death or burial.

AMERICA'S FIRST BIBLE TO AMERICA'S FIRST PEOPLE

The first Bible printed in America was not in English but in Algonquin, the language of Native Americans in Massachusetts. John Eliot, known as the "Apostle to the Indians," spent eight years learning the language before completing the translation and publication of the Bible in 1663. Until then the Algonquin language had no written alphabet. One hundred years later the first English-language Bible was printed in America.

Source: www.nationalbible.org.

ABRAHAM WASN'T JEWISH

Abraham was a Hebrew. The term "Hebrew" is derived from the name Eber, a descendant of Noah's son Shem; Abraham was Eber's descendant. Strictly speaking, Abraham was not an Israelite or a Jew, because neither existed in his time. Israelites and Jews were not identified until much later—Israelites are descendants of Isaac's son Jacob, whom God renamed Israel; Jews are descendants of Jacob's son Judah.

Source: www.keyway.ca/htm2003/20030302.htm.

ONE-HUNDRED-YEAR PRAYER MEETING

On August 27, 1727, twenty-four men and twenty-four women of the Moravian Brethren in a remote German village made a commitment to begin a "prayer watch," each person spending one hour each day in scheduled prayer. Over the next one hundred years others enlisted in the "hourly intercession," praying for world evangelization, specifically to reach those "for whom no one cared." By 1791 that small community had sent three hundred missionaries around the world.

www.ctlibrary.com/3263.

TUNE IN NEXT WEEK FOR THE REST OF THE STORY

The bracelets ask, "What Would Jesus Do?" Just where did this phrase originate? It came from the book *In His Steps*, written by Congregational minister Charles Sheldon and published in 1897.

The story began as a multipart sermon Sheldon gave to his Topeka, Kansas, congregation. Sheldon shared a few pages one Sunday and called upon members to return week after week to hear the continuation of the story. This was a practice Sheldon used frequently in his preaching.

The book tells the story of the Reverend Henry Maxwell and the moment that changed his life. A homeless man walks into his church one Sunday morning and challenges everyone's understanding of what it really means to follow Jesus. When the man dies days later—in Henry's home—Henry examines his own life and realizes that he has fallen short of what God expects of him. The next Sunday he asks for volunteers from his congregation to join him in a yearlong experiment: agree to examine every situation that arises in the coming twelve months, and before acting, ask, "What would Jesus do?"

Sheldon began his writing career at age twelve, first for newspapers and later for magazines. He earned a degree from Andover Theological Seminary and continually sought ways to combine his love of preaching and love of writing.

Once published, *In His Steps* flew off store shelves. It is still on the "top best sellers of all time" lists.

NOT DOWN AND NOT UNDER

David Smallbone was a Christian concert promoter in Australia promoting such talents as Amy Grant and Petra in the late 1970s and early 1980s. When ticket sales fell short on a major concert tour, Smallbone was out two hundred and fifty thousand dollars. He lost his business and his home to creditors. His search for work led him to another job in the music industry. A top artist offered Smallbone the opportunity to be his manager, but taking the job meant that David, his wife, and their six children had to move halfway around the world to Nashville. They decided to make the move, and in 1991 the Smallbones packed up, said good-bye to their friends, and found their way to Tennessee.

What seemed like a good opportunity turned out to be another disaster: after a couple of months, David was told that his position was "no longer available." Smallbone and his wife, Helen, told their children what happened, and together they prayed for God's help. Their rented house was sparse, with just a few cushions, a table, and a single mattress. Smallbone said they "prayed to survive"—for food and money, a car, everything they needed. Amazing things began to happen—groceries were left at their door, acquaintances took them out to dinner, furniture was donated to furnish their nearly empty house. Nashville songwriter Jon Mohr gave the Smallbones a three-month-old Toyota Previa van.

The children helped out with odd jobs—Rebecca, the oldest, and two brothers raked leaves and mowed lawns. They cleaned houses and babysat. Each member of the family did his or her part, working at whatever he or she could find to do. Then came a big break! Sixteen-year-old Rebecca was offered a recording contract by ForeFront Records after executives at the record company heard a demo of her singing. As

NOT DOWN AND NOT UNDER (CONT'D)

the daughter of a Christian concert promoter, Rebecca's talents had put her in the public spotlight when the family lived in Australia. At age twelve she had opened for Carman's Australian tour shortly before the family business hit bottom.

Rebecca took an old family name for a stage name and recorded her first album as Rebecca St. James, and the family made plans for her debut concert tour. Jon Mohr knew that meant the Smallbones would need a bigger vehicle, so he traded in the Toyota he had given them for a fifteen-passenger van. Overwhelmed by Jon's generosity, David offered him 50 percent of Rebecca's "publishing rights"—the money she earned from writing songs.

Rebecca's first music efforts were received enthusiastically, and she was distinguished as the youngest person to receive a Gospel Music Association's Dove Award nomination as New Artist of the Year. Her second album, *God*, earned a Grammy Award nomination and a Dove Award nomination for Female Vocalist of the Year. Her album *Pray* received a Grammy for the Best Rock Gospel Album. She has been named "Favorite Female Artist" in Contemporary Christian Music and one of the "Fifty Most Influential People in Contemporary Music" by *CRW* magazine. In the spotlight worldwide and winner of numerous awards, Rebecca said God has "not called me to be a star" but to be a "servant."

And what happened to Jon Mohr and his family? They left the Nashville music industry to become missionaries in the Ukraine. Royalty checks from the Smallbones help support their ministry!

Source: Luis Palau with Mike Yorkey, *It's a God Thing: Pictures and Portraits of God's Grace* (New York: Doubleday, 2001).

BIBLE BUGS

Insects and worms may not be the favorites of God's creatures to many human beings, and they certainly aren't large . . . but the Bible says people can learn a great deal from certain "bugs"!

1. *Ant.* The harvester ants referred to in Proverbs 6:6 are tiny insects that carry seed after seed into their storehouses for future use. If the stored grain gets wet, the ant carries it out into the sun to dry. Solomon said ants are worthy examples for human beings.

2. *Bee.* Of all creatures, the bee is one of the most useful. It helps pollinate plants for fruitfulness. The Promised Land was a land of "milk and honey" *(Exodus 3:8 NIV)*. Honey was highly valued for sweetness in the ancient Israelite diet. Angry bees were a sign of God's anger *(Psalm 118:12)*.

3. *Beetle.* Although translated "beetle" in the King James Bible, this quite possibly refers to a cricket. It is one of the "winged insects that walk on all fours," have "jointed legs above their feet," and are considered "clean" according to the Old Testament's dietary laws *(Leviticus 11:21–22 NRSV)*.

4. *Cankerworm.* This was most likely the larva stage of the locust. The Hebrew word is also translated as "young locust." "What the great locusts have left the young locusts have eaten" *(Joel 1:4 NIV)*.

5. *Caterpillar.* Grouped with the cankerworm and palmerworm, the caterpillar is considered a form in the life cycle of the locust. The locust was a terrifying insect to the ancient peoples because of its capacity to destroy vegetation.

6. *Flea.* The sand and dust of the Holy Land are good places for fleas to flourish. Fleas are parasites; they attach to a body, sucking blood from their host, so they have a long history of being detested! The word is also used symbolically in the Bible to refer to something very small *(1 Samuel 24:14)*.

7. *Flies.* The common housefly was among the two-winged insects referred to in the Bible as flies. The plague of flies upon the Egyptians was probably swarms of biting swamp flies or stable flies *(Exodus 8:20–32)*.

8. *Gnat.* The term for small stinging insects, such as lice, mosquitoes, or sand flies. Clouds of gnats plagued the Egyptians *(Exodus 8:16–18)*. Jesus told the Pharisees, "You strain out a gnat but swallow a camel" *(Matthew 23:24 NIV)*. Some-

BIBLE BUGS (CONT'D)

times Pharisees concentrated on the minutiae of the Law, missing the truly important.

9. *Grasshopper.* An insect with long hind legs well suited for jumping. Grasshoppers destroy crops and are considered agents of divine punishment. They are ritually clean and so, according to dietary laws, can be eaten *(Leviticus 11:22).*

10. *Hornet, or wasp.* A stinging insect. It has a poisonous, painful sting. In Bible references to the hornet, God promises to help his people in battle by "send[ing] the hornet ahead of you" *(Exodus 23:28 NIV).*

11. *Locust.* Swarms of locusts, eating every green thing and laying eggs, were one of the plagues God brought on Egypt *(Exodus 10:12–20).* The larvae fed on remaining vegetation, bringing famine from loss of food crops. John the Baptist ate locusts and wild honey *(Matthew 3:4).*

12. *Moth.* A destructive insect, the moth symbolizes destruction of worldly possessions. The moth lays eggs in wool and furs, and when hatched, the larvae feed on the fibers, leaving the clothing full of holes. Jesus says to store treasures in heaven instead of on earth, "where moth and rust destroy" *(Matthew 6:19–20 NIV).*

13. *Scorpion.* Small, eight-legged crawling arachnids with pincers and tails with poisonous stingers. In the day they hide under rocks to escape the heat, then come out at night to hunt and eat. They were a danger to the Israelites traveling through the wilderness *(Deuteronomy 8:15).*

14. *Spider.* In Scripture, the spider's web demonstrates the foolishness of those who forget God and put their confidence in something else—by comparison anything else would be as fragile as a spider's web *(Job 8:13–14).*

15. *Worm.* The Bible uses the word *worm* both literally and figuratively. Herod did not glorify God, so was eaten by worms (possibly a tapeworm) *(Acts 12:23).* Perhaps an earthworm struck at the root of Jonah's shade *(Jonah 4:7).* The psalmist cried, "I am a worm . . . and despised" *(Psalm 22:6 NIV).*

THE MOUNT OF OLIVE TREES

Why were so many olive trees planted on a hill just to the east of the old walled city of Jerusalem—an area known today as the Mount of Olives? Because the Law of Moses required that the lamps of the temple—located on the temple mount at the eastern edge of the city—be kept burning around the clock. The law stated that these lamps were to burn "pure oil of pressed olives" *(Exodus 27:20 NKJV)*. The lamps required a regular refilling by the high priest at twilight each evening *(Exodus 30:8)*. According to later traditional Jewish laws, olive presses needed to be within the prescribed number of steps allowable on a Sabbath should a priest need to get oil on the Sabbath. The trees and olive presses on the Mount of Olives were placed there for temple purposes—to be near with a sufficient oil supply.

TEACHING IN PARABLES

Jesus taught in parables, which was a method of instructing through pictures of human life. In fact, the New Testament says about Jesus during one period in his ministry, "Without a parable He did not speak to them" *(Matthew 13:34 NKJV)*. It was through the telling of parables that Jesus made his most important statements about the kingdom of God, its growth, value, relation to the world, conflict, and ultimate triumph. His parables are simple enough for a child to understand and yet deep enough for continued study by the most advanced scholars. Parables were a method of teaching in a way that was brief, to the point, and highly memorable. The most notable parables in the Old Testament are the one given by Nathan to King David as he confronted him about his adultery with Bathsheba *(2 Samuel 12:1–7)* and the one of Isaiah about the Well-beloved's vineyard *(Isaiah 5:1–7)*.

THOMAS A. DORSEY: FROM BLUES TO GOSPEL

Thomas Dorsey (1900–1993), not to be confused with the big-band leader Tommy Dorsey, was one of the foremost American songwriters and music publishers of the twentieth century. He began his musical career as a blues singer who was known for his off-color lyrics. Then Dorsey accepted Jesus as his personal Savior, and shortly afterward he turned to writing exclusively religious songs. He has been credited with coining the phrase "gospel music," and he later became widely accepted as the father of gospel music.

Dorsey wrote more than a thousand gospel songs. Two of his better-known compositions are "Peace in the Valley" and "Precious Lord, Take My Hand."

Dorsey is said to have had a strong influence on Mahalia Jackson, a popular black gospel singer for more than four decades. Jackson was active in the Civil Rights Movement and had recordings that sold millions.

For many years the "gospel" sounds of Dorsey and others were the most commercially viable form of Christian music. Read more about one of Dorsey's most popular songs on page 185.

SIBERIAN CONVERT

Fyodor Mikhaylovich Dostoyevsky (1821–1881) is considered to be one of the greatest writers in the history of literature. Among his most notable works are *Crime and Punishment* and *The Brothers Karamazov*. A Russian, Dostoyevsky began his life as an atheist. He became involved in the political activities of a very early Communist leader named Petrocheffsky, who led some of the earliest plots against the czar. This political affiliation resulted in Dostoyevsky's being labeled a political subversive in 1849, and he was exiled to twelve years of hard labor in the mines of Siberia. In 1856, much to the surprise of those who had known the pre-Siberian Dostoyevsky, he was released from prison and emerged from the mines a committed Christian!

The experience of conversion under the pressure of suffering and exile profoundly influenced Dostoyevsky's subsequent writings, including the account of his imprisonment that was published in 1860. He continued to write against a rich backdrop of Russian situations, politics, and culture, but he frequently presented human beings as a battleground between good and evil. He staunchly believed that suffering was a road that led to spiritual salvation. He is often considered a theologian, even though he was never formally trained as a theologian and never claimed to be one. One of his best-known stories, "The Grand Inquisitor," is found in his novel *The Brothers Karamazov*. In the story, Dostoyevsky pitted Jesus against the institutional church. Jesus asks difficult questions of the church and ultimately "wins" his case against it.

THE ROSE AS A SYMBOL OF FAITH

In Christian art, the rose is usually the symbol of purity or martyrdom.

However . . .

- A rose with five or seven petals is often called a "mystical rose," and it is an emblem of the Virgin Mary. Through the centuries, various people in the Roman Catholic Church have stated that the number of petals signifies Mary's joys, although no one set of "joys" has ever been declared to be authoritative. A rose without thorns is also a symbol of the Virgin Mary in Christian art.

- A rose window is a circular window with a petal-like design, usually found on the west front of a Gothic cathedral. Rose windows are generally located under a circular arch in Gothic architecture. The largest examples extend over the entire width of a cathedral's nave.

- *Rosary* is the Latin word for "rose garden."

- The "rose of Sharon" mentioned in the Bible *(Song of Songs 2:1)* is believed to be a mountain tulip—a deep-red flower that grows wild in the sandy soil of the Sharon region of Israel.

- Many Bible scholars believe that the flower called "rose" in Isaiah 35:1 *(NKJV)* is actually the narcissus—the name literally means "sweet-smelling." The narcissus is common throughout Israel, whereas the flower known commonly as a rose is not.

- In Christmas carols, the "rose" refers to Jesus.

- In the Armenian tradition, a feast called "vartavar"—literally "the festival of roses"—is celebrated to commemorate the miracle in which Jesus' face and clothes began to shine radiantly as he stood on a mountain with Peter, James, and John (a miracle called the Transfiguration—see *Matthew 17:1–9).*

GET GOD IN THE ACT!

Many movies tell stories that have to do with God or the Bible, or simply living a life of faith. (And many of those movies win Academy Awards!)

Although action flicks continue to draw large crowds, DVDs of old (and new) "religious" movies remain available for rental or purchase.

1. *King of Kings* (1927; remade in 1961). A film about the life of Jesus.

2. *Quo Vadis* (1951). Christianity triumphs over Emperor Nero's attempts to destroy it.

3. *Martin Luther* (1953) and *Luther* (2003). An account of Luther's conflict with the Roman Catholic Church.

4. *The Robe* (1953). A Roman officer becomes a believer after Jesus' crucifixion.

5. *The Prodigal* (1955). A young Hebrew leaves home for life in the big city, finds trouble, and eventually returns home.

6. *A Man Called Peter* (1955). A biography of Scottish clergyman Peter Marshall.

7. *The Ten Commandments* (1956). Moses learns that he was chosen to deliver the Israelites from Egyptian slavery.

8. *Ben-Hur* (1959). A Jewish prince, falsely accused of a crime, seeks revenge . . . until he views Jesus' crucifixion and renews his faith.

9. *Barabbas* (1962). A criminal who was freed instead of Jesus struggles with spiritual issues.

10. *Lilies of the Field* (1963). An unemployed construction worker encounters nuns and gets involved in building a church.

11. *The Greatest Story Ever Told* (1965). A film about the life of Jesus.

12. *The Bible* (1966). A movie that depicts the first chapters of the book of Genesis.

13. *A Man for All Seasons* (1966). Sir Thomas More puts faith before politics.

14. *The Cross and the Switchblade* (1970). A minister introduces New York City gang members to God.

GET GOD IN THE ACT! (CONT'D)

15. *Jesus Christ Superstar* (1973). The story of the last few weeks of Jesus' life on earth.

16. *Godspell* (1973). A musical version of the Gospel of Saint Matthew.

17. *The Hiding Place* (1975). Two sisters rise above Nazi abuse with their faith in God.

18. *Chariots of Fire* (1981). A Scottish Olympic athlete puts his faith before his sport.

19. *The Mission* (1986). Jesuit priests give their all to share their faith.

20. *Babette's Feast* (1987). A story of sacrifice. Two Danish sisters pass up opportunities to leave their minister father, and their cook gives her all to prepare them a feast.

21. *Leap of Faith* (1992). A fake preacher is confronted with a real miracle.

22. *Shadowlands* (1993). Christian scholar and author C. S. Lewis marries, then deals with the illness and death of his wife.

23. *The Gospel of John* (2003). A word-for-word retelling of the gospel.

24. *The Passion of the Christ* (2004). A film about Jesus' arrest, trial, crucifixion, and resurrection.

25. *The Chronicles of Narnia: The Lion, the Witch and the Wardrobe* (2005). A movie that illustrates the biblical themes of love, forgiveness, and sacrificing all—life itself—for the sake of others.

26. *The Nativity Story* (2006). The story of Mary and Joseph's journey; Mary's miraculous pregnancy; and the world-changing birth of Jesus.

WHAT DID HE REALLY BELIEVE?

Søren Kierkegaard (1814–1855), perhaps the most famous of the Danish existentialist philosophers, had a profound effect on the Christianity of his day. Even so, his melancholy and brooding nature, and his blending of psychological concepts and theology, have made him a mystery—and even a cause for suspicion—to many modern-day Christians. What is it that Kierkegaard really believed?

Kierkegaard was strongly opposed to what he saw as arid and lifeless Christianity in most of the established churches of his nation during the early 1800s.

At the core of his writings is the belief that a yawning gulf exists between time and eternity, the finite and the infinite, and the creature and the Creator. Kierkegaard contended that there is no "religious" bridge between these two opposites because God is wholly "other," and that the gulf was bridged only once, and for all, by Jesus' incarnation. He believed that Jesus came "incognito" and remains hidden to the masses of humanity—that he can only be discerned through the eyes of faith. Without faith, neither knowledge—which includes formulas and processes associated with "reason"—nor good works can lead a person to Jesus. A "leap of faith" is required for the believer to cross the gulf into a new kingdom. The main purpose for our temporary life on this earth is to make this leap and grasp the infinite.

A statement for which Kierkegaard is well known, "Truth is subjectivity," has been misunderstood by many. Kierkegaard made this statement in opposition to the prevailing theological philosophy of his day, which contended that a person could develop a relationship with God through group religious rituals and formalities. Kierkegaard believed that an individual could only draw close to God through a personal awareness of God achieved through a personal expression of faith. He contended that every person must come to "know the truth of Christ" totally on his own exercise of faith, and that knowing Jesus was a matter therefore of subjectivity, not objectivity. The statement was not extended by Kierkegaard to situational ethics or moral relativism, as is often implied by those unfamiliar with his full body of writings.

Kierkegaard was a well-published author. An interesting fact, however, is that he chose to publish many of his early writings under several pseudonyms. It was only in the last eight years of his life that he published more direct Christian books under his name.

O SAY, CAN YOU SING?

The first national anthem, Great Britain's "God Save the Queen," was labeled as such in 1825. Today most nations have their own anthems, and many of these songs, like Great Britain's, make mention of God in at least one verse.

Antigua and Barbuda's anthem, in verse 3, asks God to let his blessings "fall upon this land of ours," making crops grow. It also asks him to give the people "strength, faith, and loyalty."

God, says Barbados's anthem, "has been the people's guide" for three centuries, and with him on their side, they have "no doubts or fears."

The land of Botswana, its citizens sing, is a "gift to us from God's strong hand."

Fiji Islanders ask God to bless their land. "May God bless Fiji, for evermore!" the anthem's chorus concludes.

The people of Grenada, "ever conscious of God" and proud of their heritage, will move forward as one family. "God bless our nation," the anthem ends.

"Gem of God's earth" is how the Isle of Man's anthem describes this nation. "In the Lord's promise" the people will confide, trusting in his power "each single hour" and thereby warding off evil.

"Eternal Father, bless our land," begins the Jamaican national anthem. "To our leaders, Great Defender, grant true wisdom from above." Verse 2 talks about what the people need: "Give us vision lest we perish, knowledge send us, Heavenly Father."

Kenya's anthem was written by its National Commission of Musicians. Verse one is unequivocal in its appeal to the Creator, asking God to bless both the land and the people.

O SAY, CAN YOU SING? (CONT'D)

Luxembourg adopted its national anthem in 1895. The song acknowledges that the people have God to thank for their nation and refers to God as being the One who raises up nations and brings them down. The song asks for divine protection from outsiders who would enslave the people and cause them grief.

New Zealand has two official national anthems: the national anthem of Great Britain, and its own New Zealand anthem. All five verses of the New Zealand anthem end with words that ask God to defend New Zealand, and in the fourth stanza of every eight-stanza verse there is a plea that God would defend the people's "free land."

The anthem of Papua New Guinea, adopted when this nation achieved independence in 1975, speaks of "praising God" for the country. It also thanks "the good Lord above" for gifts that include kindness and love.

The Solomon Islands held a contest to choose its national anthem, which begins with the familiar "God save" our country, and "bless our people" and lands with God's "protecting hands."

Swaziland also held a competition to find an appropriate anthem. The song recognizes that God is the One who has blessed the people, thanks him for their leader and their land, asks him to bless their leaders, and requests wisdom and strength.

Although Switzerland's anthem had, for all practical purposes, been around for more than one hundred years, it was not officially adopted until 1961. Called "The Swiss Psalm," it bears a striking resemblance to a biblical psalm, saying that God, without a doubt, is alive and well in Switzerland—present at dawn, at sunset, and in darkness and mist. They can see him no matter what sort of clouds appear to stand between them and almighty God.

IRAQ IS NOTEWORTHY THROUGHOUT THE BIBLE

Israel is the nation mentioned most frequently in the Bible. But do you know which nation has the second-most-numerous references? Iraq.

Iraq is not the name used in the Bible, of course. The names in the Bible are Babylon, Land of Shinar, and Mesopotamia. The name Mesopotamia means "between two rivers," referring to the Tigris and Euphrates Rivers, which flow through Iraq. The name Iraq means "country with deep roots," and indeed Iraq has deep roots—no nation, other than Israel, has more Bible history and prophecy associated with it. Just consider:

- The Garden of Eden was in Iraq (*Genesis 2*).

- The Tower of Babel was in Iraq (*Genesis 11:1–9*).

- Noah built the ark in Iraq (*Genesis 6–7*).

- Abraham was from Ur, an ancient city many believe to have been in southern Iraq (*Genesis 11:31*).

- Babylon, which is in Iraq, destroyed Jerusalem (*2 Kings 25:8–10*).

- Nebuchadnezzar, king of Babylon, forced Jews into captivity in Iraq (*2 Kings 25:11; Daniel 1*).

- Daniel was in the lions' den in Iraq (*Daniel 6*).

- The three Hebrew children—Shadrach, Meshach, and Abednego— were thrown into a fiery furnace for failing to bow down to an image erected in Iraq (*Daniel 3*).

- Belshazzar, the king of Babylon, saw the "writing on the wall" in Iraq (*Daniel 5*).

- Ezekiel preached in Iraq (*Ezekiel 1:1*); the river Chebar was in Iraq.

- The wise men who came to pay homage to the young child Jesus were very likely from Iraq (*Matthew 2:1*).

- The fallen city (sometimes referred to as the "Empire of Man") described in the book of Revelation is Babylon, a powerful city that once existed in what is now Iraq (*Revelation 18*).

UNPOPULAR BIBLE PREACHERS

Ever felt misunderstood or unpopular because you voiced a godly opinion? Some of the best-known people in the Bible had the same problem!

1. *Enoch.* In a time of great wrongdoing, Enoch preached an unpopular message of judgment against the perpetrators and all the bad things they had done and all the harsh words they had spoken against God (*Jude 14–15*).

2. *Noah.* Noah's critics had an easy target. He predicted rain, when it had never rained before. For 120 years he built a watertight vessel on dry land. All the while, he warned his friends and neighbors to watch out for the coming catastrophe, but they didn't listen (*Genesis 6–7*).

3. *Joseph.* Joseph was the son of Jacob and Rachel. Unpopular with his siblings, he brought his father a bad report about his brothers *(Genesis 37:2)*. In his dream his brothers were serving him. When he told the dream to them, they hated him all the more *(Genesis 37:5)*.

4. *Moses.* The message from Moses to Pharaoh was, "Let my people go!" *(Exodus 8:1)*. That got Moses into a lot of trouble. Moses led the Israelites out of captivity, but on their way to the Promised Land, God's people were not always happy campers and gave Moses a lot of grief.

5. *Nathan.* Nathan preached an unpopular word to a popular king. After David arranged Uriah's death to cover David's adultery with Uriah's wife, Bathsheba, Nathan confronted the king with his crime. Nathan prophesied calamity to David's household. The good news is, David admitted his wrongdoing and repented (*2 Samuel 12:7–13*).

6. *Elijah.* Elijah has been called a "prophet of gloom." He preached God's judgment against the prophets of the false god Baal. He didn't pray that God would bless the land; he prayed that God would "shut up the heavens" and withhold rain unless the people repented (*James 5:17*).

7. *Elisha.* No one applied for the job of prophet; it was a call of God. Some young boys teased Elisha, saying, "Go away, you baldhead!" Elisha put a curse on them, and they were mauled by two bears (*2 Kings 2:23–25 NLT*).

8. *Micaiah.* Micaiah prophesied disaster for the king of Israel and called his popular prophet peers "liars" (*2 Chronicles 18:22*). For that he got bread and water and jail time. But his message proved true.

9. *Jeremiah.* Known as "the Weeping Prophet" because he agonized over the nation of Israel, Jeremiah was beaten, thrown into a pit, and put into stocks, but he couldn't keep quiet. The word of God was like "a burning fire" in him. Jeremiah's "doom and judgment" message was heard but not heeded (*Jeremiah 20:8–9*).

10. *Amos.* Amos, the small-town prophet, spoke God's word to God's people, denouncing idol worship, corruption, and oppression. Amos was not invited to dine with the rich and famous (*Amos 7:12*). They were his target—they became wealthy at the expense of the poor. But their good times would soon be over, just as Amos warned.

CHRISTMAS BOOKENDS

The Christmas season, for many, begins with Christmas shopping and store decorations sometime in November and ends with the opening of gifts on Christmas Day, or even with the day-after-Christmas sales and exchanges. Traditionally, however, it's not retailers and shoppers that mark the beginning and end of Christmas but the seasons of Advent and Epiphany.

According to the official church year, Advent, which begins on the fourth Sunday before Christmas, marks the start of the Christmas season. The four weeks of Advent are intended to be a time of expectation and anticipation, and preparation of the heart and soul for the celebration of Christmas Day.

December 25 is actually the first day of the Twelve Days of Christmas, which end with Epiphany on January 6. Observances during the Twelve Days of Christmas are an opportunity to reflect on the meaning of Jesus' incarnation— his presence in the world in human form.

The Feast of Saint Stephen is celebrated on December 26. Stephen was the first Christian martyr and one of the first seven deacons of the church *(Acts 6–7)*. As a deacon, Stephen's responsibility was to distribute goods to those in need. December 26, then, became a day to show generosity to the poor. On this day people in many countries give gifts of food and clothing to those in need.

The following day, December 27, commemorates Saint John the Evangelist. John, the author of one of the Gospels, three epistles, and the book of Revelation, was the only one of the twelve disciples who did not die a martyr. John was a witness and proclaimer of the life of Jesus. He gave testimony to the Incarnation in his gospel: "The Word [Jesus] became flesh and made his dwelling among us" *(John 1:14 NIV)*.

CHRISTMAS BOOKENDS (CONT'D)

The Holy Innocents are also a part of the Christmas story. These children who were murdered by order of King Herod are commemorated on December 28. When the wise men came from the East to Jerusalem asking, "Where is He who has been born King of the Jews?" *(Matthew 2:2 NKJV)*, Herod was alerted to a potential threat to his kingdom. To rid himself of the threat, he ordered his troops to Bethlehem to kill every male child under the age of two. The slaughter did not accomplish what Herod intended. Joseph was forewarned in a dream to flee Bethlehem. He, Mary, and the young child Jesus traveled to Egypt and escaped Herod's brutal slaughter.

Reflecting on the lives of Stephen, John, and the Holy Innocents is an opportunity to examine ways in which daily choices can be more Christlike.

The true end of the Christmas season is Epiphany. The word *epiphany* means "to show," "to make known," or "to reveal." As celebrated in the church, Epiphany recalls the coming of the wise men with gifts to visit the child Jesus, an event that revealed Jesus to the world as Lord and King. They were the first Gentiles to acknowledge Jesus as King, indicating that Jesus came for all people and that the work of God in the world would not be limited to a few. It is a time to look ahead to the mission of the church in reaching others by showing Jesus as the Savior of all people.

Sources: www.ctlibrary.com/12062; www.cresourcei.org/cyepiph.html; justus.anglica.org/resources/bio/21.html.

DYNAMIC DUO

Life in ancient Palestine depended on the supply of rain, so it's no wonder that there was strong appeal to worship Baal the weather god. Baal worship intensified in the ninth century BC under King Ahab and his wife, Jezebel. This was also the time of Elijah and Elisha, two prominent prophets of God. They performed a series of miracles that successfully routed the Baal worshippers and turned the hearts of many Israelites back to the one true God.

Elijah's Miracles

1. The rain was stopped (*1 Kings 17:1*).
2. Ravens fed him bread and meat (*1 Kings 17:6*).
3. The widow's food was multiplied (*1 Kings 17:13–16*).
4. The widow's son was brought back to life (*1 Kings 17:17–24*).
5. Fire came down from heaven (*1 Kings 18:30–39*).
6. The rain was restored (*1 Kings 18:41–46*).

Elisha's Miracles

1. The Jordan River was divided (*2 Kings 2:14*).
2. The springwater was purified (*2 Kings 2:21*).
3. Ditches were filled with water (*2 Kings 3:15–26*).
4. The widow's oil was multiplied (*2 Kings 4:1–7*).
5. The Shunammite woman became pregnant (*2 Kings 4:14–17*).
6. The Shunammite's son was raised from the dead (*2 Kings 4:32–37*).
7. Poisonous stew was made edible (*2 Kings 4:38–41*).
8. One hundred men were fed with twenty barley loaves (*2 Kings 4:42–44*).
9. Naaman's leprosy was healed (*2 Kings 5:1–19*).
10. Gehazi was cursed with leprosy (*2 Kings 5:20–27*).
11. An iron ax head floated (*2 Kings 6:1–6*).
12. Elisha's servant saw the angelic army (*2 Kings 6:15–17*).
13. The Aramaean army was blinded (*2 Kings 6:8–23*).

PRIVATE GARDENS

In the first century, many wealthy families of Jerusalem owned small gardens located just a few hundred yards from the city's gates. In these private, walled, and gated gardens the people could grow a few vegetables, vines, fruit trees, and flowering plants. The garden was intended to offer peace, quiet, and beauty for those who lived and worked in the hustle and bustle of the large city. The gardens were used for small social gatherings, for private meetings, and for personal times of reflection and rest.

The Garden of Gethsemane was such a garden at the base of the Mount of Olives. Jesus and his disciples had been given the key to the garden's gate so they might pray there on the night Jesus was betrayed and arrested. Apparently, the owner of the garden had loaned his property to Jesus in times past, since Judas knew exactly where Jesus could be found that night. (See *Mark 14:32.*)

AN AMAZING ROD

One of the things God gave Moses to show his authority before Pharaoh was a rod that would turn into a snake when it was thrown down and then become a rod again when the tail of the snake was picked up. This rod was entrusted to Aaron, Moses' brother, who spoke on Moses' behalf before Pharaoh.

The image of a cobra was a royal symbol in Egypt—it appeared on the front of the headdress worn by the pharaohs. The Egyptians worshipped and feared serpents. The use of a serpent as a first sign before Pharaoh was a surefire way to capture his attention!

Pharaoh's magicians controlled serpents—they also were able to throw down their rods and have them become serpents. But Aaron's serpent-rod ate the serpents produced by the pharaoh's magicians! This was a strong sign that the power given to Aaron was stronger than all forms of magic, fortune-telling, astrology, reading of omens, witchcraft, and necromancy. (See *Exodus 7:8–13.*)

WHAT DID YOU CALL THAT?

The objects in churches and cathedrals—especially very old cathedrals in Europe, Turkey, and northern Africa—are often very familiar by sight but totally unfamiliar by name. See if you can guess the meaning of the object name before reading the definition. Some of these words and phrases may be useful to those who like to play the word game Scrabble!

1. *Trendle* (TREN-dul). A wheel or circular object hung in a church, on which candles are placed.

2. *Exonarthex* (ex-o-NAR-thex). The porch opening of a church out onto a street.

3. *Triptych* (TRIP-tick). A painting that has three panels or "wings," the outer two of which close over the central part.

4. *Duomo* (du-O-mo). Another word for cathedral.

5. *Cutty Stool* (CUT-tee stool). A seat or area in a Scottish church where, allegedly, immoral persons were forced to sit.

6. *Arca* (AR-kuh). Usually an elaborately decorated, freestanding tomb or coffin, often raised on columns or figures, that serves as both a tomb and a shrine.

7. *Alabastron* (al-a-BAS-tron). The glass or metal vessel in a Byzantine church that holds holy oil for christening.

8. *Thurible* (THUR-i-bul). A metal vessel for the ceremonial burning of incense; it is suspended on chains so it can be swung back and forth.

9. *Rood* (rud). A cross or crucifix, often a large one made of wood and set in stone, highly decorated with carvings or statues; the rood is frequently part of a screen that divides the main part of a cathedral (nave) from the choir area.

10. *Pall* (pol). Usually a square piece of cardboard covered with linen that is placed over the chalice (cup) prior to the cup's being used in a Communion service; the word can also refer to a black, purple, or white velvet piece of cloth spread over a coffin.

11. *Chasuble* (CHAZ-u-bul). A sleeveless poncho-style outer garment worn by those who are leading a Communion service (Eucharist)—it is intended to symbolize charity.

12. *Chazranion* (chaz-RAY-nee-on). A bishop's staff, especially in the Byzantine tradition, usually a decorated ebony stick with a knob of ivory or silver at the tip.

WHAT DID YOU CALL THAT? (CONT'D)

13. *Apse* (aps). The end of a sanctuary that is covered by a half dome and is usually semicircular or polygonal in shape; usually found in a basilica-style church.

14. *Cuthino* (cuh-THEE-no). A vestment worn by clergy in the Syrian church, usually embroidered with many crosses.

15. *Custodia* (cus-TOE-dee-uh). Usually an elaborately designed, small, closed cupboard near an altar, for housing bread blessed for use in Communion services.

16. *Navicula* (nav-ICK-u-lah). A vessel for carrying incense in order to replenish a censer, sometimes called a "boat."

17. *Easter candle*. A large ornamental candle that is kept lit from the Saturday before Easter to Ascension Day.

18. *Cope* (kope). Not to be confused with a cape, a cope is a floor-length, sleeveless cloak made of elaborate, often embroidered or brocaded fabrics fastened at the chest with a clasp, worn by a priest on major religious feast days.

19. *Maesta* (my-ES-tuh). A form of painting often found in cathedrals, in which the Virgin Mary appears enthroned holding the infant Jesus on her arm or lap, or as queen of heaven surrounded by angels.

20. *Manuterge* (MAN-oo-terg). The finger towel used by presiding clergy prior to conducting a Eucharist or Communion service.

21. *Ombrellino* (om-BREL-ee-no). A small canopy of white silk carried over Communion elements if they are carried from one place to another.

22. *Yefe tsami qob* (Yef-uh za-mee kob). The name of the tall white hat worn by Ethiopian monks.

23. *Frontal*. A panel of embroidered cloth that hangs in front of the altar, usually in the color associated with the liturgical season.

24. *Kamelavchion* (kam-e-LOV-kee-on). The name of the black cylindrical hat worn by monks and clergy in the Eastern Orthodox Church—in the Greek church, the hat has a projecting brim around the top; in the Russian church the hat has no brim, but the diameter of the hat at the top is greater than at the bottom.

25. *Lich Gate* (LICK gate). A covered gateway in a churchyard wall.

WHAT A GUY!

Jesus came from heaven, so he was 100% God. But he was also 100% human (God's math, not people's). Here are ten aspects of his humanity recorded in the New Testament:

1. He was born to a woman (*Matthew 1:18–21*).
2. He grew up (*Luke 2:40*).
3. He was tempted (*Matthew 4:1*).
4. He got hungry and thirsty (*Matthew 4:2; John 4:7*).
5. He got tired (*John 4:6*).
6. He got angry! (*Matthew 21:12–13*).
7. He cried when he was sad (*John 11:32–36*).
8. He was obedient (*Philippians 2:5–8*).
9. He felt physical pain (*1 Peter 4:1*).
10. He died (*Mark 15:37*).

FOLLOW THE LEADER?

Since the beginning of time, humans have let their leaders know when they aren't happy. While it's all right to disagree, God makes it clear in the Bible that he expects people to respect their leaders. Even leaders who seem unworthy of respect can serve a purpose.

1. God created everything, including rulers, for his own purpose (*Colossians 1:16*).
2. "Render unto Caesar"—that is, pay your taxes (*Matthew 22:15–21*).
3. God has put every ruler in his position, so obey that person (*Romans 13:1*).
4. Show your leaders honor and respect (*1 Peter 2:13–17*).
5. Be thoughtful of your leaders; they work hard to try to do what's right (*1 Thessalonians 5:12–13*).
6. Even when you don't agree with something like a tax, paying is the right thing to do (*Matthew 17:24–27*).
7. Be subject to rulers and show humility to all (*Titus 3:1–2*).
8. Obeying rulers is a matter of conscience (*Romans 13:5*).
9. When you obey your leaders, their work will be a joy, which benefits all —and leaders ultimately answer to God (*Hebrews 13:17*).
10. Go the extra mile—pray for those in authority (*1 Timothy 2:1–2*).

LIGHTEN UP

Laughter is good medicine. Researchers estimate that laughing one hundred times a day is equal to a ten-minute workout on a rowing machine or fifteen minutes on an exercise bike.

Laughter is healthy. What modern research has scientifically proven, biblical wisdom has taught for hundreds of years: "A cheerful heart is good medicine" *(Proverbs 17:22 NIV)*.

Besides good health, humor makes for good relationships. People laugh when they feel comfortable with one another—and laughter increases their comfort level. A shared moment of laughter can bring people together. As author Steve Sjogren says, "Where the Spirit of the Lord is, there is fun."

People often laugh at absurdities of life. Abraham and Sarah laughed when God told them they were going to have a baby in their old age. When their son was born, Sarah said, "God has brought me laughter, and everyone who hears about this will laugh with me" *(Genesis 21:6 NIV)*. The name Isaac, which Abraham and Sarah gave to their son, literally means "he laughs."

Jesus said, "Blessed are you who weep now, for you will laugh" *(Luke 6:21 NIV)*. The promise of heaven is the promise of everlasting joy and laughter.

Source: people.howstuffworks.com/laughter7.htm.

TRUTH IS STRANGER THAN FICTION

In many bookstores, the Bible holds two distinctions. First, it is one of the best-selling books of all time. Second, it is also one of the most shoplifted books of all time. One speculation is that perhaps people think the Bible should be available to everyone free of charge.

Sources: www.unmc.edu/Community/ruralmeded/RCBfile/bible_facts.htm; www.didyouknow.cd/fastfacts/religion.htm.

LITTLE-KNOWN BIBLE WORD FACTS

The word *eternity* occurs only once in the King James Bible. The word *Christian* appears only three times. *Grandmother* can be found just once. The book of Esther does not contain the word *God*. Cats are not mentioned; dogs are. The last word in the Bible is *Amen*.

GEZHUNDHEIT!

The expression "God bless you," associated with a sneeze, began in the sixth century by order of Pope Gregory the Great. A deadly plague raged through Italy, and sneezing was one of the symptoms indicating imminent death. The pope advised healthy people to pray for the sick, and if no one was available, the sneezer was to exclaim out loud, "God help me!"

LIFE AT THE TOP

The pope is the head of the Roman Catholic Church and considered the successor of Saint Peter as bishop of Rome. He acts either alone or with a council in making laws and defining doctrine for the church. He is addressed as "His Holiness the Pope" and "Your Holiness" and has many titles: Bishop of Rome, Vicar of Jesus Christ, Successor of Saint Peter, the Prince of the Apostles, Supreme Pontiff, Patriarch of the West, Primate of Italy, Archbishop and Metropolitan of the Roman Province, and Sovereign of the State of Vatican City.

When a man becomes pope, he loses his family name and most of his ties to his native land. His daily life is regulated down to the smallest details. The pope has his own confessor and makes weekly visits to confess his sins and receive absolution. The pope receives no salary and does not have a bank account.

Pope John Paul II, who served from his election in 1978 to his death in 2005, kept this general daily schedule at the Vatican: awaken at 5:30 a.m., have prayers and attend morning Mass, have audiences with visiting groups and individuals, spend hours at work in his office, and then hold a late-afternoon staff meeting. All his meals were working meals. He said prayers at 10:30 p.m. and ended his day at 11:00 p.m.

When the pope is in residence at the Vatican, general audiences are scheduled every Wednesday. Requests are made through the Vatican office by telephone or by fax.

Source: Nino Lo Bello, *The Incredible Book of Vatican Facts and Papal Curiosities: A Treasury of Trivia* (Liguori, MO: Liguori, c1998).

HOW TO SPELL PARADISE? H-E-A-V-E-N

Peace. Joy. Beauty. Harmony. Total satisfaction. And plenty of face time with God! That's heaven. But what exactly is it? What's it about?

1. It's for those who have realized that they need God (*Matthew 5:3*).
2. It is also called the New Jerusalem (*Revelation 21:2*).
3. There's no temple, because God and Jesus are its "temple" (*Revelation 21:22*).
4. It's a place of purity (*Revelation 21:27*).
5. It's a city that's "pure gold, as clear as glass" (*Revelation 21:18 NLT*).
6. Its length, width, and height are all the same—perfectly proportioned (*Revelation 21:16*).
7. It will be daytime all the time there (*Revelation 21:25*).
8. There's enough room for everyone who is going there (*John 14:1–2*).
9. Thousands of angels live there (*Hebrews 12:22*).
10. The sun and moon won't be necessary, because God's glory will light up everything (*Revelation 21:23*).
11. Its street is made of pure gold (*Revelation 21:21*).
12. It's God's throne (*Isaiah 66:1*).
13. It has twelve gates (made of pearl) that will never be shut (*Revelation 21:21, 25*).
14. It is also called "Zion," and it is beautiful (*Psalm 50:2*).
15. It has a "river of life" (*Revelation 22:1*).
16. No one will cry there (*Revelation 21:4*).
17. Death will be a thing of the past (*Revelation 21:4*).
18. Pain will be eradicated (*Revelation 21:4*).
19. It will never perish, and neither will those who live there (*1 Corinthians 15:50*).
20. Hunger and thirst? Not a problem there (*Revelation 7:16*).
21. There's a "tree of life" whose leaves will wipe out sickness (*Revelation 22:2*).
22. When those who love God get there, they will finally understand everything perfectly (*1 Corinthians 13:12*).
23. The "gate" into it is small (*Matthew 7:13–14*).
24. It's better than earth, a place that those who love God can call home (*Hebrews 11:13–16*).
25. It is a place of rest for those who love God (*Revelation 14:13*).

OPEN HEARTS AND OPEN HOMES

Hospitality isn't about picture-perfect table settings, or even entertaining. Anyone who has ever welcomed a stranger has shown hospitality. In the Bible, God instructed his people to welcome the stranger because "you were strangers in the land of Egypt" *(Exodus 22:21 AMP)*. Abraham fed three strangers who turned out to be angels announcing Isaac's birth *(Genesis 18; Hebrews 13:2)*. Rahab was blessed for showing hospitality to Joshua's spies *(Joshua 2)*. The Shunammite woman welcomed the prophet Elisha into her home *(2 Kings 4)*.

Extending hospitality to strangers is a mark of the hospitality of God, who says that whoever will come is welcomed into his household.

A TEN-DOLLAR WORD FOR "WORK TOGETHER"

The words *ecumenical* (adjective) and *ecumenism* (noun) come from a Greek word meaning "relating to, or representing, the whole of a body of churches." One author has described ecumenism as the effort to focus on those beliefs that denominations have in common and to celebrate their common faith.

"Ecumenical relations," therefore, refers to the efforts of churches of different denominations to work together.

Ecumenical relationships are often formed within a community to provide a more consolidated, effective attack on social ills such as poverty, homelessness, illiteracy, or broken homes, as well as to help those stricken by natural disasters such as hurricanes and earthquakes. Sometimes these efforts extend beyond the local community to the national or worldwide community.

Ecumenical groups are also often formed to help promote understanding and healing for racial and religious conflicts within communities.

WHAT NOT TO
WORSHIP

God, it's fair to say, is a jealous God. He said so himself: "Do not worship any other god, for the LORD, whose name is Jealous, is a jealous God" *(Exodus 34:14 NIV)*. He made a similar point as he was giving the Israelites the Ten Commandments *(Exodus 20:5)*.

At that time in history, many of the nations surrounding Israel worshipped idols made to gods such as Baal, Asherah, and Dagon. God wanted to bless his people and share a loving relationship with them, but the Israelites couldn't resist temptation. Seduced by the Canaanites and others, God's people began to desire a god they could see instead of the God they couldn't see. God repeatedly warned his people not to make carved images or idols.

When God rescued the Israelites from slavery in Egypt, he warned them not to make images of animals, birds, or fish to worship *(Deuteronomy 4:15–18)*. He didn't want them bowing down to the sun, moon, or stars either *(v. 19)*. And what sort of penalty did God tell Moses to carry out on the ones who served or worshipped other gods? "Stone the man or woman to death" *(Deuteronomy 17:5 NRSV)*.

In talking to the prophet Jeremiah, God mentioned that some of his people had paid homage to trees and stones. They "turned their backs to Me" in doing so, God said *(Jeremiah 2:26–29 AMP)*.

At the time of the prophet Ezekiel, there were women who were making up prophecies and wearing "magic" charms on their wrists. They were pretending to be all-wise and all-knowing. God was not at all pleased *(Ezekiel 13:17–23)*. King Manasseh of Judah sacrificed his son, built altars for false gods,

WHAT NOT TO
WORSHIP (CONT'D)

consulted mediums and psychics, and practiced sorcery and divination *(2 Kings 21:1–6)*. God called him evil.

Making idols was forbidden, but so was speaking their names and eating food that had been offered up to them *(Exodus 23:13; 34:15)*.

Although the people were told time and again that they'd pay a high price for their idol worship, they refused to listen. King David had an insightful comment to make about the idols people were worshipping in his era. He said they had a mouth and eyes but couldn't speak or see. They had ears and a nose but couldn't hear or smell, hands and feet but couldn't feel or walk. Those who made them and trusted them were "just as helpless as those useless gods" *(Psalm 115:4–8 CEV)*.

Not everyone in the Old Testament hopped on the idol-worshipping bandwagon, however. The prophet Daniel and three of his friends remained true to God, even when threatened with death, and lived to tell about it *(Daniel 3:1–27; 6:1–22)*.

NERO THE DEPRAVED

Roman emperor Nero (AD 37–68) is the most famous persecutor of believers in history. Nero was suspected of starting the great fire of Rome in AD 64, which burned for ten days and left much of the city in ruins. To clear himself of rumors that he had started the fire to make space for his palace, Nero blamed the fire on the followers of Jesus.

As punishment for a crime they didn't commit, Nero had many believers arrested, tortured, and crucified. Some were burned alive—tied to posts and set afire to provide torch-style "lighting" for Nero's garden. Others were sent to the Coliseum, where they were torn to pieces by wild animals.

Christian tradition teaches that both Peter and Paul were martyred in Rome on orders from Nero. Because of his well-documented persecutions, Nero is considered one of the most depraved and cruel of the Roman emperors.

Sources: www.roman-emperors.org/nero.htm; www.wsu.edu:8080; www.religionfacts.com/christianity/history/persecution.htm.

SHEMA YISRAEL

Hear, O Israel: The LORD our God, the LORD is one" (*Deuteronomy 6:4 NIV*). This is perhaps the closest of all Jewish sayings to being the creed and declaration of the Jewish religion. These ancient words comprise a Jewish confession of faith and are recited several times daily by devout Jews. The pronouncement "The LORD is one" sums up Jewish monotheism and rejects the multiple false gods and idols of ancient and modern culture.

In Judaism, this verse is called the Shema, which is Hebrew for "hear." Jewish prayer is always an opportunity to speak and to listen. Listening is regarded as being equally important to speaking, perhaps more important. The Shema is recited with three sections of the Torah that are central to Jewish belief: Deuteronomy 6:4–9, about the nature of God; Deuteronomy 11:13–21, about reward and punishment and the truth that human actions have significance; and Numbers 15:37–41, which declares God's desire for his people to be consecrated to him, reminding them to live as belonging to him alone.

IN TIMES OF TROUBLE, CALL ON THE BIG GUY

Life is most certainly not a bowl of cherries. Even those born with the proverbial silver spoon in their mouths are not trouble-proof. Fortunately, help is not just on the way; it's here. That's what many men and women such as the ones quoted below have found to be true down through the ages:

1. "As sure as ever God puts his children in the furnace, he will be in the furnace with them."—*Charles Spurgeon (British preacher, 1834–1892)*

2. "God often puts us in situations that are too much for us so that we will learn that no situation is too much for him."
   —*Erwin W. Lutzer (American pastor, 1941–)*

3. "How often we look upon God as our last and feeblest resource! We go to him because we have nowhere else to go. And then we learn that the storms of life have driven us, not upon the rocks, but into the desired haven."—*George MacDonald (Scottish preacher and author, 1824–1905)*

4. "If you carry the cross willingly, it will carry you. If you are forced against your will to carry the cross, then you make it difficult for yourself, adding to your load. No matter what attitude you have, you must bear the burden. If you manage to throw away one cross, you will certainly find another, and it may be even heavier."
   —*Thomas à Kempis (Christian monk and author, 1380–1471)*

5. "The greater the difficulty, the more glory in surmounting it. Skillful pilots gain their reputation from storms and tempests."
   —*Epicurus (Greek philosopher, 341–270 BC)*

6. "Great trials seem to be necessary preparation for great duties."
   —*Edward Thomson (American bishop, 1810–1870)*

7. "Take everything that comes into your life as being from the hand of God, not from the hand of man."
   —*Madame Guyon (French mystic, 1648–1717)*

8. "The great thing, if one can, is to stop regarding all the unpleasant things as interruptions of one's own or real life. The truth is of course that what one calls the interruptions are precisely one's real life—the life God is sending one day by day. What one calls one's real life is a phantom of one's own imagination."—*C. S. Lewis (British author, 1898–1963)*

9. "As the sea is subject to storm and tempests, so is every man in the world."—*John Donne (English poet, 1572–1631)*

10. "Men think that God is destroying them when he is tuning them."
    —*Henry Ward Beecher (American clergyman, 1813–1887)*

11. "In times like these, it helps to recall that there have always been times like these."—*Paul Harvey (radio journalist, 1918–)*

FACETS OF PRAISE

Praise is the natural response to who God is. Hebrew and Greek, two of the original ancient languages of the Scriptures, have more than one word that means "praise." Each word gives added insight into what it means to praise God.

Hebrew

1. *Halal.* To boast, make a show, to celebrate, to act clamorously foolish. The word *hallelujah* comes from *halal* (*Psalm 113:1–3*).

2. *Yadah.* The extended hand, to throw out the hand, to worship with extended hand (*Genesis 49:8*).

3. *Zamar.* To pluck the strings of an instrument. Joyful expressions of music with musical instruments (*Psalm 57:8–9*).

4. *Shabach.* To shout, address in a loud tone, a loud adoration; proclaim with a loud voice, to glory, to command and to triumph (*Isaiah 12:6*).

5. *Barak.* To kneel down, to bless God as an act of adoration (*1 Chronicles 29:20*).

Greek

1. *Aineo.* To sing praise; used only of God (*Luke 2:20*).

2. *Epaineo.* To praise or applaud; applied to God and to people (*Ephesians 1:6*).

3. *Eulogeo.* To praise, bless, speak well of; regarding God, persons, and things. Basis of the word *eulogy* (*Matthew 21:9*).

4. *Doxazo.* To esteem, glorious, honor, magnify, dignity, full of glory. Basis of the word *doxology* (*Luke 18:43*).

5. *Humneo.* To sing praise to God in celebration. Basis of the word *hymn* (*Hebrews 2:12*).

UNCEASING PRAISE!

Praise is the most natural response to God when a person becomes aware of who God is. The book of Psalms is a songbook of praises. But throughout Scripture, exuberant praise marks the people who follow God:

1. Moses and the Israelites praised God for deliverance through the Red Sea (*Exodus 15*).

2. Deborah praised God after the defeat of the Canaanites (*Judges 5*).

3. Hannah praised God for her son Samuel (*1 Samuel 2:1–10*).

4. David praised God for his deliverance from Saul (*2 Samuel 22*).

5. Habakkuk praised God for his majesty and goodness (*Habakkuk 3*).

6. Mary praised God for choosing her to give birth to Jesus, the Messiah (*Luke 1:46–55*).

7. The angels praised God for the birth of Jesus (*Luke 2:13–14*).

8. Paul praised God for his wisdom (*Romans 11:33–36*).

MRS. GOODNEST

Timmy was a five-year-old boy whose mother was a worrier. Mom was especially worried for Timmy's safety as he walked to kindergarten two blocks away. She walked him to school the first couple of days, but at the end of the week Timmy complained that he wanted to be like the "big boys," and none of their mothers walked with them. She agreed that he could walk with another neighbor boy who lived several doors away.

Mom also knew that her neighbor, Mrs. Goodnest, often took an early morning walk, pushing her baby in his carriage with her toddler daughter walking alongside them. Mom asked Mrs. Goodnest if she would mind casually following Timmy to school for a few days without letting Timmy know what she was up to. Mrs. Goodnest was more than happy to help, and the next morning she and her little girl, Marcy, and baby Jamie in the carriage, set out following Timmy as he walked to school with his friend. She did this the entire week. Timmy's friend noticed the same lady following them every morning. Finally he asked, "Do you know that lady and little girl who follow us to school?" Timmy nonchalantly replied, "Yeah, that's our neighbor Shirley Goodnest and her daughter, Marcy."

"Well, why is she following us?"

Timmy replied, "Every night Mom makes me say Psalm 23 with my prayers. Psalm 23 says, 'Shirley Goodnest and Marcy shall follow me all the days of my life,' so I guess I'll just have to get used to it."

Source: This story has appeared on several Web sites in recent years, always with the citation "author unknown." This entry was adapted slightly from a version found on forums, dealofday.com.

HANDS THAT BRING HEALING

Growing up in a Detroit ghetto in the 1950s was not easy, especially for African-American children—and especially for children in single-parent homes.

Ben Carson rose above it all, however, thanks to a determined mother and faith in God.

Ben attended a Seventh-Day Adventist church when he was eight and decided that from then on he would do his best to live a life that pleased God—to become a follower of Jesus. He also decided to become a doctor.

There were plenty of obstacles in Ben's path, including a bad temper. One day in ninth grade he became so angry, he almost killed a good friend with a knife. Shaken, he prayed and asked God to cure him of his temper. Since that day, he says, "I have never had a problem with my temper."

Ben worked hard in school and was accepted to Yale and later graduated from the University of Michigan medical school. He became the director of pediatric neurosurgery at Johns Hopkins University Hospital in 1985 and made medical history in 1987 when he and his team became the first to successfully separate Siamese twins born joined at the back of their heads.

Ben says he always tells his patients to say their prayers before surgery, because he wants to "remind them of God's loving presence." Then he trusts God to use him—and his "divine gift" of excellent eye-and-hand coordination—to bring healing to those who turn to him for help.

Source: Ben Carson with Cecil Murphey, *Gifted Hands: The Ben Carson Story* (Grand Rapids, MI: Zondervan, 1990).

THE PERFECTION OF PARADISE

*P*aradise is a word of Persian origin, meaning a garden, orchard, or other enclosed place that is filled with beauty and delight. The word does not appear in the Old Testament but is applied figuratively in the New Testament to the heavenly home of the righteous *(Luke 23:43)*. Through a parable, Jesus taught that paradise and hades are separated by an unbridgeable fixed chasm *(Luke 16:19–31)*. The word *paradise* is used as an allusion to the Garden of Eden *(Revelation 2:7)*. Paradise is perfect in every way—a complete reversal of all that occurred after Adam and Eve disobeyed God.

MORE BALM, PLEASE

*B*alm is a common name for a number of oily, resinous substances that flow spontaneously, or by incision, from certain trees or plants. In Bible times the production of balm was particularly associated with the region of Gilead, a mountainous area east of the Jordan River *(Genesis 37:25)*. The gum of the balsam tree was specifically called "the balm of Gilead" *(Jeremiah 8:22)*. This particular gum was very costly and fragrant, and it was used extensively for centuries in the Middle East as a medicine and as a cosmetic. The so-called "balm of gilead" tree in the United States is not the same as the balsam tree in the Middle East.

CITY OF REFUGE

*A*s the Israelites settled Canaan, Moses established six "cities of refuge" under jurisdiction of the Levites: Kedesh, Shechem, and Kirjath-arba, Bezer, Ramoth, and Golan (in Bashan). If a person unintentionally was involved in the death of another person, he could flee to one of these cities and live while his offense was investigated. If he was found not to have hated the victim in the past, he was allowed to remain alive. On the other hand, if he was found guilty of the death—by premeditation, past hatred, acting as an accomplice, or outright murder—he could be turned over to the victim's tribe and slain.

AMERICA'S FIRST CHURCH

Christ Church, in Philadelphia, is believed to be the first church built on U.S. soil. Founded in 1695, it was the first Anglican parish in Pennsylvania. After the American colonies won independence, the church became the center of the birth of the Episcopal Church in America.

Christ Church is often recognized as "the Nation's Church" because of its ties to many of the country's Founding Fathers, including Betsy Ross, Robert Morris, Absalom Jones, Benjamin Rush, John Penn (William Penn's grandson), and Francis Hopkinson. During the final years of the eighteenth century, Philadelphia served as the capital of the young nation, and the commander in chief of the Continental Army, George Washington, was perhaps the most famous of Christ Church's worshippers. Benjamin Franklin, said to be the best-known American of his day, and his wife were also parishioners. The nearby Christ Church Burial Ground became the final resting place for Mr. and Mrs. Franklin.

The original church structure was a small brick-and-wooden structure that fit into its Quaker-dominated surroundings in the late 1600s. Construction on the current Christ Church building began in 1727 and continued until 1744. However, it was another decade before the tower and steeple were completed. Benjamin Franklin organized a lottery to finance the steeple, and the impressive structure was the tallest structure in the colonies for eighty-three years.

Although the church is a regular stop for tourists throughout the year, it continues to be a very active parish with regularly scheduled services.

Sources: www.christchurchphila.org/; www.oldchristchurch.org/history/; content.ancestry.com/iexec/?htx=List&dbid=6413&offerid=0%3a7858%3a0.

SELF-CONTROL

According to the apostle Paul, self-control is possible only if one yields to God and receives his help in controlling one's behavior. Self-control is therefore considered a "fruit of the Spirit" *(Galatians 5:22–23).*

1. "If you would learn self-mastery, begin by yielding yourself to the One Great Master."—*Johann Friederich Lobstein (German surgeon and anatomist, 1736–1784)*

2. "Conquer thyself. Till thou hast done this, thou art but a slave; for it is almost as well to be subjected to another's appetite as to thine own."—*Richard E. Burton (American author and professor, 1861–1940)*

3. "He who reigns within himself and rules his passions, desires, and fears is more than a king."—*John Milton (English poet, 1608–1674)*

4. "The man whom Heaven appoints to govern others, should himself first learn to bend his passions to the sway of reason."—*James Thomson (Scottish poet, 1700–1748)*

5. "To rule self and subdue our passions is the more praiseworthy because so few know how to do it."—*Francesco Guiccardini (Italian statesman and historian, 1483–1540)*

6. "What is the best government? . . . That which teaches us to govern ourselves."—*Johann Wolfgang von Goethe (German poet, dramatist, and philosopher, 1749–1832)*

7. "More dear in the sight of God and His angels than any other conquest is the conquest of self."—*Arthur P. Stanley (English clergyman and dean of Westminster, 1814–1881)*

8. "The truest conquest is where the soul is bringing every thought into captivity to the obedience of Christ."—*John Caird (Scottish clergyman, 1822–1898)*

9. "The most precious of all possessions, is power over ourselves; power to withstand trial, to bear suffering, to front danger; power over pleasure and pain; power to follow our convictions, however resisted by menace and scorn; the power of calm reliance in scenes of darkness and storms."—*John Locke (English philosopher, 1632–1704)*

10. "What we do upon some great occasion will probably depend on what we already are; and what we are will be the result of previous years of self-discipline."—*Henry P. Liddon (English clergyman, 1829–1890)*

11. "He that would be superior to external influences must first become superior to his own passions."—*Samuel Johnson (English author, 1709–1784)*

WHO NAMES
THIS CHILD?

For centuries the giving of a name to a child was part of a family's "Christian witness." Naming a child after a Bible character or a saint in the church was considered part of "claiming" that child for Jesus. To give a child a Christian name was to send a signal that the child was part of a Christian family. Thus, the names Mary and John became the most popular ones for children born to believing parents, and remained so for more than a thousand years! Other popular girl names throughout the first two millennia included Sarah, Rachel, Rebecca, Hannah, Anna, Elizabeth, and Catherine. And for the boys, the names David, Joshua, Paul, Mark, Luke, Matthew, Abraham, Isaac, Jacob, and Jeremiah were also very popular.

In Greece, children are given not only a "family name" but also the name of a saint—and the saint's day is remembered by the family and child with even greater celebration than the child's natural birthday.

Most people in the United States today are named by their parents, who choose names they like or that are traditional in their families. The official names are often announced publicly and verbally at a religious baptism or dedication ceremony, in addition to being printed in public records and a local newspaper. In other parts of the world, it sometimes takes a village to name a child! The naming has little to do with a religious ceremony.

As an example, Acholi children in northern Uganda and southern Sudan undergo an elaborate name-giving ceremony. A baby and its mother are isolated for several days in the hut where the mother gave birth, along with a woman called a

WHO NAMES
THIS CHILD? (CONT'D)

"celebrant." When the three emerge from the hut, they engage in a symbolic tasting of the baby's first food, and the infant's head is shaved. Water from the infant's "first meal" is poured at the door of the birth-hut, and then the mother and child reenter the hut. The celebrant pays a visit to the child's grandparents, who whisper to the celebrant names that she shares privately with the mother upon her return.

The celebrant then goes to gather the village together for the formal naming ceremony. After calling the village together, the celebrant returns and knocks on the door of the hut and asks the mother to call out the names that are to be given to the child. The mother responds, and if there is a consensus of those assembled outside that these are the appropriate names for the child, the full name of the child is formally announced by the celebrant, and the child is thus officially named. A child from the village is selected to enter the hut and carry out the infant.

The names given to Acholi children always have a personal "history" and often are related to significant circumstances surrounding the child's birth. All of this must occur before the child is baptized in a religious ceremony or before the child can engage in any other social functions.

FRINGE BEREFT

Why was David so guilt-ridden after he cut off the edge of King Saul's garment (*1 Samuel 24:4–6*)? The garment fringe indicated the rank of the wearer. King Saul's fringe indicated his status as king; when he discovered it had been cut off, he knew that his days as king were numbered. In this defiant act, David stripped Saul, God's anointed, of his authority as king. David repented of this before God and King Saul.

Sources: www.bibletopics.com/biblestudy/14.htm; www.thegoldenreport.com/.

PSALMS 24/7

Continual prayer was one of the chief activities of medieval monasteries. The first thing required of new monks or nuns was to learn to read; the next requirement was to memorize the entire book of Psalms. Most Benedictine monks and nuns chanted all 150 psalms once a week in the seven daily times of prayer, throughout the day. That tradition continues today.

Source: Denis Martin, "Scripture-Drenched Life," *Christian History*, no. 49; January 1, 1996, p. 26.

ALL IS FORGIVEN . . . 350 YEARS LATER

Galileo Galilei (1564–1642) created a firestorm of controversy when he asserted that earth was not the center of the universe; the sun was.

Since ancient times, humankind—including the Catholic Church—had believed that everything revolved around the earth.

In his day, Galileo couldn't convince church authorities that he was right. Ultimately, he was arrested and forced to say he was wrong.

The church reviewed its decision in 1992 and officially forgave Galileo—admitting that theological advisers had erred, but not that the church had done anything wrong.

CAN'T GET ENOUGH OF PRAYER

> Early to bed,
> Early to rise,
> Makes it possible to pray,
> Seven times a day.

The apostle Paul's admonition to "pray without ceasing" *(1 Thessalonians 5:17 NKJV)* was taken fairly literally by the "father of Western monasticism," Saint Benedict of Nursia, who was born in the late fifth century and started the Benedictine order of monks.

Saint Benedict is best known for the "Benedictine Rule," which was adopted by many monasteries across Europe. It outlined a serious, sensible, godly way of life for the monks who followed it.

Prayer was central to the Rule. It drove every activity at the monastery, including the manual labor and study expected of all members. Seven formal times of prayer were required each day, known as "the offices." This number may have come from Psalm 119:164, which says, "Seven times a day I praise You" *(NKJV)*.

The prayer life of a monk usually began before dawn. Times of day could vary from monastery to monastery, but generally speaking, a monk might pray at 3:00 a.m. (matins and lauds), 6:00 a.m. (prime), 9:00 a.m. (terce), 12:00 noon (sext), 3:00 p.m. (none), 6:00 p.m. (vespers), and 9:00 p.m. (compline). Prayers were both spoken and sung. Some prayers, oftentimes psalms, were prayed regularly in unison by all who were gathered together. This came to be known as "common prayer"—prayers voiced in common.

The influence of monasteries has waned, but the importance of prayer has been recognized by believers down through the centuries.

RUBY BRIDGES: BRIDGE BUILDER

As six-year-old Ruby prepared for school, her mother said, "I want you to behave yourself today, Ruby, and don't be afraid." That was good advice for the young girl facing her first day at a new elementary school.

It was 1960 and Ruby Bridges lived in New Orleans. She was about to become the first African-American child to desegregate an elementary school. Dressed in her new school outfit, Ruby joined her mother in a car driven by federal marshals, who took them to William Frantz Elementary School. Driving up to the building, Ruby saw a large crowd of people shouting and throwing things. Not realizing the significance of what was happening, young Ruby thought it was Mardi Gras! Escorted by federal marshals, Ruby made history walking into the school. One of the marshals, Charles Burks, said, "She showed a lot of courage. She never cried. She didn't whimper. She just marched along like a little soldier. And we're all very proud of her."

Once inside the school, Ruby and her mother spent most of the day in the principal's office because of the uproar around them. It wasn't until the following day that Ruby went to her classroom. The teacher was there, but otherwise the classroom was empty. Angry parents had taken their children out of school, and for the entire year Ruby was the only child in that class.

Among those in the crowd watching Ruby outside the school was child psychiatrist Dr. Robert Coles. He was amazed at Ruby's strong and dignified demeanor. Ruby's teacher, Barbara Henry, said, "A woman spat at Ruby but missed; Ruby smiled at her. A man shook his fist at her; Ruby smiled at him."

RUBY BRIDGES: BRIDGE BUILDER (CONT'D)

Ruby's mother had told her, "Ruby, if I'm not with you and you're afraid, then always say your prayers." So Ruby prayed on the way to school. She later said, "Prayer was my protection." One day Mrs. Henry observed Ruby talking to the crowd, and asked her, "I saw your lips moving, but I couldn't make out what you were saying to those people." Ruby explained, "I wasn't talking to them, I was praying for them." On her way to school each day, she would pray for the people in the crowd. But that day she had forgotten until she was actually in the crowd. Then she prayed for God to be with her and with those people. She prayed God would forgive them.

Dr. Coles interviewed Ruby about her experience. She mentioned that she "prayed and hoped God would do something." Coles could not account for the child's extraordinary courage. Ruby explained why she prayed: "Because they need praying for." Eventually Coles concluded that prayer does something beyond "mere psychological explanations."

Ruby and Mrs. Henry both had perfect attendance that year. When Ruby returned the next fall, things were different. There were no crowds or protests, and no federal marshals. Instead there were other kids—both black and white—in her classroom.

Ruby's mother and father had prayed before sending her to William Frantz Elementary. Ruby's mother wanted a better education for her oldest daughter. Her father, who eventually lost his job over this incident, thought they were "asking for trouble." Eventually they decided to take this step forward— not just for Ruby's benefit but for the benefit of all black children.

Source: www.pbs.org/newshour/bb/race_relations/jan-june97/bridges_2-18.html.

"UP" WITH GOD!

There are dozens of uses of the word *up* in our language. Since up is the direction usually assigned to heaven, today is a good day to align yourself with heaven's "upbeat" way of life!

1. **Wake up to a good day.** Decide that today is "the day the LORD has made" to "rejoice and be glad in it" *(Psalm 118:24 NKJV)*.

2. **Dress up your heart.** Put a smile in your heart. God said, "People judge others by what they look like, but I judge people by what is in their hearts" *(1 Samuel 16:7 CEV)*.

3. **Shut up.** Listen first, talk second. "He who guards his mouth preserves his life" *(Proverb 13:3 NKJV)*.

4. **Line up.** Set goals that are in keeping with God's plan for your life, and then trust God to help you reach them. "I can do all things through Christ who strengthens me" *(Philippians 4:13 NKJV)*.

5. **Stand up.** Continue to give your time, money, and effort toward accomplishing those things you know are right to do. "Let us not grow weary while doing good, for in due season we shall reap if we do not lose heart. Therefore, as we have opportunity, let us do good" *(Galatians 6:9–10 NKJV)*.

6. **Make up.** Come to peace with your enemies right away! "Agree with your adversary quickly" *(Matthew 5:25 NKJV)*.

7. **Get up.** Refuse to let the devil keep you down. "In the name of Jesus Christ of Nazareth, rise up and walk" *(Acts 3:6 NKJV)*.

8. **Speak up.** Speak out for what is true and right. "He who speaks truth declares righteousness. . . . The tongue of the wise promotes health" *(Proverbs 12:17–18 NKJV)*.

9. **Laugh it up.** Stay joyful and rely on God's strength. "A merry heart does good, like medicine" *(Proverbs 17:22 NKJV)*.

10. **Raise up.** Establish and restore the righteous traditions that may have been forgotten or destroyed. "They shall rebuild the old ruins, they shall raise up the former desolations, and they shall repair the ruined cities" *(Isaiah 61:4 NKJV)*.

11. **Study up.** Know what the Bible says so you will know what to obey and teach. "Study to show thyself approved unto God, a workman that needeth not to be ashamed, rightly dividing the word of truth" *(2 Timothy 2:15 KJV)*.

12. **Look up.** Look to God for your direction. "Trust in the LORD with all your heart, and lean not on your own understanding; in all your ways acknowledge Him, and He shall direct your paths" *(Proverbs 3:5–6 NKJV)*.

13. **Lift up.** Cry out with a loud voice the good tidings of God's saving grace. "Lift up your voice with strength, lift it up, be not afraid; say . . . 'Behold your God!'" *(Isaiah 40:9 NKJV)*.

14. **Pray up.** Stay in prayer about everything. "Be anxious for nothing, but in everything by prayer . . . with thanksgiving, let your requests be made known to God" *(Philippians 4:6 NKJV)*.

15. **Hands up.** Keep your hands lifted toward God in praise, expecting him to lift you up as a father lifts up a beloved child. "I will lift up my hands in Your name" *(Psalm 63:4 NKJV)*.

FROM THE BOTTOM TO THE TOP

Slavery. It caused overwhelming suffering to countless men, women, and children. In the midst of this spirit-crushing travesty, men like Richard Allen nonetheless found their way to God.

Richard was born a slave in Philadelphia in 1760. At age twenty he decided to serve God for the rest of his life. He began preaching at age twenty-two. His master, who eventually became a believer as well, allowed Richard to attend Methodist Society meetings and permitted him to buy his freedom in 1786.

When the local Methodist church refused to let Richard worship God there, Richard walked out and started his own church. In 1794 he founded the Bethel African Methodist Episcopal Church. Joining forces with other African Methodist churches, Richard helped start the African Methodist Episcopal Church in 1816 and was later ordained as its first bishop.

According to the denomination's official Web site, the AME Church that Richard started now has more than two million members.

LADY SINGS THE "GO AWAY, BLUES!"

Growing up in New Orleans in the early 1900s, Mahalia Jackson was bombarded with both jazz and gospel music.

This child with the big voice, who later became the "Queen of Gospel Song," took elements of jazz, mixed them with gospel, and created a style all her own.

Mahalia said she began singing almost from the time she learned to walk and talk. Early training came through the church choir.

At age sixteen Mahalia moved to Chicago, where she opened two businesses. Music remained her passion, however. By the time she was thirty, the world knew of this contralto. People urged her to sing the blues, but she said no. Gospel's "songs of hope," she said, had the power to lift one's burdens.

Through radio, television, concerts, and records, Mahalia's renown grew. She joined the fight for civil rights but will always be best remembered for remaining gospel-true until her death in 1972.

WHAT KIND OF CHARIOT WOULD
YOU HAVE DRIVEN?

Two types of chariots are mentioned in the Bible. The first type, used by princes and high officials, was usually elaborately decorated with gold, silver, brass, and costly jewels. The other type, used in war, was protected with sheets of iron and sometimes had blades attached to the axletrees. This latter type was referred to as a "chariot of iron," although the chariot was only partially plated with iron.

Both kinds of chariots were drawn by horses, and their construction was somewhat similar to a two-wheeled cart. The first Bible mention of chariots is in Genesis 41:43, where Joseph is said to have been placed, as a mark of distinction, in Pharaoh's second chariot. Later Joseph went in his own chariot to greet Jacob upon his arrival in Egypt from Canaan *(Genesis 46:29)*. Chariots also formed part of Jacob's funeral procession, possibly as an honor guard *(Genesis 50:9)*.

The first military mention of chariots occurs at the Israelites' crossing of the Red Sea, when six hundred chariots of Pharaoh were destroyed *(Exodus 14:7)*. The Canaanites were enabled to resist the Israelites in some of their valleys because they had chariots of iron *(Joshua 17:18)*. Jaban, king of Canaan, had nine hundred chariots *(Judges 4:3)*.

David captured one thousand chariots from Hadadezer *(2 Samuel 8:4)* and seven hundred chariots from the Syrians *(2 Samuel 10:18)*. Prior to this, the Hebrews had few or no chariots. Solomon maintained a force of fourteen hundred chariots and horses, which he imported from Egypt *(1 Kings 10:26)*.

MEMORY LIKE AN ELEPHANT

Did you ever forget something really important? Did you know it was important? Throughout the Bible, God makes it clear that there are facts and promises he wants those who believe in him to remember:

1. The Sabbath *(Exodus 20:8)*.
2. God's wonders and works *(1 Chronicles 16:12)*.
3. Their Creator *(Ecclesiastes 12:1)*.
4. His people's wrongdoings are forgotten, because of their close relationship with God *(Hebrews 8:12)*.
5. His people's mutually binding agreement with him *(Psalm 111:5)*.
6. The day the Israelites left Egypt and slavery *(Exodus 13:3)*.
7. Abraham, Isaac, and Jacob, and God's promise to them *(Exodus 32:13)*.
8. The land God promised them *(Leviticus 26:42–43)*.
9. The fish! (Actually, God wanted his people to forget the fish) *(Numbers 11:4–6)*.
10. God's commandments *(Numbers 15:39)*.
11. God's promise to exile those who disobeyed him, but bring them back when they admitted their wrongdoing *(Nehemiah 1:8–9)*.
12. God gives them the ability to gain wealth *(Deuteronomy 8:18)*.
13. The old days when God assigned the tribes their land *(Deuteronomy 32:7–8)*.
14. God's power *(Psalm 78:42)*.
15. God's patience with people; he doesn't want anyone to perish *(2 Peter 3:9)*.
16. Although his people suffer for their faith sometimes, they benefit in the end *(Hebrews 10:32–36)*.
17. What happened in the past *(Isaiah 46:8–9)*.
18. Lot's wife—she disobeyed and was turned into salt *(Luke 17:32)*.
19. The poor *(Galatians 2:10)*.
20. Prisoners *(Hebrews 13:3)*.
21. No "servant" is greater than his "master" *(John 15:20)*.
22. What God did to Pharaoh and the Egyptians *(Deuteronomy 7:18)*.
23. God gave Miriam leprosy when she criticized Moses *(Numbers 12:9–10)*.
24. God kept his people in the desert for forty years to see if they could be trusted to obey him *(Deuteronomy 8:2)*.
25. Jesus is a descendant of David *(2 Timothy 2:8)*.

"HIGHEST PRAISE" IN
THE NATION'S CAPITAL

Regardless of which party is currently occupying the White House or the seats of the U.S. Congress, criticism is a Washington way of life, and lasting praise is a rare commodity. Yet many otherwise well-informed citizens might be very surprised to know that the capital's tallest structure contains a source of "permanent" praise, and not just for the statesman whose legacy the structure honors but also for God.

The Washington Monument, honoring the first U.S. president, George Washington, rises 555 feet above the National Mall. An aluminum point crowns the apex of the monument with its four sides facing north, south, east, and west. According to the National Park Service, the north, south, and west sides contain the names of people and dates of special significance to the creation of the monument.

The east side bears the simple Latin words *Laus Deo*, which are translated "Praise be to God."

But that's not the only place in the structure where God's importance to Washington and an emerging nation have been acknowledged.

On the twelfth landing is a blessing offered by the city of Baltimore: "May heaven to this union continue its beneficence. May brotherly affection with union be perpetual. May the free constitution which is the work of our ancestors be sacredly maintained and its administration be stamped with wisdom and virtue."

The twentieth landing contains a eulogy to George Washington, carved in Chinese characters, which was presented by a group of Chinese Christians from mainland China.

"HIGHEST PRAISE" IN
THE NATION'S CAPITAL (CONT'D)

On the twenty-fourth landing are presentations made by Sunday school children from the Methodist Episcopal Church in New York and Sabbath school children of the Methodist Episcopal Church in Philadelphia, which quote Proverbs 10:7; Luke 18:16; and Proverbs 22:6, then say, "A preached Gospel" and "A free press," then close with "Washington, we revere his memory."

An open Bible carved on the monument includes the verses Luke 18:16, which reads, "Suffer the little children to come unto me," and Proverbs 22:6, which says, "Train up a child in the way he should go, and when he is old, he will not depart from it."

On July 4, 1848, when the cornerstone was laid, several dozen items were placed inside, including a Bible presented by the Bible Society.

Also displayed at the monument is a prayer adapted from a letter written by George Washington to the governors of the thirteen states on the occasion of his retirement from command of the Continental Army and public life. It says in part:

> Almighty God: We make our earnest prayer that Thou wilt keep the United States in Thy holy protection; that Thou wilt incline the hearts of the citizens to cultivate a spirit of subordination and obedience to government; and entertain a brotherly affection and love for one another and for their fellow citizens of the United States at large.
>
> And finally that Thou wilt most graciously be pleased to dispose us all to do justice, to love mercy, and to demean ourselves with that charity, humility, and pacific temper of mind which were the characteristics of the Divine Author of our blessed religion, and without a humble imitation of whose example in these things we can never hope to be a happy nation.

GOING ROUND IN CIRCLES

Labyrinths were created because it was just too dangerous to go to Jerusalem.

In the Middle Ages, devout believers made a practice of making a pilgrimage to the Holy Land—to "walk where Jesus walked" so they could understand him better and feel closer to him. Then along came the Crusades, and the trip became too risky.

Believers could still go to churches, of course, but a labyrinth (a circular path painted on the floor or laid out on the ground) was an innovation that helped a pilgrim focus on God.

There were many aspects of walking the labyrinth that gave it real meaning. As with the pilgrimage to Jerusalem, the pilgrim had to make a conscious decision to "do the walk." He did not need any special equipment; it was "come as you are," which is what God says to those who are thinking of developing a relationship with him.

Walking in a circle had the effect of making one quiet, which was good for prayer and meditation. The path was perfectly laid out—no need to bring a map or plot a course. Again, it reflected God's "showing the way" to the pilgrim.

Once the pilgrim reached the center, he could look back and think about where he started. He recognized that he was not the same person as a result of completing the walk.

Last, there was no staying in the center; he had to go back out and share his insights with others.

WHAT ABOUT "NO" DON'T YOU UNDERSTAND?

Why are some prayers answered and others not? That is one of the big questions people say they want to ask God when they get to heaven. These Bible people may be asking God the same thing!

1. **Saul.** Saul was in a battle for his life and his kingdom. Terror filled his heart as he faced the Philistine enemy. He was so far removed from God that he said God "no longer answers me" (*1 Samuel 28:15 NIV*). In desperation, Saul turned to a medium for guidance.

2. **Job.** Job's name is synonymous with suffering. In one day's time Job went from being the wealthiest man around to losing it all. He didn't forsake God, although he felt forsaken: "I cry out to you, O God, but you do not answer" (*Job 30:20 NIV*).

3. **Jeremiah.** God gave Jeremiah a word for his people to clean up their act so he could make his home with them. The people refused to listen, refused to change. God instructed Jeremiah, "Do not pray for this people . . . for I will not listen to you" (*Jeremiah 7:16 NIV*). It wasn't that Jeremiah's prayer was unanswered; the problem was that the people failed to obey. So God told Jeremiah he might as well not pray, because God was not going to listen.

4. **David.** David prayed, pleaded, and fasted for his son's life. He wouldn't eat or get up from the floor, but the child died. This was the child of his adultery with Bathsheba. The prophet Nathan had said that because of David's wrongdoing the child would die (*2 Samuel 12:13–23*).

5. **Elijah.** Elijah fled Jezebel's revenge, then prayed to die. All God's other prophets had been put to death; he might as well be dead too. But God had more for Elijah to do. Elijah never died but went to heaven in a whirlwind (*1 Kings 19; 2 Kings 2*).

6. **Jonah.** Jonah prayed for God to take his life. God's mercy on the enemy Ninevites made Jonah mad. God said Jonah didn't have any right to be angry, let alone wish he were dead (*Jonah 4:3*).

7. **James and John.** These two disciples of Jesus requested that they be given positions of high prestige and rank in God's kingdom. Jesus answered that this was not his to give. Before greatness is bestowed, the faithful must first be servants of one another (*Mark 10:35–45*).

8. **Jesus.** "Everything is possible for you. Take this cup from me," Jesus pleaded three times to God (*Mark 14:36 NIV*). Jesus also prayed, "Your will be done" (*Matthew 26:42 NIV*). It was God's will that Jesus drink the "cup" of crucifixion for the wrongs of the world.

9. **Paul.** Paul prayed that his "thorn in the flesh" would be removed, but it was not. "My grace is sufficient for you," God told Paul. The tormenting "thorn" would help keep Paul from becoming conceited (*2 Corinthians 12:7–10 NIV*), and ultimately Jesus would be glorified, not Paul.

FIGURATIVELY SPEAKING

Words from the Bible should be interpreted in the sense intended for them, but that sense is not always literal. For example, Isaiah 26:4 says, "The LORD GOD is an everlasting rock" *(ESV)*. Obviously, *rock* does not have its usual, literal sense. In this context, *rock* is figurative, to picture strength, steadfastness, or refuge. Saying God is a "rock" does not define God but describes God figuratively as "rocklike."

Figurative language adds color to communication and often speaks more vividly than straightforward, literal description. What was meant figuratively should be interpreted figuratively, and context is the key to recognizing when words are used figuratively. Among several types of figurative language, the following are the most important:

Simile

Simile is a nonliteral comparison between two things, using *like* or *as* to paint a mental picture. Something figurative is being said about one of the things being compared. When Robert Burns says, "My love is like a red, red rose," his point is not to define love but to suggest beauty, delight, and perhaps delicacy associated with the one he loves or the emotions he is feeling. The image evoked in the mind of the reader is what is important. One of many examples of simile in the Bible is Jeremiah 23:29: "'Is not my word like fire,' declares the LORD, 'and like a hammer that breaks a rock in pieces?'" *(NIV)*. Psalm 42:1 provides another example: "As the deer pants for streams of water, so my soul pants for you, O God" *(NIV)*.

Besides being frequent throughout Scripture, especially Old Testament poetry, similes are basic to Jesus' teaching. Parables are extended similes, and Jesus often introduced them with the words: "The kingdom of God/heaven is like. . . ." Even without the explicit introduction, parables work as similes, presenting an earthly picture from which to learn a spiritual truth.

Metaphor

A metaphor can be understood as a simile without *like* or *as*. "God is a rock" is an example. Metaphor may be less obvious than simile, and

FIGURATIVELY SPEAKING (CONT'D)

context is vital in recognizing it. A well-known metaphor is "The LORD is my shepherd" *(Psalm 23:1 NIV)*.

Anthropomorphism

Anthropomorphism is a subcategory of metaphor. This is figurative language that gives human physical characteristics or movements to things that are not human. When the Bible refers to "the hand of God" *(1 Samuel 5:11 NKJV)*, for example, it usually means the power or the activity of God. A reference to Jesus' hand, however, can be literal and not an example of anthropomorphism *(see Matthew 8:3)*. Another example of anthropomorphism is Isaiah 55:12, in which trees clap their hands.

Hyperbole

Obvious exaggeration for rhetorical effect is called hyperbole. This is not misleading language, because the context indicates it is not meant literally. Two examples in the Bible: 2 Chronicles 28:4, in which the term "every" tree emphasizes pervasiveness, and Matthew 7:3, in which a "plank" or "board" in the eye is an absurd impossibility, but the image makes Jesus' point about judging others even more vivid and memorable.

Irony

Irony is language used to mean the opposite of its literal sense. Recognizing irony depends on detecting sarcasm in the context. An example is Job's response to his friends: "Doubtless you are the people, and wisdom will die with you!" *(Job 12:2 NIV)*. In fact, Job was scoffing at their arrogance, since their answers were no better than his. Another example is 1 Corinthians 4:8: "Already you have all you want! Already you have become rich! You have become kings—and that without us!" *(NIV)*. Paul's true intention was to point out to the members of the church in Corinth that they were not as smart or powerful as they thought.

BEGGING OFF

Human nature wants to shift blame, get out of tight spots, or turn a good light on one's own poor behavior or mistakes. These paraphrased excuses are among the most memorable found in the Bible.

1. "The woman you put here gave it to me." Adam's excuse for disobeying God (*Genesis 3:12*).

2. "The devil made me do it." Eve's excuse for disobeying God (*Genesis 3:13*).

3. "Evil will follow me to the mountains and kill me." Lot's excuse to the angels for wanting to stay in doomed Sodom (*Genesis 19:19*).

4. "I'm a poor speaker; what if they say you didn't really speak to me?" Moses' excuse for not wanting to go to Pharaoh to demand freedom for the Israelites (*Exodus 3:11; 4:1, 10*).

5. "You were gone and you know these people are evil. I just threw the gold into the fire, and a calf came out!" Aaron's excuse to Moses for constructing the golden calf (*Exodus 32:22–24*).

6. "We can't attack them; we're no match for them." The ten Israelite spies' excuse for not entering the Promised Land (*Numbers 13:31–33*).

7. "You're old and your sons are evil. Besides, all the other nations have one." Israel's excuse to Samuel for wanting a king (*1 Samuel 8:5*).

8. "You didn't show up on time, my men were fleeing, and the battle was about to begin, so I took things into my own hands and presented the burnt offering for God's favor." King Saul's excuse to Samuel for assuming the prophet's priestly duties (*1 Samuel 13:11–12*).

9. "We saved the best for sacrifices to the Lord." Saul's excuse to Samuel for not destroying God's enemies and all their possessions—including livestock—in battle, as God had instructed (*1 Samuel 15:21*).

10. "I'm the only prophet left and the queen is out to kill me." Elijah's excuse for hiding in a cave (*1 Kings 19:10*).

11. "I just bought property and need to go see it." In Jesus' parable, guest number one's excuse for not attending a wedding (*Luke 14:18*).

12. "I have a new yoke of oxen and I want to try them out." In Jesus' parable, guest number two's excuse for not attending a wedding (*Luke 14:19*).

13. "I can't come; I just got married!" In Jesus' parable, guest number three's excuse for not attending a wedding (*Luke 14:20*).

14. "You're hard to please, so I didn't want to take any chances." The unfaithful servant's excuse for returning only the original amount of money given to him, which he was supposed to have invested (*Matthew 25:24–25*).

15. "I've heard enough! Go away, and don't call me—I'll call you." Felix's excuse for not responding to Paul's preaching of the gospel (*Acts 24:25*).

AT THE CORNER OF SHIPHRAH AND PUAH

The first chapter of the book of Exodus tells that a king came into power in Egypt "who did not know Joseph" *(Exodus 1:8 NKJV)*. This king noted that the Israelites were growing in numbers and power, and he ordered that the people be afflicted with heavy labor—building cities and monuments as well as working in the fields. He also ordered the two main Hebrew midwives, Shiphrah and Puah, to kill all the male babies they delivered. The midwives refused, fearing God more than the pharaoh. They told the Egyptian rulers that the Hebrew women delivered their babies very quickly, giving the midwives no opportunity to arrive in time to assist with the delivery. God honored the actions of these midwives and "provided households for them" *(Exodus 1:21 NKJV)*.

Today these midwives are honored in a unique way in Israel. One of the nation's foremost maternity hospitals is located at the intersection of avenues named Shiphrah and Puah!

ALL IN A NAME

The word *Bible* is not in the English version of Scripture! The word comes from the Greek word *biblia*, which means "books."

The Greek translation of the Old Testament in the first century—called the Septuagint—translated Daniel 9:2 as *ta biblia*, or "the books." The Septuagint also translated the Hebrew word as "the holy books." The first-century believers picked up on this idea and used the term "the Books" to refer to all sixty-six books of the Old Testament. Later, the early church extended the term to include the New Testament books as well.

Clement, one of the early-church leaders, wrote in the middle of the second century about "Ta Biblia"—The Books. Later, Jerome, who was an early-church leader in the fourth century, called the Old Testament "the Divine Library." It wasn't until the thirteen century that "the Books" became known as simply "the Book," or the Bible.

APPARITIONS OR INSPIRATIONS?

The apparent spontaneous appearance of religious symbols on everyday objects is nothing new, but a proliferation of such claims has been reported by local and national news media over the past few years. Most of the time, identification of the supposed subjects is highly subjective, but they attract both attention and in some cases high bids at auctions. Here are a few to make you say, "Hmmm":

1. *The Pope Pancake.* Myrna Kincaid's Sunday breakfast turned out to look a lot like a well-known photograph of Pope John Paul II leaning on his staff with a cross at the top (reported October 2005).

2. *Virgin Mary Grilled Cheese Sandwich.* Diana Duyser made the sandwich ten years before it netted her $28,000 at auction in November 2004. The unevenly browned sandwich bore the image of the Virgin Mary and has remained mold-free despite its age and the lack of any effort to preserve it.

3. *Jesus Tailgate.* In November 2002, Texan Julio Rudillo discovered the apparent image of Jesus in the dirt covering his pickup's tailgate. News spread, and over 150 people gathered to see the image, bringing candles, portraits of Jesus, and other artifacts to the site.

4. *Jesus Window.* Crowds flocked to a hardware store in Rio Grande Valley, Texas, in July 2004 to see an image of Jesus that appeared on a tinted store window. Viewers agreed that the image resembled portraits of Jesus with a crown of thorns.

5. *Madonna and Child Window.* A second-story window at Milton Hospital in Boston, Massachusetts, was the site of the 2003 appearance of a standing Madonna holding the baby Jesus in her arms. Perhaps caused by condensation or chemicals between the double panes of glass, the apparition was especially controversial because the hospital was considering allowing its doctors to perform abortions.

6. *Virgin Mary Window.* A former Clearwater, Florida, bank building was the site of the spontaneous appearance of a three-story-tall image of the Virgin Mary spread over nine adjacent windowpanes. Discovered by customers in 1996, the image was vandalized by acid in 1997 but recovered after a good rain. In 2004 vandals shattered the top three panes. Bulletproof glass now covers the remaining image.

7. *Elian's Virgin Mary #1.* A video taken in the room where six-year-old Cuban refugee Elian Gonzales was staying with Miami relatives supposedly shows the image of the Virgin Mary in a mirror (March 2000).

8. *Elian's Virgin Mary #2.* Also in March 2000, crowds of people flocked to see the image of the Virgin Mary that appeared in a bank window in the neighborhood where Elian was staying. Some claimed it was a sign that Elian should not be sent back to his family in Cuba.

9. *Fireworks Cross.* A parishioner taking pictures of a fireworks display in front of St. John's Lutheran Church in Norfork, Nebraska, was shocked

APPARITIONS OR INSPIRATIONS? (CONT'D)

to find in one of the photos not fireworks but the clear image of a giant cross over a wing of the church. The 2002 event was a celebration of the church's one-hundredth birthday.

10. *Jesus Tree #1.* A cemetery on the Mississippi River (directly west of Springfield, Illinois) has a tree whose trunk looks like a life-sized sculpture of Jesus holding a lamb. Pictures show a very distinct and identifiable image in three dimensions on the side of the tree.

11. *Jesus Tree #2.* Ella Huffin looked out her Wisconsin kitchen window one snowy morning in 2002 and saw the image of Jesus on a tree in her backyard. The tree had been damaged many years before and was decaying in one area near the ground. Apparently, the snow and her distance from the tree enhanced the image's visibility. As newspaper pictures proved, however, the image resembles Jesus holding a baby.

12. *Jesus Tree #3.* October 2005 was the first time anyone in Rochester, New York, had noticed a tree growing on North Clinton Avenue, but it quickly became a local landmark after several dozen believers said they saw the image of Jesus on the tree's trunk. The image is formed by variations in coloring on the silver maple's bark. Yomaira Otero brought six members of her family to view the tree in a pouring rain one morning. She pointed out the facial features she found obvious, including the beard formed by the tree's bark. Speaking in her native Spanish, Yomaira declared that the Jesus figure appeared to be snoozing.

13. *Jesus Church Door #1.* In 1999 parishioners at the Church of the Good Shepherd in Warehem, Massachusetts, were restaining a set of cupboard doors inside the church. As the wood stain soaked in, the previously unnoticed image began to emerge—a face with familiar long hair, parted in the middle, and a beard. The image shows a long-faced Jesus in the rich grain of the birch doors.

14. *Jesus Church Door #2.* In January 2006, members of the Reigning Light of the Healing Chapel in North Vernon, Indiana, discovered what they believe is the image of Jesus in the wood patterns of a door in the church. People from across Indiana have come to view the door that many compare to the Shroud of Turin (an ancient cloth believed by many throughout the world to bear the likeness of Jesus after his death).

15. *Jesus Tortilla.* In October 1977, Maria Rubio discovered that the thumbprint-sized skillet-scorching formed an image on the tortilla she used to make a breakfast burrito for her husband, Eduardo. The configuration of skillet burns resembled the face of Jesus. The tortilla has since been enshrined in its own tiny building near the town of Lake Arthur, New Mexico, forty minutes south of Roswell.

16. *Blue Chip Virgin Mary.* Elizabeth Gould said that "a strange sensation overwhelmed her" as she ate from a bag of blue-colored potato chips on a JetBlue Airlines' flight from New York to Florida in February 2006.

APPARITIONS OR INSPIRATIONS? (CONT'D)

She was amazed to see a head-and-shoulders portrait of the Madonna on the potato chip. At last word, Ms. Gould was considering putting the chip up for auction.

17. *Overpass Mary.* A small shrine developed under a Chicago freeway overpass in April 2005 after passersby began noticing the apparent image of the Virgin Mary on a water-stained concrete wall. Beside the image is an artist's rendering of the Virgin Mary in a pose some see echoed in the stain.

18. *Pierogi Jesus.* A Toledo, Ohio, family was preparing an Easter breakfast of pierogies when one of the fried pies developed the image of Jesus on one side. Thinking it was too good to eat, the family froze the pie and sold it in an online eBay auction for $1,775. "We choose to believe, because it was Easter, it's Jesus," said the cook, Donna Lee. Apparently, someone with $1,775 did too.

19. *Soybean Tank Portrait.* An image widely thought to look like Jesus appeared on the side of a soybean storage tank in rural Fostoria, Ohio, in 1986. A month after the image was reported, vandals attacked the tank with paint balloons. The remaining image has since faded.

20. *Frying Pan Portrait.* Texan Juan Pastrano was cooking breakfast on a Sunday in February 2005 when he saw what appeared to be the silver-dollar-sized likeness of Jesus in his skillet. Juan has no plans to sell the pan.

21. *Jesus after the Storm.* A photo taken of the sky over Frankenmuth, Michigan, immediately after a 1996 tornado appeared to display the image of Jesus. The full-length figure is seen in profile with one arm reaching forward. The picture must be rotated ninety degrees for the figure to stand upright; otherwise the figure seems to be reclining forward with the arm reaching toward the ground.

22. *Jesus in the Shadows.* The thorn-crowned head of Jesus appears nightly on a corrugated fence in Port Germein in South Australia. The shadow is caused by a streetlight above a tree and has been attracting hundreds of tourists to the town. The district council has assured locals that the tree will not have its routine trim, to preserve the image as long as possible.

23. *Cash Register Image.* When bartender Rosalind Knaff took the last dime out of the cash register, she was shocked to see on the dime tray the image of Jesus, which she said was unmistakable. The owner of the Akron, Ohio, establishment placed tape over the image when it was first spotted, but when the tape was removed, the image was even more pronounced. Declared one patron, "It proves that Christ is everywhere."

24. *Band-Aid Jesus.* An Internet posting showed the scanned image of a used bandage from the knee of a ten-year-old girl who had recently had her first Communion. The blood stains seemed to show the face of a smiling Jesus. A T-shirt with a blown-up photo of the dirty bandage was made available for purchase online.

PUTTING ON THE FEEDBAG

There's physical hunger and thirst, and there's hunger and thirst for a deeper kind of satisfaction in life. There's also a time to feed others:

1. Feed your enemy if he's hungry; there's a reward in it for you (*Proverbs 25:21–22*).

2. God is so good! He feeds people when they are hungry (*Psalm 107:9*).

3. A good man gives his food to the hungry (*Ezekiel 18:5, 7*).

4. When you have sympathy for the hungry and feed them, it's as if you are feeding Jesus himself (*Matthew 25:35–40*).

5. When you meet Jesus and decide to go through life with him, he'll make sure you never go hungry (*John 6:35*).

6. If you are thirsty for a solid relationship with God, God will make it happen (*Matthew 5:6*).

7. Paul said he and the other apostles were going hungry and thirsty because the church wasn't living up to its obligations (*1 Corinthians 4:11*).

8. Lazy people go hungry (*Proverbs 19:15*).

9. When King David needed help, he told God, "My soul thirsts for you" (*Psalm 143:6 NIV*). God protected him.

10. How did God say he'd take care of Israel? By satisfying their thirst for a life that would please him; blessings for everybody (*Isaiah 44:3*)!

CRY ME A RIVER

Do real men cry? They did in Bible days. Crying is a natural reaction when something terrible happens, or when someone experiences pain or injury. These Bible men all had good reason to cry:

1. Esau cried because his brother Jacob betrayed him, deceived their father, and stole Esau's birthright (*Genesis 27:34, 38*).

2. Joseph cried when revealing his true identity to his brothers—who years before had sold him into slavery—after they came to him for food during a famine (*Genesis 45:14–15*).

3. Saul cried when he learned that David had a chance to kill him but instead spared his life (*1 Samuel 24:16*).

4. Hezekiah cried when the prophet Isaiah told him he was going to die (*2 Kings 20:2–3*).

5. Jesus cried over Jerusalem, a city that did not recognize him or accept him as the Messiah (*Luke 19:41*).

6. Peter cried over his denial of Jesus (*Matthew 26:75*).

CLOSE ENCOUNTERS

Have you ever thought about what you would do in a face-to-face encounter with God? Learn what some Bible heroes did when they experienced God "up close and personal":

Fell on their faces. Moses was preparing Aaron and his sons for priestly ordination. Aaron brought offerings for God on behalf of himself and all the people. Then he and Moses entered the Tent of Meeting. When they came out, they blessed the people, and God's glory appeared to all the people. Fire came out from God and when the people saw it, they shouted for joy and fell facedown in worship *(Leviticus 9:24).*

Stood up. Ezekiel fell on his face when he saw God's glory, but when God said, "Stand up," the Holy Spirit came and raised Ezekiel to his feet *(Ezekiel 2:1).*

Took off their shoes. When Moses approached the burning bush, God called to him, saying, "Moses! Moses!" Moses replied, "Here I am." God told Moses to take off his sandals because he was standing on holy ground *(Exodus 3:4–5 NIV).*

Built an altar. God appeared to Jacob, telling him that his name would be Israel and confirming to him the covenant promises made to Abraham. Jacob set up a stone pillar, presented an offering, and named the place Bethel *(Genesis 35:14–15).*

THE STAR THAT NEVER STEERED THEM WRONG

When Moses told Pharaoh that God was going to send plagues to devastate the Egyptians, it seems as if Pharaoh might have listened. After all, in those days the Egyptians had priests who made predictions. Every year the Nile River flooded the land. Somehow the priests always seemed to know when it would happen. How did they know? They learned to look up. When Sirius, the Dog Star, appeared in the predawn sky, Nile flooding wasn't too far behind.

Source: William A. Gutsch Jr., *1001 Things Everyone Should Know About the Universe* (New York: Doubleday, 1998), 165.

SABBATH REST

Remember the Sabbath day" is one of the Ten Commandments, but there's more to the story. Through the centuries, the word for *Sabbath* also took on a Babylonian flair. The Babylonians had something called "sabattu," which happened every seventh day. Work was forbidden. The Jews, conquered by the Babylonians in 586 BC, already observed a Sabbath, or worship day. In Babylonia, this day became known by the Jews as Shabbat, meaning "cease" or "desist."

KNOW HOW TO FOLD 'EM

Folding an American flag properly involves twelve folds. Some of those folds have a spiritual meaning. Fold two symbolizes belief in eternal life. Fold four acknowledges the need to turn to God in peace and war. To the Jews, fold eleven represents "the lower portion of the seal of King David and King Solomon," glorifying "the God of Abraham, Isaac, and Jacob." To believers, fold twelve, an "emblem of eternity," exalts God the Father, Son, and Holy Spirit.

Source: www.legion.org/?section=our_flag&subsection=flag_folding&content=flag_symbols.

"AND WHERE DO YOU GO TO CHURCH?"

Steeples, stained glass, pews, and choir lofts are what come to mind when most people think of church. But how about drive-in movie theaters, nightclubs, coffee shops, and barns? These are some of the venues for "church" today.

Some churches simply can't afford to buy their own property and find that renting space in shopping malls or school buildings is an expedient way to hold worship services until they can purchase property. Other churches, however, are venturing into the unconventional church venue to reach people who are not attracted to traditional church buildings.

Mosaic, a nondenominational church in Los Angeles, moved out of a traditional church building to be accessible to people from all walks of life. Mosaic has three venues: a nightclub, a high school, and a university campus. Its congregation is growing.

Probably one of the fastest-growing venues of today's church is the multisite church. A multisite church is defined as "one church meeting in many locations." Music, worship, and prayer are "live" at each location; the pastor's message is reproduced at each site through video technology. Life Church in Oklahoma is one example of a multisite church. It has five campuses and fourteen thousand members. New locations are intentionally small to retain the intimacy of a small church while providing the benefits of a large church.

The multisite venue is considered a development of the megachurch phenomenon. The large campus is not for everyone, and now there are options.

Sources: www.washingtonpost.com; Jscms.jrn.columbia.edu; www.sptimes.com.

A DIFFERENT ORDER

The Hebrew Bible puts its books in a different order than the Christian Bible (Old Testament). The Hebrew Bible begins with the Torah (the Law). The Prophets follow, then the Twelve Minor Prophets. The book ends with the Writings. The Christian Old Testament starts with the Historical Books, continues with the Poetic Books, and concludes with the Prophetic Books. The two orders are contrasted below, showing the individual books of each Bible in the sequence they appear:

THE HEBREW BIBLE

The Torah
Genesis
Exodus
Leviticus
Numbers
Deuteronomy
The Prophets
Joshua
Judges
1 Samuel
2 Samuel
1 Kings
2 Kings
Isaiah
Jeremiah
Ezekiel
The Twelve Minor Prophets
Hosea
Joel
Amos
Obadiah
Jonah
Micah
Nahum
Habakkuk
Zephaniah
Haggai
Zechariah

Malachi
The Writings
Psalms
Proverbs
Job
Song of Songs
Ruth
Lamentations
Ecclesiastes
Esther
Daniel
Ezra
Nehemiah
1 Chronicles
2 Chronicles

THE CHRISTIAN OLD TESTAMENT

The Historical Books
Genesis
Exodus
Leviticus
Numbers
Deuteronomy
Joshua
Judges
Ruth
1 Samuel
2 Samuel
1 Kings

2 Kings
1 Chronicles
2 Chronicles
Ezra
Nehemiah
Esther
The Poetic Books
Job
Psalms
Proverbs
Ecclesiastes
Song of Songs
The Prophetic Books
Isaiah
Jeremiah
Lamentations
Ezekiel
Daniel
Hosea
Joel
Amos
Obadiah
Jonah
Micah
Nahum
Habakkuk
Zephaniah
Haggai
Zechariah
Malachi

AH-H-H-H-H . . .

The word *peace* is so often heard in the course of a day that it may seem unnecessary to define it. The Bible, however, speaks of peace in terms that are deeply personal and unrelated to war or interpersonal conflicts.

Scriptural peace exists within, with little or no regard to the situation around a person. Even when daily life is chaotic, Scripture assures believers that they may have an inner peace that defies logic. Jesus said, "Peace I leave with you; my peace I give you. I do not give to you as the world gives. Do not let your hearts be troubled and do not be afraid" *(John 14:27 NIV).*

Scientific studies have shown that people who are filled with inner peace handle crises better, have better leadership skills, and have fewer health problems than people who cannot attain true inner peace.

EVENSONG

Evensong is a service meant to help a person reflect on the day that is ending, meditate on the spiritual lessons learned in it, and offer thanksgiving to God for his presence throughout the day. Sometimes called vespers, this service of the church usually includes hymns, Scripture readings, and prayers. The service occurs in the early evening as daylight ends, and often as the light coming from church windows gives way to candlelight in the sanctuary.

While evensong traditionally features music, churches and cathedrals that do not have a choir available year-round may have spoken services.

Evensong is especially popular in the Anglican tradition, and the service is held in Anglican cathedrals throughout England for most of the year.

"WITH MALICE TOWARD NONE, WITH GRATITUDE FOR ALL"

Visit a public library and marvel anew at the large number of volumes devoted to America's sixteenth president, Abraham Lincoln. For a man who was born before the age of mass communication, much is known about the preserver of the Union.

Lincoln's early life was hardscrabble. He was born in a log cabin to a pioneer father and a religious mother. It's unclear what gave him a hunger for education, but given the wording of his future speeches and comments in letters, it's obvious that like many other men and women of his era, he had a good working knowledge of the Bible.

Even before Lincoln officially took office as president, several Southern states had seceded from the Union. Throughout his time in office, he dealt with a situation that no American president had ever before faced: a civil war. And although he never joined a church, it's clear from his October 3, 1863, proclamation that this gifted politician and commander in chief gave God his due. He also gave the nation one of its most popular holidays: Thanksgiving.

Lincoln's Thanksgiving Proclamation

It is the duty of nations as well as of men to own their dependence upon the overruling power of God; to confess their sins and transgressions in humble sorrow, yet with assured hope that genuine repentance will lead to mercy and pardon; and to recognize the sublime truth, announced in the Holy Scriptures and proven by all history, that those nations are blessed whose God is the Lord.

Know that by His divine law, nations, like individuals, are subjected to punishments and chastisements in this world. May we not justly fear that the awful calamity of civil war

"WITH MALICE TOWARD NONE, WITH GRATITUDE FOR ALL" (CONT'D)

which now desolates the land may be a punishment inflicted upon us for our presumptuous sins, to the needful end of our national reformation as a whole people?

We have been the recipients of the choicest bounties of heaven; we have been preserved these many years in peace and prosperity; we have grown in numbers, wealth and power as no other nation has ever grown.

But we have forgotten God. We have forgotten the gracious hand which preserved us in peace and multiplied and enriched and strengthened us, and we have vainly imagined, in the deceitfulness of our hearts, that all these blessings were produced by some superior wisdom and virtue of our own. Intoxicated with unbroken success, we have become too self-sufficient to feel the necessity of redeeming and preserving grace, too proud to pray to the God that made us.

It has seemed to me fit and proper that God should be solemnly, reverently and gratefully acknowledged, as with one heart and one voice, by the whole American people. I do therefore invite my fellow citizens in every part of the United States, and also those who are at sea and those who are sojourning in foreign lands, to set apart and observe the last Thursday of November as a day of Thanksgiving and praise to our beneficent Father who dwelleth in the heavens.

Initially, Thanksgiving occurred each year by virtue of presidential proclamation. It wasn't until 1941 that Congress stepped in and declared Thanksgiving to be an official holiday. This happened after President Franklin Roosevelt switched the date to the next-to-last Thursday in November. Now it's the last Thursday in November.

MODERN ILLUMINATION

Royal calligrapher Donald Jackson, scribe to the queen of England, heads an international team of artists and scholars creating the first handwritten, illuminated Bible since the invention of the printing press. Jackson uses hand-carved goose quills, handmade inks, and calfskin parchment, the tools and materials employed by scribes for thousands of years. The seven-year project was commissioned by the Benedictine monks of St. John's Abbey and University in Minneapolis.

The finished pages are gilded with twenty-four-karat gold leaf. When complete, *The Saint John's Bible* will be two feet tall, three feet wide, with nearly eleven hundred pages bound in seven volumes. The Bible translation being used is the New Revised Standard Version *(NRSV)*.

The book is being called "America's Book of Kells" after the famous twelve-hundred-year-old illuminated manuscript in Dublin, Ireland.

Source: www.saintjohnsbible.org/people/jackson.htm.

LIFT EVERY VOICE

A song highly associated with the struggle for racial equality in America is the anthem "Lift Every Voice and Sing." The stirring hymn has words that convey a sense of birthright and heritage as well as faith in God. The hymn was written in 1900 by noted black author, poet, and Civil Rights leader James Weldon Johnson and his brother, J. Rosamond Johnson, who was a successful composer. A Jacksonville, Florida, attorney at the time, Rosamond originally composed the piece for use in a program given by a group of Jacksonville schoolchildren to celebrate Lincoln's birthday. It is often referred to as the "Negro National Anthem"* and is frequently sung at the opening of public gatherings that celebrate black heritage, culture, and heroes. Part or all of the anthem has been included in various denominational hymnals in recent years, including *The United Methodist Hymnal.*

*As described by the NAACP at www.texasnaacp.org/history.htm#lift.

TALK ABOUT HEAVEN

Although there is no empirical proof that heaven exists, millions of people through the centuries have believed firmly that heaven not only exists in eternity but can or will be established on earth. Here are some famous quotes about heaven:

1. "Heaven will be inherited by every man who has heaven in his soul." —*Henry Ward Beecher*

2. "Give me one hundred preachers who fear nothing but sin and desire nothing but God, and I care not whether they be clergymen or laymen, they alone will shake the gates of Hell and set up the kingdom of Heaven upon Earth." —*John Wesley*

3. "We send missionaries to China so the Chinese can get to heaven, but we won't let them into our country." —*Pearl S. Buck*

4. "I hope with all my heart there will be painting in heaven." —*Jean-Baptiste Corot*

5. "Those are dead even for this life who hope for no other." —*Johann Wolfgang von Goethe*

6. "Seek first the kingdom of God and His righteousness, and all these things shall be added to you." —*Jesus (Matthew 6:33 NKJV)*

7. "Aim at heaven, and you will get earth thrown in; aim at earth, and you will get neither."—*C. S. Lewis*

8. "Everybody wants to go heaven, but nobody wants to die." —*Joe Louis*

9. "We talk about heaven being so far away. It is within speaking distance to those who belong there. Heaven is a prepared place for a prepared people."—*Dwight L. Moody*

10. "I had a million questions to ask God, but when I met Him, they all fled my mind—and it didn't seem to matter." —*Christopher Morley*

TALK ABOUT HEAVEN (CONT'D)

11. "I tell you the truth, unless you change and become like little children, you will never enter the kingdom of heaven." —*Jesus (Matthew 18:3 NIV)*

12. "The main object of religion is not to get a man into heaven, but to get heaven into him."—*Thomas Hardy*

13. "To get to heaven, turn right and keep straight." —*Author Unknown*

14. "Heaven goes by favor; if it went by merit, you would stay out and your dog would go in."—*Mark Twain*

15. "The doctrine of the Kingdom of Heaven, which was the main teaching of Jesus, is certainly one of the most revolutionary doctrines that ever stirred and changed human thought."—*H. G. Wells*

16. "What you do in your house is worth as much as if you did it up in heaven for our Lord God. We should accustom ourselves to think of our position and work as sacred and well-pleasing to God, not on account of the position and work, but on account of the word and faith from which the obedience and the work flow."—*Martin Luther*

17. "Upon a life I did not live, upon a death I did not die; another's life, another's death, I stake my whole eternity." —*Horatius Bonar*

18. "Ah, but a man's reach should exceed his grasp, or what's a heaven for?"—*Robert Browning*

19. "When we all get to heaven, what a day of rejoicing that will be! When we all see Jesus, we'll sing and shout the victory." —*song lyrics by Eliza Hewitt, 1898*

20. "Heaven is a city without a cemetery."—*Author Unknown*

SOUNDS LIKE A JOB FOR THE HOLY SPIRIT!

God and Jesus have received plenty of publicity in today's world, but the Holy Spirit has not. Who exactly is he, and what is he responsible for? Here's the scoop:

1. He participated in Creation *(Genesis 1:1–2).*
2. He gave Jesus a body *(Luke 1:35).*
3. He anointed Jesus and gave him power *(Acts 10:38).*
4. He has the power to drive out demons *(Matthew 12:28).*
5. He helps people pray *(Romans 8:26–27).*
6. He gives believers instructions and information *(Acts 20:22–23).*
7. He cleans up people's lives so they can have a healthy relationship with God *(Titus 3:4–7).*
8. He frees people from the power that wrongdoing has over them *(Romans 8:2).*
9. He reveals to people the truth about who Jesus is *(John 15:26).*
10. He gives believers the power to share their faith with others *(Acts 1:8).*
11. He calls people to specific ministries *(Acts 13:2–4).*
12. He prays on behalf of believers, in perfect agreement with God's will *(Romans 8:26–27).*
13. He guides people into knowing the truth *(John 16:13–15).*
14. He convicts believers of spiritual errors *(John 16:8).*

THE TO-LOVE LIST

Jesus commanded his followers to love God with their whole spirit, mind, soul, and strength—and to love their neighbors as themselves *(Matthew 22:34–40).* In all, however, the Bible presents a fairly long list of things and people that believers are to love if they call themselves the children of God. To love means choosing to pursue something—or a relationship with someone—with passion, willful purpose, and consistency. It means giving time, energy, attention, and devotion to acquiring that prized attribute in your life or to nurturing a relationship with that person you highly value. The Bible's list includes:

1. God *(Deuteronomy 6:5)*
2. Neighbors *(Leviticus 19:18)*
3. Strangers *(Deuteronomy 10:19)*
4. Salvation *(Psalm 40:16)*
5. God's name *(Psalm 69:36)*
6. God's Word *(Psalm 119:97)*
7. Wisdom *(Proverbs 4:6)*
8. Good *(Amos 5:15)*
9. Mercy *(Micah 6:8)*
10. Truth *(Zechariah 8:19)*
11. Peace *(Zechariah 8:19)*
12. Enemies *(Matthew 5:44)*
13. Fellow believers *(John 13:34–35)*
14. Spouse *(Titus 2:4; Ephesians 5:25)*
15. Children *(Titus 2:4)*

A MOUNTAIN-SIZED DILEMMA

In 1973, when Grace Baptist Church in Netcong, New Jersey, built a new church on a rise called Kingtown Mountain, the congregation was dismayed when the township's planning board sent word that permanent occupancy of the building would not be granted until there was sufficient parking at the rear of the structure to accommodate the anticipated congregation. The area behind the church was occupied by a "mountain" that had to be removed if a parking lot were to be placed there, and the congregation simply didn't have the budget for the removal of so much dirt.

The next Sunday morning the pastor, Ray Crawford, reminded the congregation of Jesus' promise in Matthew 17:20, which says, "I tell you the truth, if you have faith as small as a mustard seed, you can say to this mountain, 'Move from here to there' and it will move. Nothing will be impossible for you" (NIV). According to church records, the pastor added, "If you believe that, come on Wednesday night to pray with me that God will move this mountain in back of our church."

The next morning the local telephone company called to say that a building they were erecting nearby was located on swampy ground and needed a good deal of landfill before they could proceed. They asked whether the church might be willing to sell them some dirt. In about a month the phone company had leveled the mountain, leaving room for three parking lots and paying the church more than twenty-five thousand dollars for the dirt.

Source: www.gracechurchnj.org/Profile_Final_Web.pdf.

THE ETERNITY MAN

Anyone watching televised millennium celebrations as the year 2000 dawned around the world would have a hard time forgetting the view of Australia's Sydney Harbour Bridge. Strung across the bridge's span in lights were fancy letters spelling out "Eternity." Many older celebrants that night in Sydney remembered seeing a similar display in yellow chalk on city sidewalks when they were children. Written in an elegant hand, it was the work of Arthur Stace.

Born in 1884, Arthur was raised by alcoholic parents who neither cared for nor disciplined him. He stole and rummaged through garbage to eat. By age fifteen he was a hardened drunkard and spent his adult years as a street bum. His schooling was almost nonexistent, and he was barely literate.

Arthur entered a church one evening in search of food but was forced to listen to a sermon first. The experience led Arthur to turn his life around; he stopped drinking, found work, and became a respected member of the community.

Later he was deeply moved as he listened to another preacher wish aloud that he could warn the entire world that they faced eternity. Making his way home from the church, Arthur found a piece of yellow chalk in his pocket and was inspired to stoop and write, "Eternity" in large beautiful letters across the sidewalk, a remarkable act in view of his near inability to write his own name.

Every morning for the next thirty-seven years until his death, Arthur repeated that act on other sidewalks as he crossed the city, ultimately leaving the reminder as a legacy to the world as it was seen around the planet during Sydney's millennium celebration.

Sources: catalog.lexpublib.org/TLCScripts/interpac.dll?SearchForm&
Directions=1&Config=pac&Branch=,0,&FormId=0;
www.pastornet.net.au/stace/Rahme1A.htm.

SOMETHING'S MISSING

The Greek word for evil is *poneros*, which comes from the word *ponos*, meaning "pain." The root word for *ponos* is *penes*, which means poor or lacking in something essential. A person lacking in righteousness is a person marked by wrongdoing—he is "poor" in righteousness, and the result is consequences that produce pain. A person lacking in health is marked by sickness—he is "poor" in health, and the result is painful disease. A person lacking in sufficient material goods is "poor" in finances or provision, resulting in painful deprivation. Evil, according to the Bible's use of the word, is manifested in every form of wrongdoing, sickness, and poverty that keeps a person from living in the fullness of God's original intent for humankind.

GET IT RITE

The life of faith is not a do-it-yourself makeover. In fact, God intends for people to rely on him for everything needed to live it. Sacraments—religious rites practiced in many churches—are one provision for believers to receive God's help for living. According to Saint Augustine (AD 354–430), a sacrament is "an outward and visible sign of an inward and spiritual grace." By taking part in the sacraments, a person acknowledges both a need for God and the insufficiency of self in living the life of faith and receives the grace God wants to give. Evangelical and mainline Protestants practice the sacraments of baptism and Communion. Roman Catholics and Anglicans also regard confirmation, marriage, holy orders, penance, and anointing of the sick as sacraments.

Source: www.newadvent.org.

NOT A THING TO WEAR

Most people's knowledge of biblical dress comes from movies and Christmas plays. But garments play a key role in some Bible stories, so knowing a little more about Bible wardrobes can be helpful in understanding the stories.

For instance, the earliest and simplest garment mentioned in the Bible is the apron of fig leaves assembled by Adam and Eve to cover their nakedness as they tried to hide from God. It's reasonable to assume that plant life continued to be used for body cover after the couple left the Garden of Eden. Later, animal skins, wool, and linen were also used in making garments.

As time passed, garments became not only practical but also symbolic of a person's status or job. Most garments were the color of the material used—usually natural white or ecru, but purple and scarlet robes were the marks of the wealthy, and the Israelites learned to dye and use decorative needlepoint from various neighboring countries and traveling traders. Weaving the fine linen used in the vestments of the high priest was probably an art learned by the Jews when they were Egyptian captives.

Clothing worn by biblical men and women was very similar in form and function. The undergarment or "coat" was made of wool, cotton, or linen as a close-fitting tunic secured by a sash, and a person wearing only his coat was regarded as naked. A fine linen cloth wrapper was used as a nightshirt—in fact, the Old Testament word for it is translated "sheets."

The outer tunic, or "mantle," was longer than the tunic and consisted of a piece of woolen cloth worn wrapped around the body, thrown over the shoulders like a shawl, with the ends hanging down in front, or thrown over the head to conceal the face. A girdle secured it at the waist and, with the fold formed by overlapping the robe, created a handy pocket.

In short, Hollywood's version of biblical clothing is probably fairly accurate when it comes to the form, but few Bible characters could have afforded the bright lengths of cloth we usually see on the actors.

Sources: home.messiah.edu/~hb1175/mf.html; www.keyway.ca/htm2002/clothing.htm.

CASE CLOSED

A quote from an anonymous source says, "Some people treat God as they do a lawyer; they go to him only when they are in trouble." Then there are those who recognize his omnipotence and accord him the respect he is due. This includes men of letters, mathematicians, and men of science—not just men of the cloth.

1. "Belief of God is acceptance of the basic principle that the universe makes sense, that there is behind it an ultimate purpose."
   —*Carl Wallace Miller (professor of physics, 1893–1975)*

2. "Nature has some perfections to show that she is the image of God, and some defects, to show that she is only His image."
   —*Blaise Pascal (French mathematician, 1623–1662)*

3. "This most elegant system of suns, planets and comets could only arise from the purpose and sovereignty of an intelligent and mighty being. . . . He rules them all, not as a soul of the world, but a sovereign lord of all things."
   —*Sir Isaac Newton (mathematician, 1643–1727)*

4. "If we could really conceive God we could no longer believe in Him because our representation, being human, would inspire us with doubts."
   —*Pierre Lecomte du Noüy (French biologist, 1883–1947)*

5. "Everything is permissible if God does not exist, and as a result man is forlorn, because neither within him nor without does he find anything to cling to. He can't start making excuses for himself."
   —*Jean Paul Sartre (novelist/philosopher, 1905–1980)*

6. "I believe in the incomprehensibility of God."
   —*Honoré de Balzac (French novelist, 1799–1850)*

7. "To the reverent scientist . . . the simplest features of the world about us are in themselves so awe-inspiring that there seems no need to seek new and greater miracles of God's care."—*Carl Wallace Miller*

CASE CLOSED (CONT'D)

8. "I believe in God the Father Almighty because wherever I have looked, through all that I see around me, I see the trace of an intelligent mind, and because in natural laws, and especially in the laws which govern the social relations of men, I see, not merely the proofs of intelligence, but the proofs of beneficence."
—*Henry George (American political economist, 1839–1897)*

9. "The existence of a Being endowed with intelligence and wisdom is a necessary inference from a study of celestial mechanics."
—*Sir Isaac Newton (mathematician, 1643–1727)*

10. "There is a God. The plants of the valley, and the cedars of the mountain bless his name; the insect hums his praise; the elephant salutes him with the rising day; the bird glorifies him among the foliage; the lightning bespeaks his power, and the ocean declares his immensity. Man alone has said, 'There is no God.'"
—*Vicomte de Chateaubriand (French statesman and writer, 1768–1848)*

11. "Whoever considers the study of anatomy, I believe will never be an atheist."
—*Edward Herbert (English philosopher, 1583–1648)*

12. "Science has sometimes been said to be opposed to faith and inconsistent with it. But all science, in fact, rests on a basis of faith, for it assumes the permanence and uniformity of natural laws—a thing which can never be demonstrated."—*Tryon Edwards (1809–1894)*

THERE'S NOTHING TO FEAR

Scary books feature two-headed monsters.

Believe it or not, the Bible contains the story of creatures with four faces.

These "living creatures" were in a vision the prophet Ezekiel had *(1:4–24)*. The faces were those of a man, to whom God gave charge over earth's riches; a lion, who is king of the beasts; an ox, who is tops among domesticated animals; and an eagle, who is unequaled among birds. And yet, as God made clear, these powerful creatures were not on his level; he created them.

The creatures appear again in the book of Revelation *(4:6–8)*. In this instance they were standing around God's throne in heaven, praising him.

Some early-church fathers decided that the four creatures correspond to the four men who wrote the Gospels: Matthew, Mark, Luke, and John. (The Gospels are the Bible books telling the "good news" about Jesus.)

Thus, Matthew's symbol is the man, because his book begins by talking about the humanity of Jesus.

Mark's symbol is the lion, because his book contains the account of John the Baptist, who boldly spread the word that Jesus was coming to earth soon.

Luke's symbol is the ox, because at the beginning of his book, he discusses the priest Zacharias at the altar where sacrifices were made; the ox represented domesticated animals that were used for sacrificial purpose.

The eagle is John's symbol, because he is seen as the messenger who took the gospel message far and wide.

IS IT IN THE BOOK?

Many people refer to the Bible as the "Good Book," but are you aware that there are a number of books that have been equally well-known in the church for centuries? In some denominations, these books are consulted regularly for guidance about what can and can't be done by members, or for information about what should and shouldn't be done as part of worship services. In other cases, the books have great historical importance to a particular denomination.

Several of the better-known books are:

The Book of Advertisements. This book's official title is among the longest on record: *Advertisements, Partly for Due Order in Public Administration of Common Prayers and Using the Holy Sacraments, and partly for the Apparel of All Persons Ecclesiastical by Virtue of the Queen Majesty's Letters Commanding the Same.* The book was issued by Archbishop Matthew Parker in 1556. Among the thirty-nine "advertisements" in the book are instructions to wear a surplice when celebrating the Eucharist and to kneel when receiving Communion elements.

The Book of Common Order. This book was first prepared by John Knox in 1556 for the English Protestant congregations in Geneva, and from there it was taken by Knox to Scotland. It is commonly known as John Knox's Liturgy. It is essentially a guide for how to conduct services, but it does include a collection of metrical psalms for use in services. It was approved for use in Scotland by the General Assembly in 1562 and continued in general use until 1645, when it was replaced by a Directory of Public Worship. In 1994 a new service book was adopted, entitled simply *Common Order.*

The Book of Common Prayer. This service book for Anglican churches was produced under Edward VI in 1549. It has been

IS IT IN THE BOOK? (CONT'D)

the official service book of the Church of England since then, undergoing several major revisions (notably in 1552, 1559, and 1662). The book has services for morning and evening prayer, forms for administering the sacraments, the complete book of Psalms, and the prayers and forms of worship used in congregational services. The book was originally compiled by Archbishop Thomas Cranmer to replace three of the five main Latin service books: the Breviary, the missal, and the manual. (The other two Latin service books were ones Cranmer thought to be unnecessary.) Anglican churches outside England have produced their own versions of the Book of Common Prayer, especially Scotland, the United States, Canada, Ireland, South Africa, and the nations of the Indian subcontinent: India, Pakistan, Myanmar, and Sri Lanka.

The Book of Concord. This is the collective Lutheran confession of faith, first published in German at Dresden in 1580. It includes the Nicene, Athanasian, and Apostles' Creeds, the Augsburg Confession and its Apology, the Smalcald Articles, the tract "Concerning the Power and Primacy of the Pope," Martin Luther's "Small Catechism" and "Large Catechism," and the "Epitome and Thorough Declaration of the Formula of Concord," among other testimonies from the Scriptures and writings of the early-church fathers.

The Book of Discipline. This is the title chosen for separate and distinctive collections of doctrines and procedures published by both The United Methodist Church and the reformed Church of Scotland.

The Book of Confessions. This is the confessional standard of the Presbyterian Church, USA. The book is a collection of eleven creeds and confessional documents from the early church, Reformation period, and twentieth century.

MAKE A JOYFUL NOISE

German preacher Martin Luther (1483–1546) is best known as the man whose teachings led to the formation of Protestant churches.

Most people probably also know that Luther wrote the hymn "A Mighty Fortress Is Our God," but they might not know that he is also credited with taking church music out of the choir loft and "restoring it to the people." Hymns became more spontaneous and more joyful in nature, thanks to Luther.

GOD AND THE PLEDGE

The Pledge of Allegiance is not recited as it once was.

Several revisions were made after the pledge was written in 1892, such as changing "my flag" to "the flag" and adding "of the United States of America."

In 1954 President Dwight D. Eisenhower authorized another change: adding "under God" to the pledge. It was an era when Communism, and its atheistic tendencies, was feared by many Americans.

STILL VIVID AFTER ALL THESE YEARS

If only house paint were as tough as the paint used nearly five hundred years ago in Romania.

In the fifteenth and sixteenth centuries, monasteries in northern Moldova painted frescoes on the outside of their buildings. The frescoes contained scenes from the Bible. Even illiterate people could "read" them.

But what was the paint made of? The frescoes still look freshly painted. Scientists say the paint contains honey and vinegar, but no one has figured out all the ingredients.

WHAT'S THAT RINGING SOUND?

Around the year 400, it is said, Paulinus, the bishop of Nola, Campania, in Italy, decided to put a bell on top of a meetinghouse. Within three hundred years church bells had made their way from Italy to England and other parts of Europe, and they've been a-pealing ever since.

As time went by, bells got larger and larger and acquired a more prominent role in religious services.

Early bells were four-sided, made of sheets of metal held together with rivets. Later, metal was melted and poured into molds, which revolutionized bell making.

Churches started out with single bells and then began to add more for a variety of tones. Bell makers—"founders"— learned how to tune bells and figured out how the diameter and thickness could change a bell's tone.

Bell ringing actually became a popular diversion in nations such as England. Each man was assigned a bell; each bell corresponded to a note on the musical scale (C, D, E, F, G, A, B, or C). The bells were rung in order, from the high C to low C, and this was known as "Round Ringing."

Bells have also been credited with changing the architecture of church buildings. In order for bells to be heard as they sounded a call to worship, they needed a special structure—a tower—to house them. Some churches hung bells in towers that sat beside the church. In Italy those are called campaniles. Most churches, however, created towers for bells atop the church structure.

Source: Satis N. Coleman, *The Book of Bells* (New York: John Day, 1938).

GOD'S PLAN AND A
BET GONE WRONG

Judges 14–16 tells of the Bible's strongest man, Samson, and God's plan to use him to free Israel from the Philistines.

Samson was a man meant to be of special service to God. From his miraculous birth to a childless couple to his calling to set himself apart as a Nazirite *(Judges 13)*, he was to be a unique servant of God. Under the Nazirite vow, he refrained from various activities that included eating and drinking certain foods and cutting his hair. As he grew, he began to experience great spiritual and physical strength. Eventually he became so well known for his courageous physical feats that the enemies of Israel feared him.

Yet despite his vow to serve God, Samson made some awful choices.

First, he was mesmerized by a woman from among the enemies of Israel. Despite strong objections from his family, he determined to marry her anyway. So wedding plans were made, and Samson and his family traveled into enemy territory for the event.

En route to the wedding, Samson found the dried-out carcass of a lion he had killed some weeks earlier; inside was a swarm of bees and lots of honey. In spite of his vows to God, Samson violated Nazirite purity and dietary laws by scooping out and eating the honey. He even made his parents accomplices to his sin by sharing the honey with them while hiding the fact that it had been taken from a dead animal.

Yet the oddity of eating such sweetness from a beast that earlier would have eaten him seemed an intriguing conundrum to Samson and the basis for a riddle that would be his undoing.

GOD'S PLAN AND A
BET GONE WRONG (CONT'D)

As the seven-day wedding celebration began, there was, no doubt, a sense of uneasiness between the two families from enemy camps. Perhaps Samson even felt a little inferior in the presence of the opulence displayed by the bride's party. So Samson enacted his plan; he made a "sure bet" with the Philistine wedding groomsmen, one he knew would net him a free wedding wardrobe.

By the celebration's end they were to solve this riddle: "Out of the eater, something to eat; out of the strong, something sweet" *(Judges 14:14 NIV)*. Each groomsman would get a new set of clothes if the riddle was solved, but Samson would net thirty sets of clothes for himself if they failed.

As time ran out, the frustrated groomsmen threatened to murder the new bride's family unless she obtained the answer for them. Samson was quickly betrayed, and his thirst for revenge led to a series of disastrous events. His new bride was given to his best friend. Later she and her family were brutally murdered by the Philistines.

Yet Samson single-handedly killed a thousand of the enemy and became a champion of his nation.

Were God's purposes thwarted by Samson's ego and disobedience? In spite of Samson's waywardness, God's plan to use him to rout Israel's oppressors was fulfilled. But Samson was not spared the pain and humiliation he created for himself.

IT'S ALL IN THE NAME

Names in the Hebrew culture identify something about the essence or character of a person. In their original languages, the Scriptures give us many different names for God. In each of these names in the Old Testament Scriptures, God has revealed part of his nature:

1. **Elohim.** A general name for God, particularly used when referring to his transcendence and majesty. The name is often used to describe God as Creator.

2. **Jehovah, or Yahweh.** Jehovah, or Yahweh, is actually the proper personal name of the one true God. In Jewish tradition, this name is too holy to speak.

3. **Jehovah-Jireh** ("God Will Provide"). This name occurs once in the Old Testament, in Genesis 22:14, when God provided a ram for Abraham to sacrifice instead of his son Isaac.

4. **Jehovah-Rapha** ("God Who Heals"). The name Jehovah-Rapha indicates that God is the Great Physician who heals his people.

5. **Jehovah-Nissi** ("God Our Banner"). In Exodus 17:15, when the Hebrews defeated the Amalekites, Moses built an altar named Jehovah-Nissi, acknowledging God's hand in their victory.

6. **Jehovah-Shalom** ("God Our Peace"). *Shalom* means "completeness" or "wholeness." God alone provides shalom for his people.

7. **Jehovah-Ra'ah** ("God My Shepherd"). This is used in the well-known Psalm 23. *Ra'ah* means "shepherd," one who feeds his flock or leads it to pasture.

8. **Jehovah-Tsidkenu** ("God Our Righteousness"). God alone is righteous, and he makes his people righteous. This name is used in Jeremiah as a prophecy of Jesus, the coming Messiah.

9. **Jehovah-Shammah** ("God Is Present"). This is used only once in the Old Testament, in Ezekiel 48:35.

10. **Jehovah-M'kaddesh** ("God Who Sanctifies"). God alone pays the price it costs to forgive wrongdoing, purifying his people, setting them apart to belong to him.

11. **Jehovah-Sabaoth** ("The Lord of Hosts"). *Sabaoth* means "armies" or "hosts." The name Jehovah-Sabaoth can mean "the Lord of Armies," indicating God's reign over every army in heaven and on earth.

12. **El Elyon** ("The Most High God"). The word *El* is translated as "God" and with *Elyon* means "the Most Exalted God."

13. **Adonai** ("Lord," "Master"). God has authority and dominion. This name is first used in Genesis when Abram addresses God, "O Sovereign LORD" *(Genesis 15:2 NIV)*.

14. **El Shaddai** ("Almighty God," "The All-Powerful One"). God revealed himself as El Shaddai when he appeared to Abram and said, "I am God Almighty" *(Genesis 17:1 NIV)*.

15. **Olam** ("The Everlasting God"). *El* is a word used for God. *Olam* means "forever," "eternity," "everlasting."

A UNIVERSITY FOR THE NEW WORLD

The second-oldest university in the U.S. began as a mission for a Scotsman. The Reverend James Blair was an ordained minister in the Church of England. Sent to the Virginia Colony as a missionary in 1685, Blair was given the task to "revive and reform the church" there. He served as rector of the Parish of Henrico at Varina, where he quickly gained the respect and trust of prominent families in the area.

Blair's mission reached far beyond his local parish when, at the urging of Virginia Colony leaders, he returned to England in 1691 and successfully petitioned the monarch for a new college. After Blair returned to Virginia, the new college's trustees bought a parcel of 330 acres at Middle Plantation, and Blair began guiding the physical and academic development of the school.

He was named the college's first president and presided over one of the nation's premier institutions—the College of William and Mary—for the next fifty years.

BILLY SUNDAY: FROM STOLEN BASES TO TEMPERANCE

William Ashley "Billy" Sunday was born in Iowa in 1862. A professional baseball player in the National League, he gained national recognition when he became the first player to run the bases in fourteen seconds and set records for stealing bases.

In 1886 Sunday committed his life to Jesus and entered the ministry. He reportedly turned down salaries of $500 to $2,000 a month (the average was $480 per year) to continue his ministry. Later he was offered $1 million to be in the movies but again declined.

Sunday is remembered for his energetic preaching style and large evangelistic campaigns across the United States. Remarkably, Sunday addressed more than 100 million people in his lifetime without the aid of loudspeakers, TV, or radio.

Evangelizing from 1896 to 1935, Sunday made an attack on alcohol the mainstay of his campaigns. Perhaps his most famous quote is, "Whiskey and beer are all right in their place, but their place is in hell."

Sunday died of a heart attack at age seventy-three.

Sources: "Billy Sunday," The Columbia Electronic Encyclopedia, 6th ed. (New York: Columbia Univ. Press., 2003); www.answers.com/topic/billy-sunday;en.wikipedia.org/wiki/Billy_Sunday.

HOW SECURE WERE THEY?

A number of cities in the Bible are described as being fortified. Generally, fortifications were stone walls—sometimes with towers, gates, and bars—intended to defend a city against attack. The most effective fortifications were for cities built atop steep hills.

Walled cities were built in the Middle East from 3000 BC. The spies Moses sent into Canaan reported that "the people who live there are powerful, and the cities are fortified and very large" *(Numbers 13:28 NIV)*. When Joshua led the Israelites into the Promised Land, many Canaanite cities were destroyed, usually by enticing the people in the city to come out onto an open field and doing battle with them there. Walled cities were not built by the Israelites until the time of David and Solomon *(1 Kings 9:15)*. Solomon's successors also fortified cities and towns against attack from foreign invaders *(2 Chronicles 11:5–12)*.

At times fortifications included two or more parallel walls made of stone, sometimes fifteen to twenty-five feet thick and thirty-five or more feet high. A trench was sometimes dug near a wall. The lower part of some walls was constructed to have a gradual slope, sometimes covered with plaster, which made attack with a battering ram difficult. Towers were often built at the corners of a city wall. Entrance to a city was guarded by a series of gates.

Some fortified cities in later times were defeated by sieges intended to starve the city into submission, or by direct attack with battering rams. The Romans used catapults and mobile towers to attack walled cities.

THEY SAW ANGELS

Angels paid visits to people throughout the Bible. In one case, a donkey saw the angel before his rider did. Here are twenty-five of the most notable Bible people to whom angels appeared:

1. Abraham (*Genesis 22:11–12*)
2. The apostles (*Acts 1:10–11*)
3. Balaam (*Numbers 22:21–35*)
4. Cornelius (*Acts 10:1–8*)
5. David (*2 Samuel 24:17*)
6. Elijah (*1 Kings 19:5*)
7. Gideon (*Judges 6:11–22*)
8. Hagar (*Genesis 21:17*)
9. Isaiah (*Isaiah 6:1–7*)
10. Jacob (*Genesis 28:10–19*)
11. Jesus (*Matthew 4:11*)
12. John (*Revelation 1:1; 5:2–7*)
13. Joseph (*Matthew 1:20–21; 2:13*)
14. Joshua (*Joshua 5:13–15*)
15. Lot, his wife, and his daughters (*Genesis 19:1–22*)
16. Mary (*Luke 1:26–38*)
17. Moses (*Exodus 3:2*)
18. Nebuchadnezzar (*Daniel 3:25*)
19. Paul (*Acts 27:23*)
20. Peter (*Acts 5:19; 12:7–10*)
21. Philip (*Acts 8:26*)
22. Shadrach, Meshach, and Abednego (*Daniel 3:25–28*)
23. Shepherds (*Luke 2:8–14*)
24. Women at Jesus' tomb (*Matthew 28:2–7*)
25. Zacharias (*Luke 1:5–20*)

The Song Heard Around the World

The beautiful hymn "How Great Thou Art" is probably one of the most widely recognized hymns in the world. In fact, the hymn as we know it today has been pieced together from different parts of the world in an interesting fashion.

The song was first born in 1885 as the work of a Swedish minister, Carl Boberg. Originally penned in Swedish and titled "O Store Gud" ("O Mighty God"), the song began as a poem Boberg wrote after witnessing a magnificent display of nature during a visit to a beautiful country estate. While strolling the grounds, he was caught in a sudden thunderstorm and witnessed the awesome violence of the thunder and lightning. Then, as suddenly as it had begun, the storm was gone, and the clouds quickly parted to allow the sun to light the majestic landscape once again. A calm breeze and the sound of birds chattering in excitement as the rain disappeared must have accented the scene, for these sights and sounds are noted in the words he penned.

Boberg's poem later became nine stanzas of the current song, and Swedish congregations began to sing it as a hymn, using one of their traditional folk songs for the tune. The text was later translated into German and Russian, and the song spread across Western Europe and the Ukraine. It was in the Ukraine that English missionaries S. K. Hine and his wife first heard the song. They were responsible for translating the existing text into English. Hines changed the melody to better fit the English wording. He also added at least one verse.

When World War II broke out, the Hines returned to England. In 1939 they introduced the song to an English audience and added the final verse to the song, which begins,

THE SONG HEARD AROUND
THE WORLD (CONT'D)

"When Christ shall come with shout of acclamation. . . ." The hymn quickly became popular in England.

In 1954 George Beverly Shea, bass-baritone soloist for the Billy Graham Crusades, heard the song for the first time during the crusade in London. Mr. Shea introduced the song to North America the following year during the Billy Graham Crusade in Toronto, Ontario. The song gained even greater fame at the New York Crusade in 1957 when Shea, accompanied by a massive choir, sang "How Great Thou Art" ninety-nine times. It became a hallmark of the Billy Graham Crusades thereafter.

Since the 1950s, the song has appeared in the hymnals of many different denominations, and it has been recorded and sung by artists from nearly every musical genre. Even people who have never been in a church often know at least part of the song by heart because it was recorded by Elvis Presley on his album titled *How Great Thou Art*. This album was the second gospel album Presley recorded and the only album he recorded between 1966 and 1968. In his later years, Elvis Presley's live stage performances almost always included a rendition of "How Great Thou Art."

Sources: catalog.lexpublib.org/TLCScripts/interpac.dll?SearchForm&Directions=
1&Config=pac&Branch=,0,&FormId=0;www.sermonaudio.com/hymn_details.asp?PID
=howgreatthouart.

ARE WE THERE YET?

The forty-year trek from Egypt to the Promised Land—made by perhaps three million people (Exodus 12:37 says there were six hundred thousand Israelite men, plus women and children)—was no joyride. The Israelites grumbled when provisions got scarce, and built a golden calf when they tired of waiting for Moses. God knew the way was not easy. He performed miracle after miracle for the Israelites throughout the whole journey. Here are ten of the major miracles:

1. *The burning bush (Exodus 3:1–6)*. The Israelites had been enslaved for four hundred years when God summoned Moses to lead his people out of Egypt. While tending flocks in the desert, Moses saw a bush that was on fire but did not burn up. When he stepped closer, God spoke to him out of the bush: "Moses! Moses!" *(v. 4 NIV)*.

2. *Moses' staff (Exodus 4)*. To confirm the call to Moses to deliver the Israelites out of Egypt, God changed Moses' staff into a snake and told Moses to "perform before Pharaoh all the wonders I have given you the power to do" *(v. 21 NIV)*.

3. *Ten plagues (Exodus 7–11)*. God inflicted the Egyptians with calamities to convince Pharaoh to let the Israelites go. After each of nine plagues, Pharaoh relented, then would not let God's people leave Egypt. When each household suffered the loss of the firstborn, Pharaoh told Moses and the Israelites to get out of the country.

4. *Pillar of cloud and pillar of fire (Exodus 13:21–22)*. God miraculously led the Israelites, guiding them by a pillar of cloud by day and a pillar of fire by night.

5. *The Red Sea parted (Exodus 14)*. Pharaoh sent his armies to pursue the fleeing Israelites. With Egyptian armies on one side and the Red Sea on the other, the Israelites appeared doomed. But God told Moses to stretch his hand over the sea, and when he did, the waters parted, and the Israelites walked through the sea on dry ground.

ARE WE THERE YET? (CONT'D)

6. *Waters of Marah (Exodus 15:22–25).* After three days of desert travel, the Israelites found water at Marah. But when they tasted the water, it was bitter and they couldn't drink it. God told Moses to throw a piece of wood into the water to make it sweet.

7. *Miraculous manna (Exodus 16).* When the hungry Israelites began complaining about not having enough food, God told Moses he would "rain down bread from heaven" *(v. 4 NIV).* For the next forty years the Israelites ate manna six days a week. The word *manna* literally means "What is it?"—it was a sweet, grain- or seedlike substance not known before or since.

8. *Water from the rock (Exodus 17:1–7).* The thirsty Israelites complained to Moses when they had no water. God told him to strike the rock with his staff. When he did, enough water flowed out to satisfy all the people.

9. *Shoes and clothes that lasted (Deuteronomy 29:5).* For forty years the Israelites did not have to replace their clothes or shoes, because they did not wear out.

10. *The glory of God (Exodus 34:29–35).* Whenever Moses met with God, his face afterward would be radiant with God's glory—so much so that he had to wear a veil across it. Later, the glory of God "filled the tabernacle" *(Exodus 40:34–35 NIV).*

PREPRESS PRODUCTION

Before the printing press, the only way to duplicate a book or document was to copy it by hand. The first "documents" were engraved on a rock, or for a less-permanent copy, on beeswax using a sharp, pointed tool called a stylus. Once ink or dye was invented, early scribes wrote on animal hides, which could be scrubbed, cleaned, and used again.

Book production took a giant leap forward with the Egyptians' invention of papyrus. Papyrus was ancient writing paper. In fact, the word *paper* derives from the word *papyrus.* The tall papyrus plant grew along the Nile. It was harvested, cut into strips, soaked in water, and pressed into sheets. The papyrus sheets were sewn together and placed between two pieces of wood that became "book" covers. These books were known as a codex. The term "bible" actually comes from the Greek word for "papyrus plant," which is *biblos.* The oldest surviving manuscript for any part of the New Testament is a papyrus fragment that contains part of John 18, dating from about AD 125. That papyrus fragment is in the John Rylands Library in Manchester, England.

In the early 300s, papyrus was replaced by parchment made from sheepskin or goatskin. About the same time, the Roman emperor Constantine became a believer and authorized copies made of the Scriptures. The Codex Sinaiticus, considered the world's oldest Bible, dates from this time. It contains the earliest surviving copy of the complete New Testament and the earliest and best copies of some of the Hebrew Scriptures. The Codex Sinaiticus was preserved for many centuries at St. Catherine's Monastery near the foot of Mount Sinai in Egypt; a portion of it is now on display at the British Library in London.

PREPRESS PRODUCTION (CONT'D)

Bibles were copied in their original languages of Greek and Hebrew until the first translation into Latin about the year 175. By the year 600, the Gospels were available only in eight different languages. The first definitive translation was completed in 405 by the great scholar Jerome under orders by Pope Damascus I. That translation is called the Vulgate. It was the "popular" version of the Bible for nearly a thousand years.

In the Middle Ages, monks in monasteries across Europe undertook the task of copying the Scriptures. Teams of scribes and artists worked in rooms called scriptoriums or writing rooms, where they produced thousands of beautiful Bibles. By the late Middle Ages, professional copyists took on the production of both religious and secular texts. The commercial book trade took off, and booksellers sold their books in shops near universities and cathedral schools. Complete Bibles were huge and expensive and affordable only by universities and the very wealthy.

Two events served to help make the Bible more available to the general population. The first was the translation of the Bible into English through the work of Oxford scholar John Wycliffe. With the help of his followers and other faithful scribes, Wycliffe produced dozens of English language manuscripts. The next milestone event in the history of the Bible is Gutenberg's invention of the printing press in 1455. Books could be "mass-produced" instead of individually copied and handwritten.

Sources: www.ibs.org/bibles/about/18.php;
www.ibs.org/bibles/about/20.php.

PREVENT SPIRITUAL IDENTITY THEFT

One of the ways believers get discouraged is to doubt who they are. The Creator knows his children best, and it is his opinion that counts the most! If you are a believer, you can prevent spiritual identify theft by holding tightly to what God says and reminding yourself of the following truths:

1. You are God's child *(John 1:12)*.

2. As a disciple, you are a friend of Jesus *(John 15:15)*.

3. You have been justified *(Romans 5:1)*.

4. You are united with God, and you are one with him in spirit *(1 Corinthians 6:17)*.

5. You have been bought with a price, and you belong to God *(1 Corinthians 6:19–20)*.

6. You are a member of Jesus' body *(1 Corinthians 12:27)*.

7. You have been chosen by God and adopted as his child *(Ephesians 1:3–8)*.

8. You can do all things through Jesus, who strengthens you *(Philippians 4:13)*.

9. You are complete in Jesus *(Colossians 2:9–10)*.

10. You are God's workmanship *(Ephesians 2:10)*.

11. You are a citizen of heaven *(Philippians 3:20)*.

12. You are free from any accusation brought against you *(Romans 8:33–34)*.

13. You cannot be separated from the love of God *(Romans 8:35–39)*.

14. You have been established, anointed, and sealed by God *(2 Corinthians 1:21–22)*.

15. You are hidden with Jesus in God *(Colossians 3:1–4)*.

16. You are a work in progress *(Philippians 1:6)*.

ENJOY THE SABBATH

The word *Sabbath* does not come from the Hebrew word for "seventh," as many people think. The Hebrew word for Sabbath is *shabbath*, which refers to an intermission or a cessation of work. The root word is *shabath*, which means to "repose," "desist from exertion," or "rest." In the Bible, the Sabbath was observed on different days at various times in the Old Testament—on the first day *(Leviticus 23:39)*, the seventh day *(Exodus 20:8–10)*, and the eighth day *(Leviticus 23:39)*. It was also observed for different lengths of time—as one day long *(Exodus 16:23–29)*, two days long *(Leviticus 23:6–8, 15–22)*, one year long *(Leviticus 25:4)*, and for eternity *(Hebrews 4:9)*. A Sabbath day was intended to be a day of delight, rest, and worship *(Isaiah 58:13)*—never a burden. It was to be observed as "unto the LORD" *(Exodus 16:25 KJV)* and be regarded as holy *(Exodus 16:23)*.

ARE YOU HIGH OR LOW CHURCH?

The term "Low Church" originally referred to the liberal wing of the Church of England. Those who were Low Church were considered to be nonconformists who were opposed to the priesthood and sacraments as being central to worship. The term was later applied to evangelicals.

Today those considered "High Church" tend to be Episcopal or Anglican churches that emphasize tradition and ritual. Some definitions classify Protestants as High Church if they use Roman Catholic practices during Mass and honor the Virgin Mary.

Within the Roman Catholic tradition, a "High Mass" is the traditional form of the Catholic Mass, usually with the chanting of the gospel and the use of incense. A "Low Mass" is considered to be one in which the person conducting the Communion service reads the gospel and the Epistle, and no part of the service is sung.

And what about "Low Sunday"? That's the name traditionally given to the first Sunday after Easter, often a very low-attendance day!

THE PERFECT GIFT

God is a giver, and the people of God are to be givers as well. In fact, believers are to give cheerfully; those are the people God loves. Not all gifts are given with a pure motive, but even those gifts can bless others.

1. *Tithes (Genesis 14:17–20).* Abraham (aka Abram) gave a gift of tithes, 10 percent of his wealth, to the priest Melchizedek.

2. *Gold, silver jewelry, and clothing (Genesis 24:53).* Abraham's servant gave these gifts to Rebekah when he asked her to become Isaac's wife.

3. *Female and male goats, ewes and rams, camels and their young, cows and bulls, and female and male donkeys (Genesis 32:13–15).* Jacob gave this gift of livestock to his brother Esau to make up for cheating him out of his family blessing.

4. *Balm, honey, spices and myrrh, pistachio nuts, and almonds (Genesis 43:11).* Jacob sent the best products of the land of Canaan as gifts to win Joseph's favor in Egypt.

5. *Field and springs (Joshua 15:17–19).* Acsah, Caleb's daughter, received a field from her father as her marriage gift; she also asked him to give her "springs of water" *(v. 19 NIV)*, which he did.

6. *Silver plates and sprinkling bowls, gold dishes, incense, bulls, rams, male lambs, and goats (Numbers 7:84–87).* Leaders of the twelve tribes of Israel brought these gifts for the tabernacle, their place of worship.

7. *Priesthood (Numbers 18:6–8).* God gave the Levites the gift of serving as priests for the nation of Israel.

8. *Gift in proportion to the blessing (Deuteronomy 16:16–17).* At the Feast of Unleavened Bread, the Feast of Weeks, and the Feast of Tabernacles, each man was to bring a gift "in proportion to the way the LORD your God has blessed you" *(v. 17 NIV)*.

9. *Spices, jewels, almugwood, and gold (1 Kings 10:10–11).* Inquiring about accounts of Solomon's vast wealth, the queen of Sheba visited Solomon, bringing gifts to him and securing good relations between the nations.

10. *Gold, silver, robes, weapons, spices, horses, and mules (2 Chronicles 9:23–25).* These were the gifts given to Solomon by all the kings of the earth when they sought audience with him to hear the wisdom God had put in his heart.

11. *Silver, gold, and clothing (2 Kings 5:4–6).* The Syrian king gave these gifts to an Israelite king to secure the healing of Naaman, his army commander.

12. *Forty camel-loads of all the best products of Damascus (2 Kings 8:7–10).* King Ben-Hadad sent these gifts to Elisha to receive a favorable oracle from God.

THE PERFECT GIFT (CONT'D)

13. **Gold, silver, bronze, iron, wood, onyx, turquoise, stone, and marble (1 Chronicles 29:1–9).** David and the people of Israel brought these materials as gifts for the building of the temple.

14. **Silver and flocks (2 Chronicles 17:10–11).** The Philistines and the Arabs brought these gifts and more to Jehoshaphat, godly king of Judah. "The fear of the LORD fell on all the kingdoms of the lands surrounding Judah" *(v. 10 NIV)*, and they did not war with him.

15. **Valuable gifts (2 Chronicles 32:22–24).** Hezekiah, king of Judah, prayed to God for deliverance from the hand of the Assyrians. In gratitude and honor, many brought these gifts to the king.

16. **Presents of food and gifts to the poor (Esther 9:20–22).** Mordecai sent letters to the Jews in celebration of deliverance from their enemies, telling them to observe days of feasting and joy and giving of gifts.

17. **Gold, frankincense, and myrrh (Matthew 2:11).** The wise men brought these costly gifts to the young child Jesus.

18. **Alabaster jar of expensive perfume (John 12:1–8).** Mary of Bethany brought pure nard with which to anoint Jesus' feet.

19. **Two copper coins (Luke 21:1–4).** A poor widow gave two small coins to the temple treasury. Her contribution was all she had, and therefore Jesus considered it greater than the gifts of the rich.

20. **Gifts to the poor (Acts 10:1–4).** Cornelius gave gifts to the poor, and his generosity was considered a memorial offering to God.

21. **Help for the poor (Acts 11:29–30).** The prophecy of a widespread famine prompted the believers in Antioch to send gifts "according to their ability" *(v. 29 NRSV)* to help the poor of Judea.

22. **The body (Romans 12:1).** The gift of one's body is given as a living sacrifice to serve God.

23. **Spiritual gifts (Acts 2:38; 1 Corinthians 12:1–11).** The Holy Spirit is a gift and gives spiritual gifts to each one for the common good— wisdom, knowledge, faith, healing, miracles, prophecy, discernment, speaking in tongues (suddenly speaking in a foreign language without the prior ability to do so, or speaking in a spiritual language), and interpretation of tongues.

24. **Gifts to the poor (2 Corinthians 8; 9:5).** On Paul's instruction, Titus established a relief fund for the poor in Jerusalem. The Macedonians "urgently pleaded . . . for the privilege of sharing in this service to the saints" *(2 Corinthians 8:4 NIV)*.

25. **Jesus (John 3:16).** God gave his beloved Son, Jesus, as a gift to all people.

DO YOU GO TO CHURCH?

A preacher was standing at the door as he always did after services on Sundays. As he shook hands with various parishioners, he suddenly grabbed one man's hand and pulled him aside.

The pastor said, "You need to join the army of the Lord!"

The man replied, "I'm already in the army of the Lord, Pastor."

The pastor asked, "How come I don't see you except at Christmas and Easter?"

The man whispered back, "I'm in the secret service."

Source: www.AhaJokes.com.

AWAKE ALL NIGHT

Bill: Hi, Joe! You look a little tired today.

Joe: I am, with good reason!

Bill: What's the reason?

Joe: Well, you know I'm an insomniac dyslexic agnostic.

Bill: So?

Joe: Last night I was awake all night wondering if there really is a dog!

THE CHURCH CHANDELIER

A new young minister got his first charge—a tiny church way out on the prairies. He traveled from the big city early to familiarize himself with the parish and visited the church on Wednesday. It was dark and dreary inside and, remembering the suggestion that he find a cause to get the congregation working together, he got the bright idea that they should raise funds to buy a chandelier to hang in the middle of the sanctuary. On Sunday he delivered a stirring sermon designed to inspire the congregation to work together for a common cause.

The next week he met with the church trustees to see if they had made any progress on the project.

"Well, Reverend," the head trustee began, "we've decided that the chandelier isn't what this church needs. First, we don't have anybody here who can spell it. Second, we don't have anybody who can play it. Besides, what we really need is more light."

THE SUBSTITUTE ORGANIST

The minister was upset because he had to tell his congregation they'd have to come up with more money than they were expecting for repairs to the roof of the church. To top it all off, the regular organist was sick that day, and a substitute had been called at the last minute. She arrived just before the service was to start and asked the minister what she should play.

"Here's a copy of the service," he said impatiently. "But you'll have to come up with something on your own after I make the announcement about the finances. Play something inspiring."

At the end of the service, the minister paused and said, "There's one thing more. I have a special announcement to make. The repairs we are making to the roof of the church are costing twice as much as we expected, and we need four thousand dollars more. Anyone who can pledge one hundred dollars or more, please stand up."

At that moment the substitute organist broke into "The Star-Spangled Banner."

And that is how the substitute became the regular organist.

PAY ATTENTION!

A church arranged to have a well-known, scholarly preacher come visit and speak. Every seat was taken at the special afternoon service, which lasted about three hours.

The next day, the preacher ran into one of the church members at a local restaurant where both men were having lunch.

"Good to have you at our church yesterday," the man said, shaking the preacher's hand.

"Thank you," the preacher said. "If you don't mind my asking, what did you think of my sermon?"

"I have to admit, I couldn't sleep after you spoke," the man said.

"Really? All that talk about heaven and hell really got to you?" the preacher asked.

"No," the man said. "It's just that I can't sleep at night after sleeping so much during the day."

THE B-I-B-L-E

Some people think the Bible isn't so much the title of a book as it is an acronym for the content: Basic Information Before Leaving Earth.

Giggle and Groan

Q. Who was the greatest financier in the Bible?

A. Noah—he was floating his stock while everyone else was in liquidation.

Q. Who was the greatest female financier in the Bible?

A. Pharaoh's daughter—she went down to the bank of the Nile and drew out a little prophet.

Q. What kind of man was Boaz before he got married?

A. Ruth-less.

Q. What kind of motor vehicles are in the Bible?

A. God drove Adam and Eve out of the Garden in a Fury. David's Triumph was heard throughout the land. Honda . . . because the apostles were all in one Accord. And 2 Corinthians 4:8 (NIV) describes going out in service in a Volkswagen Beetle: "We are hard pressed on every side, but not crushed."

Q. Who was the greatest comedian in the Bible?

A. Samson—he brought the house down.

Q. What happened in the first baseball game in the Bible?

A. In the big inning, Eve stole first, Adam stole second. Cain struck out Abel, and the Prodigal Son came home. The Giants and the Angels were rained out.

Q. How did Adam and Eve feel when expelled from the Garden of Eden?

A. They were really put out.

Q. What is one of the first things that Adam and Eve did after they were kicked out of the Garden of Eden?

A. They raised Cain.

Q. What excuse did Adam give to his children as to why he no longer lived in Eden?

A. Your mother ate us out of house and home.

THE B-I-B-L-E (CONT'D)

Q. The ark was built in three stories, and the top story had a window to let light in, but how did they get light to the bottom two stories?

A. They used floodlights.

Q. Who is the greatest babysitter mentioned in the Bible?

A. David—he rocked Goliath to sleep.

Q. Why was Goliath so surprised when David hit him with a slingshot?

A. The thought had never entered his head before.

Q. If Goliath is resurrected, would you like to tell him the joke about David and Goliath?

A. No, he already fell for it once.

Q. What do they call pastors in Germany?

A. German shepherds.

Q. Which servant of God was the most flagrant lawbreaker in the Bible?

A. Moses, because he broke all of the Ten Commandments at once.

Q. Which area of Palestine was especially wealthy?

A. The area along the Jordan River—the banks were always overflowing.

Q. How do we know that Job went to a chiropractor?

A. Because in Job 16:12 *(NIRV)* we read, "Everything was going well with me. But he broke me into pieces like a clay pot. He grabbed me by the neck and crushed me."

Q. Where is the first tennis match mentioned in the Bible?

A. When Joseph served in Pharaoh's court.

Q: Which Bible character had no parents?

A: Joshua, son of Nun.

Q: Why didn't Noah go fishing?

A: He had only two worms!

SEES ALL AND KNOWS ALL

A blind man was standing on a street corner in the dead of winter, holding out a tin cup and imploring passersby to contribute something for his comfort.

Many men and women walked past, but in their hurry to get home or to work, they ignored the poor blind beggar.

Finally a woman noticed the blind man and put a handful of change in his cup, causing a satisfying *clink-clank*.

"Oh, thank you!" the man exclaimed, reaching out and patting the woman's arm. "The minute I saw you, I knew you were a generous person!"

WHY WASTE TIME?

There was a man named Bob who was admired and respected by his friends, in large part because he had quite a head for business. Over time, Bob did very well in the stock market, earning great gains and building an impressive portfolio.

One unfortunate day, there were some political upheavals and economic disasters in other parts of the world that scared the boys and girls on Wall Street and caused nearly all of Bob's portfolio to go up in smoke.

One of Bob's friends heard about this disaster and decided to go comfort him. How distraught he must be, the friend thought.

What a shock it was, then, to see Bob smiling!

"Aren't you upset?" the friend asked. "Think of what you lost!"

"Oh yes, I was upset," Bob said. "But God has blessed me with a fast-forward brain. What other people spend days and weeks thinking and worrying about, I can get over in just one hour!"

BIBLICAL THEME SONGS

Noah: "Raindrops Keep Falling on My Head"

Adam and Eve: "Strangers in Paradise"

Lazarus: "The Second Time Around"

Esther: "I Feel Pretty"

Job: "I've Got a Right to Sing the Blues"

Moses: "The Wanderer"

Jezebel: "The Lady Is a Tramp"

Samson: "Hair"

Salome: "I Could Have Danced All Night"

Daniel: "The Lion Sleeps Tonight"

Joshua: "Good Vibrations"

Peter: "I'm Sorry"

Esau: "Born to Be Wild"

Shadrach, Meshach, and Abednego: "Great Balls of Fire!"

The Three Kings: "When You Wish Upon a Star"

Jonah: "Got a Whale of a Tale"

Elijah: "Up, Up, and Away"

Methuselah: "Stayin' Alive"

Nebuchadnezzar: "Crazy"

TWENTY-FIVE PEARLS OF WISDOM

1. If you're too open-minded, your brains will fall out.

2. Age is a very high price to pay for maturity.

3. The cardiologist's diet: If it tastes good, spit it out.

4. Artificial intelligence is no match for natural stupidity.

5. If you must choose between two evils, pick the one you've never tried before.

6. My idea of housework is to sweep the room with a glance.

7. Not one shred of evidence supports the notion that life is serious.

8. It is easier to get forgiveness than permission.

9. For every action, there is an equal and opposite government program.

10. If you look like your passport picture, you probably need the trip.

11. Bills travel through the mail at twice the speed of checks.

12. A conscience is what hurts when all your other parts feel so good.

13. Eat well, stay fit, die anyway.

14. Men are from earth. Women are from earth. Deal with it.

15. No husband has ever been shot while doing the dishes.

16. A balanced diet is a cookie in each hand.

17. Middle age is when broadness of the mind and narrowness of the waist change places.

18. Opportunities always look bigger going than coming.

19. Junk is something you've kept for years and throw away three weeks before you need it.

20. There is always one more imbecile than you counted on.

21. Experience is a wonderful thing. It enables you to recognize a mistake when you make it again.

22. By the time you can make ends meet, they move the ends.

23. Thou shalt not weigh more than thy refrigerator.

24. Someone who thinks logically provides a nice contrast to the real world.

25. Blessed are those who can laugh at themselves, for they shall never cease to be amused.

THE PATH TO HEAVEN

This is the path to heaven and eternal life; all you have to do is decode it. (Hint: Every letter has been replaced by the letter immediately after it in the alphabet; for instance, A=B, B=C, C=D, etc.) All the Scriptures are from the King James Version.

1. "GPS BMM IBWF TJOOFE, BOE DPNF TIPSU PG
   "__ ___ ____ _____, ___ ____ _____ __
   UIF HMPSZ PG HPE."
   ___ _____ __ ___."

2. "GPS UIF XBHFT PG TJO JT EFBUI."
   "___ ___ _____ __ ___ __ _____."

3. "CVU HPE DPNNFOEFUI IJT MPWF UPXBSE VT,
   "___ ___ _____ ___ ____ _____ __,
   JO UIBU, XIJMF XF XFSF ZFU TJOOFST, DISJTU
   __ ____, _____ __ ____ ___ _____, _____
   EJFE GPS VT."
   ____ ___ __."

4. "XIBU NVTU J EP UP CF TBWFE? BOE UIFZ
   "____ ____ _ __ __ __ _____? ___ ____
   TBJE, CFMJFWF PO UIF MPSE KFTVT DISJTU,
   ____, _____ __ ___ ____ _____ _____,
   BOE UIPV TIBMU CF TBWFE."
   ___ ____ _____ __ _____."

5. "CVU BT NBOZ BT SFDFJWFE IJN, UP UIFN
   "___ __ ____ __ _____ ___, __ ____
   HBWF IF QPXFS UP CFDPNF UIF TPOT PG HPE,
   ____ __ _____ __ _____ ___ ____ __ ___,
   FWFO UP UIFN UIBU CFMJFWF PO IJT OBNF"
   ____ __ ____ ____ _____ __ ___ ____"

6. "GPS XIPTPFWFS TIBMM DBMM VQPO UIF OBNF
   "___ _____ _____ ____ ____ ___ ____
   PG UIF MPSE TIBMM CF TBWFE."
   __ ___ ____ _____ __ _____."

7. "HPE CF NFSDJGVM UP NF B TJOOFS."
   "___ __ _____ __ __ _ _____."

8. "GPS XIBU TIBMM JU QSPGJU B NBO, JG IF
   "___ ____ _____ __ _____ _ ___, __ __
   TIBMM HBJO UIF XIPMF XPSME, BOE MPTF IJT
   _____ ____ ___ _____ _____, ___ ____ ___
   PXO TPVM?"
   ___ ____?"

9. "XIPTPFWFS UIFSFGPSF TIBMM DPOGFTT NF
   "_____ _____ _____ _____ __
   CFGPSF NFO, IJN XJMM J DPOGFTT BMTP CFG
   _____, ___ ____ _ _____ ____ ___
   PSF NZ GBUIFS XIJDI JT JO IFBWFO."
   ___ __ _____ _____ __ __ _____."

(Answers to The Path to Heaven are on page 382.)

A PROPHET'S JOB

Unscramble the names of prophets in the column to the left to discover the primary role of a prophet. Clues from the Bible are below. Spellings are based on the King James Bible.

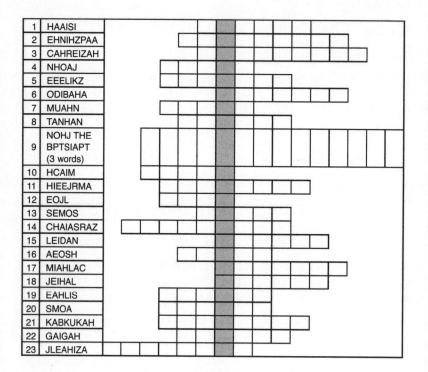

1	HAAISI
2	EHNIHZPAA
3	CAHREIZAH
4	NHOAJ
5	EEELIKZ
6	ODIBAHA
7	MUAHN
8	TANHAN
9	NOHJ THE BPTSIAPT (3 words)
10	HCAIM
11	HIEEJRMA
12	EOJL
13	SEMOS
14	CHAIASRAZ
15	LEIDAN
16	AEOSH
17	MIAHLAC
18	JEIHAL
19	EAHLIS
20	SMOA
21	KABKUKAH
22	GAIGAH
23	JLEAHIZA

Clues

1. His descriptions of the coming Messiah are among the most vivid in the Old Testament.

2. His primary theme was the "day of the LORD."

3. He ministered to the residents of Jerusalem after they returned from exile in Babylon.

4. He is perhaps best known for being swallowed by a great fish.

5. His prophecies consist almost entirely of visions and prophetic oracles that include parables, poetry, and allegories.

6. His prophecy is the shortest book of the Old Testament.

7. He prophesied that the Assyrian Empire would be destroyed.

A Prophet's Job (cont'd)

8. He confronted King David about David's affair with Bathsheba.

9. He prophesied the immediate arrival of the Lamb of God.

10. His prophecy was uttered in poetic verse.

11. He said God had formed him as a prophet "in the womb."

12. His main concepts were ruin, repentance, and restoration.

13. He foretold what would happen if the Israelites kept the commandments of God in the Promised Land, and what would happen if they did not.

14. He prophesied about his own son, John the Baptist.

15. He interpreted the dreams of Babylonian kings and boldly prayed even if it meant spending a night in a lions' den.

16. His marriage to an unfaithful woman named Gomer depicted the way God loved his people.

17. His prophetic words calling the people to renewed faithfulness are the last book in the Old Testament.

18. He outran Ahab's chariots after defeating four hundred prophets of Baal on Mount Carmel.

19. He received a "double portion" of the prophetic power of Elijah.

20. He was a sheep-breeder in Tekoa when the word of the Lord came to him.

21. His prophecies gave hope and comfort to people in the midst of certain disaster.

22. He admonished the Israelites to obey the Lord by rebuilding the temple.

23. He spoke God's command to Jehoshaphat at a time when Jerusalem was surrounded by enemy troops.

(Answers to A Prophet's Job are on page 382.)

BE AN ACTION HERO

Jesus was not a slacker. He was a man of action. He expected his followers to be the same way. The book of Matthew, and the opening lines in Acts, are full of his instructions to do something. The life of faith is not intended to be a passive activity!

Match the "action" verbs on the left with the appropriate numbered clues. Then write the verbs in the corresponding numbered blocks on the facing page. Find them all and reveal a hidden "action message" in the gray column.

ask
disciple
drink
eat
give
listen
love
rejoice
repent
sell
stay
study
watch
witness

1. Apologize for breaking God's laws and decide to never do it again *(Matthew 4:17 NRSV)*.

2. Take nourishment *(Matthew 26:26 NRSV)*.

3. Pose a question *(Matthew 7:7 NRSV)*.

4. Be generous *(Matthew 5:42 NLT)*.

5. Ponder something until you know it *(Matthew 24:32 CEV)*.

6. Become a follower of a teacher *(Matthew 4:19 NIV)*.

7. Tell others what you know to be true *(Acts 1:8 NIV)*.

8. Pay attention with your eyes *(Matthew 24:4 NIV)*.

9. Put something on the market *(Matthew 19:21 NLT)*.

10. Be very glad! *(Matthew 5:12 NIV)*.

11. Take liquid refreshment *(Matthew 26:27 CEV)*.

12. Care very deeply *(Matthew 5:44 CEV)*.

13. Use your ears *(Matthew 13:18 NIV)*.

14. Don't move from this spot *(Matthew 26:38 NLT)*.

BE AN ACTION HERO (CONT'D)

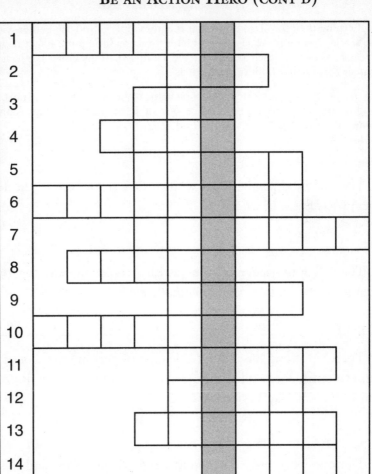

(Answers to Be an Action Hero are on page 383.)

JESUS, AKA THE VINE

Keeping the Holy Trinity straight is fairly simple—God the Father, God the Son, and God the Holy Spirit. But it takes a little more effort to look at specific names for each person of the Godhead. Jesus alone is given many names that further flesh out who he is.

In this puzzle, the last letter of the first name is the first letter in the next name, and so on. How appropriate, since one of Jesus' names is "the Alpha and Omega"—the Beginning and the End *(Revelation 22:13)*!

— — — — — — —

The one God promised to send to deliver, or rescue, the Jewish people. *(John 4:25–26 AMP)*

— — — — — — — — — —

The religious leader of the Jewish people; he was the one in charge at the temple. *(Hebrews 6:20 AMP)*

— — — — — — — — — — —

There's nothing false about this type of person; you would want him to testify for you in court (as you will want Jesus to do for you on Judgment Day!). *(Revelation 3:14 AMP)*

— — — — — —

The one who rescues mankind from certain death and destruction. *(Luke 2:11 AMP)*

— — — — — — — —

The one who makes amends for others' failures or wrongdoing. *(Job 19:25 AMP)*

JESUS, AKA THE VINE (CONT'D)

— — — — — — —

A solid, immovable boulder. *(Psalm 18:2 AMP)*

— — — — — — — — — — —

The ultimate monarch of monarchs. *(1 Timothy 6:15 AMP)*

— — — — — — — —

The male offspring of a human. *(Matthew 8:20 AMP)*

— — — — — — — —

This name for Jesus is derived from the name of his hometown. *(Matthew 2:23 AMP)*

— — — — — — — —

The Supreme Being who will live forever. *(Deuteronomy 33:27 AMP)*

— — — —

He's the way into heaven—knock, knock! *(John 10:9 AMP)*

— — — — — — — —

A popular Valentine's flower, found in a plain named for a woman. *(Song of Solomon 2:1 AMP)*

Answers

Messiah, High Priest, true Witness, Savior, Redeemer, Rock, King of kings, Son of Man, Nazarene, eternal God, Door, rose of Sharon.

WHICH WOMAN?

Both the Old and New Testaments have numerous very vivid and dramatic stories about women. Test your knowledge of these stories by taking the quiz below.

1. Which woman scared the birds away from the bodies of her sons after they had been killed by enemy troops?

   a. Rachel
   b. Rhoda
   c. Rizpah

2. Which woman hung scarlet yarn in the window of her home to escape being killed after the walls of Jericho fell?

   a. Ramona
   b. Rahab
   c. Rebekah

3. Which woman killed an enemy general by driving a tent peg through his skull?

   a. Jael
   b. Jedidah
   c. Jezebel

4. Which woman risked her life to invite her husband to a dinner party at which she might expose an evil plot of her husband's most trusted adviser?

   a. Esther
   b. Vashti
   c. Herodias

5. Which woman led the Israelites in singing and dancing after a successful crossing of the Red Sea?

   a. Susanna
   b. Miriam
   c. Naamah

6. Which woman risked the wrath of her husband to take a peace offering of food to King David?

   a. Abishag
   b. Abigail
   c. Adah

WHICH WOMAN? (CONT'D)

7. Which woman was willing to travel several hundred miles to become the bride of a man she had never met?

    a. Sarah
    b. Rebekah
    c. Rachel

8. Which woman was willing to go to the tomb where Jesus' body had been taken, even though Jesus' disciples were in hiding, fearing for their lives?

    a. Naomi
    b. Elizabeth
    c. Mary Magdalene

9. Which woman traveled more than a thousand miles to negotiate a trade deal with King Solomon and to see for herself the splendors of his court?

    a. The queen of Sheba
    b. Candace of Ethiopia
    c. Cleopatra of Egypt

10. Which woman took it upon herself to engineer the "escape" of one of her sons who had outwitted his older brother and father?

    a. Rachel
    b. Sarah
    c. Rebekah

Answers

1. c (Rizpah's story is in 2 Samuel 21:7-14.)
2. b (Rahab's story is in Joshua 2; 6:17-25.)
3. a (Jael's story is in Judges 4:17-23.)
4. a (Esther's story is in Esther 2-8.)
5. b (Miriam's story is in Exodus 15:20-21.)
6. b (Abigail's story is in 1 Samuel 25:2-42.)
7. b (Rebekah's wedding story is in Genesis 24.)
8. c (Mary Magdalene is mentioned in Matthew 28:1.)
9. a (The queen of Sheba's story is in 1 Kings 10:1-13.)
10. c (Rebekah's story is in Genesis 27:1-45.)

MATCHED PAIRS

These are biblical people whose names are strongly associated with another name in the Scriptures. See how many you can match. Hint: Remember that some people in the New Testament had the same name as Old Testament characters. You will use each answer only once.

1. Adam and _____
2. Ahab and _____
3. Ananias and _____
4. Balaam and _____
5. Boaz and _____
6. David and _____
7. Delilah and _____
8. Elijah and _____
9. Elimelech and _____
10. Esau and _____
11. Herod and _____
12. Jonathan and _____
13. Joseph and _____
14. Leah and _____
15. Mahlon and _____
16. Mary and _____
17. Naomi and _____
18. Priscilla and _____
19. Saul and _____
20. Shechem and _____

a. Ahab
b. Aquila
c. Rachel
d. David
e. Kilion
f. Eve
g. John the Baptist
h. Samson
i. Saul
j. Jonathan
k. Naboth
l. Naomi
m. Balak
n. Ruth (as wife)
o. Potiphar
p. Martha
q. Bathsheba
r. Ruth (as daughter-in-law)
s. Jacob
t. Dinah

Answers

1. f (Genesis 3:20 NIV)
2. k (1 Kings 21:1 NIV)
3. i (Acts 9:17 NIV)
4. m (Numbers 22:5 NIV)
5. n (Ruth 2:8 NIV)
6. q (2 Samuel 12:24 NIV)
7. h (Judges 16:6 NIV)
8. a (1 Kings 18:15 NIV)
9. l (Ruth 1:2 NIV)
10. s (Genesis 25:26 NIV)
11. g (Mark 6:14 NIV)
12. d (1 Samuel 18:1 NIV)
13. o (Genesis 39:1-19 NIV)
14. c (Genesis 29:16 NIV)
15. e (Ruth 1:2 NIV)
16. p (John 11:1 NIV)
17. r (Ruth 1:22 NIV)
18. j (Acts 18:2 NIV)
19. j (1 Samuel 13:16 NIV)
20. t (Genesis 34:11-26 NIV)

NAME THAT ENEMY

The Bible has a number of stories of war, and a few stories of enemies who sidestepped major battles through interesting means. Some of the stories are famous, others are not. See how many of the "enemies" below you can identify correctly:

1. Goliath of Gath—defeated by a young shepherd named David—was part of this enemy group that came to do battle against the Israelites.

    a. Amonites   b. Gathites
    c. Philistines   d. Cretans

2. These people should have been enemies destroyed by the Israelites in the Promised Land, but they claimed to be from a "far country," and their lives were spared.

    a. Gibeonites   b. Hittites
    c. Perizzites   d. Hivites

3. His chariots, horses, and horsemen chased the Israelites but were destroyed when the parted waters of the Red Sea came together again.

    a. Adoni-Zedek of Jerusalem   b. Pharaoh of Egypt
    c. King of Lachish   d. Reul of Midian

4. As they wandered in the wilderness, the Israelites defeated Og and Sihon, kings of these people who descended from Lot's younger daughter.

    a. Canaanites   b. Hivites
    c. Ammonites   d. Levites

5. Deborah the prophetess and Barak led the Israelites in defeating this enemy king.

    a. Ehud of the Moabites   b. Hazor the Kenite
    c. Shamgar leader of Hazor   d. Jabin king of Canaan

6. Gideon and a band of three hundred men with trumpets and pitchers with torches inside them drove these enemies from the land.

    a. Midianites   b. Amorites
    c. Pelegits   d. Canaanites

7. They were the lifelong enemies of Samson.

    a. Canaanites   b. Philistines
    c. Amorites   d. Egyptians

Answers

1. c (1 Samuel 17:1–4)
2. a (Joshua 9:3–15)
3. b (Exodus 14:28)
4. c (Deuteronomy 31:4)
5. d (Judges 4)
6. a (Judges 7)
7. b (Judges 16:23–31)

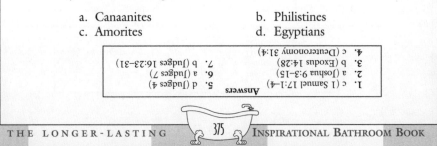

ALL WRAPPED UP

How much do you know about the Bible's givers and gifts?

1. What gifts did Abraham's servant give to Rebekah, Isaac's future wife?
   - a. articles of clothing
   - b. cattle
   - c. gold and silver jewelry
   - d. both gold and silver jewelry and articles of clothing

2. Who said, "Thanks be to God for his indescribable gift"?
   - a. Peter
   - b. Titus
   - c. Paul
   - d. John

3. Of the gifts given to the child Jesus by the Magi, which come from a tree?
   - a. gold
   - b. frankincense
   - c. myrrh
   - d. both frankincense and myrrh

4. In the book of Revelation, which event prompts the earth's inhabitants to send one another gifts?
   - a. the end of the judgments that were announced by trumpet
   - b. Satan is bound for one thousand years
   - d. the false prophet is killed
   - c. the two witnesses are slain

5. Proverbs says that a man who boasts of gifts he does not give is like
   - a. clouds and wind without rain
   - b. a constant dripping of water
   - c. a barren ox
   - d. one who lies down in the midst of the sea

6. On their way back to Canaan to get Benjamin, what did Joseph's brothers find hidden in their sacks of grain?
   - a. snakes
   - b. Joseph's coat of many colors
   - c. money
   - d. mice

7. According to Proverbs, "A gift given in secret . . ."
   - a. will be made known
   - b. soothes anger
   - c. is bribery
   - d. accomplishes nothing

8. Jesus asked, "If your son asks for a fish, will you give him a ____?"
   - a. net
   - b. serpent
   - c. lizard
   - d. stone

Answers

1. d (Genesis 24:53)	5. a (Proverbs 25:14)
2. c (2 Corinthians 9:15)	6. c (Genesis 42:27)
3. d (Matthew 2:11)	7. b (Proverbs 21:14)
4. c (Revelation 11:3–11)	8. b (Matthew 7:10)

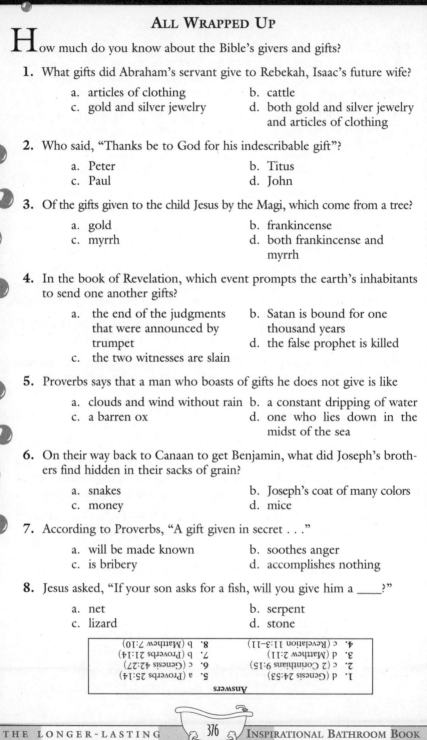

BIBLE BRAIN TWISTER

H ow many books of the Bible can you find in the text below?

Bible Brain Twister by John Kezer

I once made a remark about the hidden books of the Bible. It was a lulu, kept people looking so hard for facts, and for others it was a revelation. Some were in a jam, especially since the names of the books are not capitalized, but the truth finally struck home to numbers of readers. To others, it was a real job. We want it to be a most fascinating few moments for you. Yes, there will be some really easy ones to spot. Others may require judges to help them. I will quickly admit it usually takes a minister to find one of the seventeen, and there will be loud lamentations when it is found. A little lady says she brews a cup of tea so she can concentrate better. See how well you can compete. Relax now, for there really are the names of seventeen books of the Bible in this puzzle.

Source: http://jmm.aaa.net.au/articles/16032.htm. © John Mark Ministries, used by permission.

Answers

Bible Brain Twister by **John** Kezer

I once made a re**mark** about the hidden books of the Bible. It was a **lulu,** kept people looking **so** hard for **facts,** and for others it was a reve**lation.** Some were in a **jam,** especially since the names of the books are not capitalized, but the **truth** finally struck home to **numbers** of readers. To others, it was a real **job.** We want it to be **a most** fascinating few moments for you. **Yes, there** will be some really easy ones to spot. Others may require **judges** to help them. I will quickly admit **it usually** takes a minister to find one of the seventeen, and there will be loud **lamentations** when it is found. A little lady says s**he brews** a cup of tea so she can concentrate better. See how well you can com**pete. Relax** now, for there really are the names of seventeen books of the Bible in this puzzle.

ARE YOU SURE?

Do you know the Ten Commandments? Test yourself on this multiple-choice test, and find out how much you know!

1. The Ten Commandments can be found in which books of the Bible?

   a. Matthew and Luke   b. Leviticus and Numbers
   c. Exodus and Deuteronomy   d. Genesis and Exodus

2. God gave the Ten Commandments to which Old Testament leader?

   a. Noah   b. Moses
   c. Esther   d. David

3. Where did God give the Ten Commandments?

   a. Mount Sinai   b. Mount Nebo
   c. Jordan River   d. Massada

4. The first commandment says, "You shall have no other _____ before me."

   a. Religion   b. Gods
   c. Love   d. Altar

5. The second commandment says, "You shall not make for yourself an _____."

   a. Ebenezer   b. Unleavened bread
   c. Idol   d. Offering

6. The third commandment says, "You shall not take the _____ of the Lord your God in vain."

   a. Sacrifice   b. Word
   c. Commandments   d. Name

7. The fourth commandment says, "Remember the _____ by keeping it holy."

   a. Law   b. Sabbath
   c. Lord's Supper   d. Altar

8. The fifth commandment says, "Honor your _____."

   a. Father and mother   b. Sister and brother
   c. Scribes and Pharisees   d. Urim and Thummim

9. The sixth commandment says, "You shall not _____."

   a. Dance   b. Borrow money
   c. Divorce   d. Murder

ARE YOU SURE? (CONT'D)

10. The seventh commandment says, "You shall not commit _____."

    a. Perjury   b. Adultery
    c. Suicide   d. Crimes

11. The eighth commandment says, "You shall not _____."

    a. Steal   b. Take an oath
    c. Pass "Go"   d. Take offense

12. The ninth commandment says, "You shall not give false testimony against your _____."

    a. Butcher   b. Neighbor
    c. In-laws   d. Tax collector

13. The tenth commandment says, "You shall not _____."

    a. Covet   b. Lie under oath
    c. Trade a lame camel   d. Use dishonest weights

14. The original stone tablets of the Ten Commandments were broken into pieces because _____.

    a. They were dropped on the way down the mountain.   b. There was a mistake in the tablets.
    c. The Israelites were worshipping a golden calf.   d. God was angry with the people for their complaining.

15. The Israelites kept the Ten Commandments in the _____.

    a. Upper Room   b. Qumran caves
    c. Ark of the covenant   d. Outer court of the temple

16. Another name for the Ten Commandments is the _____.

    a. Dead Sea Scrolls   b. Decalogue
    c. Logos   d. Septuagint

Answers

1. c	9. d
2. b	10. b
3. a	11. a
4. b	12. b
5. c	13. a
6. d	14. c
7. b	15. c
8. a	16. b

TRAVELOCITY BIBLE STYLE

Biblical people used many different modes of transportation. Match the mode with the traveler/trip:

1. Mary going to Bethlehem, where Jesus was born
   a. Boat
   b. Donkey
   c. Horse
   d. We don't know

2. Death's carrier in Revelation
   a. Flying carpet
   b. Dragon
   c. Horse
   d. Chariot

3. Paul's trip to Italy
   a. Horse
   b. Camel
   c. We don't know
   d. Ship

4. Jacob and his extended family on their trip to Egypt
   a. Camel caravan
   b. Pharaoh's carts
   c. Walked
   d. Slave-carried litters

5. Ishmaelite merchants traveling from Gilead to Egypt
   a. Camel caravan
   b. Horse-drawn carts
   c. Walked
   d. Donkeys

6. Son of the widow of Nain when Jesus met him
   a. Donkey
   b. Pallet
   c. Cart
   d. Coffin

7. Shem, Ham, and Japheth on their trip to the mountains of Ararat
   a. Ark
   b. Camels
   c. Donkey
   d. Walked

8. Philip's trip with the Ethiopian
   a. Fishing boat
   b. Camel caravan
   c. Horse
   d. Chariot

9. King Amaziah of Judah on his final trip home to Jerusalem for burial
   a. Horse
   b. Royal bier
   c. Coffin
   d. Jar (after being cremated)

10. Moses' first ride on the Nile River
    a. Pharaoh's barge
    b. Small boat
    c. Inner tube
    d. Basket

Answers

1. d (Luke 2:4–7)
2. c (Revelation 6:8)
3. d (Acts 27:1)
4. b (Genesis 46:5)
5. a (Genesis 37:25)
6. d (Luke 7:11–17)
7. a (Genesis 7:13)
8. d (Acts 8:26–39)
9. a (2 Chronicles 25:27–28)
10. d (Exodus 2:1–8)

JACOB'S BOYS

Find all twelve sons of Jacob in the grid below by searching in all directions.

1. Asher
2. Benjamin
3. Dan
4. Gad
5. Issachar
6. Joseph
7. Judah
8. Levi
9. Naphtali
10. Reuben
11. Simeon
12. Zebulun

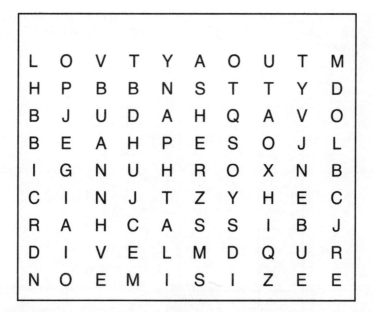

(Answers to Jacob's Boys are on page 383.)

Answers to The Path to Heaven (page 365) from the King James Version of the Bible.

1. Romans 3:23—FOR ALL HAVE SINNED, AND COME SHORT OF THE GLORY OF GOD

2. Romans 6:23—FOR THE WAGES OF SIN IS DEATH

3. Romans 5:8—BUT GOD COMMENDETH HIS LOVE TOWARD US, IN THAT, WHILE WE WERE YET SINNERS, CHRIST DIED FOR US

4. Acts 16:30–31—WHAT MUST I DO TO BE SAVED? AND THEY SAID, BELIEVE ON THE LORD JESUS CHRIST, AND THOU SHALT BE SAVED

5. John 1:12—BUT AS MANY AS RECEIVED HIM, TO THEM GAVE HE POWER TO BECOME THE SONS OF GOD, EVEN TO THEM THAT BELIEVE ON HIS NAME

6. Romans 10:13—FOR WHOSOEVER SHALL CALL UPON THE NAME OF THE LORD SHALL BE SAVED

7. Luke 18:13—GOD BE MERCIFUL TO ME A SINNER

8. Mark 8:36—FOR WHAT SHALL IT PROFIT A MAN, IF HE SHALL GAIN THE WHOLE WORLD, AND LOSE HIS OWN SOUL

9. Matthew 10:32—WHOSOEVER THEREFORE SHALL CONFESS ME BEFORE MEN, HIM WILL I CONFESS ALSO BEFORE MY FATHER WHICH IS IN HEAVEN

Answers to A Prophet's Job, page 366:

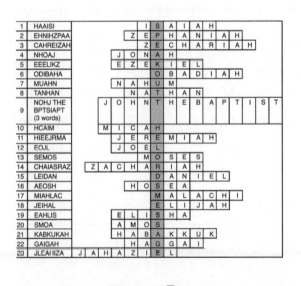

#	Scramble	Answer
1	HAAISI	ISAIAH
2	EHNIHZPAA	ZEPHANIAH
3	CAHREIZAH	ZECHARIAH
4	NHOAJ	JONAH
5	EEELIKZ	EZEKIEL
6	ODIBAHA	OBADIAH
7	MUAHN	NAHUM
8	TANHAN	NATHAN
9	NOHJ THE BPTSIAPT (3 words)	JOHN THE BAPTIST
10	HCAIM	MICAH
11	HIEEJRMA	JEREMIAH
12	EOJL	JOEL
13	SEMOS	MOSES
14	CHAIASRAZ	ZACHARIAH
15	LEIDAN	DANIEL
16	AEOSH	HOSEA
17	MIAHLAC	MALACHI
18	JEIHAL	ELIJAH
19	EAHLIS	ELISHA
20	SMOA	AMOS
21	KABKUKAH	HABAKKUK
22	GAIGAH	HAGGAI
23	JLEAIIIZA	JAHAZIEL

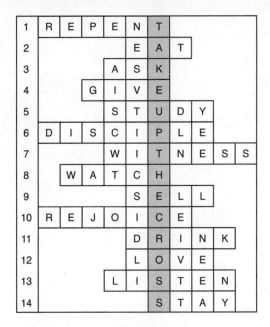

Answers to Be an Action Hero, page 369:

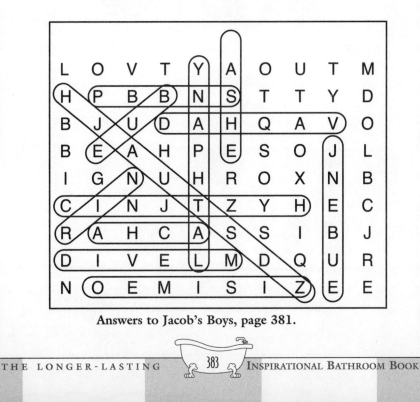

Answers to Jacob's Boys, page 381.

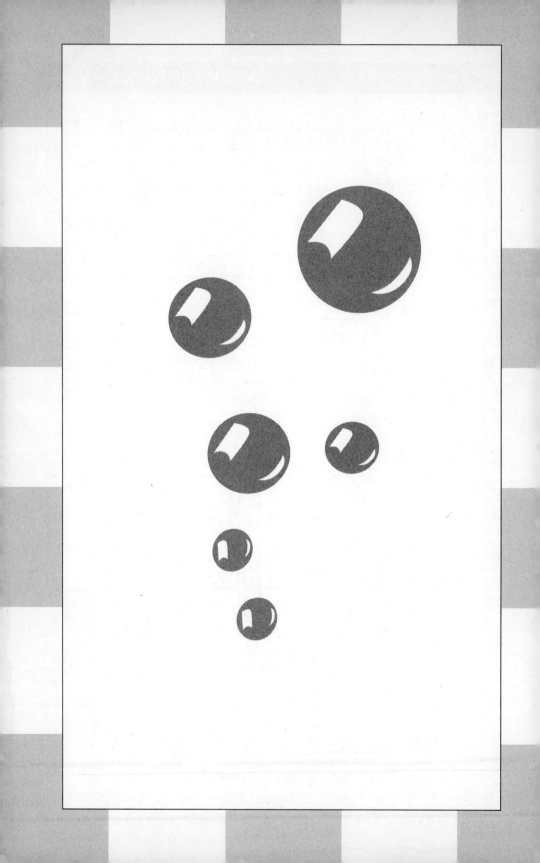